FALLING

FLAT

A REFUTATION OF
FLAT EARTH CLAIMS

DR. DANNY R. FAULKNER

First printing: August 2019

Copyright © 2019 by Danny Faulkner. All rights reserved. No part of this book may be used or reproduced in any manner whatsoever without written permission from the publisher, except in the case of brief quotations in articles and reviews. For information write:

Master Books®, P.O. Box 726, Green Forest, AR 72638

Master Books® is a division of the New Leaf Publishing Group, Inc.

ISBN: 978-1-68344-206-6
Library of Congress Number: 2019910854

Cover by Felicia Joyce Designs, LLC

Unless otherwise noted, Scripture quotations are from the ESV® Bible (The Holy Bible, English Standard Version®), copyright © 2001 by Crossway, a publishing ministry of Good News Publishers. Used by permission. All rights reserved.

Scripture quotations noted NASB are from the NEW AMERICAN STANDARD BIBLE®, Copyright © 1960, 1962, 1963, 1968, 1971, 1972, 1973, 1975, 1977, 1995 by The Lockman Foundation. Used by permission.

Scripture quotations noted YLT are from Young's Literal Translation.

Scripture quotations noted KJV are from the King James Version of the Bible.

Please consider requesting that a copy of this volume be purchased by your local library system.

Printed in the United States of America

Please visit our website for other great titles:
www.masterbooks.com

For information regarding author interviews,
please contact the publicity department at (870) 438-5288.

Master
Books®
A Division of New Leaf Publishing Group
www.masterbooks.com

Dedicated to Teddy, a lifelong friend and companion. May we have many more adventures together.

Contents

Chapter 1

Why Write About Flat Earth?

Many people probably wonder why it is necessary to write a book about the flat earth. After all, didn't we settle that question more than five centuries ago when Christopher Columbus proved that the earth is round? Well, no, Columbus didn't settle that question, and therein lies a major part of the problem — but more about that later. Beginning around 2012, there has been a major resurgence in interest in the flat earth. Much of this was started by Eric Dubay, who began posting on the Internet and published two books on the subject, *The Flat-Earth Conspiracy* and *200 Proofs the Earth Is Not a Spinning Ball*. Soon, others took up the cause, and a movement was born. Much of this has been promoted on the Internet, particularly through social media. Some of the more prominent leaders in the flat-earth movement are Mark Sargent, Jeran Campanella, Robbie Davidson, and Rob Skiba. The last two are notable because they promote a Christian version of the flat earth based upon their understanding of the cosmology of the Bible.

There is a wide diversity of theological beliefs within the flat-earth movement — conservative Christians, New Agers, deists, and pantheists, to name just a few. Flat-earthers often remark that there are no atheists in their ranks. I suppose that's because the flat-earth model is so contrived, no one would seriously suggest it evolved. However, belief that there is a creator doesn't necessarily lead one to faith in Jesus Christ, or, for that matter, belief in the Bible.

In this book, I will be most concerned about the Christian version of the flat-earth movement because I see it as a great threat to true Christianity today. I want to provide answers for people who, when confronted with arguments that the earth is flat, may not know how to respond. Since I learned of the flat-earth movement in February 2016, I have conducted extensive study of the phenomenon. I've read numerous books on the subject, read much material online, and watched far more videos about the flat earth on the Internet than I'd care to admit. I also attended the first International Flat Earth Conference in November 2017, as well as the second one in 2018. I'm confident that this study, combined with my knowledge of astronomy and physics, as well as my understanding of the aspects of the sky developed over a half-century as a serious student of the sky, uniquely qualifies me to tackle this task. Since the Christian version of flat-earth cosmology ostensibly is built upon a biblical foundation, I must respond to the biblical arguments put forth for flat earth as well. I doubt that the other theological persuasions within the flat-earth movement will be interested in that part.

I will discuss some topics relative to the Bible in this chapter. However, I will defer a fuller discussion of biblical passages that allegedly teach that the earth is flat until chapters 10 and 11. For those more interested in that, please feel free to skip ahead to those chapters. Some of my friends thought that the biblical discussion ought to appear earlier in this book. However, a certain amount of introductory material, such as historical context, must be addressed first. That also necessitated a sort of logical progression in the order of material in this book. That would defer the biblical discussion until at least chapter 3. I thought it best to conclude the book with a more detailed discussion of the supposed biblical support for the earth being flat.

Before proceeding, I want to make it clear why I use the term "flat-earthers" to refer to those who believe that the earth is flat. For a long time, that term has been thrown around as a pejorative for people who aren't terribly bright or at the very least cling to cherished old notions that no longer have relevance. I've never used the term in this manner. Therefore, I use the term "flat-earther" as a very descriptive term. At first, I was reluctant to use it, because I feared some flat-earthers would take offense, but then I found that many flat-earthers use the term to describe themselves.

Some Basics

At the outset, I also ought to describe briefly the conventional under-standing of cosmology and the flat-earth understanding of cosmology and to contrast those views. First, what is cosmology? Cosmology is the study of the structure of the universe. Unfortunately, much of what passes as cosmology today technically is cosmogony, the study of the origin and history of the universe. However, for our needs, it isn't necessary to dis-cuss cosmogony, so I will restrict my discussion to cosmology proper.

In the conventional understanding of cosmology, the earth is one of eight planets revolving around the sun. The moon is a natural satellite that orbits the earth once per month. The earth rotates[1] once per day, which causes the sun, moon, planets, and most stars to rise and set each day from the perspective of a person on earth. The sun is a star. Contrary to common misconception, the sun isn't an average star. Rather, the sun is a bit more massive, larger, and brighter than the average star. What confuses people on this count is that most stars are relatively small and dim, but the relatively larger stars are fantastically bright. There is an incredible range in stellar brightness so that if one merely compares the sun to the range in stellar brightness, the sun is average. If the sun is a star, then why do the other stars appear so faint? It is because the other stars are incredibly far away. The nearest star is 275,000 times farther away than the sun. Light diminishes with the inverse square of the dis-tance, so if the sun were as far away as the nearest star, the sun would appear 1/75 billionth as bright as it does now. But even if the sun were that much fainter, it would be among the brighter appearing stars in the sky, though not the brightest star. Other stars are much farther away than the closest star is to the sun. I could go on to include a description of the Milky Way Galaxy, a collection of billions of stars to which the sun and stars we see belong, and that there are billions of other galaxies in the universe, but that is at best tangential to the discussion of flat earth.

In the flat-earth cosmology, the earth is flat and round. The North Pole is at the center of the earth. There is no South Pole. The edge of the explored earth consists of an ice wall that we call Antarctica. This

---

1. Note that I use the terms *rotate* and *revolve* in the manner that astronomers do. That is, a rotating body turns about an axis passing through or very near the body's center. Revolution is a turning motion about an axis not passing through a body.

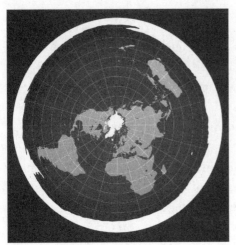

Flat-Earth Cosmology
Credit: Shutterstock

ice wall not only limits the earth as we know it, but it also keeps the oceans contained. There is disagreement among flat-earthers how far Antarctica extends. Above the earth is a dome in which the stars are embedded. The dome rests on Antarctica beyond the ice wall. The dimensions and exact shape of the dome are debated among flat-earthers. In many versions, the dome is a hemisphere, while others prefer a dome with greater radius at the center (over the North Pole) than at its edges, so that it resembles the roof of a sports arena. Each day, the dome spins around an axis passing through the earth's North Pole. This causes the stars to move in the sky. The North Star is located almost directly over the North Pole, so it remains nearly motionless while the other stars go in loops around it. In most flat-earth models, the sun and moon are above the earth but generally below the dome. They also orbit around the axis of the North Pole each day, which accounts for their daily motion. The sun and moon move at a slightly different rate from the dome, which accounts for their motion with respect to the stars. Since the sun and moon are always above the earth, they never rise or set. The sun and moon merely *appear* to rise and set due to perspective. The sun is like a spotlight shining down on the earth. When locations are under the spotlight, it is day; when the spotlight passes a location, it is night. There are variations on this theme, but I trust I have accurately portrayed the basics of the flat-earth cosmology.

A related, yet separate, issue is geocentrism. All flat-earthers are geocentrists, but not all geocentrists are flat-earthers. For several decades, there has been a small, but vocal, group of geocentric recent creationists who believe that the earth is spherical but does not move, at least with respect to space. They subscribe to the Tychonic cosmology, where the other planets orbit the sun, but the sun orbits the earth, carrying the other planets with it. This amounts to a coordinate transformation from the sun to the earth. Newtonian gravity explains the orbits of the earth and other planets, but, thanks to the coordinate transformation, the earth does not move. This coordinate transformation essentially is geocentrism by definition. The earth moves in some sense, but since space is attached to the earth, and the earth is at rest with respect to itself, the earth is at rest with respect to space. Flat-earthers don't have much in common with the Tychonic geocentrists, but flat-earthers heavily borrow from the Tychonic geocentrists' arguments.

I have found that flat-earthers frequently conflate the question of the earth's shape with the question of whether the earth moves. In the West, the majority cosmology for nearly four centuries has been that the spherical earth orbits the sun. For 2,000 years prior to that, the majority cosmology in the West was that the spherical earth was the center of the universe (generally expressed as the Ptolemaic model). As mentioned above, some people today believe in a geocentric spherical earth (generally expressed as the Tychonic cosmology). If one believes that the earth is flat, it would seem obligatory to believe in geocentrism. I suppose that it's possible to believe in a heliocentric flat-earth cosmology, but I am not aware that anyone does. How do some flat-earthers conflate these two questions? They do so by confusing the history of Western cosmology on this matter and by giving stock geocentric arguments, mistakenly thinking that the arguments also prove that the earth is flat. Those in the modern geocentric movement would strongly disagree with that. I generally won't discuss geocentric arguments, except where they directly relate to flat earth. I defer that discussion to chapter 7.

Epistemological Exercise

Epistemology is the study of knowledge. In simple terms, epistemology answers the question of "How do we know what we know?" Flat-earthers raise a good epistemological question. While most people believe the earth is a sphere, how do we know this? In my years at the university, I asked this question in my introductory astronomy classes, partly to discuss the history of astronomy, but also to motivate my students into thinking more deeply. Almost none of my students could give me a good answer. Eventually, someone would suggest photos taken from space that show the earth is spherical. However, I would ask my students whether such photos could be faked, and they all readily agreed.[2] Furthermore, since the first satellite was launched in October 1957, if this is how we know the earth is spherical, that knowledge came very late.[3] By raising this question, I challenged our cultural mythology that, until the time of Christopher Columbus five centuries ago, nearly everyone thought the earth was flat. Supposedly, with our sophistication and intelligence today, we know better than the ignorant people of the past. Most of my students were surprised to learn that the facts of history are very different from the Columbus mythology they grew up hearing. The question of the earth's true shape had been settled two millennia before Columbus. Yet rarely could any of my students give a good reason why the earth is spherical. So much for our modern smug superiority over the supposedly ignorant people of the past.

Most people have not given this question any thought because they have been taught their entire lives that the earth is spherical, so why worry about it? Consequently, with no idea of the reasons we know that the earth is spherical, most people long ago entered a complacent state of taking someone else's word for the matter. When a modern flat-earther comes along and begins to raise what appear to be simple objections to the earth's spherical shape, it doesn't take much to fluster most people. When cornered in this manner, people generally respond with the observation that we have photos from space that clearly show a spherical earth. However, the flat-earther almost certainly will respond that such photos easily can be faked (but note that I thought of this first). Indeed, because we all know that it is very easy to fake such photos, perhaps those photos don't prove much after all. Furthermore, belief in a spherical earth goes back much earlier than the space age, so obviously there must be better responses.

Once the space photos of a spherical earth are shot down, most people usually have one of two responses. The most common response is to dismiss the person asking the questions as a crank or fool because "everyone knows that the earth is round." The other response is to pay

---

2. Therefore, I was pointing this out long before the flat-earthers were, though it's not as though I believed that photos from space are faked.

3. This was three years after I was born. I think that my parents believed the earth was spherical long before I was conceived.

more attention to the flat-earthers, looking for errors in their facts or logic. However, rarely having the knowledge readily at hand to refute the case for a flat earth, most people who take this approach soon look for help (this is what this book is for). That search for help usually ends up on the Internet, whereupon they quickly find a slew of websites and videos promoting the flat earth, but precious little, if any, refuting it. Some people emerge a few hours later, their egos bruised and their intelligence a bit insulted, because they still think that the earth being flat is nonsense but are frustrated that they can't seem to answer many of the arguments they've just encountered. Still others never emerge from this rabbit hole and end up thinking that maybe the conspiracy theories that they have encountered along the way may be right — perhaps for a long time we've all been fed a whopping lie about the true shape of the earth.

Back to Columbus

Perhaps the rise of the flat-earth movement is a symptom of a deeper problem. Far too much of our educational system is geared toward rote memorization of facts without assimilation of those facts or reasoning to understand how we came to know those facts. Hence, it's understandable why most people know the earth is spherical, but don't know how we know this. This also explains why it is so easy for flat-earth arguments to fluster so many people. But compounding the problem is that some of the things we think are true aren't true. An excellent example of this is what I call our Columbus mythology. Most of us grew up learning that Columbus thought that the earth was spherical, so sailing westward from Europe to reach Asia was shorter and faster than traveling eastward. This wasn't just an academic exercise because Muslims had closed to Europeans the overland trade routes to the Far East. According to the story, nearly everyone opposed Columbus' rash plan because they believed that the earth was flat, so such a foolhardy trip would end in disaster, such as falling off the edge of the earth. It may make for a good story, but it's not true.

To the contrary, at least in the West, for 2,000 years before Columbus nearly everyone had known that the earth was spherical. Most people today are astounded to learn this. Then what was the nature of the argument about Columbus' proposal? The dispute was over the size of the earth, not its shape. People knew that one could sail westward to reach the Far East, but the question was why would you want to do that? Most people thought that there was a vast ocean all the way to Asia (they didn't know about the American continents yet), which would require a very long voyage across an open ocean without the prospect of resupply. Vessels at that time were small and rarely traveled more than a few days out of sight of land. Besides concerns about resupply, there also were concerns for safety because if a problem developed, the crew had hope of limping back toward land only if they weren't far from land. Therefore, a voyage across a large, unknown ocean was a very frightening thing, but not because of fear of falling off an edge.

By the way, a look at any globe (or map) of the earth shows that Columbus was wrong and Columbus' critics were right — the distance from Europe to Asia is much shorter going eastward (the straight-line distance from Spain is about 7,500 km, or 4,500 miles) than going westward (more than 30,000 km or nearly 20,000 miles). How did Columbus come to think that Asia wasn't that far westward from Europe? First, for centuries there had been stories of reported sightings of land to the west of Europe. For instance, the Vikings briefly settled on the far northeast coast of North America less than five centuries before Columbus' voyage, and Irish legends placed Brendan the Navigator in lands to the west four centuries before the Vikings. There are other examples. Columbus accepted such stories as true and reasoned that the lands to the west were Asia. Second, Columbus cooked the numbers to make his case. The distance to the Far East was known by subtracting the eastward distance to the Far East from the earth's circumference. Columbus reduced the earth's circumference and increased the eastward distance to Asia to get a reasonable distance for getting to the Far East by sailing west. Most people are surprised to learn that people five centuries ago knew the earth's circumference. I'll take up that topic shortly.

Confusing Heliocentrism and a Spherical Earth

Flat-earthers consistently conflate this mythology about Columbus with the Galileo affair a little more than a century later. In 1543, a half-century after Columbus' voyage, Nicolaus Copernicus published his *Revolutionibus*,[4] in which he promoted the heliocentric theory. Contrary to popular misconception, it was not immediately banned by the Roman Catholic Church. Instead, Copernicus' work was widely read and prompted much discussion. One convert to the heliocentric theory was Galileo Galilei. In 1610, Galileo published *The Starry Messenger*,[5] in which he shared his telescopic observations of the phases of Venus and four natural satellites, or moons, orbiting Jupiter, which supported the heliocentric model and disproved the geocentric Ptolemaic model, along with relevant aspects of the dominant Aristotelian physics. This book, along with Galileo's continued teaching of the heliocentric theory, aroused some opposition, but not from the theologians, as most people think. Rather, it was the other scientists who opposed Galileo, because if the heliocentric model were true, it would overturn the Ptolemaic model, which had been the dominant cosmology for 15 centuries. This opposition demanded a hearing, which led to a trial in 1616 (six years after the publication of Galileo's book). The trial resulted in banning heliocentric books, primarily those of Galileo and Copernicus. The court also instructed Galileo to refrain from teaching heliocentrism.

Galileo continued to work on his cosmology, though he didn't write on it much for two decades. However, in 1632, more than 15 years after the trial, Galileo published his *Dialogue*.[6] This book once again promoted heliocentrism, this time in the form of a discussion between three people, an advocate of the Copernican model, an advocate of the Ptolemaic model, and a supposedly neutral third person. Despite the order of the trial, Galileo had permission from Roman Catholic officials to publish the book. Those officials clearly had no idea what direction Galileo would take in his book. Rather than being in Latin, which was the usual practice of the time, the book was written in Italian to reach a larger audience. Immediately, the book was very popular, but it brought very

---

4. The full title of Copernicus' book is *De Revolutionibus Orbium Coelestium*, which, translated from Latin to English, is *On the Revolutions of Heavenly Spheres*.
5. The original Latin title was *Sidereus Nuncius*. While other important books of the time are more often known by their Latin titles, Galileo's book is better known by the English translation of its title. It may be because of the relatively short title of this book compared to others of the period, the Latin titles of which generally are shortened.
6. The full title in Italian was *Dialogo Sopra i Due Massimi Systemi del Mondo*, which translates into English as *Dialogue Concerning the Two Chief World Systems*. This book usually is referred to by the first word of its title.

swift opposition from church leaders. Galileo did lay his argument on thick. He was required to include a disclaimer that what the book taught wasn't true, but merely was an intellectual exercise. Galileo fulfilled this requirement by calling the book a fantasy, after all, he wrote, any fool knows that the earth doesn't move. Get it? Galileo subtly called anyone who disagreed with him a fool. The Ptolemaic supporter in his book was named Simplicio, which roughly translates as "simpleton." Galileo made Simplicio look foolish. To make matters worse, the pope had insisted that his views be included in the book, so since the pope believed the Ptolemaic model, Galileo put the pope's words in Simplicio's mouth. Understandably, the pope was furious. The uproar the book stirred resulted in a second trial in 1633. The pope had been sympathetic to Galileo, but Galileo's intemperate attitude had thrown that away, along with any other support he once enjoyed. Therefore, the decision of the court was a foregone conclusion. Galileo was found guilty of teaching a heretical doctrine, and he was sentenced to house arrest for the rest of his life. He further was forced to recant and was banned once again from teaching heliocentrism.

Note that Copernicus' book, which had been much read and discussed, wasn't banned for 70 years, and then only in response to Galileo's actions. Hence, contrary to common misconception, the Roman Catholic Church did not react to the heliocentric model per se. Had Galileo acted more prudently, the outcome may have been very different. Galileo wasn't quite the innocent victim of an overzealous Roman Catholic Church as many people today think. Rather, his caustic attitude invited the treatment that he received. And was that treatment so harsh? At that time, the Inquisition was executing people for real heresy or for just being Protestant, but Galileo never even came close to that sentence.

As I've previously mentioned, the question of the earth's shape and the question of whether the earth moves (geocentric vs. heliocentric) are not directly related. Yet many flat-earthers (as do many other people) consistently confuse the two. I can't begin to count the times I've heard flat-earthers blame Copernicus for introducing the spherical earth. Their ignorance of the history of cosmology is appalling. In a weird way, this faux history of man's knowledge of the earth's shape is an aid in roping people into the flat-earth camp.

One obstacle to belief in flat earth is the realization that if the earth truly is flat, many people must know that the earth is flat despite being told it is spherical, so why do these people who supposedly know better continue to lie about the earth's shape? The only answer is that there must be a vast conspiracy behind the spherical earth. Belief in all sorts of conspiracies is rampant among flat-earthers, which is a fascinating facet of the flat-earth movement, but I shall not explore it here. It seems that the flat-earth conspiracy is the grandest of all conspiracies which subsumes all others.

Why is there supposedly a conspiracy to conceal the earth's true shape? The most common answer is that it is an attempt to control people, though it isn't clear how promoting and maintaining a false belief about the earth's shape accomplishes that. To the Christian flat-earthers, belief in the spherical earth is the strong delusion spoken of in 2 Thessalonians 2:11. Belief in a spherical earth is very diabolical, supposedly linked to paganism or even Satan worship, and often it is tied in with beliefs about end times. Things really did begin to change five centuries ago, as it marked the transition from the Middle Ages to modern times. The claim is that belief that the earth is spherical ultimately led to belief in evolution, so spherical earth, not evolution, is the real root of the problem.[7] To the true believers that the earth is flat, the revival of flat-earth belief represents a return to basic values and ancient wisdom. To the Christian believers that the earth is flat, the modern flat-earth movement means even more, for it represents a return to biblical Christianity. Though, as we shall soon see, the church never taught that the earth is flat.

Ancient Greek Cosmology

Much of Western science and philosophy traces back to the ancient Greeks. Therefore, if we want to know the history of cosmology, such as beliefs about the earth's shape, we ought to start with them. The writings of many early Greek scientists, mathematicians, and philosophers do not exist today. Instead, we must rely upon much later sources that reported on their teachings. However, the writings of later Greeks, such

---

7. The flat-earthers stole this idea from the geocentrists. For many years, the geocentrists had argued that it was belief in the heliocentric theory that eventually led to belief in evolution.

as Aristotle and Ptolemy, do exist. The Greeks borrowed heavily from the Egyptians and Babylonians, though they soon built on what they borrowed and developed their own ideas. The ancient Egyptian and Babylonian cosmologies predominantly were flat earth. However, the details varied, so there were many cosmologies of the Ancient Near East (ANE). It has become fashionable now, even in some conservative circles, to believe that the Bible, being a product of the ANE, reflects the ANE cosmology. Therefore, it is reasoned, the Bible teaches that the earth is flat. I will take up this question later, but I will mention here two problems with this teaching. First, there was no single ANE cosmology, so how could the Bible reflect *the* ANE cosmology? Second, this belief undermines the inspiration and authority of Scripture.

In the early sixth century B.C., Anaximander thought that the earth was a disk with a thickness 1/3 its diameter, making him a flat-earther. However, Anaximander had the sun, moon, and stars orbit around the earth each day, passing below the earth to permit rising and setting. This is in stark contrast with the modern flat-earth cosmology. In the modern flat-earth model, the sun and moon do not rise and set, but merely appear to do so, as the sun and moon perpetually remain above the flat earth. Earlier Greek cosmologies probably were flat earth, but we have no knowledge of them.

Later in the sixth century B.C., Pythagoras proposed that there were eight concentric spheres surrounding the earth. The outermost sphere carried the stars, while the other seven spheres carried the sun, moon, and the five naked-eye planets. The spheres turned at different rates to produce the motions of the heavenly bodies. As they turned, the friction between them produced the *music of the spheres* that only the most gifted could hear. In the fourth century B.C., Eudoxus and Callippus improved upon Pythagoras' scheme by adding many more nested spheres to account for the intricacies of the motions of the sun, moon, and planets. Eudoxus' system required a total of 27 spheres, while Callippus' system required 34 spheres. Therefore, by the fourth century B.C., heavenly spheres concentric with the earth had become an integral part of cosmology in the West and would remain so for the next 2,000 years. The motions of these spheres allowed celestial objects to rise and set. This is in stark contrast to the modern flat-earth model of a flat, round earth, covered by a dome. Despite flat-earthers' claims to the contrary, almost no one in the West (of course, later including the church) believed that there was a dome over the earth. Instead, the dominant belief was that the earth was surrounded by the celestial sphere and possibly additional concentric spheres.

Pythagoras is best known for his contributions to mathematics, such as his famous Pythagorean theorem. The Greeks came to view the circle as the perfect shape, along with the sphere, which is a circle in three dimensions. The ancient Greeks may have reached this conclusion through the influence of Pythagoras. At any rate, Pythagoras thought that the earth, moon, and sun were spheres. It's not entirely clear what his reasons were, but Pythagoras, and possibly his contemporaries, Empedocles and Parmenides, are given credit with originating the idea that the earth is spherical. In his *Histories*, written in the mid-fifth century B.C., Herodotus reported that around 600 B.C., Phoenician explorers circumnavigated Africa and reported that the sun was in the northern part of the sky rather than the southern part of the sky. This is indeed what is expected as one passes south of the tropics if the earth is spherical, though not necessarily expected in a flat-earth cosmology.[8] Because of this detail, some modern scholars suggest that the ancient Phoenicians may have known of the earth's spherical shape. Unfortunately, no record of Phoenician geography survives.

By the fourth century B.C., the concept of a spherical earth was well-established in Greek thought. In his *On the Heavens*, Aristotle taught the sphericity of the earth and moon, with clear reasons for both. First, let's tackle the moon's shape. Lunar phases make sense only if the moon is a sphere. If the moon is a sphere, then half of the moon will be lit by the sun. Lunar phases are caused by the changing geometry of the moon and sun with respect to the earth. More specifically, lunar phases are determined by how much of the moon's lit half faces the earth. When the moon is opposite the sun in the sky, its lit half faces the earth, so we see the moon fully illuminated. We call this full moon. When the moon is in the same part of the sky as the sun, the lit half of the moon faces

---

8. Modern flat-earthers are sure to object that they can explain this, and indeed they can. However, I chose the words "not necessarily expected" carefully. It appears that at the time of Herodotus, those committed to the flat earth could not explain it.

toward the sun, so the moon's unlit half faces the earth. Besides the unlit half of the moon being very dim, the moon appears in the same part of the sky as the sun. The sun's glare so overpowers the very dim unlit half of the moon facing the earth that we can't see the moon for several days. We call this new moon. It takes the moon about two weeks to travel from new to full, and another two weeks to return to new from full. As the moon goes from new to full, we see progressively more of the lit half of the moon, so we call these the waxing phases. As the moon travels from full to new, we progressively see less of the moon's lit half illuminated, so we call these the waning phases. We call the division between light and dark on the moon the *terminator*. The terminator is curved, except when the moon is briefly exactly at quarter phases (which happens about half-way between new and full phases). The moon appears round to observers on earth, so obviously the moon is round in the plane tangent to the sky at its location. But is the moon round and flat, like a plate, or is it round in our line of sight as well, like a ball? The phases of the moon, and especially the curved terminator, only make sense if the moon is spherical.

Interestingly, modern flat-earthers generally deny that the moon is a sphere, insisting that it is a disk. It's not clear why they think this. For one thing, it leaves them with no explanation for lunar phases. They claim that the moon produces its own light, so it doesn't reflect the light of the sun. I guess it's something like National Geographic's product "Moon in My Room." A friend gave me one of these a few years ago. It requires AA cells to power it and a remote control as well. You mount it on the wall, and in the dark it simulates the phases of the moon by switching on various lights in compartments behind its slightly curved translucent face. I suppose that the moon *could* operate this way, but keep in mind that the "Moon in My Room" merely is an imperfect simulation of the moon's real phases. Why would God have made a flat, round moon that varies in its own light in a manner that strongly implies that the moon is a sphere illuminated by the sun? Do flat-earthers think that God is so malicious as to make the world in such a way that we so easily could be led astray on this?

Besides, what if the moon is spherical? Does that automatically mean that the earth is spherical too? Apparently, the flat-earthers think so. This brings us to one of Aristotle's arguments for believing the earth is spherical. Once Aristotle realized that the moon was spherical, he surmised that the earth was spherical too. This is an argument by analogy, so it hardly is a rigorous argument. Underlying this argument is the assumption that the earth and moon must be similar in certain respects. That is a huge assumption, and it is very clear that while the moon and earth share some common properties, they differ in many other respects. I suspect that modern flat-earthers are employing the similar argument by analogy: they know the earth is flat and round, so the moon must be flat and round, too. Either way, this argument by analogy isn't anything more than confirmation of what one already believes.

Beside the argument by analogy, Aristotle gave much better arguments for the earth's sphericity. He noted that as a ship departs, it progressively disappears hull first. If the earth were flat, the ship would appear progressively smaller as it moves away, ultimately reaching the vanishing point, but no part of the ship would disappear first. On the other hand, if the earth is spherical, then one would expect the curvature of the sea's surface progressively to obscure more and more of the ship from the bottom up. Since this is what we see, the earth must be spherical. I've always been a little skeptical of this argument, because without optical aid, this would be difficult to observe (the telescope was invented a little more than four centuries ago, long after Aristotle lived). On the other hand, Aristotle almost certainly was aware of a sort of reverse of this argument. A lookout perched atop the mast of a ship will spot approaching land long before those on the deck will. Furthermore, Greece is a hilly country with many islands. From a beach, an island some distance off shore may not be visible, but it will become visible as one ascends a bluff by the shore. This is not possible on a flat earth, but it is if the earth is spherical. I once observed this for myself on the Door Peninsula of Wisconsin. The peninsula divides Green Bay from Lake Michigan. I was on the western side of the northern part of the peninsula overlooking Green Bay with the Upper Peninsula (UP) of Michigan 18 miles away. From the beach, the tree line of the UP wasn't visible — all I saw was open water. I drove up to the top of the bluffs that overlook the beach. From there, it was easy to see the tree line of the UP.

Another argument that Aristotle invoked was the visibility of stars in the northern and southern parts of the sky as one travels north or south. Traveling northward, stars near the northern horizon climb higher in the sky, even revealing stars that were below the northern horizon when the observer was farther south. At the same time, stars near the southern horizon get lower in the sky, with some stars disappearing below the southern horizon. As one travels southward, the reverse is true. This cannot happen on a flat earth, but it is what one expects if the earth is spherical. I shall return to this topic in chapter 5.

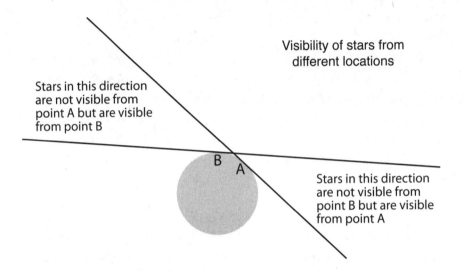

Visibility of stars from different locations

Stars in this direction are not visible from point A but are visible from point B

Stars in this direction are not visible from point B but are visible from point A

However, the best argument for the earth's sphericity from the ancient Greeks is the shape of the earth's shadow during lunar eclipses. This requires an understanding of what causes lunar eclipses — the earth passing between the sun and moon so that the earth's shadow falls on the moon. The cause of lunar eclipses was easy enough to grasp for the ancient Greeks because they were careful observers of the world around them. Lunar eclipses occur only at full moon, when the moon appears opposite the sun in the sky. While the moon being full is a necessary condition for a lunar eclipse, it is not a sufficient condition, because a lunar eclipse does not occur at every full moon. Why is that? The moon's orbital plane is tilted a little more than five degrees to the plane of earth's orbit around the sun (we call the earth's orbital plane the *ecliptic*[9]). Therefore, at most

---

9. The ecliptic, the name for the earth's orbital plane, goes back to the ancient Greeks. Its name derives from the observation that eclipses, both lunar and solar, occur only when the moon is near the ecliptic. The etymology of this name indicates that the ancients correctly

full moons, the moon passes above or below the earth's shadow so that no eclipse occurs. The *nodes* are the two places where the moon's orbital plane and the ecliptic intersect. If the moon is near a node at the time of full moon, a lunar eclipse occurs. By keen observations made over many years, the Greeks and many other ancient cultures knew about the ecliptic, the moon's orbit, and the nodes. From this information, they could anticipate when a lunar eclipse was possible. However, their information was not precise enough to predict exactly when and where eclipses would be visible. Related to this is the saros cycle, which I will discuss in chapter 3.

The earth's shadow is larger than the moon, so we cannot see the entire shadow at once. However, as the earth's shadow creeps across the moon, it always appears as a portion of a circle. The distance between the moon and earth varies, and the distance to the sun varies throughout the year, so the size of the earth's shadow changes slightly. However, to the naked eye, the size of the earth's shadow is about the same at every lunar eclipse. If the earth were round and flat, such as a disk, could it cast a circular shadow on the moon? Yes, but only when a lunar eclipse occurs at midnight, and then only in winter, when the full moon is very high, and the sun is very low below the horizon. However, if a lunar eclipse occurs at sunrise or sunset, the orientation of the disk is different, so the earth's shadow would be an ellipse or a rectangle, or some combination of both, but not a circle. The only shape that consistently casts a circular shadow regardless of its orientation is a sphere. Many flat-earthers are well aware of this problem, so they have spent time critiquing the conventional explanation of lunar eclipses. I will take up this matter in chapter 3.

I previously described how as one travels north or south, the stars change in a manner that indicates the earth is curved in the north-south direction. However, some ancient sources also noted evidence that the earth is curved in the east-west direction. There is a time difference of three hours between the east and west coasts of the United States. That is, the sun rises and sets approximately three hours earlier on the east coast than it does on the west coast. This is easily verified by anyone who has flown between the east and west coasts of the United States. Not

understood the cause of eclipses.

only will your watch show that there is a time difference of three hours, but your body will notice the difference in time as well. If one drives from one coast to the other, the trip will take several days, so our bodies will not notice the time difference as much. However, our watches reveal that the time has changed. Such rapid transportation was not possible in ancient times, nor were there watches, but the ancients could see this time difference a different way. A lunar eclipse obviously must happen simultaneously for everyone on earth, but it will be at different times at different locations. For instance, a lunar eclipse may start shortly after sunset in the eastern Mediterranean, such as in Greece. However, in the western Mediterranean, such as in Spain, the moon might already be in eclipse when the moon rose that night. This means that the lunar eclipse began before sunset/moonrise in Spain, but after sunset/moonrise in Greece. While communication was much slower in the ancient world than it is today, people did record and share their observations, so people in the ancient world were aware of this effect. This shows that the earth is curved in the east-west direction. If the earth is curved in both the north-south and east-west direction, the most likely shape of the earth is

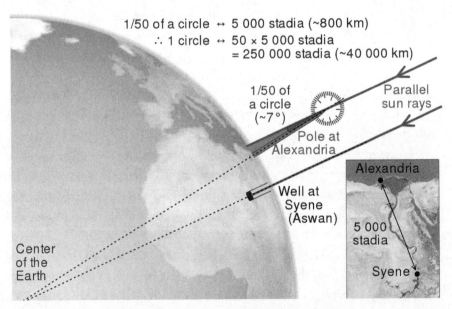

Eratosthenes' measure of earth's circumference.

a sphere.

Building on this knowledge that the earth was spherical, around 200 B.C. Eratosthenes accurately measured earth's size. Eratosthenes worked at the Great Library in Alexandria, Egypt. Eratosthenes is the father of geography because he coined the term and commissioned the creation of many maps. On the summer solstice one year, Eratosthenes was in Syene, a city (now called Aswan) in southern Egypt. Being on the northern limit of the tropics, the sun was directly overhead at noon on the summer solstice. Eratosthenes realized this because he peered into a deep well and saw the bottom. Normally, the bottom of a deep well is not visible because the sun's light does not shine directly on the bottom, but it does at noon on the summer solstice on the Tropic of Cancer because the sun is directly overhead. The sun never is directly overhead in Alexandria because it is north of the tropics. Back in Alexandria a following year, Eratosthenes measured the angle that the sun made with the *zenith*, the point directly overhead, at noon on the summer solstice. He did this by constructing a *gnomon*, a vertical pole of known height, and by measuring the gnomon's shadow at noon. Trigonometry allowed Eratosthenes to compute how far the sun was from the zenith. Eratosthenes found that the angle was about one-fiftieth of a circle. This meant that Alexandria and Aswan were separated by one-fiftieth of the earth's circumference. Eratosthenes knew the distance between those two locations (he was the father of geography, after all), so multiplying that distance by 50 gave him the earth's circumference.

Flat-earthers frequently argue that Eratosthenes didn't prove that the earth was spherical, but that Eratosthenes *assumed* that the earth is spherical. Flat-earthers further claim that they can explain Eratosthenes' result on a flat earth. Both statements are true, but flat-earthers have missed the point. Notice above that I didn't state that Eratosthenes proved that the earth was a sphere. Rather, I said, "Building on this knowledge that the earth was spherical, around 200 B.C. Eratosthenes accurately measured earth's size." Eratosthenes' observation can be explained in the flat-earth model as a parallax effect due to viewing the sun from different positions on the earth's surface. Furthermore, just as in the globe-earth model Eratosthenes' result can be used to measure the earth's circumference, in the

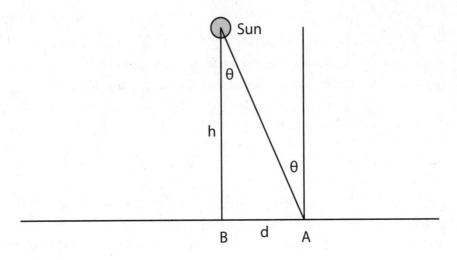

flat-earth model Eratosthenes' result can be used to measure how high the sun is above the earth.[10] This figure shows the situation. The sun is directly over Syene at point B. Meanwhile, the sun makes an angle θ from the vertical at Alexandria at point A. The angle θ also is an angle in the right triangle formed by the sun and points A and B. Let h be the height of the sun and d be the distance between points A and B. Then

$$h = \frac{d}{\tan \theta}$$

The north-south distance, d, between Alexandria and Syene is 490 miles. Eratosthenes measured θ to be 1/50 of a circle = 7.2 degrees. Therefore, the height of the sun is 3,900 miles. However, many flat-earthers, following the lead of 19th-century promoters of flat earth, claim that the sun is 3,000 miles above the earth. This is a difference of 30%. There are many different heights of the sun claimed in the flat-earth model. This is because different approaches produce different results. If the flat-earth model were true, this ought not to be the case. In recognition of this problem, many flat-earthers now simply refuse to quantify dimensions

10. Apparently, not one flat-earther has yet recognized the inconsistency of their claim here. They insist that it somehow is improper to assume a spherical earth and use Eratosthenes' result to find the earth's circumference, while at the same time claim that it is proper for them to assume a flat earth to constrain the sun's height within their model.

Ptolemy
Wikimedia

in their model.

The final word on ancient Greek cosmology was Claudius Ptolemy in the early second century A.D. Ptolemy, as he usually is called, also lived in Alexandria. He authored an exhaustive work on astronomy that in the ancient world was called the *Syntaxes Mathematica*, but it is better known today by the title medieval Arabs gave it, the *Almagest*.[11] The *Almagest* contains a good discussion and history of ancient Greek astronomy. Indeed, much of what we know of ancient Greek astronomy comes via the *Almagest*. The *Almagest* also included a star catalog of more than 1,000 stars listed among 48 constellations. Most of those constellations still survive, and with Ptolemy's coordinates and descriptions of the locations of stars within the constellations, we have a good understanding of the constellations as the ancient Greeks saw them, and we can unambiguously identify many of the stars in Ptolemy's catalog. Ptolemy clearly taught that the earth was a sphere (*Almagest*, book 1, section 4). From his observations, Ptolemy also computed the sizes and distances of the sun and moon (*Almagest*, book 5, sections 15 and 16). Ptolemy found that the earth was 3⅔ the size of the moon, and that the average distance to the moon was 59 times that of the earth's diameter. These are close to the correct values. However, Ptolemy determined that the sun was nearly 5½ times larger than the earth and 1,210 times the earth's radius away. These are woefully short of the correct values. However, these results clearly reveal how wrong the flat-earthers are on the history of cosmology.

---

11. In Arabic, *almagest* means "the greatest." Obviously, the Arabs were very impressed with Ptolemy's book.

However, the *Almagest* is best known for its system of predicting the positions of the moon and the five naked-eye planets. While the positions of the stars are relatively simple to calculate, the planets' positions are very complicated. The main difficulty is the back-and-forth motion that planets appear to trace out in the sky from time to time. We call this backward motion *retrograde motion*. Retrograde motion of *superior planets* (those planets orbiting farther from the sun than the earth) occurs as the earth passes them on its smaller, swifter orbit. Retrograde motion of *inferior planets* (planets that orbit the sun closer to the sun than the earth) happens when they lap the earth in its orbit. To model retrograde motion, Ptolemy had each of the five planets move on its own circle called an *epicycle*. The epicycle of each planet, in turn, moved along its

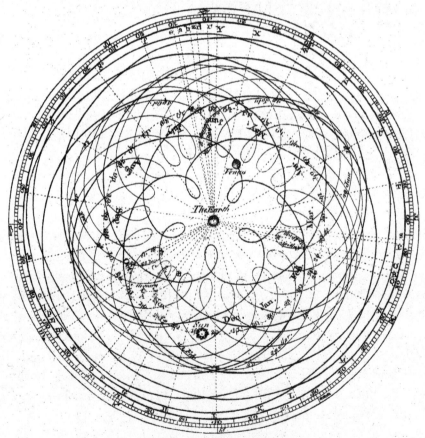

The epicycle of each planet
(Wikimedia)

own larger circle called the *deferent*. By adjusting the sizes of the epicycle and deferent for each planet, as well as the rates of the motion of each planet on its epicycle and the motion of each epicycle on its deferent, Ptolemy could match retrograde motion. Since the orbital planes of the planets are inclined slightly to the ecliptic, they bob up and down slightly with respect to the ecliptic. Ptolemy modeled this by adding an additional small epicycle for each in a plane perpendicular to the ecliptic. Thus, each planet required two epicycles. The moon also required two epicycles, and the sun required one epicycle.

The Ptolemaic model was very successful because it could predict the positions of the planets so well when no previous model could. For a long time, historians thought that most ancient Greek astronomers believed the geocentric theory, with the notable exceptions of Aristarchus and Eratosthenes, who believed the heliocentric theory. Part of their reasoning was that the heliocentric model did not require epicycles to explain retrograde motion. Now some historians are suggesting that prior to the Ptolemaic model, the heliocentric theory may have enjoyed more of a following than previously thought. However, with the success of the Ptolemaic model, any belief in the heliocentric theory soon faded. What led Copernicus and others to reconsider the heliocentric model after nearly a millennium and a half of dominance by the geocentric theory? From time to time, small discrepancies between the predictions of the Ptolemaic model and observations of planetary positions arose. The fix was the addition of more epicycles. By the late Middle Ages, these additions had accumulated to more than a hundred epicycles. Occam's razor[12] dictates that when confronted with two solutions, one simple and one convoluted, the simple explanation usually is the correct one. By eliminating the large epicycles to explain retrograde motion, the heliocentric model offered the desired simplicity.

The Early and Medieval Church on the Earth's Shape

There are examples of early church authorities who taught that the earth was a globe. Three examples are Athenagoras (late second century),

---

12. Named for William of Ockham (1287–1347), Occam's razor (notice variations in the spelling of his name) is the law of parsimony. It states that when one must decide between two competing hypotheses, the one with the fewest assumptions generally is correct.

Methodius (late third century), and Arnobius (early fourth century). However, early church fathers did not address cosmology much. There probably are at least two reasons for this. One reason was that the early church was battling some very serious issues of considerably more immediate concern. Early on, there was the influence of gnosticism that had to be driven from the church. Then there were debates about the nature of Jesus Christ. The gospels portray Jesus as fully human, yet they also record that Jesus claimed to be divine. How could Jesus be both God and man? Different answers to this question arose, and they all could not be correct. The doctrine of the trinity eventually emerged as the proper understanding. After the Council of Nicaea in A.D. 315, fundamental doctrines, including the Trinity, clearly defined orthodox Christianity. The second reason was that there probably was not much dispute about cosmology — why write about matters that don't appear to be doctrinal, especially on questions where there was no debate? Therefore, among Christians, there was not much impetus to discuss cosmology in the late ancient world and throughout the medieval period. However, discussion of cosmology began to appear more in the 13th century, as Thomas Aquinas explicitly wedded Aristotle's teaching and the Ptolemaic model to the doctrines of the Roman Catholic Church. This set the stage for the Galileo affair 3½ centuries later.

Let me reiterate that historically, the cosmology of the Church was geocentric, but not flat earth. The medieval scholar Jeffrey Burton Russell's 1991 book, *Inventing the Flat Earth: Columbus and Modern Historians*,[13] is a detailed refutation of the flat-earth myth. Admittedly, there were two individuals in the history of the church worthy of note that did indeed teach that the earth was flat. One was Lactantius, an early-fourth-century Berber who eventually became an advisor to Constantine. In chapter 24 of book III of his *Divine Institutes*, Lactantius mocked those who believed that the earth was spherical. The other was Cosmas Indicopleustes, a Greek from Alexandria, who in the early sixth century made several voyages to India and Ceylon. He later wrote *Christian Topography*, in which he argued that the earth was flat and rectangular. The heaven above was shaped like a box with a curved lid. He took his contemporary

---

13. Jeffrey Burton Russell, *Inventing the Flat Earth: Columbus and Modern Historians* (New York: Praeger, 1991).

Christians to task for believing that the earth was spherical, claiming that the spherical earth was pagan-inspired.[14] That is evidence that Christians at that time generally believed the earth to be a globe, for why would one criticize a belief that did not exist? Neither Lactantius nor Cosmas are known for anything else. If not for their odd ideas about the earth's shape, they would be more obscure than they already are. In the 19th century, critics falsely portrayed the teachings of Lactantius and Cosmas as typical of the early and medieval church. Sadly, modern flat-earthers have unquestionably accepted this faux history created by the critics.

The critics even claim that Augustine taught that the earth was flat when he clearly thought otherwise. The relevant portion of Augustine's writing is chapter 9 of book XVI of his *City of God*. That entire chapter reads:

> But as to the fable that there are Antipodes, that is to say, men on the opposite side of the earth, where the sun rises when it sets to us, men who walk with their feet opposite ours, that is on no ground credible. And, indeed, it is not affirmed that this has been learned by historical knowledge, but by scientific conjecture, on the ground that the earth is suspended within the concavity of the sky, and that it has as much room on the one side of it as on the other: hence they say that the part which is beneath must also be inhabited. But they do not remark that, although it be supposed or scientifically demonstrated that the world is of a round and spherical form, yet it does not follow that the other side of the earth is bare of water; nor even, though it be bare, does it immediately follow that it is peopled. For Scripture, which proves the truth of its historical statements by the accomplishment of its prophecies, gives no false information; and it is too absurd to say, that some men might have taken ship and traversed the whole wide ocean, and crossed from this side of the world to the other, and that thus even the inhabitants of that distant region are descended from that one first man. Wherefore let

14. Many modern flat-earth Christians raise this same objection. Perhaps they got the idea from Cosmas. At any rate, they generally would reject Cosmas' cosmology.

us seek if we can find the city of God that sojourns on earth among those human races who are catalogued as having been divided into seventy-two nations and as many languages. For it continued down to the deluge and the ark, and is proved to have existed still among the sons of Noah by their blessings, and chiefly in the eldest son Shem; for Japheth received this blessing, that he should dwell in the tents of Shem.[15]

The context, established by the adjoining chapters, is the repopulation of the world after the Flood and the confusion of languages at the Tower of Babel. Here Augustine concludes that there are no *antipodes*. Many people incorrectly assume that the antipodes refer to locations on the other side of the spherical earth, and so erroneously conclude that Augustine's rejection of the antipodes amounts to rejection of the earth being spherical. However, Augustine defined the antipodes as "men on the opposite side of the earth." The word "antipode" means "opposite feet," coming from the idea that people on the opposite side of the earth would have their feet oriented opposite to him. Furthermore, if Augustine had intended the antipodes to mean the opposite side of the earth, the singular form of antipode would have been appropriate. The fact that he used the plural is consistent with the proper interpretation. Augustine went on to state that the argument for the existence of antipodes was conjecture based upon the scientifically established fact that the earth is spherical. However, he pointed out that it doesn't follow that the other side of the globe has any land, or if that land exists there, that it is inhabited. Here Augustine reflects the geography of his day that Europe, Asia, and Africa comprised the only significant landmass on the earth.[16] Though he doesn't explicitly state it, Augustine here also reflected the widespread belief of the ancient world that it was too hot in the tropics for man safely to traverse the tropics to reach any land on the other side of the earth. Given the huge stature of Augustine in the medieval church, it is inconceivable that later students would have abandoned belief that the earth is spherical.

---

15. *The City of God*, translated by M. Dods in *Great Books of the Western World, Volume 18*, Robert M. Hutchins, editor (Chicago, IL: William Benton, 1952), p. 428.
16. The name of the Mediterranean Sea reflects this as well, for it means "middle of the earth," lying between Europe, Asia, and Africa.

In the first century B.C., Cicero wrote *The Dream of Scipio* based on the second century B.C. Roman general. *The Dream of Scipio* is just a part of a much larger work, *De re Publica*, but most of that work did not survive. However, we have all of *The Dream of Scipio* thanks to a *Commentary on the Dream of Scipio*, written by Macrobius in the fifth century A.D. This work was one of the most popular books during the Middle Ages. *The Dream of Scipio* describes a spherical earth that is much smaller than the rest of the universe. The accompanying figure comes from a 12th-century copy of the book. It shows a spherical earth divided into different climate zones.

Isidore of Seville (early 7th century) wrote about the earth being spherical in his *On the Nature of Things*. In his *On the Reckoning of Time*, the Venerable Bede (early 8th century) clearly taught that the earth is spherical. In his *Opus Majus*, Roger Bacon (13th century) indicated belief that the earth is spherical. Also in the 13th century, Johannes de Sacrobosco wrote a well-read textbook on astronomy, *On the Sphere of the World*. In this book, Sacrobosco gave reasons why the earth is spherical. The

A spherical earth divided into different climate zones

A spherical earth.

accompanying figure from a copy of the book illustrates a spherical earth. The next illustration is one of the creation, and it shows a spherical earth surrounded by water above (day two of the creation week). This image comes from a French Bible that belonged to King John the Good dating from about 1350. We know the vintage of the Bible because the English have possessed the Bible continually since they captured it as booty in the Battle of Poitiers in 1356.

In his commentary on Genesis, Martin Luther certainly indicated that the earth is spherical. He frequently referenced Aristotle in his commentary. Aristotle clearly taught that the earth was spherical, which if Luther disagreed with this, there was ample opportunity to express that.

Many flat-earthers confuse this matter by referencing a quote attributed to Luther. In the *Table Talk*, number 4638, dated June 4, 1539, we find:

> There was mention of a certain new astrologer who wanted to prove that the earth moves and not the sky, the sun, and the moon. This would be as if somebody were riding on a cart or in a ship and imagined that he was standing still while the earth and the trees were moving. [Luther remarked,] "So it

goes now. Whoever wants to be clever must agree with nothing that others esteem. He must do something of his own. This is what that fellow does who wishes to turn the whole of astronomy upside down. Even in these things that are thrown into disorder I believe the Holy Scriptures, for Joshua commanded the sun to stand still and not the earth."[17]

Again, notice that this quote is in reference to the question of whether the earth moves, not what shape the earth is. Flat-earthers persist in confusing these two issues. Though Copernicus is not mentioned by name, Copernicus likely is the astrologer mentioned (astronomers often were called astrologers then, for the two were mingled at that time). This is table talk number 4638, from June 4, 1539, four years prior to the publication of Copernicus' book. Apparently, Copernicus had been discussing the heliocentric model for a while, and news of this had spread across Europe. Note that Luther first objected on the grounds that what Copernicus proposed would overturn the whole of astronomy. This was true, as most people in the West, including Luther, subscribed to Aristotelian/Ptolemaic cosmology, which was geocentric. But that cosmology was not flat earth, as many flat-earthers consistently and erroneously seem to think. Luther's scriptural basis for rejection was secondary. However, we must note that the *Table Talks* were not penned by Luther. Rather, they were recollections by others of informal conversations published 20 years after Luther's death. And this particular conversation occurred nearly 30 years before publication. One must wonder how accurately this attribution reflected Luther's thoughts on the matter.

This discussion of the history of Western cosmology is far from exhaustive. There are many more examples that one could site that demonstrate the dominant cosmology in the West for 25 centuries has been that the earth is spherical. However, that dominant cosmology was geocentric until four centuries ago when the heliocentric theory replaced the geocentric theory. The faux history of cosmology that the flat-earthers peddle, that nearly everyone believed the earth was flat until 500 years ago, could not be more wrong. Furthermore, their repeated confusion of the geocentric model with the flat-earth model further clouds this false history.

---

17. Martin Luther, *Table Talk*, translated by Theodore G. Tappert. In *Luther's Works, Volume 54*, Helmut T. Lehmann, editor, (Philadelphia, PA: Fortress Press. 1967), p. 358–359.

Accusation Against Christianity

Since from ancient times and through the Middle Ages people in the West thought the earth was spherical, how did the widespread belief that everyone thought the earth was flat until five centuries ago come about? It is a result of a concentrated effort to discredit Christianity and the Bible. Consider the depiction of the Middle Ages as the "dark ages." That term apparently was first used by Petrarch in the 14th century. He meant it as a reference to the glory of the Greco-Roman world that obviously had disappeared by his day. By the time of the so-called Enlightenment, this term was appropriated to disparage the Church. The Age of Reason supposedly was in stark contrast to the Age of Faith, a term then applied to the Middle Ages. This thinking came to fruition in the 19th century when the flat-earth myth was concocted.

A major figure in creating the flat-earth myth was Washington Irving, who in 1828 published *A History of the Life and Voyages of Christopher Columbus*. It appeared to be an exhaustive tome, consisting of three volumes when published in the United States and in four volumes in the United Kingdom. The book proved to be quite popular, for it went through 175 editions before the end of the 19th century. Because of its length, most people assumed that it was accurate. However, Irving blended true information with many details that were not true. Today, we understand that authors frequently do this, but two centuries ago, this was a new concept. It was Irving who sold the myth that Columbus had to battle the foolish superstition of flat-earthers in demonstrating that the earth was round. For instance, Irving fabricated the dispute with religious authorities in Salamanca and the fears of Columbus' crew.

Others soon followed Irving's lead. In 1834, Jean Antoine Letronne published *On the Cosmographical Ideas of the Church Fathers*, where he falsely accused the church fathers and the medieval church of believing the earth was flat. In his 1837 book, *History of the Inductive Sciences,* William Whewell continued Letronne's false claims, citing Lactantius and Cosmas as evidence. Other historians quickly joined, though they couldn't find other examples. One would think other examples would have been easy to find if the church actually had taught that the earth was flat. This led to the *conflict thesis*, the idea that religion in general and Christianity in particular had held back progress. This was the theme of

Flammarion engraving.

John William Draper's 1874 book, *History of the Conflict Between Religion and Science*. Andrew Dickson White followed suit with his book, *The Warfare of Science*, just two years later, followed by his much larger two-volume tome, *History of the Warfare of Science with Theology in Christendom* in 1896. It was in this climate that Camille Flammarion included the engraving illustrated here in *The Atmosphere: Popular Meteorology*. Most people who have seen the Flammarion engraving think it is medieval in origin, but it first appeared in his book published in 1888.

Flat-earthers frequently quote Ferdinand Magellan as saying:

> The church says the earth is flat; but I have seen its shadow on the moon, and I have more confidence even in a shadow than in the church.

This quote certainly seems to sum up what flat-earthers claim about history. However, Magellan said no such thing. This quote actually comes from "The Great Agnostic," Robert G. Ingersoll, who in his 1873 essay "Individuality," wrote:

> It is a blessed thing that in every age some one has had individuality enough and courage enough to stand by his own convictions — some one who had the grandeur to say his say. I believe it was Magellan who said, "The church says the earth is flat; but I have seen its shadow on the moon, and I have more confidence even in a shadow than in the church." On the prow of his ship were disobedience, defiance, scorn, and success.[18]

This is the earliest known reference to this quote, indicating that it originated with Ingersoll, not Magellan. And Ingersoll wrote this at the height of the conflict thesis. The Roman Catholic Church never opposed the flat earth because no one seriously was teaching it. On the other hand, the Roman Catholic Church did oppose the heliocentric theory because the Roman Catholic Church had adopted the geocentric model, and there were people questioning that decision. Once again, this is the result of conflation of the shape of the earth with the question of whether the earth moves.

The Flat-Earth Movement Is Born

In 1838, Samuel Birley Rowbotham became convinced that the earth was flat. What prompted him to reach this conclusion? Was it because he read Irving, Letronne, or Whewell? It likely wasn't Letronne, for Letronne's book was in French. Because his book went through so many editions and was popular in the UK, it could have been Irving's book. However, Irving didn't make such a strong case that the Church taught the earth was flat. It is more probable that Rowbotham was influenced by fellow Englishman Whewell, who published his book the year before. If

Samuel Rowbotham

18. R.G. Ingersoll, *The Gods, and Other Lectures* (Washington, DC: C.P. Farrell, 1879), p. 171.

so, then instead of recognizing that Whewell was peddling a false history of cosmology and the Church, Rowbotham unfortunately accepted the lie. At any rate, Rowbotham conducted what has become known as the Bedford Level experiment on the Old Bedford River near Norfolk, England. The Bedford Level is a six-mile stretch of the river that is straight, allowing an uninterrupted view along the six miles. Furthermore, there is no gradient there, so that portion of the river amounts to a slow-flowing drainage canal. If the earth is spherical, then the drop from one end of the Bedford Level to the other is about 24 feet. That is, if one were to use a telescope at water level to view along the water on one end of Bedford Level, an object less than 24-feet high on the other end would not be visible. Rowbotham waded into the river and used a telescope held eight inches above the water to observe a rowboat with a five-foot-high mast row away. Rowbotham claimed that he could see the mast when it was six miles away, even though the spherical earth required that the top of the mast be about 11 feet below his horizon (as viewed from eight inches above the water). As is usually recounted, Rowbotham concluded that the earth must be flat based on this experiment. However, as I argued above, it is more likely that Rowbotham had already concluded that the earth was flat, so this experiment merely confirmed his thesis, at least to his satisfaction. Using the pseudonym Parallax, Rowbotham published his results in a pamphlet titled *Zetetic Astronomy: Earth Not a Globe* in 1849, which he expanded into a book in 1865 under his own name.

Rowbotham preferred to call his cosmology "zetetic astronomy," a term flat-earthers today occasionally use. As he explained at the beginning of his book, Rowbotham chose this term because:

> The term Zetetic is derived from the Greek verb *Zeteo*; which means to search, or examine; to proceed only by inquiry; to take nothing for granted, but to trace phenomena to their immediate and demonstrable causes. It is here used in contradistinction from the word "theoretic," the meaning of which is, speculative — imaginary — not tangible — scheming, but not proving.[19]

---

19. S.B. Rowbotham, *Zetetic Astronomy: Earth Not a Globe* (Forgotten Books, 1881, reprinted in 2007), p. 3.

I'll let pass Rowbotham's mischaracterization of "theoretic," an alternate word for theoretical. Instead, I wish to emphasize that Rowbotham's zetetic flat-earth model is very different from ancient flat-earth cosmologies. Many ancient flat-earth cosmologies had a dome over the earth as the zetetic model has.[20] However, unlike the zetetic model, which has the sun and moon moving in circles perpetually above the earth, ancient flat-earth cosmologies had the sun and moon passing below the flat earth each night. That is, in ancient flat-earth cosmologies, the sun and moon (as well as many of the stars) rose and set, but in the zetetic model, the sun, moon, and stars never rise or set. Modern flat-earthers must go through elaborate mental gymnastics to explain how it is possible for the sun, moon, and many stars to only *appear* to rise and set.

Why the difference? The ancient flat-earth models could account for some aspects of the sky, a subject I take up in chapter 4. However, in these ancient flat-earth models, the sun, moon, and stars had to rise and set at the same time across the flat earth. Given the lack of good timepieces in the ancient world and slow transportation as compared to the modern world, it is not surprising that many ancient cultures were not aware that different times exist at different places in the world. As I discussed earlier, the ancient Greeks became aware that time was not the same across the earth, but that time became progressively earlier as one traveled westward. This was one of the evidences that they used to argue that the earth is a sphere. In the 19th century, even Rowbotham had to admit that there were different time zones around the world, hence the need to create his model in a way that was very different from ancient flat-earth cosmologies. Hence, while ancient flat-earth models could account for certain aspects of the sky, they could not explain the existence of time zones. While Rowbotham's zetetic model can accommodate time zones, it utterly fails to explain some of the aspects of the sky that ancient flat-earth cosmologies could explain. However, the conventional cosmology of a spinning globe earth can explain all of these, and then some.

Most people ignored Rowbotham's work. However, in 1870, John Hampden, another flat-earth proponent, offered a wager of a hefty sum to anyone who could demonstrate a convex curvature of a large body of

---

20. However, by the Christian era, any domed cosmology in the West had been replaced by a sphere or spheres surrounding a spherical earth.

water, as a spherical earth would require. The famous evolutionist Alfred Russell Wallace took the challenge. Apparently aware of Rowbotham's result, Wallace altered the technique a bit. He placed two identical objects at different locations along the Bedford Level. Wallace examined each object from a telescope mounted on a bridge. He found that the nearer object appeared higher than the more distant one, consistent with the results predicted by a spherical earth.[21] Why the difference? A temperature inversion is common over bodies of water during spring and summer when these experiments were done. A temperature inversion causes light initially traveling tangent to the earth's surface to bend downward, resulting in light traveling around the earth's curvature. I shall discuss this phenomenon more in the next chapter.

As new converts joined the movement, several of them wrote books, but most aren't referenced much anymore. Two exceptions are William Carpenter's *A Hundred Proofs the Earth Is Not a Globe* (1885) and David Wardlaw Scott's *Terra Firma: The Earth Not a Planet, Proved from Scripture, Reason, and Fact* (1901). Rowbotham founded zetetic societies in England and New York in 1883, two years before his death. Lady Elizabeth Blount was perhaps the next leader in the flat-earth movement. In 1893, she founded the Universal Zetetic Society, which counted among its members the well-known British theologian E.W. Bullinger. This is a bit strange. Bullinger wrote on many topics, even some odd ones, such as the gospel in the stars and numerology, but he never wrote about the earth being flat. If Bullinger was a flat-earther, he was not outspoken about it. Perhaps Bullinger joined the society out of curiosity. The society published a journal called *Earth Not a Globe Review*. In reading flat-earth material, one sometimes sees this publication referenced. It took me a while to figure out what this publication was. Apparently, this journal was published 1893–1897. The society published another journal, *Earth*, 1901–1904. One occasionally sees this journal referenced in flat-earth material, too. Neither journal is easy to find.

An interesting case is Wilbur Glenn Voliva. In 1906, Voliva had gained control of the Christian Catholic Church based in Zion, Illinois.

---

21. The outcome of the wager was a messy affair. The referee of the wager awarded the money to Wallace. Hampden accused Wallace of cheating and sued for return of the money. Eventually, the court imprisoned Hampden for libeling and threatening to kill Wallace, but it also ordered Wallace to return the money because Hampden had retracted the bet.

Voliva amassed total power in the church, as well as the city of Zion and the industries in town. Voliva came to embrace the flat-earth cosmology, which he made a doctrine of the church. At its height, the church claimed 20,000 followers worldwide. However, by the late 1920s, Voliva's lavish lifestyle and dictatorial control had alienated many church members. This dissension and the Great Depression took its toll, and the church fell on hard times. By the time of Voliva's death in 1942, the church virtually ceased to exist. Though a few members revived and renamed the church, it never has enjoyed the following it once had. It also jettisoned flat-earth teaching.

Belief that the earth is flat probably peaked in the late 19th and early 20th centuries. From there, it underwent decline. In 1956, Samuel Shenton organized the International Flat Earth Research Society (better known simply as The Flat Earth Society) in the United Kingdom. Shenton may have been earnest in his belief, but with the advent of the space program, many people joined the society as a joke. It's ironic that at times membership of The Flat Earth Society was dominated by people who thought the earth was a globe. After Shenton's death in 1971, Charles K. Johnson of California incorporated the International Flat Earth Research Society. It never had more than a few thousand members. The society was inactive after Johnson's death in 2001, but in 2004, Daniel Shenton (not related to Samuel Shenton) began a society website. Therefore, contrary to common misconception, there is no single flat-earth society. Rather, the group has gone through several incarnations, and it's not clear how serious various leaders or its members have been.

Before moving on, I ought to mention a few other, more obscure, books about flat earth (while omitting many pamphlets and booklets). The American Alexander Gleason published *Is the Bible from Heaven? Or Is the Earth a Globe?* in 1893. Gleason is best known for his azimuthal equidistant projection map of the earth, the representation of the earth most favored by flat-earthers (I discuss this map in chapter 5). The South African Thomas Winship published *Zetetic Cosmogony: Or Conclusive Evidence That the World Is Not a Rotating Revolving Globe, but a Stationary Plane Circle* in 1898. More recently, the French woman Gabrielle Henriet wrote *Heaven and Earth*. It isn't clear when this book was published — there is no publication date on the copyright page. Its publication date often is stated as being 1958, but the last text on the final page of the book enigmatically is "1938–1956." Is 1958 the date of the English translation, and is 1938 the publication of the original French version?[22] This book failed to attract the attention that the books of the late 19th century did. These appear to be the last flat-earth books published before Dubay's two books in the second decade of the 21st century. It is interesting that the flat-earthers of today have published few books on the subject, opting instead to promote flat-earthers primarily with YouTube videos. The only other recent books about flat earth that I'm aware of are Nathan Roberts' 2017 *The Doctrine of the Shape of the Earth*, Chad Taylor's 2017 *Where Are We? Earth, According to the Bible* and Edward Hendrie's 2016 *The Greatest Lie on Earth: Proof that our World is Not a Moving Globe*.

Why I Wrote This Book

This brings me back to where I began this chapter — the revival of the flat-earth movement in the 21st century. Apparently, Dubay or others stumbled across some flat-earth writings from more than a century earlier, perhaps Carpenter's book. These 21st-century converts began to repeat and repackage flat-earth arguments. It's not entirely clear that some of the people involved in this revival believe the earth was flat. It could be that some of them merely promoted flat earth as a prank.[23] Unfortunately, as flat-earth websites proliferated on the Internet, thousands of people soon joined the movement. It's ironic that more people in the West today may believe that the earth is flat than have in two millennia.

I have interacted with a few flat-earthers in person, via email, and on a few websites. It's been impossible to convince true believers in the flat earth that the earth is a globe. They are very quick to dismiss all evidence to

---

22. I've seen Henriet credited with a 1963 book entitled *The Solid Vault of Heaven*, however, I have not been able to find a copy or a facsimile of this book. I suspect that it may be a reprinting of her earlier book with a different title.

23. I've wondered about the sincerity of some flat-earth promoters for some time. For instance, Rowbotham originally authored his ideas under the pseudonym Parallax. But Rowbotham argued that parallax, the apparent shift in position of stars due to the earth's orbit around the sun, doesn't exist. Could use of this pseudonym have telegraphed that Rowbotham wasn't being serious in his claims? Or consider Dubay's book entitled *The Flat Earth Conspiracy*. If Dubay were serious, shouldn't that title be *The Globe Earth Conspiracy*? Might Dubay cleverly be indicating that his work about flat earth merely is a joke?

the contrary. What about photos from space showing a spherical earth? There are no satellites, no astronauts, we haven't been to the moon, and so NASA has lied about everything. What about astronauts who testify that they have been in space and directly observed that the earth is a globe? They're all Freemasons, which proves that they are part of a large conspiracy (and big liars, to boot). It doesn't seem to faze in the least professing Christian believers in the flat earth when I point out that this puts them into the position of accusing several Christian brothers of lying about one of the biggest things that has happened in their lives.

My own personal observations that dispute what flat-earthers teach is met with great skepticism. I've asked several flat-earthers who question what I say on these matters if I'm lying about my evidence or if I'm just so professionally incompetent I can't properly make and interpret such observations. That question usually is left unanswered. I wish that flat-earthers would apply even an ounce of such skepticism to the flat-earth arguments that they encounter on the Internet. To my questions of flat-earthers, they often link to webpages that mock and mischaracterize the conventional (and I think correct) understanding of reality. Supposed arguments for the flat earth do much the same. For instance, one person recently posted on a Facebook (FB) page dedicated to discussing flat earth a frame from the beginning of a Three Stooges movie with the images of myself and two other creation scientists who have taken on the flat-earth movement superimposed over the faces of Moe, Larry, and Curly. For the record, I wasn't offended. In fact, I was amused, because I like lampoon. However, this sort of thing hardly constitutes a rational argument for something. This sort of thing is all too common among promoters of flat earth. Many flat-earthers seem to think that ridicule of their opponents' position is a logical argument for their own position. If they truly think this, then that may explain why they were so easily duped into believing that the earth is flat in the first place. I haven't written this book for the benefit of these people, because I don't think anything I could possibly say could change their minds. To the contrary, one of the reasons that I wrote this book is for people who have encountered flat-earth arguments and are seeking help in deciding if those arguments are sound.

But there are two other reasons that I wrote this book. The flat-earth books of more than a century ago argued that the Bible taught that the earth was flat. Never mind the fact that almost no one for two millennia seemed to think so. When these writings recently began to circulate on the Internet, some very conservative Christians who take a hyper-literal approach to Scripture encountered these arguments and accepted them. Hence, to them, belief that the earth is flat became a question of orthodoxy. I wrote this book to counter this wrong approach to the Bible. It is no coincidence that some Christians of the 19th century began believing that the Bible teaches that the earth was flat precisely when critics of the Bible started laying that false accusation. Those misguided Christians unquestionably accepted that lie. We shouldn't believe the devil's lies.

Finally, I've always suspected that there is a hidden agenda behind the recent revival of 19th-century flat-earth belief. We biblical creationists frequently are accused of believing that everything in the Bible is literally true.[24] I think that there are people out there who are saying, "If you think it's literal, then I'll show you literal!" That is, part of the motivation behind the modern flat-earth movement is to undermine the credibility of the creation science movement. As one who has dedicated his life to sharing the reality of biblical creation with the world, I view the flat earth as a threat to my calling. Therefore, the third reason I wrote this book is to counter this attack.

---

24. As I will show in chapter 10, there are many examples of nonliteral uses in the Bible. However, that does not mean that everything in the Bible can be taken nonliterally. Far from it. It is patently false that *everything* in the Bible is literally true.

Chapter 2

Exhibit A: The Bedford Level Experiment and the Chicago Skyline

Seeing Is Believing

As I discussed in chapter 1, it was Samuel Rowbotham's 1838 Bedford level experiment that launched the 19th-century flat-earth movement. More than anything else, it probably was Joshua Nowicki's famous photograph of the Chicago skyline from more than 50 miles away that convinced people in the 21st century to believe that the earth was flat. Therefore, it is appropriate that I begin more detailed discussion of the flat earth with these two similar experiments.

To recap, Rowbotham realized that over the six miles of the Bedford level, the earth's curvature ought to obscure anything shorter than 16 feet tall (assuming the telescope used was mounted eight inches above the water). Since he could see the five-foot mast of a boat from six miles, Rowbotham concluded that the earth was flat. Similarly, one might expect that on a curved earth, the skyline of Chicago ought not to be visible from more than 50 miles. But how is this quantified?

In the accompanying, point C represents the center of the earth having radius *R*. Consider the top of an object of height *h* at point A. From that height, one can see the horizon at point B at distance *d* away. Since the line of length *d* is tangent to the earth's surface at point B, triangle ABC has a right angle at vertex B. Applying the Pythagorean theorem,

$$d^2 + R^2 = (R + h)^2$$

this reduces to

$$d^2 = h(2R + h).$$

For a given height, h, it is relatively straightforward to determine the distance, d, that the height is visible. However, finding h as a function of d is more complicated. Fortunately, we can approximate a much simpler expression. If h is much smaller than R ($h << R$), the above equation becomes

$$h = \frac{d^2}{2R}$$

Note that this is an approximation, but the approximation works well for most of the heights and distances of concern here. If the distance, d, is one mile, then using the earth's radius of approximately 4,000 miles, we find that the height, h, is eight inches. That is, at a height of eight inches, the visible horizon is one mile away. We can turn this around and note that if one's eye were located on the surface, an object one mile away that is less than eight inches tall would not be visible. Notice that h increases with the square of d. This often is expressed as the simple relation that the height that one can see is eight inches times the distance in miles squared. For instance, to see two miles, a man must have his eyes at a height of 2^2 x 8 inches, or 32 inches. To see three miles, a man must have his eyes at a height of 2^3 x 8 inches, or six feet. This is the basis of the oft-repeated fact that while standing on shore, a person can see about three miles over water, because when standing on shore, an adult's eye is about six feet above the water.

This probably is why Rowbotham placed his telescope eight inches above the water in the Bedford Level experiment. He didn't want the telescope directly on the water. Placing it eight inches high meant that the telescope's horizon would be one mile. Hence, when calculating what height could be seen at greater distances, he had to subtract one mile.

That is, at a distance of 6 miles, the correct distance to put into the above approximation is 5 miles, yielding a minimum height that can be seen of more than 16 feet. Therefore, Rowbotham ought not to have seen a 5-foot mast 6 miles away because it would have been about 11 feet too low. Similarly, from 50 miles away, nothing lower than about 1,700 feet ought to be visible. Nothing on the Chicago skyline is taller than this (the Willis Tower is 1,450 feet tall, capped by a pinnacle that extends to 1,729 feet), so nothing in Chicago ought to be visible from more than 50 miles away.

Nor are the Bedford Level experiment and the Nowicki photograph the only examples of things that ought not to be visible on a spherical earth. Many of the 100 proofs of a flat earth in Carpenter's book are examples of distant objects, such as lighthouses, islands, and peaks of land, far enough away to be beyond the earth's curvature, yet sometimes are visible. In an obvious update of Carpenter's book, the 21st-century flat-earther, Eric Dubay, has published a book entitled *200 Proofs That the Earth Is Not a Spinning Ball*. I guess by doubling the number of "proofs," Dubay might think that his book is twice as good as Carpenter's book. Dubay repeats many of Carpenter's arguments, including examples of distant objects that are beyond the distance that they ought to be seen (plus, Dubay added a few more), if the earth is spherical. This argument for the earth being flat is so simple to understand, it is no wonder that so many people have been convinced of the earth being flat primarily based on this one argument. Therefore, it requires an explanation.

The Explanation

First, note that if the earth is truly flat, then seeing very distant objects over such great distances ought to be a common occurrence on every clear day. Alas, it is not. Right away, this suggests that maybe something else is at play. Also, notice that these observations are almost always, if not always, done over water. Generally, this is because water, being a liquid, rapidly sinks to its own level, producing a surface of uniform height.[1]

---

1. On a flat earth, the surface level of a large body of water is in a plane, while on a globe earth, the surface level of a large body of water is on the surface of a sphere. At any point on the sphere, the surface is in a plane tangent to the sphere at that point. Since the earth's radius is so large, local curvature is not noticeable. Therefore, the flat-earth and spherical-earth models aren't that different on the local scale. I shall discuss this topic more in chapter 6.

This contrasts with land, where obstructions can block one's view of distant objects. But viewing over bodies of water is key in explaining what is going on in these experiments. Rowbotham was a victim of a superior mirage, and this is the explanation of the other similar experiments in which objects beyond the horizon are visible. When flat-earthers hear this, they normally respond by dismissing this as impossible, because they claim that mirages are inverted images, but Rowbotham saw the boat right side up the entire time. Likewise, other similar experiments show erect views as well. However, this confuses superior and inferior mirages. What is the difference? For one thing, superior mirages are mostly seen over water, while inferior mirages are most commonly seen over land. To understand both, we must discuss the physics of light a bit.

In a vacuum, light travels at 299,792,458 m/s. In all other media, the speed is less than in a vacuum, with the speed depending upon the medium. We usually express this behavior reciprocally as the index of refraction, n:

$$n = c/v\,,$$

where c is the speed of light in a vacuum, and v is the speed of light in any medium. Notice that since the speed of light is greatest in a vacuum, all indices of refraction are greater than one. In the situations that we are discussing, the medium is air. In air, the speed of light is only slightly less than it is in a vacuum. The speed of light in air depends upon several factors, the most important being the temperature and pressure of the air. We can express this as the index of refraction of air as a function of pressure and temperature:

$$n(P,T) = 1 + 0.000293 \left(\frac{P}{P_0}\right)\left(\frac{T_0}{T}\right)$$

where P and T are the pressure and temperature of air, and P_0 and T_0 are the standard values of one atmosphere of pressure and 300 K. Pressure is a function of height, and since with mirages there is no appreciable height difference, pressure differences are negligible, and so the temperature difference dominates differences in the indices of refraction. When light travels from one medium to another, the path of the light is refracted, or bent. This is what causes the "bent stick" appearance of a long object partially inserted in water, such as a pole placed into the water of a pool. This behavior is described by Snell's law:

$$\frac{\sin\theta_1}{\sin\theta_2} = \frac{n_2}{n_1}$$

where θ_1 and θ_2 are the angles that the light rays make with the perpendicular to the interface between the two media, and n_1 and n_2 are the indices of refraction of the two media (see figure Snell's Law). Depending upon which direction the light is traveling, one of the angles is the angle of incidence, and the other angle is the angle of refraction.

For most media and angles of incidence, the light transmits from one medium to the other. However, when passing from a medium of higher index of refraction into a medium of lower index of refraction at a sufficiently high angle of incidence, there may not be a real value for the angle of refraction in Snell's law. When this happens, the light cannot pass into the second medium. Instead, the light is reflected off the interface and back into the first medium. We call this phenomenon total internal reflection. Many devices make use of total internal reflection. Total internal reflection allows a prism with two 45-degree angles and one 90-degree angle to reflect light at a right angle. One could use a mirror

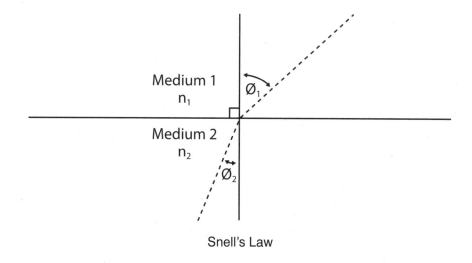

Snell's Law

mounted at a 45-degree angle to do the same thing, but total internal reflection is nearly 100% efficient, while the best mirrors are perhaps 85% efficient. Many optical devices, such as binoculars and periscopes, make use of this. Fiber optics are thin wires of glass. Being so thin, fiber optics are flexible and about as easy to handle as metal wire. Glass has a relatively high index of refraction, so light shining down a fiber optic is totally reflected internally by the walls of the fiber optic, if the fiber optic is not bent too sharply. We use fiber optics every day with telephones, cable TV, and Internet connections.

What must be the angle of incidence for total internal reflection to occur? Let medium 1 be the medium with the higher index of refraction. As θ_1 increases, θ_2 also increases, albeit at a faster rate. When θ_2 reaches 90 degrees, there is total internal reflection, and there is no transmission of light. The corresponding angle of incidence, θ_1, is the critical angle where total internal reflection occurs. Let the critical angle be θ_c. Substituting into Snell's law:

$$\sin \theta_c = \frac{n_2}{n_1}$$

For instance, for a 45°-45°-90° prism (the kind used in binoculars and many other optical devices), light impinges on the reflective surface at 45°, so the critical angle is 45°. For total internal reflection, the index of refraction of the prism must be at least $1/\sin(45°) = 1.414$. All glass has an index of refraction greater than this.

However, in layers of air the indices of refraction are very close to one another, so the critical angle must be very close to 90°. From the second equation above, the index of refraction at one atmosphere of pressure and a temperature of 310 K (50 degrees F) is 1.000284, while the index of refraction at one atmosphere of pressure and a temperature of 320 K (68 degrees F) is 1.000275. These values yield a critical angle of 89.76 degrees. Hence, when at one atmosphere of pressure light attempts to pass from air at 310 K (50 degrees F) to air at 320 K (68 degrees F), the light will be totally internally reflected if the angle of incidence is greater than 89.76 degrees, or less than about a quarter of a degree from grazing incidence. If the temperature difference is greater, the critical angle will be less; hence, the angle from grazing incidence will be greater. If the temperature difference is less, the angle from grazing incidence will be less.

Inferior Mirages

Inferior mirages are the most commonly noticed type of mirage; therefore, in the minds of most people, it is the only type of mirage. An inferior mirage occurs when there is a layer of warm air in contact with the ground, with layers of much cooler air just above. This condition exists over land in the afternoon on nearly every sunny day, but particularly in the summer. As the sun's radiation is absorbed by the ground, the air in contact with the ground heats. Air a short distance above the ground remains cooler, so a large temperature difference can exist between these two layers. Because this temperature difference is most pronounced when the sun is as high in the sky as possible, this condition is most likely to occur in the early afternoon in late spring and into summer. The type of surface exposed to sunlight is very important, too, because dark, flat surfaces, such as pavement, rock, and sand are most efficient at heating air this way. Surfaces with much vegetation, such as grass, are far less efficient in doing this. Because of its high specific heat and great optical depth, water generally is very poor at producing conditions conducive to an inferior mirage. The above example of a 10-degree difference in air temperature is rather modest — much greater temperature differences occur under ideal conditions of early summer, decreasing the critical angle and increasing the angle above grazing where an inferior mirage can happen. With these conditions, light from a distant object near but above the horizon reflects off the warmer air (see figure).

One of the most common objects reflected in this way is blue sky, which our brains interpret as light reflecting off a body of water. The reflected image appears below the object, which is why we call this an inferior mirage. The layer of warm air near the surface acts much like an ordinary mirror. As a mirror mounted vertically, as on a wall, reverses direction left to right, a mirror mounted horizontally, as with an inferior mirage, reverses direction from top to bottom (you see the same thing with a vertical mirror if you tilt your head 90 degrees and look

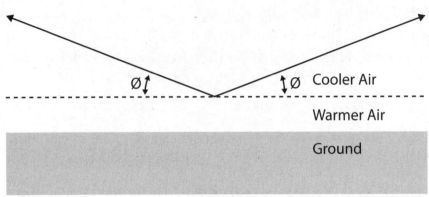

Inferior Mirage

at reflections in the mirror or place a mirror on the floor). The reversal happens because light from the top of a distant object will reflect closer to the observer than light from the bottom of the object. Therefore, inferior mirages usually appear inverted. Early in the morning or late in the afternoon, solar heating of the ground is not nearly as great, so inferior mirages are less likely to happen then. The sun is much lower in the sky even at noon during autumn and winter than in summer, so inferior mirages are much less common outside of summer.

The warm surface air that causes inferior mirages tends to expand. As air expands, it becomes less dense, producing buoyancy. Buoyant force causes warm air to rise, and the air at ground level must be replaced, usually with downward motion of cooler air aloft. This is an unstable condition, which leads to upward and downward motion of air (turbulence). Light passing through pockets of air at different temperatures and different indices of refraction is randomly deflected, producing blurring of images. The turbulence varies where these pockets are, which causes time-varying blurriness. We see this as shimmer. Therefore, it is unusual for an inferior mirage to be steady.

Superior Mirages

As previously mentioned, the reaction of bodies of water with sunlight is very different from that of land. Being largely transparent, light penetrates deeply into water so that the sun's light is absorbed throughout a thick layer from the surface to some depth rather than just on the surface, as with land. Additionally, water has a high specific heat, which means that its temperature increases very slowly as heat is added. Consequently, water exposed to sunlight does not change temperature appreciably throughout the day, so there is no heating of air in contact with the water. If anything, during summer afternoons, when land is rapidly heating, bodies of water frequently are cooler than air temperature. The cooler water chills the air in direct contact with it, so the air lying just above water often is cooler than air higher up. Since air temperature normally decreases with height, this temperature reversal from the norm is called a *temperature inversion*. Temperature inversions are common over bodies of water during late spring and throughout summer and into autumn. Since this temperature structure is the reverse of what causes inferior mirages, inferior mirages are far less commonly seen over water than over land.

Consider light from a distant object that is emitted horizontally, parallel to the water's surface at the location of the object (see figure). With increasing distance from the object, the earth's curvature causes the surface of the water to fall away from the beam of light. Over one mile, the amount of drop is eight inches, but the drop increases quadratically with distance. Consequently, after three miles, the drop is 6 feet, and after six miles, the drop is 24 feet. This is the point of the Bedford Level experiment — the curvature of the earth ought to intervene to prevent the mast of the boat being visible from much more than three miles, let alone six miles. However, for the light from the distant object not to be visible, it would have to travel in a straight line. But with a temperature inversion, straight-line motion would carry the light from a cooler layer of air into a warmer layer of air at nearly a grazing angle. The light cannot do this,

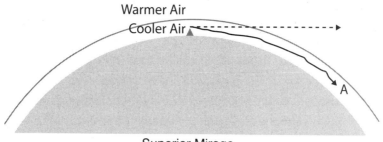

Superior Mirage

so it continually is refracted downward, causing the light to bend around the edge of the earth. Therefore, with a temperature inversion, one can see objects that lie well beyond the edge of the earth's curvature when viewing close to the surface of water. This assumes that all the rays of light from the object begin within the inversion layer. What about tall objects, the tops of which may lie above the inversion layer? Being so tall, some rays of light from the top will be directed with a slight downward component. As those rays travel, they will enter the temperature inversion, which is permitted by Snell's law, but they will be refracted downward toward the water, hence, they can curve around the earth's surface as well.

Since this image is visible above where the object is, it is called a superior mirage. Because cooler air has no physical reason to rise, a temperature inversion is a stable situation, with little convection as with the condition that produces an inferior mirage. Therefore, superior mirages can be very steady, much steadier than inferior mirages. Furthermore, since the refraction acts almost continually rather than reflecting at one point, superior mirages normally are erect rather than inverted. If one gains a little altitude, one can get out of the inversion layer, and thus avoid seeing a superior mirage. In chapter 1, I pointed out that this is what Alfred Russell Wallace did when he repeated the Bedford Level experiment. Wallace did not see the distant object that was his target, which is consistent with a spherical earth. Wallace correctly accounted for the effect of a temperature inversion, but Rowbotham did not.

Variable refraction due to temperature inversions explains the other similar experiments, such as the Nowicki photograph. However, there is a further test. The difference in the indices of refraction depend upon how great the temperature inversion is. Therefore, how far one can see distant objects over the earth's curvature depends upon the amounts of temperature inversion present. Nowicki has produced many photographs showing various heights of the Chicago skyline across Lake Michigan. In some photographs, the lower parts of buildings are obscured, while in others, most, if not all, of the buildings are visible. He even has produced a time-lapse video of photos taken over several minutes that show the Chicago skyline bouncing up and down. Other photos show no buildings in Chicago, but he generally doesn't publish those because they aren't nearly as interesting. This variable visibility of Chicago buildings is difficult for flat-earthers to explain. They don't even try, perhaps because they don't know about them.

If the rate of increase of air temperature with height is great enough, a temperature inversion can even cause objects in the distance to appear above the horizon. In 1896, Ulysses Grant Morrow conducted an experiment similar to the Bedford Level experiment on the Old Illinois Drainage Canal. A very strong temperature inversion produced results consistent with the earth being curved concavely. There are people who think that the earth's surface is the inside of a shell. This experiment is their exhibit A.

My Own Experiment

Inspired by the Nowicki photos, flat-earthers have posted many other examples of the visibility of distant objects, such as ships, that are fully visible. Most, if not all, of these are taken during warm weather, such as late spring and summer, when the water is likely to be cooler than the air, producing a temperature inversion. However, what would happen if one were to repeat this experiment over water that is warmer than the air temperature? Since there is no temperature inversion, the hulls of ships ought to disappear as the ships move away. This condition is likely to prevail on cool days in late autumn and early winter, when water temperatures are higher than air temperatures. These conditions also can produce inferior mirages, though not nearly as pronounced as over land on sunny summer days.

On November 12, 2016, I had the opportunity to conduct this experiment. I was near the water's edge, just beyond the surf, at Virginia Beach from middle to late afternoon. When I began, the air temperature was 50 degrees F, and the temperature dropped a degree or two by the time that I was done, near sunset. The water temperature was 62–64 degrees F, so the air immediately above the water was at least ten degrees warmer than the air temperature a short distance above the water. I photographed two cargo ships as they made their way out to sea from the port at Hampton Roads. I mounted a digital SLR camera (a Nikon D3200) on a 3.5-inch Questar telescope, having a 1,320-mm focal length. The ISO setting on the camera was 100 for all photographs, though the exposure times varied according to light levels. The images produced here are the JPG images produced by the camera. There was no processing of the images.

The first photograph (Photo 1) is of a cargo ship bearing the name of the company on its hull. The company is the NYK line, a major Japanese shipping company. Notice that the bottoms of the letters are not visible. The letters on the hulls of cargo ships generally do not extend to the waterline, even when fully loaded, so clearly, the bottom of the hull is not visible. This is consistent with what we would expect on a spherical earth, but not on a flat earth. Notice the white bridge castle to the left. The shipping containers are multicolored, and they are stacked at least seven high above the hull directly in front of the bridge castle. Below the visible tiers of the multicolored containers, there is a level of what appears to be gray containers. It is not clear why the containers in this layer are the same color. It is more likely that this is the siding of the ship immediately above the hull. Finally, notice that the image is a bit blurry. This is because of turbulence in the air between the ship and shore. With increasing distance, the turbulence will get worse, and the images will get blurrier.

In the next and succeeding photographs, the ship is farther away, as indicated by the decreasing apparent size of the ship. In Photo 2, an inferior mirage is starting to show up. At the edge of the water, you can see a gray line, which is an inferior mirage of the grey row right above the hull. On the right side of the ship, you can see the inferior mirage of the bow. The hull protrudes forward there, and the small white patch just

Photo 1

Photo 2

above is a small portion of the forecastle. Notice that the inferior mirage of the bow is inverted, as one would expect. It is difficult to see here, but the lettering on the hull also is undergoing an inferior mirage, too.

In the next photograph (Photo 3), the lettering on the hull is no longer visible. The layer of gray containers is even more visible in the inferior mirage, and the first layer of multicolored containers is now beginning to appear in the inferior mirage. In the next photograph (Photo 4), the light from the gray layer of containers and its inferior mirage are beginning to merge. The first layer of the multicolored containers above it is clearly visible in the inferior mirage. The white of the bridge castle is starting to show up in the inferior mirage. In Photo 5, the layer of gray containers no longer is visible. The bottom of the bridge castle and its inferior mirage have merged. None of the hull is visible. In the next photograph (Photo 6), the ship has turned, so we see the back of the bridge castle and containers on the stern. Much of the bottom of what appears to be the ship is an inferior mirage of the upper containers. At any rate, the hull is

Photo 3

Photo 4

Photo 5

clearly not visible. Finally, in Photo 7, no containers are visible. All that we can see is the back of the bridge castle, merged with the upside-down inferior mirage. Notice the symmetry between the two.

Another container ship made its way outward, as shown in Photo 8, a photograph taken through the supports of a pier at Virginia Beach. You can clearly read the name of the shipping company, Maersk Line, on the

Photo 6

Photo 7

hull. What appears to be stains under the letters are the beginnings of an inferior mirage of the letters. Instead of a level of gray immediately above the hull as on the first ship, the layer right above the hull on this ship appeared a deep red (dark gray here in black and white). As with the other ship, in each succeeding photograph this ship is farther away, as evidenced by the decreasing apparent sizes of the containers and the ship.

In Photo 9, the ship now appears beyond the pier. Notice that the inferior mirage of the lettering on the hull is much more obvious now. In Photo 10, the lettering and its inferior mirage have now merged. In Photo

Photo 8

Photo 9

Photo 10

Photo 11

Photo 12

11, the lettering is difficult to see. This probably is because most of the lettering is below the horizon, and what at first appears to be the bottom of the hull, is an inferior mirage of the top of the hull. This is clearly seen by the inferior mirage of the layer of red (gray here in black and white) below the color of the hull. In Photo 12, the inferior mirage of the bottom layer of containers is more obvious, and the inferior mirage of the bottom of the bridge castle is beginning to show up. Clearly, at least half of the color of the hull visible here is an inferior mirage. Most of the hull is below the curvature of the earth. Unfortunately, at this point, the sun was about to set, so light levels were dropping quickly, forcing me to use longer exposures. Soon, I stopped taking photographs.

These photographs clearly reveal that the hulls of these two ships progressively disappeared as the ships moved farther away. This is consistent with what we would expect if the earth is spherical, but this cannot be explained if the earth is flat. Therefore, this is good evidence that the earth is spherical. Some flat-earthers have attempted to explain my results by claiming that the light from the ships has been refracted downward into the sea, merely giving the impression that the bottoms of the ships are blocked by the earth's curvature. However, the well-understood physics says otherwise — such refraction takes place only when there is a temperature inversion. But there was no temperature inversion that day, as indicated by water and air temperatures. Furthermore, the presence of weak inferior mirages testifies to the fact that there was no temperature inversion that day. It is ironic that flat-earthers dismiss the effect of refraction in explaining their observations but attempt to use the same effect to explain my observation. By doing so, they clearly indicate that they do not understand optics.

The results presented here contradict the many photos on the Internet of objects beyond the horizon that supposedly prove that the earth is flat. Those alleged proofs are flawed because they fail to take account of atmospheric refraction due to temperature inversions. By conducting this experiment when there was no possibility of a temperature inversion, I avoided that complication. The fact that inferior mirages consistently showed up in the photographs prove that there was no temperature inversion, indicating instead that there was a warm layer of air in contact with the water, with cooler air above. Like most people, flat-earthers prefer going to the beach on warm, sunny days. But this is when temperature inversions are almost guaranteed. Therefore, to get results that are not affected by a temperature inversion, one must do their due diligence and conduct this experiment when it isn't comfortable, on cold autumn and winter days (I certainly wasn't comfortable when I did my experiment).

Responses from Flat-Earthers

As I previously mentioned, flat-earthers typically dismiss this explanation, insisting that mirages are inverted. However, as I also pointed out, this conflates inferior and superior mirages. I suspect that many flat-earthers simply do not understand the difference between the two. Nor do I think many flat-earthers understand the physics and math underlying the formation of either type of mirage. Flat-earthers continue to take new images with total disregard for the warnings against doing so when there are temperature inversions. Even when flat-earthers take images when there is no temperature inversion showing clear evidence of the earth's curvature, they interpret the images otherwise.

An example of this is Dean Odle, pastor of Fire and Grace Church of Opelika, Alabama. On April 30, 2017, Odle and a group of his parishioners went to Mobile Bay, where they took images of the Port of Mobile docks a dozen miles across the bay. Odle computed that the docks should have been obscured by the earth's curvature if the earth was spherical, and since he could see all the way down to the water, he reasoned that this proved that the earth was flat. I checked the water temperature that day and the air temperature at the time of Odle's experiment, and I found that conditions then were conducive for producing a temperature inversion. In November 2017, I briefly spoke to Odle, and I suggested that he repeat the experiment when there was no temperature inversion. He didn't seem interested, so I was surprised when he repeated the experiment on February 3, 2018. The weather was cold that day, so this was a good time to repeat the experiment. I looked up the water and air temperatures that day, as did Odle. Early in the morning, the water temperature was warmer than the air temperature. But Odle took his images in early afternoon, when the air temperature was close to the water temperature, if not slightly warmer. Not to worry, since it was so cold that morning, it would have taken time to produce a temperature inversion, and so even if a temperature inversion did exist at the time of Odle's experiment, it would have been mild anyway. But this is what Odle had to say on his Facebook page:

> Here's a picture from the telescope at 12 miles across Mobile Bay after the water temperature was below the air temperature. Crystal clear picture of a crane and shipping containers sitting on the dock. Should have been hidden by 60 feet of earth curvature . . . but it wasn't. And this was not refraction as we waited for the conditions to be opposite of what it takes for temperature inversion.

Picture across Mobile Bay from Dean Odle's post.

Odle explained this in more detail in a sermon he preached the following day at his church. From his sermon, it is very clear that Odle doesn't know what a temperature inversion is. Even in his brief discussion reproduced here, he has completely reversed what a temperature inversion is — he thinks that it occurs when the air temperature is cooler than the water temperature. Of course, this is wrong, because a temperature inversion happens when the air temperature is warmer than the water temperature. But, as I already pointed out, that doesn't matter, because if there was a temperature inversion that day, it was very mild and brief.

Let us look at an image that Odle described above taken from his Facebook page. In the photograph, you can see two cranes and a portion of a third. Stacked cargo containers also are visible. Because they block the view of the cranes, it is very clear that the stacked containers are in front of the cranes. I examined several photographs of the cranes at the Port of Mobile on the Internet, but I couldn't find a good one that I could use here. However, I did find an excellent photograph (see following page) of the cranes at the Port of Rotterdam that are similar to the ones at Mobile and many other ports. Notice in this photograph that the cranes are located on the dock very close to the water. Ships that are to be loaded or unloaded are berthed in the water next to the dock. The cranes

Cranes at the Port of Rotterdam (Photo credit: M.M. Minderhoud)

are on wheels that allow them to move along the side of the ship while loading and unloading. The containers are stored a short distance away in the yard lying inland from the crane. The yard typically has a rail siding and a road that allows overland transport of the containers to bring them to be loaded onto a ship or to deliver them after they are offloaded from a ship. The important thing to realize is that when viewed from the water, the yard where containers are stored is *beyond* the cranes, not in front of the cranes. There is too little room to stack containers between the crane and the ship. Even if there were enough room, it would impede access to the ship, as well as block the view of the people loading or unloading the ship. Furthermore, there is no rail or easy road access there. Temporary storage of containers is what the much more spacious yard is for.

So, if the stacked containers in front of the cranes are not sitting on the dock, where are they? A clue to answering that question is provided by the white structure just right of center in the photograph. It, too, blocks the view of the cranes, so the white structure must be in front of the cranes. But some of the stacked containers block the view of the white structure, so it must lie between the cranes and at least some of the stacked containers. Compare the white structure's appearance to the photos of the cargo ships that I took at Virginia Beach. Obviously, the white structure is the bridge castle of a cargo ship. Therefore, there must be a cargo ship moored next to the cranes, with cargo containers partially stacked on it, or possibly the ship is a little offshore. In either case, the ship clearly lies between the observer and the cranes on the dock. In the video of his sermon, Odle said that the structure under the containers was the side of the dock. However, it is more likely that this is the siding lying just above the hull of the cargo ship (the same structures were gray on the NYK ship and red on the Maersk ship that I photographed).

Speaking of the hull, where is it? Obviously, it must lie below the containers and the siding below the containers, but it isn't visible. All that is visible below is water. This is exactly what we would expect to see if the earth is spherical — when viewed from enough distance, the hull of the ship will be obscured by the earth's curvature. This interpretation is confirmed by the single bottom of the crane supports visible to the right (the other supports are obscured by the ship and its cargo). The cranes rest on a base with wheels below that sit on a thick concrete pavement some distance above the water. However, none of this is visible in the photograph. Instead, the crane appears to be in water. Again, this is what we expect to see if the earth is spherical, but not at all what we expect to see if the earth is flat. To the right of the support are what appear to be buildings floating on water. Again, this is what we would expect if the earth is spherical, but not at all what is predicted by the flat-earth model. Lest anyone doubt my interpretation of this photograph, I discussed it with a retired Coast Guard rear admiral. With his 32-year career, he certainly is familiar enough with ships and ports to be a competent judge of what this photograph reveals.

The fact that Odle did not properly interpret his photograph is stunning. Here he had conducted an experiment that disproved his belief that the earth is flat, yet he interpreted his data otherwise. When I pointed this out to one of Odle's parishioners, he responded that not enough of the cranes and dock were obscured — by his calculation (or, more likely Odle's, because the parishioner probably consulted with Odle first) there should have been more obscured if the earth were spherical. However, this neglects the fact that the view of *some* of the dock and crane *was* blocked. How can a flat-earther explain that? He can't. The parishioner merely ignored it. However, the amount of refraction present is a complex function of the temperature inversion. A temperature inversion is highly variable in both location and time. Therefore, how much is obscured changes over time. Atmospheric refraction due to a temperature inversion isn't a quantum state, either on or off. Rather, there can be mild or severe temperature inversions, resulting in mild or severe atmospheric refraction. I have found that flat-earthers generally are so convinced of their position that no data will convince them that they are wrong. As I stated in chapter 1, I wrote this book for the benefit of people honestly exploring the question of the whether the earth is flat, not those who won't listen to arguments that say it is not.

When confronted with the argument that ships disappear hull first, one response that flat-earthers have is to claim that it merely is an illusion as the result of perspective. They say that the ship only looks like it is disappearing hull first to the naked eye, but with magnification, the entire ship is brought back into view. But magnification does not magically bring into view things that are otherwise obscured. All magnification does is make an image appear larger. It cannot bring into view things that are not in the view (image) to begin with. The photographs that I took at Virginia Beach demonstrate that, when no temperature inversion is present, ships do indeed disappear hull first, just as the spherical-earth model predicts.

Warship Fire Control

A variation on this theme among flat-earthers is the claim that large guns and other weaponry on warships could not be aimed long range against enemy ships if the earth were spherical because the ships are beyond the curvature of the earth, and, hence, could not be seen. Large guns on warships typically have a maximum range of about 20 miles. Depending upon the shell used, that range can extend to nearly 30 miles, but those typically aren't used against other ships. It is typical for a large warship to have a mid-ship tower where the spotters are located. The spotters use range finders and other equipment to fix the distance and azimuth of the target ships. These spotters can be 150 feet above the waterline. At that height, the horizon is 15 miles away. But the target ships also have superstructures that extend above the hull. At an additional distance of only 5 miles (a total distance of 20 miles away), only the bottom 17 feet of an enemy ship would be obscured by the earth's curvature to an observer 150 feet above the waterline. This would obscure the lower part of the hull of an enemy ship, but it would leave the entire ship above the hull visible to spotters. The spotters relay the information to fire control, which, in turn, computes the necessary parameters for hitting the target. Therefore, while the crew on the deck of a ship may not see much or even any of the target ship, they don't need to. The crew operating the guns don't look outside where they are firing anyway. All they do is follow the instructions issued by fire control.

The situation has changed considerably in modern warfare. While spotters using radar and other devices may be present aboard a ship, aircraft that are much higher in the sky can target ships that are considerably farther away. It would not be uncommon now for a ship to fire on a target that no one aboard has even detected.

Chapter 3

Eclipses and the Flat Earth

As described in chapter 1, the earth's circular shadow during a lunar eclipse was one of the earliest proofs that the earth is spherical. Even today, observing a lunar eclipse is one of the simple tests that anyone can conduct for themselves to see that the earth is spherical. Obviously, for those who are convinced that the earth is flat, this won't do, because the conventional explanation of lunar eclipses directly contradicts the flat-earth model. A lunar eclipse occurs when the earth comes between the sun and moon so that the earth's shadow is cast on the moon. But in the flat-earth model, the sun and moon always are above the earth, so it is impossible for the earth to come between the sun and moon. Therefore, it is understandable why flat-earthers spend so much time denying the cause of lunar eclipses.

However, it is not so clear why most flat-earthers dismiss the cause of solar eclipses. A solar eclipse happens when the moon passes between the earth and sun so that it blocks the light of the sun. Since in the flat-earth cosmology the sun and moon are contained within a dome above the earth, there is no reason why the conventional explanation for solar eclipses would not work in a flat-earth cosmology. Perhaps flat-earthers fear that if they admit that the conventional explanation of solar eclipses works, then it would undermine their argument against the cause of lunar eclipses.

The (True) Causes of Eclipses

Let us begin with a description of how a lunar eclipse happens. The accompanying figure shows the situation of a lunar eclipse, but keep in

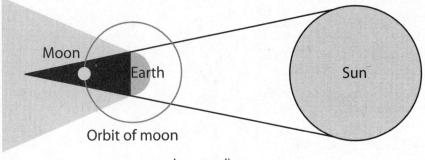

Lunar eclipse

mind that it is not to scale. For instance, the earth is 4 times larger than the moon, but the sun is more than 100 times larger than the earth (so, the sun is 400 times larger than the moon). The distance between the earth and moon is 30 times the earth's diameter. Furthermore, the sun is about 400 times farther away from the earth than the moon is. Obviously, it is difficult to show the proper relationship of sizes and distances in a diagram that would fit in this book.

Since the earth's shadow points away from the sun, the only time that a lunar eclipse is possible is when the moon is opposite the sun in our sky. This coincides with full moon, so the moon must be in this phase for a lunar eclipse to occur. However, there are no lunar eclipses during most full moons. This is because the moon's orbit is tilted a little more than five degrees to the earth's orbit around the sun. Therefore, when full, the moon usually passes above or below the earth's shadow so that no eclipse occurs. Only if a full moon occurs when the moon is near one of the *nodes*, the two points of intersection of the two orbits, does a lunar eclipse happen. There are two times per year, separated by six months, when the *line of nodes* (the line connecting the two nodes) points toward the sun and eclipses are possible. These *eclipse seasons* last a little more than a month, so at least one lunar eclipse must happen each eclipse season.

The earth's shadow has two parts, the *umbra* and the *penumbra.* The umbra is the inner portion of the shadow where the sun's light is completely blocked[1] (this is shown as the black region in the figure). The penumbra is the outer portion of the earth's shadow where the sun's

---

1. This isn't exactly true, as the earth's atmosphere refracts some light into its umbra. Therefore, total lunar eclipses are rarely totally dark.

light is only partially blocked (this is shown by the light gray region in the figure). The figure is only a two-dimensional representation. In three dimensions, the umbra is a cone having the earth's circumference as its base, with its apex pointing away from the sun. The penumbra is a truncated cone oriented the other direction. The penumbral cone is truncated by the earth's circumference. If the cone of the penumbra were extended, its apex would lie beyond the earth toward the sun. A plane perpendicular to the axes of these cones intersects the two cones in two concentric circles. Therefore, at the moon's distance from the earth, the umbra appears as a circle, with the penumbra appearing as a larger concentric circle.

If the moon's motion is such that at some point the moon is entirely immersed in the umbra, we say that it's a *total lunar eclipse.* Depending upon the moon's path through the umbra, totality can last anywhere from a moment to a little more than 100 minutes. For instance, the July 27, 2018, lunar eclipse had totality lasting 103 minutes, the longest totality of a lunar eclipse in the 21st century. Sometimes the moon passes only partially through the moon's umbra, causing a *partial lunar eclipse.* Even a total lunar eclipse is preceded and followed by partial phases, as the umbra slowly creeps across the lunar surface. These partial phases last for about an hour. There is a third type of lunar eclipse, a *penumbral eclipse.* A penumbral eclipse occurs when part of the moon passes through the earth's penumbra, but the moon misses the umbra entirely. The moon dims a little, but it's hardly noticeable to the naked eye.

This diagram demonstrates how a solar eclipse occurs. As before, the sizes and distances of the sun, moon, and earth are not to scale. Like the

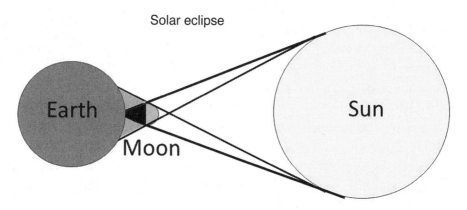

earth's shadow, the moon's shadow has two parts, the umbra and penumbra, and they are shaded in this diagram as well. For places within the moon's umbra, the sun is totally blocked, producing a *total solar eclipse*. On either side of the umbra there is a wide swath covered by the moon's penumbra, where the sun is partially blocked. These locations experience a *partial solar eclipse*. The moon's orbit around the earth is elliptical, which means that the moon's distance varies. When the moon is near *apogee*, the most distant part of its orbit, the moon's umbra doesn't quite reach the earth. For locations beyond the apex of the moon's umbra, the sun's surface is mostly blocked, but a ring is left along the perimeter. This is an *annular* eclipse. The path of totality, or annularity, for solar eclipses is not very wide — typically a hundred miles or even less. However, the regions on either side where a partial solar eclipse is visible is very wide.

Investigating Some of Dubay's Claims

Two of the supposed proofs of the flat earth in Dubay's book, *200 Proofs Earth Is Not a Spinning Ball* (p. 26), directly mentioned both lunar and solar eclipses. He also discussed eclipses in his other book, *The Flat-Earth Conspiracy* (p. 124–130). In both books, Dubay repeated several false things. For instance, he stated that Ptolemy's model is that the earth is flat and stationary. The stationary part is correct, for the Ptolemaic model was geocentric, but it hardly was flat, for early in his book, *The Almagest* (book 1, section 4), Ptolemy explicitly described his model as a spherical earth in the center of the universe. He also gave several reasons why the earth is a sphere. This is a manifestation of the common conflation of flat earth with geocentrism among flat-earthers.

Dubay further claimed that not only Ptolemy, but many other ancient civilizations, accurately predicted eclipses with a flat-earth model. Many other flat-earthers repeat this. This simply isn't true. Ptolemy had a method for predicting eclipses (book 6, sections 9 and 10). But his method was based upon the theory of a spherical moon orbiting a spherical earth, casting its shadow on the earth. Modern flat-earthers reject every part of this model. While the Ptolemaic method could predict the general times of both types of eclipses with some reliability, the precise times of either types of eclipse wasn't possible, nor could it predict the paths of total solar eclipses. The first reasonably accurate prediction of a solar eclipse was when Edmund Halley predicted the path of the May 3, 1715, total solar eclipse just a few months before the eclipse. Halley's predicted path was off by only 20 miles and the time of totality was correct within four minutes. In doing this, Halley presaged the modern technique of predicting solar eclipses that Friedrich Bessel greatly improved a little more than a century later, and William Chauvenet further refined. The technique is to compute the size and motion of the moon's shadow in the *fundamental plane*, the plane perpendicular to the direction of the moon's umbra and passing through the (spherical) earth's center. The projection of the moon's shadow and its motion in the fundamental plane to the earth's spherical surface provides detailed predictions of the circumstances of a solar eclipse. This method remains in use today. A similar technique now is applied to predicting lunar eclipses. Flat-earthers accept the reality of eclipses and the predictions of when and where eclipses will be visible. However, flat-earthers don't seem to realize that the accurate predictions of eclipses, both lunar and solar, are based upon a spherical earth in the heliocentric model and with the conventional understanding of how eclipses happen. That is, there is no theory of eclipses in a flat-earth model, and, hence, there are no flat-earth predictions of eclipses.

Is there any basis at all to Dubay's claim, often repeated by other flat-earthers, that ancient cultures predicted eclipses? Sort of, as Dubay mentioned an 18-year cycle in which eclipses repeat. Dubay undoubtedly is relying upon Rowbotham's *Zetetic Astronomy* (p. 151–154) for this information. This cycle is the saros cycle, an 18-year, $11\frac{1}{3}$ day period over which eclipses repeat, though not exactly. How does the saros cycle work? Recall that a lunar eclipse can happen only when the moon is full. Similarly, with a solar eclipse, the moon must be new. When an eclipse of either type happens, the moon will next be at the proper phase for another eclipse after one *synodic month*, the orbital period of the moon with respect to the sun. The average length of the synodic month is 29.530588 days. However, after one synodic month, the moon likely will not be near enough to a node to produce an eclipse again. The *draconic month*, the orbital period with respect to its nodes, is 27.212220 days, more than two days shorter than the synodic month. The synodic and draconic months come into and out of phase, producing eclipses from time to time, but something interesting happens over a little more than

18 years. After 223 synodic months, 6585.321 days have transpired. At the same time, 242 draconic months is equal to 6585.357. These two lengths of time are within an hour of one another and are roughly equal to 18 years, 11⅓ days. Therefore, a very similar eclipse will repeat after one saros cycle. But the ⅓ day means that the visibility of the eclipse will shift by eight hours on the earth's surface. After a second saros cycle, a similar eclipse will repeat about 16 hours shifted on the earth's surface. After three saros cycles, 54 years and about a month, the eclipse will be visible in a similar part of the world again. For instance, on April 8, 2024, there will be a total solar eclipse visible in the eastern United States. The path will be similar to a total solar eclipse that was visible on the southeastern U.S. coast on March 7, 1970, albeit shifted to the west and a little to the south. These two eclipses are separated in time by three saros cycles.

Many ancient cultures around the world independently figured out the saros cycle, but not the way Dubay and other flat-earthers think. Flat-earthers are under the impression that ancient cultures merely observed many eclipses and spotted the periodicity. But there are many simultaneous saros families of eclipses going on, and many of the eclipses within any family won't be visible from any given location. This makes it impossible to spot the regularities hidden in the data. Instead, ancient cultures figured out the real cause of eclipses, the earth coming between the sun and moon for a lunar eclipse, and the moon coming between the sun and earth for a solar eclipse. Knowing this, ancient cultures realized that there were two requirements for eclipses: the moon being at the proper phase, and the moon being near a node. By careful observation over many years, they determined the lengths of the synodic and draconic months. After that, it was a relatively simple matter to see the periodicity of the saros cycle, even if many of the eclipses of any eclipse family were not observed. But with knowledge of the saros cycle, it is possible to predict eclipses only in a crude way, without the precision that we have today.

Flat-earthers often mention that Thales predicted an eclipse around 600 B.C., apparently as evidence that the ancients could predict eclipses accurately. We have no writings of Thales, so what we know of him and his accomplishments come from much later sources. The ancient Greeks highly regarded Thales, so their accounts may have been embellished. Herodotus is the source of the story of Thales and the eclipse. Herodotus wrote about this incident a century-and-a-half later,[2] giving no details of how Thales might have predicted the eclipse. It is tempting to suggest that Thales knew of the saros cycle, and so could have anticipated that a solar eclipse was possible on the date in question, but could not predict the location or exact time where the eclipse was visible. However, it is generally thought that in Thales' lifetime, ancient Greek astronomy had not yet developed to the point that the cause of eclipses, and, hence, even the saros cycle, was known. Most historians discount the story of Thales and the eclipse, among some other things that Herodotus wrote.

Selenelions

Dubay's primary argument against the conventional explanation of eclipses is that lunar eclipses sometimes are observed when both the sun and moon are visible in the sky. He reasoned that if lunar eclipses happen when the earth is exactly between the sun and moon, this would be impossible. Here Dubay has included some true information, but that information is very misleading. First, Dubay claims that this is a common occurrence. It isn't. Second, he seemed to imply that both the sun and moon are relatively high in the sky when this phenomenon occurs. They aren't. What Dubay described here is a *selenelion*. The main problem with Dubay's claims is that he assumed that the moon, the sun, and the earth's umbra are points. They aren't. Both the sun and moon subtend an angle of about ½ degree. At the moon's distance from the earth, the diameter of the earth's umbra is about 2.6 times the moon's diameter, approximately 1.3 degrees.

During every lunar eclipse, there is a lune-shaped region of the earth's surface where the eclipse begins at sundown. Suppose that sunset is just beginning with the sun's bottom *limb* (edge) on the western horizon. Therefore, the center of the sun is perched ½ degree above the horizon. This would place the center of the earth's umbra 180 degrees away, ½ degree below the eastern horizon. However, since the earth's umbra is 1.3 degrees in diameter, the top edge of the umbra could be as much as 0.8 degree above the horizon. If the partial phase of the eclipse is beginning at this instant, then the top of the moon's limb could be as high as 1.3 degrees above the horizon, with a small part of the moon's

---

2. The earliest manuscript of Herodotus' history that we have is from the 10th century, 1,400 years after the death of Herodotus. This great time gap could have allowed the introduction of much embellishment.

lower limb partially eclipsed. That is, both the sun and the moon could be visible above the horizon, but in nearly opposite parts of the sky, and only briefly, as the sun, moving its apparent diameter every two minutes, could set within two minutes, with the moon simultaneously rising higher. Additionally, atmospheric refraction tends to raise objects that are on the horizon by about ½ degree, improving the odds of witnessing a selenelion.

Similarly, there is another lune-shaped region on the earth where the lunar eclipse occurs at sunrise. By the same reasoning, the sun can be rising in the east, while the end of the partial phase of the eclipse is setting in the west. Obviously, viewing a selenelion at any given lunar eclipse requires being situated within one of the two lune-shaped regions. These regions encompass only a small part of the earth's surface. But it also requires a good exposure in directions of both the rising and setting objects. Furthermore, the sky must be extraordinarily clear, because any clouds or high humidity would obscure either the moon or the sun when so low in the sky. Given these caveats, while it is theoretically possible to witness a selenelion at every lunar eclipse, actually seeing one is a relatively rare event. I've never seen one, though I've seen many lunar eclipses, with some of those occurring at sunset or sunrise.

Other Flat-Earth Claims About Eclipses

The curved shadow on the moon

In chapter 1, I mentioned that one of the proofs that the earth is spherical is the round shadow that the earth casts on the moon during a lunar eclipse. Flat-earthers have posted some creative videos on the Internet that supposedly demonstrate that this is wrong. Some of these videos feature a spherical object, such as an orange, in a dark room illuminated by a light source. A person passes the edge of a straight object, such as a ruler, through the path of the light so that the shadow of the object falls on the sphere. Having a straight-edge, the object's shadow has a border that is a line, yet the shadow moving across the orange appears curved. The narrators on these videos then lead viewers to the conclusion that a curved shadow doesn't prove that the eclipsing body is a sphere after all. It is easy to understand why so many people are easily convinced with these videos, but there are several things wrong with these demonstrations. First, the shadow on the moon during a lunar eclipse isn't just curved, but it is curved a particular way — it is circular.

Second, by using an orange or some other spherical object, the demonstration explicitly accepts that the moon is a sphere. But this is not what most flat-earthers think about the moon — they think that the moon is a round disk like the earth. If they repeated this experiment with an illuminated disk, like a pizza pan, they would get a straight-edged shadow, not a curved one.

A third problem is that the person moving the straight-edge doesn't continue moving it forward so that its shadow crosses the sphere. Instead, the person usually backs the straight-edge up a few times and repeats the demonstration as far as he has taken it. What would happen if the straight-edge is moved all the way across the sphere? The curve will be in the wrong direction as it moves off, hence the subterfuge of not following this experiment through.

Fourth, these videos attempt to kick up dust about the cause of lunar eclipses in the conventional understanding, but they do nothing to advance their model. What is the object that casts its shadow on the moon during lunar eclipse? They never say. The makers of these videos are trying to convince the viewer that a straight-edged object can cast a curved shadow on the moon much as a curved object can. But what is that straight-edged object?

Fifth, flat-earthers generally deny that it is a shadow falling on the moon that causes lunar eclipses. They claim that the moon has its own light, so there is no shadow falling on the moon during a lunar eclipse. If that is the case, then what is the point of these demonstrations?

Because it involves three dimensions, it is difficult to visualize and to diagram, but I will try to describe what is going on in this experiment. The shadow of any object cast onto a sphere must be projected, or mapped, onto the sphere's surface (much like the modern technique of predicting eclipses described above). Since the sphere's surface is curved, the edge of the shadow mapped onto the surface is curved, even though the edge of the shadow is a straight line. However, what we see of that mapped shadow is, in turn, a mapping onto the plane that is perpendicular to our line of sight to the sphere. That is, what we see is the result of two successive mappings, or projections. In the conventional explanation of lunar eclipses, we view the moon in the same direction that the sun's light and the earth's umbra are oriented. To see this, note that the center of the earth's umbra is exactly 180 degrees from the sun's center. Since the earth's umbra has a diameter of 1.3 degrees, the edge of its umbra extends only 0.65 degrees from the point opposite the sun. Therefore, the eclipsed part of the moon can be no more than 0.65 degrees from the axis of the earth's umbra, which lies along the direction to the sun. Under these conditions, the two successive projections cancel, and we see the same shaped shadow that we would see if the moon were flat. Therefore, the circular shadow of the earth during a lunar eclipse is a true representation of the shadow's shape. However, in the Internet videos of this demonstration, the angle measured at the orange between the direction of the light (and the shadow, too) and the direction to the camera is very large. Hence, what the viewer sees is the result of two complicated mappings. If the angle were very small (placing the camera in the same direction as the light source), the shadow of the straight-edge on the orange would appear to be a straight line. Furthermore, if the shadow of a larger ball were cast on the orange, what the viewer would see would be a circle. Hence, this demonstration is flawed. It's not clear if some of the people doing this demonstration intentionally set out to fool people or were deceived themselves.

Direction of the shadow's motion

Other Internet videos that attempt to refute the conventional explanation for lunar eclipses are made from time-lapse photos of the partially eclipsed moon as it rose or set. In these videos, the moon appears to move from left to right, but the shadow of the eclipse appears to overtake the moon from the left. The narrators of these videos argue that if a lunar eclipse is caused by the earth's shadow, then the shadow ought to fall onto the moon's right as the moon moves into the shadow. Since it doesn't, the narrators conclude that the conventional explanation of lunar eclipses is wrong. As with the other videos that I discussed above, it is easy to understand how many people could become convinced of what the narrator is saying. But, as before, this video is a misrepresentation. Let's see how.

Why does the moon appear to move left to right in these videos? The conventional explanation is that this motion is due to the earth's rotation.

It doesn't matter what the cause is, because for those viewing the sun or moon in the north temperate latitudes, the sun and moon appear to move left to right, or east to west, across the sky.[3] This is a matter of observational fact that even flat-earthers must agree with. On maps, the convention is to have north up and east to the right, so why is east to the left in the sky? It is because we are looking up at the sky, not down, as on the earth with a map. Try this yourself — stand facing roughly southward, so that south is down, and north is up. If you point to the east, you will see that it is to your left. Here are three photographs of the sun that I took on the afternoon of March 18, 2018, spanning about an hour and 40 minutes. Notice that the sun's motion is east to west (left to right). The moon's daily motion is in the same direction. Hence, the left-to-right motion in the videos of the eclipsed moon is due to the normal daily motion of the moon.

This is very important: if this left-to-right motion is due to the earth's rotation, then the earth's shadow also must move left to right at the same speed that the sun moves left to right. Of course, the earth's shadow will be 180 degrees away from the sun's location. However, the moon doesn't move left to right at the same speed that the sun does. It moves a bit

---

3. In the Southern Hemisphere, the apparent motion of the sun and moon each day across the sky is east to west too, but since they are oriented in another direction, the sun and moon appear to move right to left.

slower, losing a little more than 12 degrees on the sun per day. The conventional explanation is that the difference in the moon's apparent speed is caused by the moon's 29.5-day orbit around the earth with respect to the sun (360 degrees/29.5 days = 12.2 degrees per day). The moon's orbit is eastward, which subtracts from its apparent westward daily motion. The explanation of the moon's motion isn't important, as flat-earthers agree that the moon trails the sun by this much each day. For instance, in their models (sometimes mechanical models), they show the sun and moon orbiting over the earth at a different rate than the sun (the difference in their model also is 12.2 degrees per day).

To see the moon's eastward orbital motion from one day to the next, look at the next three photographs. I took these photographs at the same time on three consecutive mornings, March 2, 3, and 4, 2018, looking in the same direction as the sun photographs above. The moon was just past full (waning gibbous). Being so bright, the moon was overexposed in each photograph. In the first photograph, I have identified Jupiter and the bright star Spica. Both Jupiter and Spica are readily visible in the second photograph. Jupiter is obvious in the third photograph, but, due to thin clouds, Spica is difficult to see. Notice that on each successive morning, the moon progressively moved west to east (left to right), opposite the daily motion. Anyone can see this motion for themselves by noting the moon's

location in the sky over several consecutive evenings (or morning, as in this case), being sure to conduct the observations at the same time each evening.

In the next figure, I have reproduced the final photograph above, but with the location of the moon on the previous two mornings marked with white circles. Those two circles, along with the moon's image on the third morning, indicate the moon's west-to-east (right to left) motion over 48 hours. Now, suppose that the earth's shadow was located on the line between the moon's location on these two consecutive mornings,[4] as indicated by the dark circle, and that the moon was near a node. If that were the case, then between the times of the first two photographs, a lunar eclipse would have been visible somewhere in the world. Also, notice that it's the moon's monthly orbital motion right to left that causes the earth's umbra to fall on the moon. Consequently, we expect the umbra to impinge on the left side of the moon, just as the videos show. Therefore, rather than disproving the conventional explanation for lunar eclipses, these videos confirm it. As before, it isn't clear whether the people who

---

4. It wasn't on the mornings that I took these photographs because the moon was in the waning gibbous phase. Therefore, the earth's shadow was to the right of the moon in these photos. However, each month at full moon, the moon passes close to the earth's shadow, creating the possibility of a lunar eclipse.

promote flat earth via these videos are intentionally deceiving others, or they have managed to fool themselves as well.

Does the moon's umbra decrease in size with distance?

There are videos on the internet that give specious arguments against the conventional explanation of a solar eclipse as well. Several of these videos were popular about the time of the August 21, 2017, total solar eclipse seen along a narrow path from Oregon to South Carolina. The size of the path of totality is dictated by the size of the moon's umbra where it intersects the earth's surface. Many of these videos noted that the path of totality was only about 70 miles wide, while the moon is 2,000 miles across. The videos argued that the shadow of an object *always* is larger than the object, thus proving that the eclipse couldn't have been due to the moon's shadow. These videos also included demonstrations of shadows of various objects, and in the videos, the shadows indeed are larger than the objects. However, the flaw here is that the videos used very small light sources, light sources that were smaller than the objects used. This figure illustrates the shadow cast by an object from a light source that is smaller than the object.A line drawn from the top of the light source past the top of the object and a line drawn from the bottom of the light source past the bottom of the object will define the boundaries of the shadow (umbra). Notice that since the light source (the smaller, lighter circle) is smaller than the object (the larger, darker circle), the two lines drawn do not intersect beyond the object, and, hence, the shadow (the black region) increases in size with increasing distance.

However, the next figure demonstrates what happens when the light source is larger than the object casting the shadow. The line drawn from the top of the light source past the top of the object and the line drawn from the bottom of the light source past the bottom of the object define

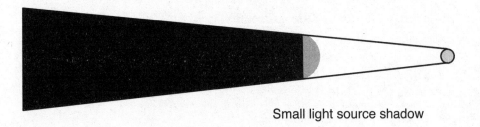

Small light source shadow

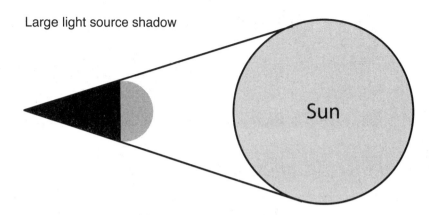

Large light source shadow

the boundaries of the shadow as before. But, unlike before, these lines intersect beyond the object, showing that the shadow diminishes in size with increasing distance, finally disappearing at the apex on the left. In this circumstance, the shadow has its maximum size at the object. Since the sun is 400 times larger than the moon, the diameter of the moon's shadow always is smaller than the moon's diameter. Therefore, the moon's shadow being only 70 miles wide is not a problem for the conventional understanding of eclipses.

On the morning of August 15, 2017, just six days before the eclipse, I did a simple experiment to test this. Assuming the conventional cosmology, I calculated that the sun shining on a volleyball a little more than eight inches in diameter would cast a shadow about half its size nearly 40 feet away. To see this, look at the figure. The diameter of the ball, D, is the base of a long isosceles triangle. Since the sun has an angular diameter of ½ degree, indicated by θ, the shadow of the ball will be a thin cone (shown as a triangle in this two-dimensional view), with its apex where

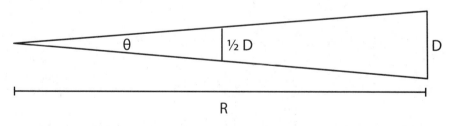

Volleyball experiment

the shadow vanishes. Since the angle is so small, the small angle approximation applies, and one may use either the sine or tangent of the angle θ to find the distance *R* where the shadow vanishes:

$$R = \frac{D}{\sin \theta} = \frac{D}{\tan \theta} = 76 \text{ feet.}$$

Here I assumed that the volleyball was eight inches in diameter, when in reality, the volleyball was slightly greater than eight inches in diameter. The triangle having base ½ *D* is similar t [theta] to find o the larger triangle. Hence, the base of the smaller isosceles triangle is located one-half the distance between the apex and the base of the larger isosceles triangle. Therefore, the shadow will be half the size of the volleyball at a distance of 38 feet from the volleyball. Since the volleyball is slightly larger than eight inches across, the distance where the shadow will be half the size of the volleyball ought to be a little more than 40 feet. However, if flat-earthers are correct, then the volleyball's shadow ought to be larger than the volleyball 40 feet from the volleyball. Therefore, we have clear, different predictions from the two models.

The sky was very clear that morning, so as soon as the sun rose above the trees on the east end of the employee parking lot at Answers in Genesis, I asked a coworker to hold the volleyball over her head so that it cast a shadow on a makeshift white screen nearly 40 feet away. The

photograph shows the setup for the experiment. I measured the dark part of the shadow (there is always a fuzzy area around the shadow). As I expected, the shadow was a little more than four inches across. Clearly, my experiment confirmed the prediction of the conventional cosmology (that the sun is an 860,000-mile-diameter sphere 93 million miles away, and the moon is a 2,000-mile-diameter sphere one quarter million miles away). On the other hand, the flat-earth prediction that the volleyball's shadow will be larger than the volleyball clearly was disproved. This is so typical of flat-earth arguments. If people would stop watching all those videos and get out and try some real experiments such as this, they'd soon see that the flat-earth videos are lying to them and misrepresenting reality.

Where is the moon during a solar eclipse?

There are other false claims made about solar eclipses. For instance, in a presentation at the first International Flat Earth Conference in November 2017, Bob Knodel said that he watched the total solar eclipse three months earlier. He said that he didn't see the moon move in and block the sun or move away afterward, so it must have been something else that blocked the sun during the eclipse. Others have made similar arguments on the Internet. If these people had any familiarity with the moon's motion and the visibility of lunar phases, they wouldn't make such statements. For instance, anyone familiar with the moon's phases knows that the moon is not visible for two to three days around new moon. Since the moon was new at the time of eclipse,[5] why would Knodel and other flat-earthers expect to have seen the moon that day? As I showed earlier, the moon moves 12.2 degrees eastward with respect to the sun each day. Therefore, in the three hours before or after the eclipse, the center of the moon would have appeared, at most, 1.5 degrees from the sun's center. Hence, it would have been impossible to see the moon move in or leave the sun's location that day.

Why is the moon not visible for two to three days around new moon? Near new moon, the moon appears faintest, while it simultaneously appears closest to the sun in the sky. Consequently, when near

---

5. Even if one rejects the conventional explanation for solar eclipses, it is an established fact that the moon was new on August 21, 2018, as well as on the dates of all other solar eclipses.

its new phase, the moon is lost in the glare of the sun. When the moon appears close to the sun but doesn't eclipse the sun, the lit portion of the moon facing the earth is a very thin sliver. But the remaining portion of the moon facing the earth isn't entirely dark. This is because when the moon is new, the moon's landscape is flooded with the light of a "full earth." Since the earth is four times larger than the moon, it has 16 times the surface area, and the earth reflects light nearly 2½ times better than the moon does, so the lunar landscape is nearly 40 times better lit than the earth's landscape at full moon is lit. *Earthshine*, as this is called, extends into the visible crescent phases of the moon. That is why the dark portion of the moon often is visible when the moon is a thin crescent. Even though the new or nearly new moon is not entirely dark, it is much too faint to be seen when so close to the dazzlingly bright glare of the sun.

Knodel and other flat-earthers dismiss the moon as the object that blocks the sun during a total solar eclipse, opting instead for something else doing the blocking. But most flat-earthers never seem to identify what that something else might be. I find this fundamental lack of curiosity amazing. A few flat-earthers have attempted to identify the blocking object as Rahu, or possibly Ketu. Rahu and Ketu come from Hindu astrology. They represent, respectively, the ascending and descending nodes of the moon's orbit. Rahu is mentioned in Buddhist texts. Obviously, this identification is problematic for those flat-earthers who claim that the heliocentric and globe earth theories are pagan in origin.

Given the fact that the moon was new during the eclipse, if it weren't directly in front of the sun, it probably was bright enough to be visible in the sky during totality. After all, brighter stars and planets were visible, but no one reported seeing the moon during the eclipse. However, there is evidence that the moon was directly in front of the sun during totality. My friend David Rives took this very long exposure photograph during the total solar eclipse, grossly overexposing the solar corona, but showing the dim light of the moon illuminated by earthshine.Many lunar features are easily identified on the moon, demonstrating that the moon was indeed in front of the sun during totality. The fact that the moon was directly in front of the sun during totality is very strong evidence that it was the moon that was blocking the sun. To insist that it was something

LUNAR DETAIL (AND OVER-EXPOSED CORONA)
TOTAL SOLAR ECLIPSE AUGUST 21. 2017
PHOTO COPYRIGHT © 2017 DAVID RIVES

David Rives Ministries
DAVIDRIVES.COM

else that blocked the sun while the moon was exactly in the same spot is an unnecessary complication.

Which direction does the moon's shadow move?

Some flat-earthers have posted on the Internet other criticisms about solar eclipses. One is the fact that the track of totality always travels from west to east on the earth. They reason that if the earth is spinning this direction, the shadow ought to move east to west as the sun appears to move across the sky. Combined with this are doubts about the speed of the moon's shadow — about 2,000 mph — as compared to the earth's maximum rotation speed of a little more than 1,000 mph.

First, let's tackle the speed of the moon's shadow. During a solar eclipse, the moon's orbital motion is perpendicular to the direction of the sun. Therefore, the moon's shadow moving across the earth will have approximately the same speed as the orbiting moon. What is the moon's average orbital speed? The semimajor axis of the moon's orbit is about 240,000 miles. Multiplying by 2π to get the circumference and dividing by the synodic period (29.5 days), the moon's average orbital velocity is 2,130 mph. Rounding this off, it matches the oft-repeated 2,000 mph speed of the moon's umbra. The actual speed varies slightly, as the moon's orbital speed varies as it moves along its slightly elliptical orbit.

From an earlier discussion, I pointed out that the moon's orbital motion is west to east, so the moon's umbra also moves from west to east. This is the direction that the earth is rotating, so the relative speed of the moon's umbra on the earth's surface is the difference between the speed of the moon's umbra and the earth's rotation speed.[6] The peak speed of the earth's rotation (a little more than 1,000 mph) is along its equator. Therefore, the relative speed of the moon's umbra across the earth's surface is slowest near the equator, which is why durations of totality tend to be longer at lower latitudes than at higher latitudes. But there is a second effect at play. The path of totality begins at sunrise at some location on the earth, races through progressively later time zones as it moves eastward, and then ends where the moon's umbra exits the earth at sunset. Near the midpoint of the eclipse track, it will be local noon. At this point, the motion of the moon's umbra is parallel to the earth's surface. However, at the beginning and ending points of the path of totality, the motion of the moon's umbra has a large component perpendicular to the earth's surface. This causes the moon's umbra to move very rapidly across the earth's surface near the beginning and ending points of the eclipse path. Thus, the duration of totality is shortest at the beginning and ending point of the eclipse, with maximum duration near the midpoint. These two effects that produce longer duration of totality, low latitude and totality at local noon, compete somewhat, so the maximum duration rarely occurs exactly at the lowest latitude or at local noon.

How Eclipses Are Computed

Anyone can check these trends, short duration at the beginning and end of paths of totality with maximum duration somewhere in between, by consulting any published maps and times of the path of totality for any total solar eclipse. This trend, among others, is a consequence of the earth's sphericity, and, hence, amounts to evidence that the earth is spherical. The Bessel/Chauvenet theory computes the motion of the

---

6. If you have difficulty seeing why this is the case, picture a vehicle driving at 60 mph overtaking a vehicle traveling at 50 mph. As the faster vehicle passes the slower vehicle, the relative speed will be 10 mph, the difference in the two speeds.

moon's umbra (and penumbra) in the *fundamental plane*. The fundamental plane is the plane perpendicular to the axis of the moon's umbra passing through the earth's center (yes, there is a geocentric element to this, but it hardly is a geocentric model). The intersection of the umbra and penumbra are circles in the fundamental plane, and their motion is uniform in the fundamental plane, making this part of the computation relatively easy. The complicated part is the projection of this motion onto the earth's spherical surface, with corrections for differences in elevation above mean sea level and the slight departures of the earth from a sphere. Hence, the prediction of the paths of solar eclipses are based upon the spherical-earth model. The irony is that flat-earthers appear to accept these predictions without realizing that the conventional explanation of eclipses and conventional cosmology are necessary for these predictions. There is no flat-earth prediction of eclipses.

In 1887, Theodor Ritter von Oppolzer published his great *Canon of Eclipses* using the Bessel/Chauvenet theory. The *Canon of Eclipses* contained detailed calculations of the visibility of all 8,000 solar eclipses and all 5,200 total and partial lunar eclipses between the years 1207 B.C. and A.D. 2161. It remained the standard reference for eclipses for more than a century. Recently, it has been superseded by the *Five Millennium Canon of Solar Eclipses: -1999 to +3000*[7] by Fred Espanak and Jean Meeus and the *Five Millennium Catalog of Lunar Eclipses*[8] by Fred Espanak. The time interval for both types of eclipses is expressed more conventionally as 2000 B.C. to A.D. 3000.[9] The greatest improvement of these later works is the better understanding we now have of the moon's orbit around the earth and the earth's slowing rotation. In predicting eclipse paths into the near future or the recent past, this isn't a problem. However, when predicting eclipse paths for possible coordination with historic events from many centuries ago, precise knowledge of the earth's slowing rotation is especially important. Without considering this factor, the predicted path and actual path of an eclipse will be displaced in longitude.

---

7. Available at https://eclipse.gsfc.nasa.gov/SEpubs/5MCSE.html.

8. Available at https://eclipse.gsfc.nasa.gov/LEcat5/LEcatalog.html.

9. When Dionysius introduced *Anno Domini* (A.D.), Latin for "year of our Lord," in A.D. 525, the concept of zero as a number was unknown in the West. Consequently, there was no year zero between 1 B.C. and A.D. 1. Computationally, it helps to view the year 1 B.C. and year number 0, with other B.C. dates as consecutive negative numbers.

Supposed Tacit Admissions on the NASA Website

In Internet videos, flat-earthers have picked at what they perceive as problems or inconsistencies in these canons of eclipses. For instance, some flat-earthers note that these canons are on a NASA website, yet have disclaimers that Fred Espanak assumes responsibility for their accuracy. Why that is a problem is a mystery to me. Espanak was employed at the Goddard Space Flight Center, a NASA facility, for more than three decades. He worked on various projects there, but one of his responsibilities was to prepare eclipse bulletins, which apparently developed into the canons of solar and lunar eclipses. It probably was Espanak who placed the disclaimer on the websites, for he assumed responsibility for his work.

Another supposed inconsistency that flat-earthers have tried to make use of is that the canons of eclipses list saros cycle numbers for individual eclipses. The flat-earthers intone that astronomers deny that they use the saros cycle for predicting eclipses, but this is a tacit admission that they do use the saros cycle to predict eclipses. As I previously discussed in this chapter, despite what flat-earthers claim, astronomers don't use the saros cycle to predict eclipses. Again, there is a misunderstanding of the saros cycle on the part of flat-earthers. Since the saros cycle is a period over which the circumstances of an eclipse nearly repeat, then we can think of eclipses as being within families, or series, of related eclipses. Eclipses are more frequent than the length of the saros cycle, so there are several simultaneous eclipse series going on at any time. The canons spanning five millennia recognized 180 saros series, with each series having about 70 members[10] (lunar eclipses are more common, so some saros families have more than 80 members). For a solar eclipse saros series, a series begins as a partial eclipse in the Arctic or Antarctic. Each subsequent eclipse in a series occurs closer to the other pole. The series progresses from partial to total and/or annular eclipse of increasing duration. Maximum duration is in the tropics, whereupon the eclipses shorten, eventually becoming partial eclipses at the other pole before ceasing. A saros series of lunar eclipses begins with penumbral eclipses that progress to

---

10. A list of all 180 saros series for solar eclipses are found at https://eclipse.gsfc.nasa.gov/ SEsaros/SEsaros0-180.html. The list of all 180 saros series for lunar eclipses are found at https://eclipse.gsfc.nasa.gov/LEsaros/LEsaroscat.html.

partial, through total, back to partial, before finally ending as a series of penumbral eclipses.

For instance, the August 21, 2017, total solar eclipse, which was visible across the United States, was eclipse number 22 of 77 in saros series 145. This series began with a partial eclipse visible in the Arctic on January 4, 1639. It wasn't until the 15th member of this series on June 6, 1891, that an annular eclipse occurred. The next eclipse in the series was a hybrid eclipse (annular and total) on Jun 17, 1909. The ensuing eclipses were total, with increasing durations of totality. The maximum duration of totality in this series will occur during eclipse number 50 on June 25, 2522. From there, totality rapidly diminishes until eclipse number 58, which will be a partial eclipse. The final eclipse in the series is number 77, a partial eclipse visible off the coast of Antarctica on April 17, 3009. I personally find this grouping by saros cycles helpful, for it allows me to trace the progression of eclipse families. For example, I hope to watch the total solar eclipse on April 8, 2024. This eclipse is number 30 of 71 eclipses in saros series 139. Its path is similar to the total solar eclipse of March 7, 1970, number 27 in this same family of eclipses. This was the first solar eclipse that I saw, though it was only a partial eclipse where I was.

A third issue that flat-earthers raise is that the plots of the paths of solar eclipses list the positions of the sun and moon at greatest eclipse in geocentric coordinates. Again, flat-earthers intone that this must be a tacit admission that NASA knows that the earth doesn't move. To see what the flat-earthers are talking about, look at the figure on the following page taken from the *Five Millennium Canon of Solar Eclipses*[11] showing the circumstances for the August 21, 2017, total solar eclipse. For both the sun and the moon, it lists the right ascension (R.A.) and declination (Dec.) of their centers at greatest eclipse, as well as their angular semidiameters (S.D). Right ascension and declination are coordinates in the sky similar to longitude and latitude on the earth. Notice that rather than being expressed in degrees, right ascension usually is expressed in hours, minutes, and seconds of time, with 15 degrees of arc being equal to one hour of time. Due to a slight parallax effect, the precise position of both the sun and the moon depends upon one's location on the earth. The standard for expressing the position of the centers of the sun and moon is the earth's

---

11. https://eclipse.gsfc.nasa.gov/SEcat5/SEcatalog.html.

Total Solar Eclipse of 2017 Aug 21

Ecliptic Conjunction = 18:31:19.6 TD (= 18:30:11.2 UT)
Greatest Eclipse = 18:26:40.3 TD (= 18:25:31.8 UT)

Eclipse Magnitude = 1.0306   Gamma = 0.4367

Saros Series = 145   Member = 22 of 77

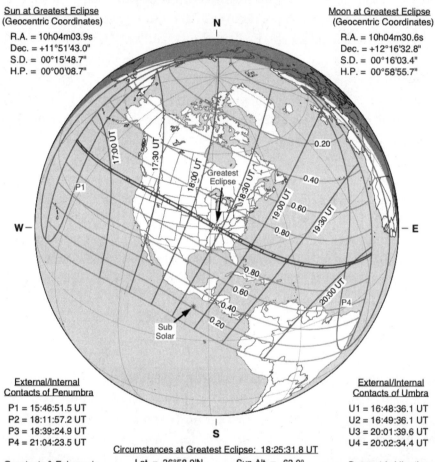

Sun at Greatest Eclipse
(Geocentric Coordinates)

R.A. = 10h04m03.9s
Dec. = +11°51'43.0"
S.D. = 00°15'48.7"
H.P. = 00°00'08.7"

Moon at Greatest Eclipse
(Geocentric Coordinates)

R.A. = 10h04m30.6s
Dec. = +12°16'32.8"
S.D. = 00°16'03.4"
H.P. = 00°58'55.7"

External/Internal Contacts of Penumbra

P1 = 15:46:51.5 UT
P2 = 18:11:57.2 UT
P3 = 18:39:24.9 UT
P4 = 21:04:23.5 UT

Constants & Ephemeris

ΔT = 68.4 s
k1 = 0.2725076
k2 = 0.2722810
Δb = 0.0" Δl = 0.0"
Eph. = JPL DE405

Circumstances at Greatest Eclipse: 18:25:31.8 UT

Lat. = 36°58.0'N   Sun Alt. = 63.9°
Long. = 087°40.3'W   Sun Azm. = 197.9°
Path Width = 114.7 km   Duration = 02m40.1s

Circumstances at Greatest Duration: 18:21:49.2 UT

Lat. = 37°35'N   Sun Alt. = 63.8°
Long. = 089°07'W   Duration = 02m40.2s

External/Internal Contacts of Umbra

U1 = 16:48:36.1 UT
U2 = 16:49:36.1 UT
U3 = 20:01:39.6 UT
U4 = 20:02:34.4 UT

Geocentric Libration
(Optical + Physical)

l = 4.64°
b = -0.57°
c = 21.90°

Brown Lun. No. = 1171

F. Espenak, NASA's GSFC
eclipse.gsfc.nasa.gov
2014 Feb 22

| 0 | 1000 | 2000 | 3000 | 4000 | 5000 |
Kilometers

center. This is what is meant by the term "geocentric" (center of the earth) here. Also listed is the half parallax (H.P.) of both the sun and moon. This is the maximum change in position that the center of the sun or moon can have, using the earth's radius as the baseline. The moon's half parallax is about 400 times greater than the sun's half parallax because the sun is about 400 times farther away than the moon is. The geocentric positions of the sun and moon, as well as their half parallaxes, are used to compute the circumstances of eclipses across the earth's surface. Espanak thought it fitting to include this information on these plots.

Therefore, the videos sniping at the eclipse website are based upon ignorance of the information presented there. It is yet another example of how flat-earthers misunderstand much of what they criticize.

The Sizes of the Umbrae of the Earth and Moon

Some flat-earthers attempt to discredit the conventional understanding of eclipses by arguing that the sizes and lengths of the umbrae of the earth and moon do not work in the conventional understanding. For instance, the moon's umbra barely reaches the earth, so the maximum diameter of the moon's umbra at the earth's surface is 167 miles.[12] Consequently, very little of the earth's surface is covered by the moon's umbra during a total solar eclipse. Meanwhile, the earth's umbra on the moon is larger than the moon so that the entire moon (over 2,000 miles across) can be immersed in the earth's shadow. Some flat-earthers claim that this is a problem. Let us examine these claims.

The figure on the following page shows the situation of the sun on the left and the shadow cast by a sphere on the right. The line BF is an extension of the line AF, which is tangent to both spheres. The line DE is parallel to line AF. Therefore, the triangles SDE and EBF are similar, and we can form the ratio

$$\frac{EF}{SE} = \frac{EB}{SD}$$

---

12. The maximum occurs when the moon is at perigee and the earth is at aphelion. This maximum diameter of the moon's umbra on the earth is in the tropics, where the axis of the moon's umbra is perpendicular to the ground. At higher latitudes, the earth's curvature causes the moon's umbra to strike the ground at an oblique angle, stretching the moon's umbra in the north-south direction.

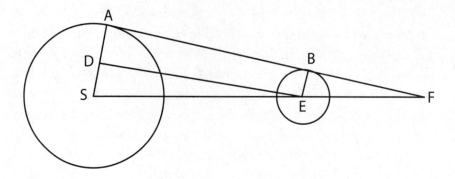

The line *EB* is the radius of the sphere, and *SD* is the difference between the radius of the sun and the sphere. The line *SE* is the distance between the sun and the sphere, while *EF* is the desired length of the umbra. Therefore,

$$EF = \frac{SE \times EB}{SD}$$

The sun's radius is 432,000 miles, the earth's radius is 3,963 miles, and distance between the sun and moon is 9.296×10^7 miles. Placing these values into the equation, we find that the length of the earth's umbra is 861,000 miles, about 3.6 times the average distance between the earth and moon. Therefore, the earth's umbra clearly extends well beyond the moon, with the diameter of the earth's umbra exceeding the moon's diameter. This is what we observe.

The moon's average radius is 1,080 miles, and its average distance from the earth is 239,000 miles. Placing these values into the above equation, we find that the length of the moon's umbra is 233,000 miles. This is very close to the average distance between the earth and moon. But the average distance between the earth and moon is the center-to-center distance — the earth's surface can be nearly 4,000 miles closer to the moon than this. Also, keep in mind that not only does the earth-moon distance vary throughout the month, but the earth-sun distance varies throughout the year. This changes the length of the moon's umbra slightly, as well as the distance that the umbra must extend to reach the earth's surface. And whether the moon's umbra reaches the earth's surface makes a large difference in the type of eclipse that is visible. When the moon's umbra reaches the earth, it just barely does. The result is a total solar eclipse. When the apex of the umbra falls short of reaching the earth's surface, locations along the extension of the axis of the moon's umbra experience an annular eclipse, where the angular size of the moon isn't quite large enough to cover the sun's photosphere entirely. This leaves a ring, or annulus, of the sun's photosphere shining around the moon's limb. Therefore, the moon's umbra just barely reaches the earth's surface, and sometimes it fails to do that, resulting in an annular eclipse. This is what we observe.

Some flat-earthers contend that this is all contrived — that the moon's umbra barely reaching the earth somehow proves that something is amiss about solar eclipses. However, flat-earthers can't seem to state clearly just what they think the problem is. The fact that the moon's umbra just barely reaches the earth's surface is a design argument. This fact, along with the tilt of the moon's orbit preventing there being a solar eclipse every month, is indication of design. The circumstances of total solar eclipses are such that total solar eclipses are very spectacular. And exceedingly rare — at any given location on the earth, a total solar eclipse occurs, on average, about once every four centuries. People who view this ultimate natural wonder either are very fortunate to live in a place and time to experience a total solar eclipse, or they go to some expense and bother to travel into the path of totality. This is the only planet in the solar system where such conditions prevail — the natural satellites of other planets either produce no total solar eclipses, or those eclipses are commonplace and not very spectacular. And this is the only planet where it matters because it is the only planet where there are inhabitants who can appreciate these facts. I see the hand of a very gracious, kind, and artistic Creator in this. It is truly a shame that so many flat-earthers are so wrapped up in their conspiratorial beliefs that they fail to see this indication of design staring them in the face.

Chapter 4

Aspects of the Sky and Flat Earth

What Are Aspects of the Sky?

What I mean by *aspects of the sky* is where astronomical bodies appear in the sky as a function of time and one's location on earth. With time, astronomical bodies change position in the sky, so their motions are part of the aspects of the sky as well. Both the spherical-earth model and the flat-earth model make specific predictions about the aspects of the sky, so the aspects of the sky provide good tests of either model. First, let us briefly review the two models.

Review of the Two Models

In modern cosmology, the spherical earth spins on its axis each day and orbits the sun each year. The rotation axis is tilted 23.4 degrees to the revolution axis. The stars are at great distance, far greater than the size of the earth or even the size of earth's orbit around the sun. However, as far as the aspects of the sky are concerned, the conventional model is indistinguishable from the concept of the *celestial sphere* from ancient Greek cosmology. The celestial sphere is a very large sphere concentric with the spherical earth on which the stars are located. We also can place the sun, moon, and planets on the celestial sphere. For simplicity, we can assume that the celestial sphere spins around the earth each day on an axis coincident with the earth's rotation axis.

Some flat-earthers may gleefully object that I've changed the model here. To the contrary, while the ancient Greeks believed this model to

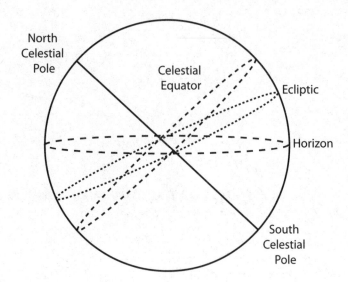

be true, we don't today. However, even if this model isn't true, it doesn't mean that it isn't useful. In science, we often use models that we don't believe are true, but nevertheless are descriptive. For instance, we treat electrical current as a fluid traveling from positive (where there is an excess of the fluid) to negative (where there is a deficit of the fluid). However, we know that electrical current isn't a fluid but rather is motion of particles (electrons). Furthermore, the electrons have negative charge, so their motion is in the opposite direction to our convention. But the fluid model of electricity works well to describe many aspects of electricity because many of its predictions don't differ from what we think is the correct theory. Similarly, the predictions of the modern cosmology and the cosmology of the celestial sphere are indistinguishable when it comes to aspects of the sky, as defined above. However, when one investigates other areas of astronomy, such as spectroscopy and astrometry, the celestial sphere model proves to be woefully inadequate.

The axis of the celestial sphere's spin intersects the celestial sphere in two places. We call these points the *north celestial pole* and the *south celestial pole*. Halfway between the two celestial poles is the *celestial equator*. As the earth spins west to east each day, the celestial sphere appears to spin east to west around the north and south celestial poles. Meanwhile, the sun appears to move west to east on the celestial sphere about a degree per day. This motion is along the ecliptic, which is tilted 23.4 degrees to the celestial equator. This annual apparent motion of the sun is due to the earth's yearly orbit around the sun. The moon orbits west to east once each month on the celestial sphere on a path that is inclined a little more than five degrees to the ecliptic. The five naked-eye planets appear to move along paths that are slightly inclined to the ecliptic. The apparent motion of the planets is a combination of their orbital motion and the earth's orbital motion.

In the flat-earth model, the earth is a flat disk with a dome above. The edge of the dome rests beyond the ice wall of Antarctica. The dome spins each day around an axis passing through the North Pole at the center of the round, flat earth. The sun and moon also are above the earth, but in most flat-earth models, they are below the dome. The sun and moon orbit around the same axis that the dome spins, but the radii of their motions change. This accounts for the changing position of the sun in the sky with respect to the seasons, as well as the moon's motion throughout the month. Though I have yet to see a flat-earther make the case, the concept of the ecliptic could be incorporated into this model very easily.

The flat earth model

The sun and moon are not spheres, but instead are round and flat like the earth. The shape of the dome varies in flat-earth models. In some versions, the dome is hemispherical. In others, the dome is squashed so that it resembles the dome of an indoor sports stadium. In this way, the dome has its least radius of curvature at its edges and its greatest radius of curvature above the North Pole. One may notice immediately that the sun always is above the horizon, so how does the flat-earth model explain night? The answer is that the sun's light is directed like a spotlight so that there is a cone of illumination below the sun. Once the sun moves far enough away from one's location, the observer is no longer in the cone, and night falls. Daylight returns when the sun's position is such that the observer is back in the cone of light.

Most flat-earthers are not explicit about the dimensions of their model. Flat-earthers generally seem to accept most distances measured on the earth. Therefore, since it's nearly 11,000 miles from the North Pole to the ice wall of Antarctica, the dome must be a minimum of 22,000 miles across. However, if the dome is shaped like the roof of an indoor sports arena, then the height of the dome over the North Pole may be much less than 11,000 miles. Flat-earthers generally agree that the sun and moon are about the same size and height above the earth. However, many flat-earthers aren't specific about what that size and height are. The most common belief among flat-earthers is that the sun and moon are 32 miles across and 3,000 miles high. For my purposes here, I will use these dimensions. However, in some cases, the exact dimensions will not matter.

Sunrise and Sunset

How do sunrise and sunset happen in the conventional model? Start with the sun in the sky, above the plane of the horizon defined by an observer's location.[1] As the earth spins (or alternately, as the celestial sphere spins), the sun is carried to a location in the sky where it passes through the plane of the horizon. In other words, the sun sets. Later, the rotation (it doesn't matter which is rotating, the earth or the celestial sphere), carries the sun to a location where it once again crosses the plane of the horizon. This is sunrise.

---

1. The plane tangent to the earth's surface at a given location defines the plane of the horizon.

Right away, one can spot a problem for the flat-earth model. Imagine the flat-earth model with a dome covering the surface of a round, flat earth underneath. A line can be drawn from *any* point on the dome to *any* point on the disk below. Therefore, from any location on the earth, a person can *always* see every point in the sky. Since there is no place on the dome that cannot be viewed directly from any point on the earth, the sun always is above the horizon. Therefore, the sun cannot rise or set in the flat-earth model. Flat-earthers understand that they have a problem. Indeed, the suggestion that the sun acts as a spotlight was offered to overcome at least part of this problem. But the sun, whether directly visible or not, is still above the horizon, so how could it appear to rise or set? As when the hulls of ships disappear first, flat-earthers appeal to perspective to explain how the sun can rise and set. And as with ships, this doesn't work here either. Perspective makes things in the distance appear smaller. As an object recedes into the distance, we could draw a line connecting a point on that object at different distances. If we do the same for other points on the object, the lines will appear to meet at the *convergent point*. Since all the lines meet at the convergent point, if the object reached the convergent point, it would appear to have zero dimension. Of course, the object never reaches the convergent point, though it may approach it very closely. However, at no time is the object obscured. Therefore, the sun always will appear above the horizon.

Let me demonstrate the folly of this answer with some numbers. I live in northern Kentucky near Cincinnati, which is at latitude 39 degrees north of the equator and 84.5 degrees west longitude. Within the flat-earth model, when would the sun be most distant from my location? That would be at local midnight on the winter solstice. In both the flat-earth and conventional models, at that time the sun would be directly overhead at latitude -23.4 degrees south of the equator and at longitude 95.5 degrees east (it would be local noon there). How far is that location from Cincinnati? In either model, the shortest distance would be directly north past the North Pole and then continuing due south. Flat-earthers appear to accept measurements of latitude and longitude. One degree of latitude is equal to 69 miles. Therefore, it is (90 – 39) x 69 miles = 3,519 miles from Cincinnati to the North Pole. Continuing, it would be another 90 x 69 miles = 6,210 miles to the equator, and then another

23.4 x 69 miles = 1,615 miles to the point in where the sun is directly overhead. Therefore, the total distance is 11,344 miles. Taking the often-stated flat-earth model height of the sun of 3,000 miles, the angle that the sun would make above the horizon would be the arctangent of 3,000/11,344, which is 14.8 degrees. That is, according to the flat-earth model, the sun ought to be 14.8 degrees above my horizon at midnight on the winter solstice. Interestingly, this places the sun within a degree of the ecliptic north pole, one of the two points in the sky where the axis of the earth's orbit intersects the celestial sphere. But the sun perpetually is 90 degrees from the ecliptic north pole. Therefore, the prediction of the flat-earth model is not correct. And the calculation presented here is for the most distant, and, hence, the lowest in the sky, that the sun would ever appear. It would be higher in the sky on any other night. This obviously is not the case.

The Changing Apparent Size of the Sun

A true understanding of perspective allows us additional, more rigorous and quantitative tests of the two models. Throughout the day, the sun rises, gets higher in the sky, and then it gets lower in the sky and sets. When the sun is highest in the sky, we say that it is *noon*, and the day is half over. In either model, we are closest to the sun at noon and farthest from the sun at sunrise and sunset. Therefore, throughout the day, the apparent size of the sun ought to change, with the sun appearing largest at noon and smallest at sunrise and sunset. Let's quantify this. In the conventional model, we are, at most, 4,000 miles (the radius of the earth) closer to the sun at noon than at sunrise or sunset. How much will the sun change in apparent size throughout the day in the conventional model? Since the sun is 93 million miles away, the sun's apparent size will change by the factor of 4,000/93,000,000 = 0.000043, or 0.0043%. Obviously, this is imperceptible, so the conventional model predicts that there will be no change in the sun's apparent size throughout the day.

What does the flat-earth model predict? Since the sun is much closer to us, its apparent size must change throughout the day. And flat-earthers agree with this. Though I haven't yet seen a flat-earther quantify a prediction of the change in the apparent size of the sun in their model, I have seen numerous videos on the Internet promoting this very phenomenon as proof of the flat-earth cosmology. These videos are time-lapse movies of the sun sinking in the sky toward sunset, showing that the sun appears smaller as it sets (alternately, some videos show the same sort of thing in reverse at sunrise). It is understandable why these videos might convince some people, but there is a flaw. These images aren't taken through appropriate solar filters, so when the sun is high in the sky, the sun is dazzlingly bright. The sun is so bright that it is grossly overexposed, causing its light to bleed into surrounding pixels. The overexposed image is much larger than the true apparent size of the sun. As the sun gets lower in the sky, atmospheric extinction greatly dims (and reddens) the sun's light. Thus, right at sunset, the sun's image is not overexposed, and it more accurately portrays the correct apparent size of the sun. If the sun were properly exposed, then the sun would show no change in apparent size. It's not clear if the people making and posting these videos on the Internet know what they are doing and, hence, are intentionally misleading people.

It is not difficult to quantify the prediction of the flat-earth model. Let the sun be at some distance, d, above the earth's surface (figure 2). If the sun's altitude (the angle that the sun makes with the horizon) is θ, then s, the distance of the sun from an observer, is

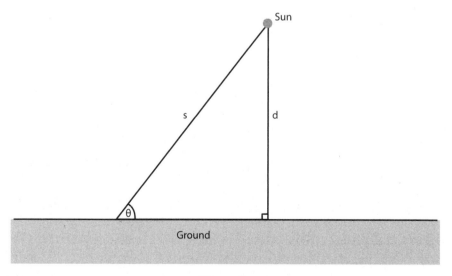

Figure 2

$$s = \frac{d}{\sin \theta}$$

Notice from either figure 2 or this equation that, as the altitude of the sun decreases, the distance to the sun increases.

Let D be the diameter of the sun. The angular size of the sun, α (figure 3), in radian measure, will be

$$a = \frac{D}{s}$$

Conversion to degrees is done by multiplying by 57.3 degrees, but, as I shall demonstrate, this is not necessary. Combining these two equations, we find

$$a = \frac{D}{d} \sin \theta_1$$

This equation is best expressed in the form of a ratio of measurements made at two different times. Let α_1 and α_2 be the sun's angular diameters at altitudes θ_1 and θ_2, respectively, then,

$$a_1 = \frac{D}{d} \sin \theta_1$$

and

$$a_2 = \frac{D}{d} \sin \theta_2$$

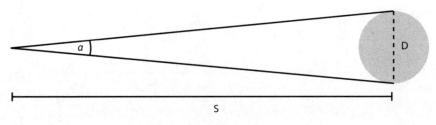

Figure 3

Dividing the equation for α_1 by the equation for α_2, the common terms in D and d cancel, leaving

$$\frac{a_1}{a_2} = \frac{\sin \theta_1}{\sin \theta_2}$$

This equation is very useful for two reasons. First, it does not rely upon any particular flat-earth model because both the sun's size and its height above the earth factor out when expressed as a ratio. Second, because this is a ratio, there is no need to convert the angular sizes from radians to degrees.

Testing the Predictions

On Wednesday, August 3, 2016, I took photographs of the sun at Johnson Observatory on the grounds of the Creation Museum in Northern Kentucky. I shot the photos with a digital SLR camera attached to the observatory's Questar 3.5-inch telescope. The focal length of the telescope is 1,380 mm. Of course, photographing or looking at the sun is very dangerous, and neither should be attempted without a proper filter. The Questar telescope comes equipped with a very safe filter that fits on the front, preventing most of the sun's light from entering the telescope. I took the first photograph (figure 4) at 7:30 a.m. ET, when the sun was at an altitude of eight degrees. I took the second photograph (figure 5) at 1:45 p.m. ET. I chose the time of the first photograph because that was when the sun first rose above the trees to the east of the observatory (a small branch of a tree can be seen silhouetted against the sun to the lower right). I selected the time of the second photograph because it was when the sun was

Figure 4

Figure 5

highest that day as it transited the celestial meridian. The celestial meridian is an imaginary line that passes north-south through the zenith (the point directly overhead). When the sun passes through, or transits, the meridian, it is local noon. There are several reasons why local noon was not at 12 o'clock, the chief two reasons being that daylight-saving time was in effect and Northern Kentucky is in the Eastern Standard Time Zone when it ought to be in the Central Standard Time Zone. The sun's altitude at the time of the second photograph was 63 degrees. Both exposures were 1/200 of a second with an ISO setting of 200. Notice that the image of the sun on the first photograph is fainter than on the second photograph. This is because of the dimming and reddening due to atmospheric extinction. I could have produced the same color and brightness by changing the exposure time and/or the ISO setting, but I wanted the settings of the exposures to be the same. Processing, such as with Photoshop®, could have equalized the color and intensity of the two photographs, but neither photo was processed. Rather, these are the JPG images produced by the camera in fine mode.

The flat-earth model and the conventional model make very different predictions about the relative sizes of the two images. Using the above equation and the angles of 8 and 63 degrees, we get

$$\frac{a_1}{a_2} = \frac{\sin 63°}{\sin 8°} = 6.4.$$

Therefore, the flat-earth model predicts that the sun's image on the later photograph (figure 5) ought to be 6.4 times larger than on the earlier photograph (figure 4). On the other hand, as previously mentioned, the conventional model predicts that the images ought to be about the same size.

Examine the sizes of the sun's image on each photograph. Notice that the images appear to be the same size. I printed the images on 8x11-inch paper and measured the horizontal diameter of the sun's image on each photograph. The diameter on the earlier image was 237 mm, while the diameter on the later image was 240 mm. This is a ratio of 1.0126, or a difference of 1.26 percent. Clearly, the prediction of the flat-earth model fails, unquestionably disproving the flat-earth theory. One may object that the two images are not *exactly* the same size, so the conventional model is disproved, too. However, the printing process is not exact due to several factors. For instance, while being printed, the paper may have stretched, compressed, or wrinkled slightly, or the feed may not have been 100 percent consistent. A variance of a little more than 1 percent is not surprising. Therefore, the conventional model is confirmed within the errors likely inherent in the experiment.

We can take this discussion further. What would be the angular size of the sun when it is at an altitude of one degree as compared to the sun's angular size at 63 degrees? From the equation, it ought to appear 51 times larger at 63 degrees than it would at an altitude of one degree. At one-half degree altitude, the ratio is 102. Due to atmospheric extinction, it is relatively safe on some occasions to look at the sun as it is rising or setting and has this altitude. Because many people have done this, they have some idea of how large the sun appears at the horizon. Does the sun really appear 50–100 times larger when much higher in the sky? It is interesting that those who promote the flat-earth model never quantify their predictions in this manner, because if they did, their predictions would not match what we observe.

We can apply similar reasoning to the moon; for, in the flat-earth model, the moon is the same size and distance above the earth as the sun. Therefore, when the moon is high in the sky, it ought to appear much larger than it does when rising or setting. However, as all can easily verify for themselves, the moon does not look larger when high in the sky compared to when it is low in the sky. If anything, the moon appears larger when rising or setting than it does when it is high in the sky. This is due to the moon illusion, a well-known effect that occurs in the brain that is not entirely understood. Photographs of the moon when taken either high or low in the sky show no appreciable difference in size, proving that the moon illusion indeed is an illusion.

But there is a second effect of perspective that makes a prediction that we can test. If the earth is flat and the sun appears to set because of perspective, perspective also ought to cause both the sun and the moon to move most quickly when they are nearest (near the zenith) and move most slowly when farthest away (near the horizon). We frequently observe this effect — a vehicle speeding by very close to us appears to move much faster than a vehicle far away moving the same speed. Of course, we do not observe this with the sun and moon as they rise or set. For instance, when viewing the sun with the Questar telescope as I did on the day I took these photographs, I normally use the clock drive. The clock drive compensates for the sun's apparent motion across the sky by turning the telescope around an axis aligned with the axis of rotation at the uniform rate of one revolution per day. If the flat-earth model were true, this would not be possible because the rate or motion would not be uniform. Apparently, this prediction of the flat-earth model has not occurred to its supporters.

The Midnight Sun

The midnight sun is the phenomenon of the sun remaining above the horizon for at least 24 hours. This happens only in the Arctic (along the Arctic Circle and northward) and the Antarctic (along the Antarctic Circle and southward).[2] Flat-earthers tend to think that only their model can explain the midnight sun, so they spend some time discussing it. For instance, Dubay dedicated four of his *200 Proofs*[3] (numbers 56–59) to the midnight sun. How do flat-earthers explain the midnight sun? They reason that when the sun is at the summer solstice, the sun is closest to the North Pole. People at locations in the Arctic not only see the sun during the hours near noon, but also 12 hours later, because they are not too far from where the sun is overhead, and light from the sun shines over the Arctic to their locations.

Let us quantify this. The Arctic Circle is at latitude 66.6 degrees. On the summer solstice, the sun is directly overhead at noon at latitude 23.4 north of the equator. From here, the shortest distance to the point on the Arctic Circle where the midnight sun is visible is northward through the North Pole and then continuing southward to the Arctic Circle. The difference in latitude between the North Pole and 23.4 degrees north latitude is 90 – 23.4 = 66.6 degrees. The Arctic Circle is 23.4 (90 – 66.6) degrees from the North Pole. Therefore, the shortest distance from the subsolar point to the Arctic Circle at midnight is through 90 degrees of latitude.

---

2. Atmospheric refraction raises the sun about ½ degree when on the horizon, so the range that the midnight sun can be seen may extend a little out of the Arctic and Antarctic regions.

3. E. Dubay, *200 Proofs Earth Is Not a Spinning Globe* (Morrisville, NC: Lulu.com., 2015), p. 11–12.

Again, multiply by 69 miles, the distance is 6,210 miles. If the sun is at height 3,000 miles above the earth, then the angle the midnight sun will make with the northern horizon is the arctangent of 3,000/6,210, which is 25.8 degrees. However, observation shows that midnight sun on the Arctic Circle is on the horizon, not 25.8 degrees above the horizon. Clearly, in the flat-earth model, people well outside the Arctic Circle ought to see the midnight sun. Since they don't, this disproves the flat-earth model.

Flat-earthers seem to think that the midnight sun cannot happen on a spherical earth. For instance, Dubay's proof number 56 makes the claim that on a spherical earth, the midnight sun would be visible only at the North Pole. The problem with his understanding is revealed by the figure accompanying his proof number 59 — it shows no tilt to the earth's axis. The correct situation is shown in this diagram. On the summer solstice, the earth's Northern Hemisphere has its maximum tilt toward the sun. Consider an observer on the Arctic Circle. At point A, it is noon, and the sun is as high in the sky as it can be, nearly 47 degrees. To an observer facing the sun with the North Pole to his back, the sun would appear in the southern part of the sky. However, 12 hours later, the earth's rotation will take the observer to point B. This will be at midnight. As you can see, the sun's rays pass over the North Pole and reach point B tangent to the earth's surface. The sun's rays being tangent

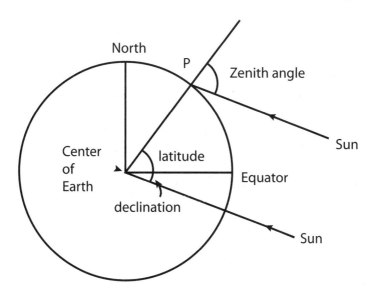

to the earth's surface means that the sun is on the horizon. Since the observer must face the North Pole to view the sun, the sun is in the northern part of the sky.

On the Arctic Circle, the midnight sun is visible only on the summer solstice. At higher latitudes, the midnight sun is visible for more days. At the earth's North Pole, the sun is above the horizon for six months. The sun does not appear to bob up and down each day at the North Pole. Instead, the sun appears to circle each day at about the same altitude. Actually, the sun rises on the vernal equinox and slowly gains altitude until the summer solstice, whereupon the sun slowly descends again until it sets on the autumnal equinox. The sun's maximum altitude on the summer solstice is 23.4 degrees.

Dubay's proof number 59 is merely a quote from Gabrielle Henriet's 1957 book, *Heaven and Earth*. That quote asserts that if the earth were a sphere, all parts of the earth would experience 12 hours of light and 12 hours of dark throughout the year. If the earth's axis had no tilt, this would be true. However, within the conventional cosmology, there is a 23.4-degree tilt to the axis. Hence, Dubay's case against the conventional model is a straw-man argument. In his proof number 58, Dubay quoted from a Belgian Antarctic expedition that at 71 degrees south latitude, the sun sets on May 17 and does not rise again until July 21. He went on to assert that this is not possible on a spherical earth, but that the flat-earth model supposedly can explain this. This apparently plays off the common mistaken belief that the sun perpetually is above the horizon for six months at all points in the Arctic (this is the case only at the North Pole). Therefore, as with proofs 56 and 57, Dubay utterly fails to understand how a spinning spherical earth with a 23.4-degree tilt explains this. And, as before, this is a false assertion in support of a straw-man argument.

Dubay illustrated his discussion with two series of images showing the midnight sun. There also are many time-lapse videos on the Internet promoting flat earth that show the same thing. They show the sun moving rightward along the horizon, slowly bobbing up and down once each day. In his proof number 57, Dubay correctly states that in the conventional model, the midnight sun ought to be visible in the Antarctic as well, but he says this is not seen because in the flat-earth model, this is impossible. This claim is repeated on the Internet as well. As it turns out, there are videos on the Internet showing the midnight sun from Antarctica. These are very similar to the videos from the Arctic, except that the sun is going leftward rather than rightward, as is expected. What is the response of flat-earthers to these videos? Flat-earthers claim that these videos are faked. This is so common with flat-earthers — they dismiss any evidence that contradicts their model as fake, but they utterly fail to understand that flat-earthers can and do fake data. How can one rationally discuss a topic when the other side dismisses data so cavalierly?

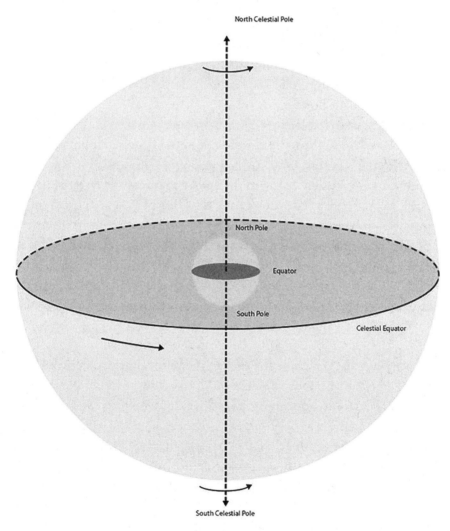

Figure 1A Celestial sphere

The North Star and Other Circumpolar Stars

The horizon is the horizontal plane tangent to the earth at one's location. Since the earth is at the center of the celestial sphere and is much smaller than the celestial sphere, the horizon bisects the celestial sphere. Those objects in the half above the celestial sphere are visible, while those objects in the lower half are not. You may have noticed that planetariums have hemispherical ceilings — this makes a good backdrop on which to project images that mimic what the sky looks like.

Figure 1a shows the celestial sphere surrounding the earth. Keep in mind that the sizes of the earth and the celestial sphere are not to scale because the earth is much smaller than the theoretical celestial sphere. The north celestial pole is inclined to the northern horizon by an angle equal to one's latitude. The south celestial pole is the same angle below the southern horizon.

The distance to the closest star (other than the sun) is six billion times the earth's radius, so the radius of the celestial sphere is at least six billion times the earth's radius. Obviously, if the figure were to scale, the earth would not show up at all. Due to the earth's rotation, the celestial sphere appears to spin around the earth each day. Just as the earth spins on an axis passing through the earth's North Pole and South Pole, the celestial sphere appears to rotate each day around an axis passing through its *north celestial pole* and its *south celestial pole*. The celestial poles are the points where the earth's axis intersects the celestial sphere. Halfway between the celestial poles is the *celestial equator*. The celestial equator is the intersection of the earth's equator with the celestial sphere.

To an observer at the North Pole (on top of the earth in the figure), the north celestial pole is at the *zenith*, the point directly overhead. The celestial equator lies along the horizon. Everything south of the celestial equator is below the horizon because the earth would block the view of anything below the celestial equator. As the earth rotates, the sky appears to spin around the north celestial pole. Therefore, all stars that are above the celestial equator are always above the horizon, while stars below the celestial equator are always below the horizon. Stars that never rise or set are said to be *circumpolar*, meaning *around the pole*. From any location, there are generally two circumpolar regions, one region whose stars are

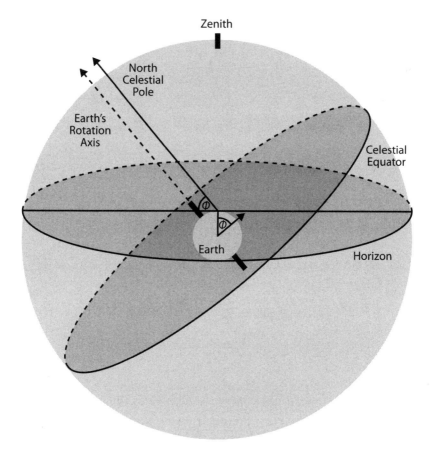

Figure 2a

always visible, and another whose stars are never visible. (The exception is the earth's equator — from locations on the earth's equator, there are no circumpolar regions). At the North Pole, stars above the celestial equator are always visible, placing them in the visible circumpolar region. Stars below the celestial equator are in the non-visible circumpolar region. The situation is reversed at the South Pole: the south celestial pole is at the zenith. Stars below the celestial equator are always visible, and stars above the celestial equator are never visible.

Figure 2a illustrates the situation for an observer located in the Northern Hemisphere at latitude ϕ. The north celestial pole makes an angle ϕ with the northern horizon. As the celestial sphere spins, stars within angle ϕ of the north celestial pole are always above the horizon. This defines the

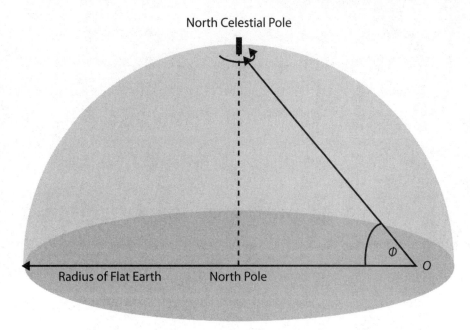

Figure 3a

visible circumpolar region. Likewise, stars within angle φ of the south celestial pole are never above the horizon, defining the non-visible circumpolar region. The celestial equator intersects the horizon due east and west, making an angle equal to the complement of the latitude. Stars not in either circumpolar region rise at some angle along the eastern horizon and set at the same angle along the western horizon. A similar thing happens in the Southern Hemisphere, but the south celestial pole appears above the south direction, making an angle equal to one's latitude with the visible circumpolar region centered on the south celestial pole.

As one moves northward, the latitude increases so that the angle that the north celestial pole makes with the northern horizon increases. There is a corresponding loss of stars visible to the south. Thus, both circumpolar regions increase in size. This change in appearance occurs because the earth is spherical. People in the ancient world were familiar with this phenomenon, and this was one of the arguments that ancient people, such as Aristotle, gave for the earth's spherical shape.

Contrast this to the flat-earth model, as illustrated in figure 3a. In the flat-earth model, the earth is round and flat with the North Pole at its center. There is no South Pole. Above the earth, there is a dome on which the stars and other astronomical bodies are located. The north celestial pole is directly above the earth's North Pole. The dome of the sky is thousands of miles in radius, comparable in size to the radius of the flat earth. The earth does not rotate, but rather the dome of the sky spins around the north celestial pole each day. Because the dome of the sky is only thousands of miles across, an observer, such as at point O, will see the north celestial pole at an angle ϕ above the northern horizon. At the North Pole, ϕ will be a right angle, but ϕ will decrease with increasing distance from the North Pole. Notice that ϕ will always be greater than zero degrees, so the north celestial pole will be visible from all locations on the earth. Notice that since a line may be drawn from any point on the flat earth to any point on the dome of the sky, the entire dome is visible from all locations on the earth. That is, there are no stars that are visible from some locations, but not from others. However, at different locations, particular stars will be visible in different parts of the sky. There is no south celestial pole, so all motion will be around the north celestial pole.

How well do these predictions of the flat-earth model match what we see in the sky? Not very well. The star Polaris is within a degree of the north celestial pole. Being so close to the north celestial pole, Polaris appears to move over a very tiny circle around the north celestial pole. The naked eye generally cannot discern such a small change in position over hours, so Polaris appears to remain motionless over the northern horizon, while all other stars appear to spin around it. This is why we call Polaris the North Star. Being so close to the north celestial pole, the North Star can act as a sort of stand-in for the north celestial pole. There is no bright star near the south celestial pole, so there is no *South Star*.[4] In the Southern Hemisphere, stars appear to spin around the south celestial pole (I have made numerous trips to the Southern Hemisphere and observed this for myself). However, in the flat-earth model, there is no south celestial pole, so this cannot happen. The simple observation that

---

4. Some people refer to the rather faint fifth magnitude Sigma Octantis, lying a little more than a degree from the south celestial pole as Polaris Australis, or the South Star.

stars in the Southern Hemisphere indeed appear to spin around the south celestial pole devastatingly disproves the flat-earth model.

The North Star is not visible south of the earth's equator. This is a matter of observational fact. For observers in temperate regions of the Southern Hemisphere, there is a circumpolar region surrounding the north celestial pole that is never visible. This region contains the North Star, the Big Dipper, and the Little Dipper. On a rafting trip in the Grand Canyon, a man from Australia was delighted for me to point out the Big Dipper and the North Star to him, for, though he had heard about them, he had never seen these before. In similar manner, there are stars near the south celestial pole that people in most northern temperate latitudes cannot see. One example is the Southern Cross. Alpha Crucis, the southernmost star in the Southern Cross, is within 27 degrees of the south celestial pole, meaning that it is not visible farther north than 27 degrees north latitude. The northernmost star in the Southern Cross, Gamma Crucis, is 33 degrees from the south celestial pole, so it can be seen no farther north than 33 degrees north latitude. Of course, the stars in question only briefly rise above the horizon at these minimal locations. This fact, along with adverse conditions near the horizon, such as obstructions, would make practical observations very difficult. Even closer to the south celestial pole are two satellite galaxies of the Milky Way, the Large Magellanic Cloud (LMC) and the Small Magellanic Cloud (SMC). While the LMC is technically above the horizon as far north as 18 degrees north latitude and the SMC technically is above the horizon at 16 degrees north latitude, given their diffuse nature, these beautiful objects are not readily visible except in the Southern Hemisphere.

These circumstances of visibility are easily explained in terms of a spinning spherical earth, as illustrated in figure 2a, because there are circumpolar regions of invisibility in each of earth's hemispheres. However, with the flat-earth model, as in figure 3a, there are no regions of the star dome that are not visible from every location on earth. Therefore, the North Star, the Big Dipper, and the Southern Cross ought to be visible from all locations on the earth. They demonstrably are not visible from all over the earth, so the flat-earth model must be false. Some flat-earthers understand this problem, so they claim that the North Star is visible well

Ark star trails

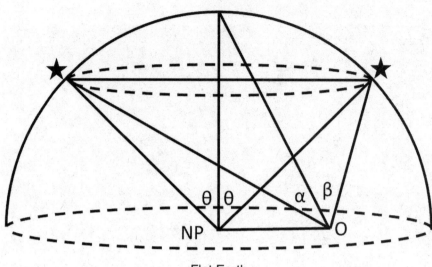

Flat Earth

south of the earth's equator. Simply asserting false information does not suffice for a good argument for the earth being flat. But there is more.

Star Trails

Long-exposure photographs of stars show that throughout the night, stars sweep out circular paths centered on the north celestial pole. The figure Ark Star trails shows a half-hour exposure of star trails taken over the Ark Encounter. Proponents of the flat-earth model frequently claim that these circular star trails cannot be explained with a spinning, spherical earth, but can easily be explained by a flat, non-spinning earth, thus proving the flat-earth model. Actually, the reverse is true. Consider the conventional cosmology, that the earth is a spinning globe, and the stars are billions of times farther away than the earth's diameter. As the earth spins, a person's position changes so minutely compared to the distances of the stars that the stars will appear to maintain a constant angular radius from the north celestial pole. Therefore, the stars will appear to move in circles around the north celestial pole each sidereal day.[5] This is what we see.

But what does the flat-earth model predict? Since the stars are far closer to the earth than in conventional cosmology, parallax effects

---

5. The sidereal day is the rotation period of the earth with respect to the stars.

because one's changing distance to the stars come into play. In the accompanying figure, the flat earth is a disk with the North Pole (indicated by NP) at its center. On the dome of the sky directly above the North Pole is the north celestial pole (NCP). Consider a star at an angular distance of θ from the NCP as observed from the NP. As the dome of the sky rotates each day, the star will sweep out a circle of radius θ as seen from the NP. Consider an observer at point O at some distance from the NP so that the NCP makes an angle φ with the horizon. What shape will the star sweep out from the perspective of an observer at point O? From point O, the circle that the star sweeps out will be projected so that the observed motion of the star will not be a circle. To see this, consider the angle α, the angle that the star makes with the NCP when closest to point O, and the angle β, the angle that the star makes with the NCP when farthest from point O. Using high school geometry and trigonometry, we find:

$$a = \tan^{-1} \left(\frac{\cos \theta}{\cot \varphi - \sin \theta} \right) - \varphi,$$

$$\beta = \varphi - \tan^{-1} \left(\frac{\cos \theta}{\cot \varphi + \sin \theta} \right).$$

By inspection, one can see that these angles are not the same, but let us consider a few examples. In each example, let φ be 39 degrees, which is the value of φ where I live in Northern Kentucky. If θ = 10 degrees, α = 3.9 degrees, while β = 4.0 degrees. Notice that this is not a circle, for while the star will appear to orbit the NCP, the star will be farther from the NCP when it appears above the NCP than when it appears below the NCP (a circle, by definition, has a constant radius). Next, consider a star for which θ = 30 degrees. Now α = 10.7 degrees, while β = 12.5 degrees. Again, this cannot be a circle because the angles are different. If θ = 60 degrees, α = 14.6 degrees, while β = 25.6 degrees. The apparent motion of the star is even more distorted from a circle than in the previous two examples. The point is, since the angles α and β are different, star trails predicted from the flat-earth model are decidedly not circular, but rather some complicated loop.

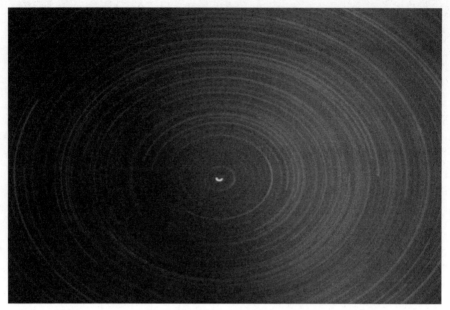

Flat earth star trails

I used the Stargazers Planetarium at the Creation Museum to demonstrate what sort of star trails the flat-earth model predicts. We set the system so that the north celestial pole was at the zenith, with the sky spinning at the rate of once per minute. A person at the center of the room would see in 60 seconds what a person at the earth's North Pole would see in 24 hours — all the stars spinning in a circle around the north celestial pole. To show what a person not at the North Pole would see, I set up a digital SLR camera on a tripod near the plane defined by the bottom of the planetarium dome, located some distance from the center of the room, but still under the dome. The figure Flat Earth Star Trails is a 30-second photograph. Since this is one-half the rotation rate, the planetarium stars followed one-half of a rotation around the dome. The bright half-loop near the center is the North Star. Notice that the star trails are clearly not circular. The paths of the planetarium stars resemble an ellipse with its major axis in the horizontal direction because the motion in the line of sight on either side is foreshortened, while the motion in the other direction is not. However, the shape is not exactly elliptical because, as the discussion above demonstrated, the angular radius of motion above and below the north celestial pole (along what would be the minor axis) is not the same. Therefore, despite claims to the contrary made by flat-earthers, photographs of star trails prove the conventional cosmology and disprove the flat-earth cosmology. Flat-earthers couldn't be more wrong about this.

Equatorial Mounts and Sidereal Drives

Many astronomical telescopes are equipped with equatorial mounts that, when properly aligned with the NCP, allow for a single motion around the polar axis to counteract the earth's rotation. A sidereal drive is a motor that turns the telescope around the polar axis at a rate of one rotation per sidereal day (about four minutes shorter than a solar day) to keep objects viewed through the telescope centered with no need to adjust position throughout the night. This works very well with the rotating spherical earth with the stars very far away, because in that model, stars turn at a uniform rate (one revolution per sidereal day) at the same angular distance from the NCP. However, as demonstrated here, with the flat-earth model, the angular distance from the NCP would change throughout the night so that stars would drift in the north-south direction. Furthermore, in the flat-earth model, stars would appear to move in the east-west direction more quickly when observed above the NCP than when observed below the NCP. Therefore, stars would drift in the east-west direction with a sidereal drive if the earth were flat and the stars relatively close to us. I frequently do research with a camera mounted on a telescope with a sidereal drive. This work requires that the telescope precisely track the stars that I observe over many hours. The field of view of the camera is typically 15 arcminutes or less. An arcminute is ¼ of a degree. Obviously, the examples considered here demonstrate that a sidereal drive would do a miserable job of keeping any star in the field of view of the camera, let alone centered, if the flat-earth model were true. But this is not the case, so the flat-earth model must be false.

The Changing Aspect of the Sky Each Season

The figure on the following page shows a meme taken from Nick Havok's Facebook page. The meme begins with the statement:

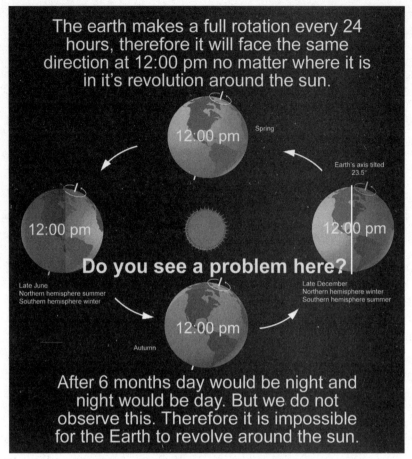

Graphic from Nick Havok's Facebook page

The earth makes a full rotation every 24 hours, therefore it will face the same direction at 12:00 pm no matter where it is in it's revolution around the sun.

The meme goes on to ask the question:

Do you see a problem here?

Followed by the answer:

After 6 months day would be night and night would be day. But we do not observe this. Therefore it is impossible for the Earth to revolve around the sun.

Other flat-earth memes on the Internet present similar diagrams and ask something like this:

> Why don't our clocks have to change by a full 12 hours between Summer and Winter Solstice to account for the fact that we are on the opposite side of the sun?

Grammar issues aside, the first part of Nick Havok's meme introduces something false in its first statement. We usually express time of day in terms of the *solar day*, the average length of time it takes for the earth to spin on its axis with respect to the sun. Since time of day is defined with respect to the sun, then it is no surprise that it is noon when we are centered on the side of the earth facing the sun. However, the solar day is not the true rotation period of the earth. The true rotation period of the earth is the *sidereal day*, the length of time that it takes the earth to spin with respect to the stars. The sidereal day is nearly four minutes shorter than the solar day. Consequently, the stars gain about four minutes per day on the sun, meaning that the stars rise and set about four minutes earlier each day. In a week, the stars rise and set nearly a half-hour earlier. In a month, the stars rise and set about two hours earlier. And in six months, the stars rise and set about 12 hours earlier. There is where the 12 hours have gone.

Look at the meme again. Suppose that it is noon on the summer solstice. That would place the earth on the left side of this figure, with the observer on the right side of the earth, facing the sun. If six months later it is again noon, then the earth would be on the right side of this figure, with the observer on the left side of the earth, again facing the sun. We would reckon that it is noon on either date, even though we are facing opposite directions in space. Now suppose that it is midnight on the summer solstice. At that time, the earth will be on the left side of this figure, with the observer on the left side of the earth. The observer will see stars that are to the left of this figure. Stars to the right side of the figure will not be visible because the earth will be in the way. Twelve hours later, the observer will be on the right side of the earth, but it will be daytime, so stars to the right of the figure will not be visible. However, at midnight six months later, on the winter solstice, the earth will be on the right side of the figure, with the observer on the right side of the earth. Stars to the right of the figure will now be visible, but the stars on the left side of the figure will not be visible.

Rather than disproving the conventional cosmology, flat-earthers who employ this argument have stumbled upon the reason why the stars we see at night change with the seasons.

Chapter 5

Astronomy and Flat Earth

Pythagoras, Egypt, Heliocentrism, and the Occult

In chapter 1, I gave a little history of cosmology as it relates to belief in the earth being flat. It is necessary here to revisit this history. Flat-earthers frequently malign the conventional understanding of cosmology, a spherical planet earth orbiting the sun, as occultic. They claim that this cosmology arose as a form of sun worship. Flat-earthers further claim that this worship of Helios, the sun god, began in ancient Egypt, and that Pythagoras (a Greek) got this teaching from Egypt. Therefore, flat-earthers conclude, belief in the conventional cosmology is a form of pagan worship, the sort of thing that Scripture forbids. There are several false bits of information here.

First, this confuses the question of the earth's shape and whether the earth orbits the sun (heliocentrism). This is a common misconception among flat-earthers, as well as the public. For instance, while Pythagoras was among the first in the West to teach that the earth was spherical, there is no evidence that he was a heliocentrist. About a century after the death of Pythagoras, Philolaus was the first in the West to teach that the earth moved. However, Philolaus thought that the earth orbited a central fire, not the sun. Apparently, Philolaus still thought that the sun orbited the earth. Nearly a century after Philolaus, people in the West began to consider that the earth may orbit the sun, but that apparently never was the dominant cosmology until about four centuries ago.

Second, while the ancient Greeks obtained some of their mathematics and astronomy from ancient Egypt, flat-earthers have included some false attributions. The cosmology of ancient Egypt was very much that of a flat earth with a dome over the top. The dome was the nude body of the goddess Nut with stars affixed to her body. Each day, the sun god Ra traveled across this dome. When the sun set, Ra passed under the earth to rise in the east the next day. In later dynasties, the god Ra was combined with other deities. Furthermore, flat-earthers call this worship of Helios, but Helios was the Greek god of the sun. If anything, it is the flat-earthers who have adopted the pagan cosmology of ancient Egypt. It is very bold for them to accuse others of what they are guilty of.

Parallax

If the earth orbits the sun, then we view stars from different vantage points throughout the year. Consequently, the apparent positions of stars ought to shift on an annual basis, an effect we call *parallax*. Stars lying perpendicular to the ecliptic, the plane of the earth's orbit, ought to go in small circles once per year. Stars in the plane of the ecliptic ought to move back and forth. Stars that lie between these two extremes ought to move through ellipses, with the amount of flattening of the ellipses being dependent upon ecliptic latitude.

Some ancient astronomers considered the heliocentric theory, and so they were aware of this prediction. Consequently, ancient astronomers looked for parallax. When they didn't see parallax, being good scientists, most ancient astronomers concluded that the earth did not orbit the sun. A few ancient astronomers thought otherwise. So, how did they explain the lack of parallax? They reasoned that the stars were so far away that stellar parallax was too small to measure. It turns out that they were right.

By 1700, nearly everyone had abandoned the Ptolemaic model in favor of the heliocentric model. There were several reasons for this. By the 17th century, the Ptolemaic model had been the dominant cosmology for 1,500 years. During this time, discrepancies between the model predictions and observations required the addition of many tweaks, making the Ptolemaic model very complicated. The heliocentric model, with simple improvements made by Johannes Kepler, was much simpler. Occam's razor suggested that the heliocentric model was more likely correct. Another reason was that by 1610, Galileo Galilei had viewed Venus through a tele-scope, and he saw that Venus goes through phases. Venus could not do this in the Ptolemaic model because its phases could be explained only if Venus orbited the sun. It did not automatically follow that the earth orbited the sun, but it was highly suggestive. Finally, there was the elegant Newtonian physics that gave a very powerful theory as to how the sun's gravity com-pelled the earth, the other planets, and comets to orbit the sun. This also applied to the natural satellites, or moons, of the planets. This theory not only had descriptive power, but it also had predictive power. Still, there was not yet direct evidence that the earth orbited the sun.

In 1725, James Bradley began a series of observations to measure par-allax. For his study, Bradley chose 2.4-magnitude Gamma Draconis, the brightest star to pass directly through the zenith near London. Bradley fastened a telescope at the bottom of a chimney pointed at the zenith. The tall, narrow opening of the chimney allowed Bradley to observe Gamma Draconis night and day. Soon after embarking on his program, Bradley saw a small shift in the position of Gamma Draconis. This pleased him, for he thought he was seeing evidence of parallax. However, a few more months of observation revealed that the direction of the shift in Gamma Draconis was off by 90 degrees. Parallactic shift ought to be directed toward the sun and perpendicular to the direction of the earth's motion. However, the observed change was in the direction of the earth's revo-lution around the sun. This baffled Bradley for a while, but, eventually, he realized that this was a consequence of the finite speed of light. As we move through space, we must tilt our telescopes very slightly in the direc-tion of our motion. Not only did this *aberration of starlight* provide the first direct evidence of the earth's orbital motion, it also provided a crude measurement of the speed of light. The maximum amount of aberration of starlight is 20.5 arcseconds. The amount of aberration of starlight for any given star depends upon the star's location in the sky.

On the other hand, parallax is smaller than this. Parallax has an inverse relationship with distance, so unlike aberration of starlight, the amplitude of stellar parallax is different for each star and doesn't depend on a star's location in the sky. The closest star, Alpha Centauri, has a parallax of 0.76 arcseconds, about 4% of the amplitude of aberration of starlight. Given its small value, the first parallax measurements were a little more than a century after Bradley's discovery of the aberration of starlight. In 1838, Friedrich Bessel was the first to measure stellar parallax. The star he measured was 61 Cygni, which had been suspected of being a nearby star for more than 30 years. This suspicion came from the large *proper motion* of 61 Cygni. Proper motion is the apparent movement of a star across the sky. Proper motion is determined by comparing precise measurements of stellar position over several decades. Unlike parallax, proper motion accumulates, so the longer the baseline of time, the greater the change in position, and, hence, the easier and more accurate measurement of proper motion. For a given velocity in space, a nearby star will have greater proper motion than a more distant star. Therefore, proper motion studies are valuable in determining which stars are most likely to have large parallaxes and, hence, are good targets of parallax studies.

Parallax measurements of other stars soon followed, and by the end of the 19th century, scores of stars had known distances by this method.[1] Classical techniques of parallax measurements are limited by the blurring effect of the earth's atmosphere. By these techniques, astronomers could measure parallax with 20 percent error or less within 20 parsecs, about 65 light years. Fortunately, there are a few hundred stars within this limit, most of which were measured by the classical techniques. Parallax measurements have been revitalized in the past 30 years. Part of this has been accomplished by new techniques from the ground. However, the greatest boon has been getting above the earth's atmosphere. There have been two spacecrafts with dedicated parallax instrumentation working above the earth's atmosphere. The Hipparcos mission (1989–1993) provided high-precision parallax measurements of more than 100,000 stars, but the less precise catalogue provided parallax measurements of more than a million stars. The Gaia mission (launched 2013) is providing precise position measurements of more than a billion astronomical objects, and will yield parallax measurements for millions of stars, giving accurate distance measurements for stars out to 6,000 light years.

This is an impressive body of data collected over the past 180 years, so what do flat-earthers have to say about it? Flat-earthers rarely discuss

---

1. For a discussion of the state of stellar parallax measurements from a century ago, see F.W. Dyson, "Measurements of the Distances to the Stars," *The Observatory*, 1915, 38:292–299.

parallax. One of the few who does discuss it is Eric Dubay in his book, *200 Proofs*. His proof 19 reads:

> Tycho Brahe famously argued against the heliocentric theory in his time, positing that if the Earth revolved around the Sun, the change in relative position of the stars after 6 months orbital motion could not fail to be seen. He argued that the stars should seem to separate as we approach and come together as we recede. In actual fact, however, after 190,000,000 miles of supposed orbit around the Sun, not a single inch [sic] of parallax can be detected in the stars, proving we have not moved at all.[2]

The first part of this is basically correct[3] — Tycho did make this argument against the heliocentric model. But Tycho died more than 400 years ago, about a decade before the invention of the telescope, and more than two centuries before the first parallax measurement. Therefore, it's a mystery as to why what Tycho thought on this matter is relevant. Also, notice that Dubay's response is simply to assert that there have been no parallax measurements. He offered no proof. He offered no evidence. He offered no refutation. He simply asserted that no one has ever measured a single star's parallax. This is typical of so many flat-earth arguments — they simply assert their case. They understand that if parallax measurements have been made, it would contradict their model. Since they firmly believe that the earth is an unmoving flat disk with a dome over the top, there can be no stellar parallax. Ergo, no one has ever measured stellar parallax. It is impossible to reason with people who are, well, so unreasonable.

There also is a small irony here. Samuel Rowbotham used the pseudonym "Parallax" in writing his original pamphlet that he eventually expanded into his book *Zetetic Astronomy*. In *Zetetic Astronomy*, Rowbotham discussed parallax in his Experiment 4. His discussion amounts to mining of sources from about the time the first parallax measurements

---

2. Dubay, *200 Proofs Earth Is Not a Spinning Globe*, p. 4.
3. However, I must correct the notion that parallax causes the stars to appear to separate and come together as we alternately approach and recede from the stars. Rather, parallax causes an apparent shift in position.

were made, from which he concluded that no parallax measurements exist. Why did Rowbotham use the pseudonym "Parallax?" Flat-earthers are quick to argue that those promoting the earth as a globe leave obvious clues to the contrary in plain sight. Two can play that game. How do we know that by using the pseudonym "Parallax" that Rowbotham wasn't cleverly revealing that he was pulling our legs about the earth being a flat, motionless disk? After all, by Rowbotham's own words, parallax doesn't exist.

Historic Measurements of the Speed of Light

The above discussion of Bradley's discovery of the aberration of starlight is a good segue into the speed of light and how it relates to flat-earth cosmology. From ancient times, there had been debate as to whether the speed of light was finite or that light traveled instantly. The first demonstration that light traveled with finite speed was Ole Rømer's 1675 discovery that the timing of eclipses of Io, the innermost Galilean satellite of Jupiter, had a periodicity that was in phase with Jupiter's changing distance from earth. This indicated that it took time for light to travel across the earth's orbit. Rømer's data suggested that light travel time across the earth's orbit was about 22 minutes. This was a first measurement, and as is common with first measurements, it is off from the correct value. Within 25 years, this had been refined to the point that in 1704, Isaac Newton stated that light took 7–8 minutes to reach the earth from the sun. This is close to the correct value.

Though it wasn't Rømer's purpose to use this information to find the speed of light, in 1768, Christiaan Huygens used Rømer's result to determine the speed of light for the first time. This determination was about 30 percent less than the modern value. The discrepancy is partly due to Rømer's initial measurement of the light travel time across the earth's orbit being too great, but it was also due to uncertainty in the size of the earth's orbit. In chapter 6, I discuss the method that permitted Copernicus to determine the orbital radii of the then-known five other planets. These sizes were expressed in terms of the *astronomical unit* (AU), the average distance between the earth and sun. The size of the AU had not been directly measured at the time, though there were some crude estimates.

For many years, the best method for calibrating the AU was to observe the rare transits of Venus. How rare are transits of Venus? They occur on a 243-year cycle, with pairs of transits eight years apart, separated by 121.5 and 105.5 years. Two widely spaced observers watching the same transit will not see Venus take the same path across the sun's disk. By comparing the two observed paths and knowing the distance between the observers, one can use trigonometry to determine the distance between Venus and the earth at the time of the transit. Since that distance can be expressed in terms of the AU, the length of the AU in traditional units, such as miles or kilometers can be found. The first to do this was Jeremiah Horrocks during the 1639 transit of Venus. Plagued by bad weather and other problems, Horrocks' determination of the AU was about two-thirds the modern value.

The transits of Venus in 1761 and 1769 were the objects of several ambitious observing programs. In 1771, Jérôme Lalande used observations from these transits to determine that the AU was 153 million km, within 2 percent of the correct value. The 1874 and 1882 pair of transits of Venus saw even more research efforts. Using results from all four transit measurements, Simon Newcomb published a new value for the AU in 1895. It was within 0.06 percent of the modern value. Since that time, other methods have made observations of transits of Venus obsolete for determining the length of the AU. With improved values of the AU, there was improved measurement of the speed of light. Certainly, with Lalande's accurate determination of the AU, the speed of light was known to be within 2–3 percent of the correct value as early as 1771.

As an aside, I must regularly correct for light travel time in my work with *eclipsing binary stars*. A binary star is a system of two stars orbiting around a common center of mass. If the earth is situated close to the orbital plane of a binary star, the two stars will eclipse, or pass in front of, one another each orbit. The stars in an eclipsing binary are so close together that we don't see the individual stars so that the stars appear as one. But twice each orbital period, the amount of light that we receive from the system fades as the stars eclipse one another. We time when eclipses occur, and if not corrected for light travel time due to our varying distance from the binary system throughout the year, the eclipses periodically are earlier or later by as much as eight minutes. The amplitude of the light travel time correction is eight minutes times the cosine of the ecliptic latitude of the star in question. The time varying portion goes as the negative of the cosine of the difference in ecliptic longitude of the star and the sun.

As I mentioned above, Bradley's measurement of aberration of starlight not only provided the first direct evidence of the earth's orbital motion, it also provided another way to measure the speed of light. Bradley pointed out that the amount of aberration of starlight that he measured indicated that light traveled 10,210 times faster than the earth in its orbit. This is very close to the modern value of 10,066. Multiplying the circumference of the earth's orbit by this number and dividing by the length of the year yields the speed of light. Bradley had Horrocks' measurement of the AU, so his value for the speed of light was one-third less than today's value. However, within a few decades of Bradley's work, Lalande's measurement of the AU produced a speed of light much closer to the true value of the speed of light.

Armand Fizeau directly measured the speed of light for the first time in 1849. Fizeau's device used a rapidly spinning toothed wheel. A beam of light passed through the gap between two teeth toward a mirror 8.67 km away. After reflecting off the mirror, the light returned to pass through the next gap as the wheel spun. Fizeau measured the rate at which the wheel turned to accomplish this (25 revolutions per second) and knowing the number of teeth on the wheel (720), Fizeau determined the amount of time the light beam required to make a round trip of 17.34 km (1/18,000 seconds). Dividing the distance by the time, Fizeau found the speed of light to be 312,000 km/s. This result is 4 percent greater than the true value for the speed of light. Fizeau and others quickly improved upon this method, and this remained the primary method for measuring the speed of light for many years.

How does all this relate to the flat-earth discussion? Direct measurement of the speed of light on earth is consistent with the speed of light implied by the aberration of starlight. Furthermore, the light travel time required by the timings of eclipses of Io and the eclipses of the other satellites of the solar system by their planets, as well as the timings of the eclipses of eclipsing binary stars, are consistent with this speed of light, but only if the scale of the solar system is properly understood, with the

AU being 150 million km (93 million miles). But these distances are far too great for the flat-earth cosmology to accommodate. For instance, it requires that the sun be 93 million miles away, but the flat-earth cosmology places the sun only a few thousand miles above the earth's flat surface.

Flat-earthers don't appear to be aware of these facts, so we don't know what their response might be. When flat-earthers are confronted with these sorts of arguments, the most common response is to ignore them. If they engage at all, flat-earthers most likely would claim that all these data are made up. But what would be the point of all this false data creation spanning centuries and involving many people? Is it part of some nefarious plot to mislead the world about the earth's true shape? Given the conspiratorial bent of so many flat-earthers, the answer to that question probably is a resounding "yes." As I previously mentioned, I have had four decades of experience with eclipsing binary stars, and in my work, I regularly see the effect of light travel time across the earth's orbit around the sun. Therefore, if flat-earthers are correct, then I must be lying about this as well. Hence, I must be part of this conspiracy. This is nonsense.

The Gleason Map

Most flat-earthers seem to accept Gleason's 1892 New Standard Map of the World. Indeed, Gleason apparently was a flat-earther, so his map must have been an attempt to provide flat-earthers with a map for their model. The Gleason map is a projection of the globe earth onto a flat plane. Here I will describe the conversion between the spherical earth to the Gleason map. Flat-earthers who may object to this approach could reverse engineer this to convert the Gleason map to the spherical earth. Either way, this conversion permits a comparison of distances in either model, allowing predictions that we can use to test the two models.

The Gleason map is a polar coordinate graph. Polar coordinates have two

Gleason's map of the world

variables: distance from the origin and an angle measured from a reference direction. Though these two coordinates can be related to latitude and longitude respectively, there are some differences. For instance, latitude is expressed as an angle, which makes sense only on a curved surface, such as on a spherical earth. It makes no sense to express radial distances on a polar coordinate graph in terms of angles. However, differences in latitude can be expressed as differences in linear distances, with one degree = 60 nautical miles = 69 statute miles. With this conversion, latitude can be expressed as linear distance from the North Pole, with the North Pole at the center of the Gleason map. If the earth is a sphere with radius R, then the outermost part of the earth that can be plotted on the Gleason map is the South Pole, one-half the circumference, πR radians (180 degrees), from the origin. Flat-earthers may object that the South Pole does not exist, and that no one knows how far the ice wall of Antarctica extends. Flat-earthers generally agree that the ice wall begins close to 70 degrees south latitude. Flat-earthers also don't think that what lies beyond the ice wall of Antarctica has been mapped. Therefore, if we avoid latitudes beyond 70 degrees south, there ought to be no complaint.

There are some differences between longitude on a spherical earth and the angular coordinate on the Gleason map. On a sphere, a meridian is a line (a portion of a great circle arc) extending from pole to pole. The prime meridian passes through the Royal Observatory in Greenwich, England. The longitude of a given location is the angle between the meridian at that location and the prime meridian. It has been common practice to express longitude in degrees either east or west up to 180 degrees. However, in some cases, it is advantageous to express longitude westward through 360 degrees. Furthermore, it is sometimes desirable to express longitude through 360 degrees, but to use hours, minutes, and seconds of time, rather than degrees, with one hour equal to 15 degrees. On a flat earth, it makes no sense to speak of meridians, so the Gleason map technically has no meridians. Instead, there are lines directed radially from the origin. The line passing through Greenwich coincides with the prime meridian on the spherical earth.

Both latitude and longitude project in this manner onto the Gleason map. Consequently, the Gleason map is useful in comparing latitudes and longitudes of various locations. However, since the Gleason map is flat, there will be distortion of linear distances when mapping the surface of a spherical earth onto a flat plane. Therefore, one must be aware of these distortions when making comparisons of different locations. Along the radial directions on the Gleason map (along meridians of longitude), there is no distortion of linear distances. However, there is distortion along circles (parallels) of latitude. This difference allows for tests between the spherical earth and flat-earth models.

Let φ be the latitude and λ be the longitude of a location on the spherical earth having radius R. Treat north latitudes as positive and south latitudes as negative. Let ρ be the linear distance from the North Pole that this point would project onto the Gleason map. Then

$$\rho = \left(\frac{\pi}{2} - \varphi \right) R,$$

where φ is expressed in radian measure rather than degrees. On both the spherical earth and the flat earth, the linear distance between points having the same longitude depends upon the difference in latitude. More specifically, if φ_1 and φ_2 are the two latitudes expressed in radian measure, then the distance between the two locations, $\Delta\rho$, is given by

$$\Delta\rho = (\rho_1 - \rho_2)R = (\varphi_2 - \varphi_1)R.$$

On the spherical earth, consider two points having the same latitude but separated by longitude $\Delta\lambda$. The linear distance between two points, Δs, is given by

$$\Delta s = \Delta\lambda R \cos \varphi.$$

However, on the Gleason map, the distance between the two points, Δs, will have a different functional dependence:'

$$\Delta s' = \Delta\lambda \left(\frac{\pi}{2} - \varphi \right) R.$$

We can express the amount of longitude distortion on parallels of latitude as $\Delta s'/\Delta s$, the ratio of linear distances on the Gleason map to linear distances on the spherical earth:

$$\Delta s' / \Delta s = \frac{\frac{\pi}{2} - \varphi}{\cos \varphi}$$

This distortion is the least (unity) at the North Pole, which can be shown by application of L'Hôpital's rule. However, in the Southern Hemisphere, the distortion rapidly increases with higher latitudes. The ratio increases without bound as latitude approaches $-\pi/2 = -90$ degrees. The table gives the distortion ratio at increments of 10 degrees latitude.

Notice that at high northern latitudes, the distortion ratio is modest — it doesn't reach 10 percent until below 50 degrees latitude. Even at 30 degrees, the distortion is only 1.21, and it is only 1.57 at the equator. There is a mathematical reason for this. The colatitude is defined as the complement of the latitude. Notice that north of the equator, the equation for $\Delta s'$ is a linear function of the colatitude. Similarly, the equation for Δs could be expressed as being proportional to the sine of the colatitude. At high latitudes, the colatitude is small, and for small angles, the sine function is approximately a linear function of the angle, with the angle expressed in radian measure. Therefore, in the small angle approximation, both $\Delta s'$ and Δs are nearly the same linear function of the colatitude. Consequently, the ratio of $\Delta s'$ and Δs is very low throughout northern temperate latitudes. However, this trend does not continue in the Southern Hemisphere. The equation for $\Delta s'$ continues to increase with increasing angular distance from the North Pole, but Δs decreases with increasing southern latitude, eventually reaching zero at the South Pole.

Lat.	Ratio
90	1.000
80	1.005
70	1.021
60	1.047
50	1.086
40	1.139
30	1.209
20	1.300
10	1.417
0	1.571
-10	1.772
-20	2.043
-30	2.418
-40	2.962
-50	3.801
-60	5.236
-70	8.165
-80	17.09
-90	------

When most land masses in the north temperate latitudes are projected this way onto the Gleason map, they do not appear that different from what one sees on a globe. That makes it easy to fool people into thinking that the Gleason map is a good representation of the earth. But anyone familiar with Southern Hemisphere land masses, such as South America and Australia, can readily see that on the Gleason map, Southern Hemisphere land masses are stretched in the east-west direction. For instance, Perth (on Australia's western coast) is at nearly -32 degrees latitude, and Sydney (on Australia's eastern coast) is at nearly -34 degrees latitude. Hence, the east-west distance between the two on the Gleason map is stretched about 2.5 times over what it is on the spherical earth. There are many maps of Australia available, so one can readily compare those maps to depictions on the Gleason map and on globes to see which one best matches the maps of Australia. It is very clear that the globe better depicts Australia.

In the light of this information, the flat-earther has three choices. One choice is to reject the flat-earth model. The second choice is to accept the linear east-west length of Australia depicted on maps as correct, but this requires rejecting the established longitudes of Australia. Apparently, Gleason, who was a flat-earther, did not choose this option, or else he would have reduced the east-west size of Australia on his map. The third option is to accept that the longitudes of Australia are correct and maintain that Australia truly is stretched by a factor of about 2½ in the east-west direction over what appears on most maps. This third option, which Gleason obviously believed, requires believing that every published map of Australia is grossly incorrect.

This third option presents a good test between the two models of the earth. Perth and Sydney are at nearly the same latitude, but their separation in longitude is 35.3 degrees. In the United States, Atlanta and Los Angeles are at similar latitude as Sydney. Their separation in longitude is 33.8 degrees, about four percent less than the longitudinal separation between Perth and Sydney. If Australia is stretched as much as the Gleason map indicates, then flights between Perth and Sydney ought to take about 2½ times longer than flights between Atlanta and Los Angeles. Prevailing winds on either continent are from the west, so westbound flights take about an hour longer than eastbound flights. If one checks flight times between the two cities on their respective continents, one quickly learns that the flight times are about the same. This test definitively disproves the Gleason map. One could revert to option two, but then one would have to explain why and how all those longitude measurements in Australia could be so wrong.

Latitude and Longitude

This discussion of the Gleason map brings up the question of latitude and longitude. Flat-earthers appear to accept established measurements of latitude and longitude, though they don't seem to be aware of how latitude and longitude are determined. Today, most surveying is done by using the GPS constellation of satellites. Of course, flat-earthers don't believe that there are any satellites, so they claim that GPS signals come from nearby cell towers. It is amazing that flat-earthers totally deny the basis of how GPS works while simultaneously accepting the results of that technology.

Comments made by some flat-earthers suggest that they think latitude and longitude measurement are the result of surveying over relatively small distances. Until the emergence of GPS satellites, surveyors generally worked from local survey markers with established latitude and longitude, so it is true that until recently, much surveying work was relative to those survey markers. However, since the emergence of GPS, this technique isn't used much anymore. Furthermore, how were those survey markers established? Undoubtedly, some of those survey markers were determined in relation to other survey markers in a sort of patchwork process. However, this survey marker system had to have a starting point or starting points. How were those initial standards established? Ultimately, original survey markers were determined by navigation techniques using astronomical bodies, such as the sun or stars. Traditionally, this is a process that surveyors were educated to do, but is probably not taught or practiced much today. This is the same process that navigators have traditionally used, but even they have abandoned the old methods in favor of GPS. However, over fear of loss of use of the GPS constellation during time of conflict, the U.S. military has returned to using celestial navigation as a backup.

Navigation by the stars or the sun is done by solving one or more spherical triangles. Astronomers use a coordinate system in the sky very similar to latitude and longitude on earth. Coplanar with the earth's equator is the celestial equator. The celestial equator divides the celestial sphere into two halves — one half north of the celestial equator and the other half south. We can draw parallels to the equator similar to parallels of latitude on the earth to express how far north or south of the celestial equator objects are. We call this coordinate *declination*. Declinations north of the celestial equator are positive, while declinations south of the celestial equator are negative. Similar to meridians of longitude, we can draw meridians of *right ascension* perpendicular to the celestial equator. The prime meridian of right ascension passes through the vernal equinox, where the ecliptic and celestial equator intersect with the sun traveling northward. Right ascension is measured eastward and, rather than expressed in degrees, right ascension normally is expressed in hours, minutes, and seconds of time. Every astronomical body has a unique declination and right ascension. For a given object, these coordinates will be the same, regardless of one's location on earth.[4]

However, the position in the sky where one observes an astronomical body, or even if the object is above the horizon at all, will depend on one's location, as well as the time. To express this, we define a second coordinate system unique to a position on the earth and the local time. The *zenith* is the point directly overhead. The *horizon* is the great circle arc 90 degrees from the zenith. If there are no obstructions, such as on a large body of water, this horizon coincides with the actual horizon, where one's view of the celestial sphere is blocked by the earth. Like the celestial equator, the horizon divides the celestial sphere into two halves — one half above the horizon and the other half below the horizon. Similar to latitude and declination, we can draw parallels to the horizon to express how high in the sky an object appears. We call this coordinate the *altitude*. We express altitude in degrees. Objects below the horizon have negative altitude. We can draw meridians of *azimuth* perpendicular to the horizon passing from the zenith to the *nadir*, the point below directly opposite the zenith. Azimuth is measured from zero to 360 degrees eastward.

An astronomical object's altitude and azimuth depend upon its declination and right ascension, as well as the observer's location (latitude

---

4. The exception is the slight parallax effect of solar system objects due to different positions on the earth's surface. Being so close to us, the moon's position is most subject to this small effect.

and longitude) and the local time. Knowing the location and time, and the right ascension and declination of an object, solution of a spherical triangle reveals the altitude and azimuth of the object. Or one can specify rising and setting (when an object's altitude will be zero degrees) and solve for the time. This is the method used for computing the time and azimuth of sunrise and sunset. As the sun's right ascension and declination change throughout the year due to our orbit, the time and azimuth of the rising or setting sun changes.[5]

Throughout the day (and night), the altitude and azimuth of all astronomical bodies change. Therefore, the altitude and azimuth of an astronomical body is unique to a specific latitude and longitude and time. Navigation makes use of this unique functional dependence. If we measure the altitude and azimuth of an astronomical body, and if we know the time, such as in Greenwich, England, then we can solve a spherical triangle to determine one's location. Since there are two unknowns (latitude and longitude), we must have two equations. Those two equations come from applying the law of sines and the law of cosines to the spherical triangle. A sextant allows for quick-and-easy measurement of altitude, but it doesn't measure azimuth. Even with a device to measure azimuth, without knowing which way north is, azimuth cannot be measured.[6] The best method is to measure the altitude of two stars in rapid succession. The altitudes of two stars will be unique to one's location and time, so solving two spherical triangles yields the latitude and longitude. Historically, navigators and surveyors using this technique could solve these equations analytically, but they usually used nomograms, a sort of paper analog computer prepared ahead of time. Today, these computations are usually done using digital computers.

This has been the basis of navigation for some time. It has also been the basis for establishing survey standards from which latitude and longitude can be measured. All of this is based upon the earth being a sphere. If the earth were not a sphere, then none of this would work. More specifically, if the earth were flat, navigation and surveying would

---

5. When the sun is near the horizon, atmospheric refraction raises the sun by about ½ degree. Computation of sunrise and sunset usually takes this into account.

6. Magnetic north deviates from true north — the difference between the two is called *magnetic declination*. Tables provide magnetic declination as a function of latitude and longitude, but until latitude and longitude are established, these tables are useless.

not work. Flat-earthers appear to be ignorant of this. If they knew this, then they would reject all navigation and all surveying that is ultimately tied to it.

While I am discussing this topic, I ought to mention that classical techniques of surveying (no GPS) provide evidence for the earth being spherical. We all know that in plane geometry, the interior angles of triangles sum to 180 degrees. Much less well-known, the interior angles of triangles on a spherical surface sum to *greater* than 180 degrees.[7] For small triangles on a spherical surface, the difference from the plane case is negligible. However, on parcels of land greater than about 200 acres, the deviation of the sum of the interior angles of a triangle are measurable using classical surveying techniques. Again, flat-earthers must be ignorant of this fact.

Out-of-Focus Stars

The Nikon P900 camera came out in 2015, about the time that the flat-earth phenomenon began taking off. Flat-earthers soon discovered the P900 camera, and its use among flat-earthers quickly spread. The P900 is a superzoom digital bridge camera. Bridge cameras bridge the gap between single lens reflex (SLR) cameras and point-and-shoot cameras. At the time it was introduced, the P900's superzoom lens was the greatest zoom lens available, and it remained so for some time. At first, flat-earthers used P900 cameras to photograph distant objects to show that those objects sometimes could be seen at great distance, even though the curvature of the earth ought to intervene. Therefore, they concluded that the earth is flat. As I discussed in chapter 2, the explanation for this is superior mirages due to temperature inversions.

However, some flat-earthers began to take zoomed videos of stars and to capture still images from those videos. Many of these images were put into Internet memes that quickly spread among flat-earthers. The images show stars as blobs of light, which flat-earthers took as evidence that stars are not what astronomers claim that they are. Instead of being distant suns that are so far that they still appear as mere pinpoints of light even through large telescopes, these images supposedly reveal that stars have physical extent, proving that they are much closer to us on

---

7. The maximum for the largest possible spherical triangles is 540 degrees.

the dome that covers the earth. Furthermore, the videos reveal that stars have different colors, and that the disks of these stars flicker quite a bit. This observation often is accompanied with a mention of 1 Corinthians 15:41, which reads:

> There is one glory of the sun, and another glory of the moon, and another glory of the stars; for star differs from star in glory (ESV).

In these videos and images, the stars certainly look different, but it is a small sample size. If one were to do this sort of thing for more stars, one would quickly end up with star images that would be difficult to distinguish from one another. So much for demonstrating the uniqueness of each star using this method. What is going on with these images? As a professional astronomer, and as a person who has used telescopes to view the sky for more than a half-century, I immediately recognized that these videos and images are out of focus.

Let me quantify this. We can express how large something appears with its angular diameter, the angle subtended by its diameter. For instance, both the sun and moon appear about ½ degree across, so their angular diameters are about ½ degree. Nearly a century ago, Albert Michaelson[8] used an interferometer on the 100-inch Hooker telescope at the Mt. Wilson Observatory (then the largest telescope in the world) to measure the angular diameter of the star Betelgeuse to be 0.044 arcseconds (the modern value is 0.050 arcseconds). That remained the record angular size for a star until 1997 when astronomers measured the angular diameter of the star R Doradus to be 0.057 arcseconds. It is unlikely that astronomers will measure any angular diameters much larger than this. A dime, when viewed at 2.2 miles, has an angular diameter of one arcsecond. Therefore, the angular diameter of R Doradus is the same as that of a dime held at 38 miles. Since this is the largest known angular diameter for a star, the stars that flat-earthers have supposedly imaged have angular diameters far smaller. With their tiny angular sizes, even with the largest

---

8. This is the same Albert Michaelson of the famed Michaelson-Morley experiment a few decades earlier. As I discuss in chapter 7, flat-earthers hail that earlier experiment because, in their minds, it proves that the earth isn't moving. However, they probably would throw Michaelson under the bus for his measurement of the angular diameter of Betelgeuse, even though both experiments used similar interferometers.

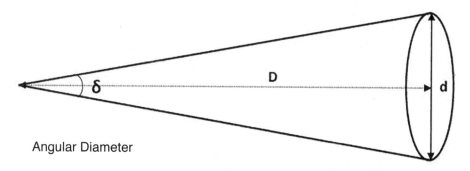

Angular Diameter

telescopes in the world with very high magnification, the stars appear as the smallest of pinpoints. Yet, we are to believe that flat-earthers, using an off-the-shelf camera with a lens that is, at most, two inches in diameter, can do what professional astronomers have never done. That's arrogant. And ignorant.

On a Facebook discussion group, I engaged some flat-earthers who posted some of these images. This prompted me to make and post my own video of the bright star Arcturus to show what a good focus and bad focus look like. I did this with my digital SLR camera attached to a 3.5-inch Questar telescope, using the telescope objective as the camera lens (1,380 mm focal length). I repeatedly took the star in and out of focus, narrating it the entire time. One person responded that, in my opinion, his images weren't focused, but that, in his opinion, my images weren't in focus. However, focus is not subject to post-modern thinking of no absolutes, where one person's focus is as good as any other person's focus. Instead, focus is a matter of objective reality — either an image is in focus, or it's not in focus. It was all for naught, for none of the flat-earthers agreed. Apparently, my half-century of experience with telescopes are trumped by what someone has put on YouTube.

One woman posted a meme featuring an image taken from a video that she had made of a bright star with her P900 camera. She even connected her photo with the vision of Ezekiel 1:4–26. In the blurry light and dark splotches of her out-of-focus image, she had identified an ox and the faces of a person, a lion, and an eagle. In addition to the Rorschach-test quality of this exercise, are we to think that Ezekiel had access to a P900 camera 2,500 years ago? No amount of interaction with this woman could convince her that her video was out of focus. She threw around some technical photography terms, but her use of those terms indicated that she didn't understand what she was talking about, though she certainly was confident that she did. She further opined that her zoomed images of the moon showed craters and other lunar features, demonstrating that the moon is much closer than the standard distance of 238,000 miles. When asked how this proved the moon was much closer than astronomers think, she didn't respond, except to remove her statement.

It is truly sad that people who don't know how to use these cameras properly post these photos and videos with preposterous claims. It's even more sad that many other flat-earthers uncritically accept these things as evidence, not because they are so convincing, but because they conform with what they've already chosen to believe. To those who understand optics, this is total nonsense.

Lunar Occultations

Flat-earthers make several odd claims about the moon. For instance, one claim is that the moon is not a sphere, but rather it is a semitransparent disk. As evidence of this, flat-earthers produce photos and videos of stars supposedly shining through the moon (this is the claim of Dubay's proof number 135). From time to time, the moon passes in front of a bright star or planet, an event we call a *lunar occultation*. Astronomers have good reasons for observing lunar occultations. I've seen some of these myself. My observation is that the stars and other objects occulted by the moon do disappear and later reappear. They *do not*, as flat-earthers claim, shine through the moon. For that matter, I've looked at the moon through telescopes probably thousands of times. I've never seen a star shining through the moon.

Where did this idea come from? Rowbotham discussed this under the heading "Moon Transparent" In his book, *Zetetic Astronomy*. Rowbotham supposedly supported his claim with some quotes from various sources. For instance, here is one of Rowbotham's quotes from a respected astronomy journal, the *Monthly Notices of the Royal Astronomical Society*, in 1860:

Occultation of Jupiter by the moon, on the 24th of May, 1860, by Thomas Gaunt, Esq.

I send you the following account as seen by me at Stoke Newington. The observation was made with an achromatic of 3.3 inches aperture, 50 inches focus; the immersion with a power of 50, and the emersion with a power of 70. At the immersion I could not see the dark limb of the moon until the planet appeared to touch it, and then only to the extent of the diameter of the planet; but what I was most struck with was the appearance on the moon as it passed over the planet. It appeared as though the planet was a dark object, and glided on to the moon instead of behind it; and the appearance continued until the planet was hid, when I suddenly lost the dark limb of the moon altogether.[9]

What?! This quote states that Jupiter disappeared behind the moon, and the distinction between the immersion and emersion of Jupiter means that Jupiter also reappeared. How does that support the idea that the moon is transparent? Here is another quote that Rowbotham offered from the same issue of the *Monthly Notices of the Royal Astronomical Society* describing another astronomer's comments on the same lunar occultation of Jupiter:

Occultation of Jupiter by the moon, May 24, 1860, observed by T.W. Burr, Esq., at Highbury.

The planet's first limb disappeared at 8h. 44m. 6.7s., the second limb disappeared at 8h. 45m. 4.9s. local sidereal time, on the moon's dark limb. The planet's first limb reappeared at 9h. 55m. 48s.; the second limb reappeared at 9h. 56m. 44.7s., at the bright limb. The planet was well seen, notwithstanding the strong sunlight (4h. 34m. Greenwich mean time), but of course without any belts. The moon's dark limb could not be detected until it touched the planet, when it was seen very sharply defined and black; and as it passed the disc of Jupiter in front appeared

---

9. Parallax (pseudonym of S.B. Rowbotham), *Zetetic Astronomy* (London, England: Simpkin, Marshall, and Co., 1881), p. 339.

to brighten. So that the moon's limb was preceded by a bright band of light, doubtless an effect of contrast.

Like the previous quote, this one stated that Jupiter disappeared and reappeared, and it even gave the times of the disappearance and reappearance of either limb of Jupiter. Apparently, Rowbotham didn't comprehend what he had read and quoted, for it says the opposite of what he claimed.

From another issue of the *Monthly Notices of the Royal Astronomical Society*, Rowbotham quoted this:

> Occultation of the Pleiades, December 8, 1859, observed at the Royal Observatory, Greenwich; communicated by the Astronomer Royal.
>
> Observed by Mr. Dunkin with the alt-azimuth, the disappearance of 27 *Tauri* was a most singular phenomenon; the star appeared to *move a considerable time along the moon's limb*, and disappeared behind a prominence at the first time noted (5h. 34m.); in a few seconds it re-appeared, and finally disappeared at the second time noted (5h. 35m.).
>
> Observed by Mr. Criswich, with the north equatorial, 27 *Tauri* was *not occulted at all*, though it passed so close to some of the illuminated peaks of the dark limb as hardly to be distinguished from them.

What is described here is a *grazing occultation*, where either the upper or lower limb of the moon barely occults a star. Mr. Dunkin was obviously along the narrow region of grazing occultation, while Mr. Criswich was in the region where the moon's limb just missed occulting the star 27 Tauri. Again, these quotes don't support Rowbotham's contention. The other references that Rowbotham included to support his claim were equally misunderstood by Rowbotham. Sadly, some flat-earthers recently have unquestioningly repeated these quotes without stopping to read and think about what the quotes actually say.

I had an opportunity to test this claim on the evening of March 4, 2017, when the moon occulted Aldebaran, the brightest star that the moon can occult. Being one of the 20 or so first magnitude stars,

Aldebaran is the 14th-brightest star in the sky and is easily visible to the naked eye, even in the most light-polluted skies. This occultation by the first quarter moon was visible in most of the United States. If the moon is a solid sphere 2,000 miles in diameter, then Aldebaran would obviously not be visible for the two hours or so that it was occulted by the moon. But if the flat-earthers are right, then Aldebaran, one of the brightest stars in the sky, would easily be visible through the moon, particularly at the beginning of the occultation when it was the unlit half of the moon that passed in front of Aldebaran.

At my location that evening, the occultation began at 11:00 p.m. The disappearance took a tiny fraction of a second. So, a few minutes before and after 11:00 p.m., I took some photos of the moon and Aldebaran with a zoom lens on my digital SLR camera mounted on a tripod. In the accompanying photo, taken shortly before 11:00 p.m., you can easily see Aldebaran to the upper left of the moon. By extending the curved edge of the lit portion of the moon, you can see that Aldebaran was just beyond the limb, or edge, of the unlit portion of the moon. I took the second photo a few minutes later, just after 11:00 p.m. Clearly, Aldebaran is not visible. Nor was it visible to the naked eye, where it had been visible just a few minutes before. Clearly, these results match the prediction of the conventional understanding of the moon, but it contradicts the prediction of the flat-earth model.

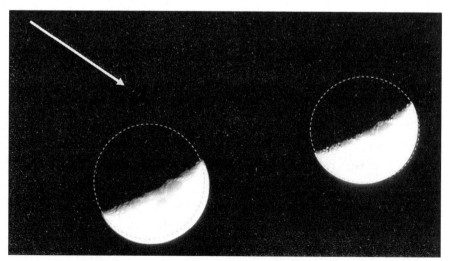

Aldebaran to the upper left of the moon

Nevertheless, most flat-earthers are undeterred, for there are videos on the Internet that ostensibly show faint stars shining through the moon. If one of the brightest stars in the sky is completely obscured by the moon when it passes over it, then what are the "stars" that flat-earthers see through the moon? It's difficult to say. None of the "stars" are identified, and since the date and time that such photos and videos were taken are not provided, I cannot begin to identify what they might be. There are at least two possibilities. One possibility is that these bright spots are noise in the camera detectors, something that is common with high gain settings. Another possibility is that these "stars" are hot pixels, a common thing in modern electronic cameras. I've seen many lunar occultations, and I know many other astronomers, both amateur and professional, who have seen many occultations. It is very strange that we never see stars shining through the moon when people who have no experience in these matters do. Or, more commonly, flat-earthers merely uncritically repeat the claims of other flat-earthers on this matter, while dismissing experienced observers who say otherwise.

Blue (in the) Moon

Another claim meant to support the idea that the moon is a semitransparent disk is that one can see the blue of the sky through the moon. Dubay's proof number 135 includes a photo to illustrate this. That photo shows a waxing gibbous moon shortly after it rose late in the afternoon. Part of the moon appears white, but other portions appear the same shade of blue that the sky around the moon does. Dubay stated that "it is possible to see the blue sky right through the Moon."[10] Or consider this photo from the International Flat Earth Research Society website also showing a waxing gibbous moon. In the original color photo, the lunar maria (the dark, round regions of the moon) have a blue hue, as does the rest of the sky. From the photo it is easy to see why someone might think that the sky is shining through the moon. So, what is going on?

First, we need to understand why, when the sky is clear, it appears blue. For that matter, why does the sky appear bright in the daytime? The answer is that molecules of air scatter light. The sun is so bright that

---

10. Dubay, *200 Proof Earth Is Not a Spinning Globe*, p. 26.

Waxing gibbous moon
Source: International Flat Earth
Research Society

the scattering of its light makes the entire sky bright, blotting out the light of stars and most of the planets (Venus is bright enough that it sometimes can be seen during the daytime). John William Strutt, better known as Lord Rayleigh, elucidated the physics of this scattering process in a series of papers in the late 19th century, so we call this *Rayleigh scattering*. Rayleigh scattering occurs when the scattering particles are much smaller than the wavelength of the light. Rayleigh scattering is inversely proportional to the inverse fourth power of the wavelength of light. Since blue light has the shortest wavelength of visible light, it is scattered most, while red light, having the longest wavelength of visible light, is scattered least. The inverse fourth power of wavelength dependence ensures that the scattered light is very blue, producing the blue light of a clear sky. Incidentally, Rayleigh scattering also explains why the sky is red near sunrise and sunset. Since the sun is very low in the sky near sunrise and sunset, its light travels through much more air than when the sun is higher in the sky. Rayleigh scattering removes shorter wavelengths of light (blue and yellow), leaving only the red, longer wavelengths of light.

Is there any evidence of this theory? Yes. The spectrum of the blue sky has the same absorption lines that the solar spectrum has. Furthermore, the theory of Rayleigh scattering predicts that the light of the blue sky is polarized[11] in a certain way. Observations of the blue sky's polarization confirm this prediction. What do flat-earthers attribute the sky's blue color to? Many of them claim that the blue is due to the color of water above the dome of the sky. However, this explanation fails to account for the spectrum and polarization of the blue light of the sky.

---

11. Polarization refers to the direction that light vibrates.

Now let us return to the photos of the moon taken during the day that show a blue color over portions of the moon. Those portions with blue color are the lunar maria, the darker regions of the moon that are visible even to the naked eye. The maria, along with the much brighter lunar highlands, give the man-in-the-moon appearance to the moon when it is full. The lunar highlands and maria appear so different because they are made of different kinds of rock. The lunar maria consist of rocks similar to terrestrial basalts, while the highlands are made of rocks more similar to terrestrial granites. Basalt generally is much darker than granite, hence the difference in brightness between the highlands and maria. The highlands are bright enough to shine through the brightness of the blue sky, though on some of these photos, there is a blue tint in the highland regions. But since the darker maria are not bright enough to shine through, the blue light scattered by the earth's atmosphere is what we see in the maria when the moon is visible in the daytime — that is, blue light that we see is in front of the moon, not behind it.

The Moon's Shape

Is the moon a disk, or is it a globe? In chapter 1, I explained that lunar phases make sense only if the moon is a ball illuminated by the sun. First, the moon's terminator usually appears curved. This is easily explained if the moon is a sphere, but it defies explanation if the moon is a disk. Second, as the spherical moon orbits the earth each month, the amount of the half-lit part of the moon facing the earth varies, producing the lunar phases. Flat-earthers generally respond by denying that this is the cause of lunar phases, insisting instead that the moon provides its own light and that something else must be the cause of the lunar phases. However, that other cause is never explained. It is amazing that flat-earthers persistently throw away perfectly good explanations, replacing them with nothing but assertions.

Another evidence that the moon is a sphere is *lunar librations*. The moon has *synchronous rotation*, meaning that it rotates and revolves at the same rate. Consequently, the same side of the moon always faces the earth. However, lunar librations are irregularities that permit us to "peek" around the moon's limb, allowing us, over time, to see more than half of the moon (58 percent of the lunar surface if we wait long enough). There are several types of lunar librations, but the most significant are librations in latitude and librations in longitude. The moon's rotation axis is tilted 6.7 degrees to its orbit around the earth. If we look at the moon when one pole of the moon is tilted toward earth, we can see a short distance over that pole. A half-month later, we can see over the other pole. This effect is called librations in latitude.

The moon rotates at a uniform rate, but because of its elliptical orbit around the earth, the moon doesn't revolve at a uniform rate. This allows us to view around the eastern and western limbs of the moon throughout the month. These are librations in longitude. The figure illustrates libration in longitude.

But there is another proof of the moon's spherical shape that anyone can do with a relatively inexpensive telescope (or lunar photographs if they trust the photographs). The one type of feature that people expect to see on the moon is craters. Craters on the earth are almost universally

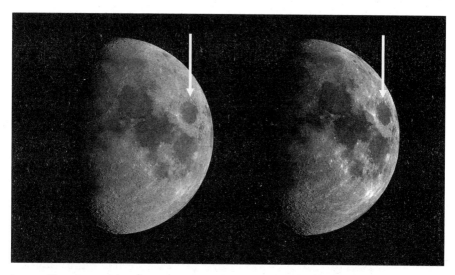

Lunar librations. The photo on the left was taken by Glen Fountain on February 27, 2015, at 7:30 p.m. EST. The photo on the right was taken by Jim Bonser on October 18, 2018, at 8:30 p.m. ET. The two photos were taken at almost the exact same waxing gibbous phase, but more than 3½ years apart. The location of Mare Crisium (the large, dark circle) is indicated with arrows. Notice that in the photo on the left, you can see more of the lunar surface to the right of Mare Crisium than you can in the photo on the right. This can happen only if the moon is a sphere. But if the moon were a disk, as many flat-earthers claim, then peeking around the moon's limb like this isn't possible.

circular. Even craters on the moon appear to be circular. At least the ones near the center of the moon. The maria are generally round, too. But what about craters and maria near the moon's limb, or edge? Look at the figure illustrating libration in longitude. In both photos, Mare Crisium appears flattened in the direction perpendicular to a radius drawn from the center of the image of the moon. But notice that in the image on the right, Mare Crisium appears noticeably more flattened than it does in the photo on the left. This is exactly what one would expect to see if craters and maria are round and the moon is a sphere — we would observe craters near the lunar limb obliquely, foreshortening them in the direction from the center of the moon's image to the limb. The closer they are to the limb, the more craters and maria appear flattened. The amount of flattening in these photos is consistent with Mare Crisium being round. Though not as obvious, craters near the lunar limb are similarly flattened, as you may be able to see in the photographs. There is no explanation for this if the moon is a flat disk, but this is exactly what we expect to see if the moon is a sphere and its craters are circles.

The Sun's Shape

A similar thing happens with sunspots — those sunspots closest to the solar limb appear flattened because they are foreshortened in the radial direction. The photograph taken during the August 21, 2017, solar eclipse shows several sunspots. Notice that the sunspots to the lower left near the sun's limb appear flattened, while the sunspots closer to the center of the sun's image do not. This demonstrates that the sun is also a sphere and not a disk, as most flat-earthers claim.

Sunspots offer a second line of evidence for the sun's sphericity. The sun rotates over the course of a month, so from day to day, sunspots appear to move. Sunspots appear to move most quickly when they are near the center of the sun's apparent disk. This is because their rotational motion is perpendicular to our line of sight. However, near the sun's limb, sunspots move more slowly because most of their rotational motion there is along our line of sight with very little component in the perpendicular direction. This simple observation is what we expect if the sun is a rotating sphere, but it has no explanation if the sun is a disk.

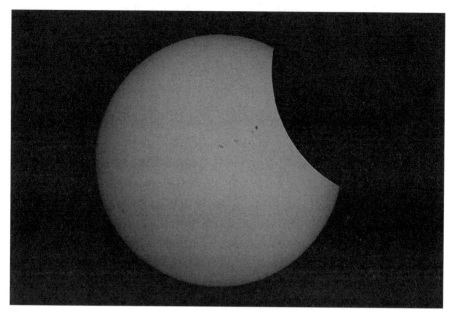

Solar eclipse

Apparently, some flat-earthers are aware of this evidence about sunspots, and so they have responded with a spurious observation. They have claimed that the only motion that sunspots have is a clockwise motion on the sun's apparent disk, thus supposedly refuting the argument about sunspots. Throughout the day, the sun's apparent disk appears to roll. Imagine a sunspot close to the sun's equator near the sun's western limb. The north orientation on the sun is always toward the north celestial pole. At noon, the north celestial pole will be vertically above the sun, causing the sunspot near the sun's western limb to appear on the right side of the sun. However, early in the morning, the direction toward the north celestial pole will be to the upper left of the sun, around the 10:30 position on the sun's apparent disk. Therefore, the sunspot will appear to be on the sun's upper right, around the 1:30 position. Near sunset, the north celestial pole will be toward the sun's upper right, about the 1:30 position, so the sunspot will appear on the lower right of the sun, around the 4:30 position. Therefore, if one does not account for this apparent rolling motion of the sun, it is easy to think that sunspots rotate clockwise throughout the day. This description is typical of views in north temperate latitudes. In the Southern Hemisphere, the directions are reversed. Notice that the sun appears to go through something less than a half-rotation throughout the day. In the tropics, the apparent rotation is closer to a half-rotation. Hence, the amount of apparent rotation throughout the day depends upon latitude and time of year.

The flat-earthers have missed another vital point here. It isn't the hourly apparent motion of spots that is important, but the day-to-day motion. If one were to look at the sun at the same time each day, the spots will not undergo apparent clockwise rotation on the sun. Instead, sunspots will move west to east as the sun rotates. It is not clear whether the flat-earthers who offer this argument are doing so knowing that it is a misdirection or if they are self-misdirected. Further, notice that flat-earthers once again offer no explanation for these observations, either throughout the day or from day to day.

Cool Light of the Moon

Perhaps the most bizarre claims about the moon that flat-earthers make is about its light. Dubay has written:

> The Sun's light is golden, warm, drying, preservative and antiseptic, while the Moon's light is silver, cool, damp, putrefying and septic. The sun's rays decrease the combustion of a bonfire, while the Moon's rays increase combustion. Plant and animal substances exposed to sunlight quickly dry, shrink, coagulate, and lose the tendency to decompose and putrefy; grapes and other fruits become solid, partially candied and persevered like raisins, dates, and prunes; animal flesh coagulates, loses its volatile gaseous constituents, becomes firm, dry, and slow to decay. When exposed to moonlight, however, plant and animal substance tend to show symptoms of putrefaction and decay.[12]

12. E. Dubay, *The Flat Earth Conspiracy* (Morrisville, NC: Lulu.com., 2014), p.79. A similar statement appears as proof number 132 in E. Dubay, *200 Proofs Earth is Not a Spinning Globe* (Morrisville, NC: Lulu.com., 2015), p. 25.

This sounds very mystical and superstitious. Where did he get such an idea? It probably came from David Wardlaw Scott's 1901 book, *Terra Firma*.

> The light which is reflected must necessarily be of the same character as that which causes the reflection, but the light of the Moon is altogether different from the light of the Sun, therefore the light of the Moon is not reflected from the Sun. The Sun's light is red and hot, the Moon's pale and cold — the Sun's dries and preserves certain kinds of fish and fruit, such as cod and grapes, for the table, but the Moon's turns such to putrefaction — the Sun's will often put out a coal fire, while the Moon's will cause it to burn more brightly — the rays of the Sun, focused through a burning-glass, will set wood on fire, and even fuse metals, while the rays of the Moon, concentrated to the strongest power, do not exhibit the very slightest signs of heat. I have myself long thought that the light of the Moon is Electric but, be that as it may, even a Board School child can perceive that its light is totally unlike that of the Sun.[13]

Rowbotham made similar statements about the moon's light.

Following this up, Dubay's proof number 133 claimed that thermometers in moonlight read cooler than thermometers in the shade where the moon's light does not fall. This supposedly proves that the moon does not reflect the sun's light, but rather has its own light. Where did this idea come from? Dubay's proof number 133 mentions an article from the March 14, 1856, issue of *The Lancet*, the British medical journal that purportedly gave experimental results that moonlight has a cooling effect, but there was no March 14, 1856, issue of *The Lancet*. *The Lancet* is a weekly publication, and the closest issue to this date was the one on March 15, 1856. The table of contents of that issue does not remotely suggest a paper of that type in it. One must wonder why *The Lancet* would publish such an article. I seriously doubt that this article exists.

---

13. D.W. Scott. *Terra Firma: The Earth Not a Planet, Proved from Scripture, Reason, and Fact* (London, England: Simpkin, Marshall, Hamilton, Kent, and Co., 1901), p. 151–152.

Dubay undoubtedly got this idea from Rowbotham, because Rowbotham included mention of the supposed article in *The Lancet*, too. However, Rowbotham also included reference to several other articles that reported experiments that showed no temperature change due to moonlight. So, which are readers supposed to believe — the one article (that incidentally doesn't exist) that claims that moonlight is cooling, or the quotes from many other articles that say there is no temperature difference between moonlight and shade? Rowbotham was obviously confused on this issue, but not most other flat-earthers, for they are confident that moonlight is cooling.

The moon's spectrum is a good match to the solar spectrum, strongly indicating that the moon does reflect the sun's light. Therefore, it may seem reasonable that since objects exposed to the sun's light are warmed, the same ought to be true of the moon's light. The apparent magnitude of the sun is -27.4, while the full moon's apparent magnitude is -12.7. That is a difference of 14 magnitudes, which corresponds to a difference in brightness of 400,000 times. Hence, an object illuminated by moonlight will receive 1/400,000 the heating that it would receive from the sun during the day. With such a large disparity in brightness, any heating from the moon's light at night would be very difficult to detect.

There is another objection to this claim that the moon's light is cooling. It contradicts everything we know about heat and light. Light contains energy that objects can absorb. Therefore, any moonlight that falls on an object will heat that object, though the amount of heat is so small that it may not be easy to detect a temperature increase as a result. Furthermore, heat can radiate from an object, but nothing sucks heat from things, as this mythical belief of flat-earthers would require. Nevertheless, flat-earthers are unperturbed by this, for there are many videos on the Internet that promote this idea that moonlight is cooler than shade. Most of these videos feature people using infrared (IR) thermometers to measure the temperature of objects in moonlight and in shadow. They seem always to find that objects in moonlight are cooler than objects in shadow, thus supporting their claims.

I have conducted this experiment myself many times. I can reproduce the results that flat-earthers get, but a moment later, I can produce the opposite result — objects in moonlight are warmer. How did I do this? Most people have no idea how IR thermometers work. They apparently think that simply pointing the device at an object will give "the temperature" of the object. This is not a bad approach for objects that are significantly warmer or cooler than their surroundings. However, IR thermometers work by measuring the IR emission from objects. When objects are close to ambient temperature, the IR emission is more of a function of the *emissivity* of the objects than anything else. Emissivity is an expression of how well an object radiates energy. Emissivity depends upon color, with darker objects emitting better than lighter objects. But emissivity also depends upon the composition of an object. Therefore, on a clear night, pavement will read warmer than grass or soil. By selecting different surfaces in shadow and not in shadow, I can produce any result that I want. In many of the videos of these experiments, there is no indication what surfaces are sampled. It is like a magic trick, where the magician will distract the audience to look at one thing (shadow or non-shadow), while he subtly does a slight-of-hand trick (changing surfaces). On some videos, it is clear that the experimenter has changed surfaces, but on most videos, one cannot see what surfaces are being sampled.

Another trick is to take the temperature on the ground under the canopy of a tree, often in shadow from the moon's light, and then take the temperature away from the canopy in the moon's light. On a clear night with little wind, objects on the ground radiate IR energy, causing their temperatures to cool, often to temperatures less than the air temperature. However, any obstruction overhead, such as the canopy of a tree, will prevent radiative loss of heat this way. Out from under a tree's canopy, radiative cooling will allow the ground or objects to cool more than under the canopy where leaves overhead block radiative losses from the ground. This is why automobiles parked under a carport or a tree with leaves usually won't develop dew on a clear night, while an automobile parked with no cover overhead will. Therefore, it is possible to get a slightly different temperature reading this way. However, if one samples both moonlight and no moonlight out from under a tree's canopy, no temperature difference likely will be found.

The videos of these experiments online are very convincing to people who do not know what is going on. Some of the people who post these videos online probably do not know what they are doing, and so stumble onto the results that flat-earthers claim. However, even a person who does not know what he is doing will sometimes stumble onto the opposite results. Since these do not appear to be on the Internet, I must assume that most of the people posting these videos are charlatans.

As I said, I have done this experiment myself many times, and I have had difficulty repeating the results claimed by flat-earthers. I will now share the results of one of my experiments done on the evening of July 24, 2018. I took temperature measurements in my front yard at 10:00 p.m. ET, about one hour after sunset. While it was still astronomical twilight, civil twilight had long ended, and possibly nautical twilight as well. At any rate, many stars were visible. The moon was waxing gibbous, 2.75 days from full. The sky was mostly clear, and the air temperature was in the mid-70s F. The display on my IR thermometer reads to 0.1°F. When I pull the trigger, the output updates every second. If I release the trigger, the display holds the current reading so that I would not bias the results. When I recorded temperature measurements, I pulled the trigger while not looking at the display, waited a couple of seconds, and then released the trigger and looked at the display to take the reading. I took multiple readings this way. I read the temperature readings aloud and recorded them on an audio recorder. All measurements were made on the grass in my front yard. There appears to be 2–3 kinds of grass in the yard, so variations in the type of grass at different locations could cause temperature variations because of differences in emissivity.

To test whether moonlight cools objects, obviously one must measure the temperatures of similar objects (grass in this experiment) in and out of moonlight. However, there is the additional factor of radiative cooling that I already mentioned. Since I am concerned that many of the results of flat-earthers may be due to this effect, I took measurements under and not under the canopy of an oak tree in my front yard as well. Therefore, I made four different temperature measurements:

1. Temperature taken in moonlight with no canopy
2. Temperature taken in moonlight with a canopy
3. Temperature taken out of moonlight with a canopy
4. Temperature taken out of moonlight with no canopy

If the flat-earth claim is correct, then the temperatures taken in cases 1 and 2 would be cooler than the temperature taken in cases 3 and 4. On the other hand, I would expect that radiative cooling would make the temperatures of cases 1 and 4 cooler than the temperatures taken in cases 2 and 3. If one wished to consider both factors (both moonlight cooling and radiative cooling), the temperatures taken in case 2 or case 4 would be cooler.

Instead of taking a single temperature measurement for each of the three cases, for each case, I took 10 temperatures that I averaged. This allowed calculation of the standard deviation of each average temperature. All temperature measurements were in Fahrenheit. The results are as follows:

Case 1: T = 62.64°F, S.D. = 0.368°F
Case 2: T = 64.60°F, S.D. = 0.22°F
Case 3: T = 63.43°F, S.D. = 0.104°F
Case 4: T = 61.71°F, S.D. = 0.45°F

While I have reproduced full accuracy here, the average temperatures and standard deviations are probably meaningless past the first place to the right of the decimal point. Hence, in what follows, I will round these to the nearest 0.1°F.

Notice that the coolest average temperatures are cases 1 and 4, in line with the expectation of radiative cooling alone. However, the expectation that moonlight cools objects is not confirmed — case 3 is the second coolest average temperature, while case 2 is the warmest average temperature. We can express this a different way by taking the average of the cases 1 and 2 average temperatures and the average of the cases 3 and 4 average temperatures. The former average temperature (in moonlight) is 63.6 F, while the latter average temperature (not in moonlight) is 62.6 F. That is, the moonlight temperature is 1.0 degree warmer than the shade temperature. This contradicts the flat-earth model prediction. On the other hand, the average of the average temperatures of cases 2 and 3 (under the canopy) is 64.0°F, while the average of the average temperatures of cases 1 and 4 (no canopy) is 62.2°F. That is, the average temperature under the canopy is 1.8 F warmer than not under the canopy, which is consistent with the expectation of radiative cooling. Therefore, the results of this experiment disprove the flat-earth prediction but are consistent with the expectation of radiative cooling.

In the four-month interval from late June to late October 2018, I did this experiment 32 times using the same methodology. The results have been similar to those here — I found no real difference in temperatures in and out of moonlight. However, I have consistently found that temperatures measured under the canopy of a tree are higher than temperatures measured with no tree canopy above. Since moonlight is frequently shaded under trees, I suspect that many of the experimental results claimed by flat-earthers are merely the result of the effect of radiative cooling rather than any effect of the moon's light. However, there may be another effect at play. Most of the videos promoting this idea fail to reveal what surfaces were sampled. It may be that different surfaces with different emissivities were sampled. If this was done intentionally, then those responsible are dishonest.

I have conducted more extensive experiments to test this idea. For instance, I have placed a piece of ¼-inch plywood six inches wide and 45 inches long on supports well above the ground, with one end in moonlight and the other end in shade. After waiting 20 minutes, I took the temperature of either end of the board. To account for possible differences between the two ends of the board, I swapped the ends of the board, waited 20 minutes, and then repeated the experiment. On another evening, I repeated this experiment, but then after swapping ends of the board, I rolled the board over, waited 20 minutes to record temperatures, then I swapped ends once again and waited 20 minutes to repeat the temperature measurements. That is, I sampled both ends of either side of the board in moonlight and not in moonlight. I found no evidence that the moonlit end of the board was cooler than the other end.

Finally, I devised a definitive test of this odd idea. I placed the bulb of an alcohol thermometer at the focal point of a fast 16-inch Newtonian telescope. I alternately exposed the bulb to moonlight and then no moonlight for five-minute intervals, taking the temperature after each five-minute exposure. I did this experiment for nearly two hours on two different nights. I found no evidence of any temperature change due to moonlight.

Conclusion

Anyone with a good knowledge of astronomy can easily see that the flat-earth model fails on so many issues. Yet most flat-earthers are unfazed by this. Apparently, they are content in their ignorance of astronomy. That is a real shame. Astronomy is one of the most thrilling of the sciences. The beauty and vastness of the universe are a wonder to comprehend. And they speak of the majesty and power of our Creator (Psalm 19:1). But flat-earthers throw this away, happy to live in a tiny encapsulated world of their own making.

Chapter 6

Physics and the Flat Earth

Many of the things that flat-earthers claim can be refuted by physics. For instance, flat-earthers sometimes mockingly ask how water can stick to a spinning ball. This question is raised in argument number 195 of Dubay's *200 Proofs* book[1] and repeated almost word for word in his *Flat-Earth Conspiracy*. Some videos demonstrating this question feature spinning balls, such as tennis balls, with water slinging off. The simple answer is gravity keeps water on the earth's surface, to which flat-earthers scoff. I shall discuss gravity shortly, but for the time being, I will discuss how much "slinging" action there actually is on a spinning earth.

The Amount of Force Required to Keep Water on a Spinning Earth

Newton's first law of motion states that

> an object at rest remains at rest, and an object in motion remains in straight-line motion, unless acted upon by an outside force.

This law has many applications, and it appears to be universally true. What causes water to sling off the surface of a spinning ball? Let us concentrate on a small amount of water on a point on the equator of the ball (the circle that is the intersection of the surface of the ball with the plane perpendicular to the rotation axis and including the center of the ball). At any given instant, the parcel of water is moving along a line tangent to the point and in the plane of the equator. If no force acts on the water,

---

1. Dubay, *200 Proofs Earth Is Not a Spinning Globe*, p. 38.

then by Newton's first law of motion, the water will continue moving along that line, thus leaving the surface of the ball along the tangent. However, if there is sufficient force, the water will remain on the ball.

How much force is required to do this? This is the subject of Newton's second law of motion:

> When a net force acts on a body, the body experiences an acceleration in the direction of the force that is proportional to the force and inversely proportional to the body's mass.

We commonly write this in equation form:

$$F = m\mathbf{a},$$

where F is the force, m is the mass, and $\mathbf{a}$ is the acceleration. I have written both F and $\mathbf{a}$ in boldface, indicating that force and acceleration are *vectors*. What is a vector? A vector is a quantity that has both magnitude (an amount) and direction. A *scalar* is a quantity that has just magnitude. In physics, we define velocity as a vector, but we define speed, the magnitude of velocity, as a scalar. In specifying speed, it is sufficient to give the magnitude, such as 60 mph. However, velocity requires specifying the direction as well, such as to the east. If one is concerned merely with magnitudes of force and acceleration, then they are written in normal type. The mass refers to how much matter is in the parcel of water. How do we evaluate the acceleration? If the water stays on the ball, then it is exhibiting circular motion, with radius r, the radius of the ball. Since this isn't straight-line motion, Newton's first law of motion dictates that the water requires an acceleration toward the center of motion. Physicists call this kind of acceleration *centripetal acceleration*, meaning "toward the center." It is a straightforward matter to show that the centripetal acceleration a_c is given by

$$a_c = \frac{v^2}{r} = \frac{4\pi^2 r}{T^2}$$

where v is the velocity, T is the period to complete one revolution, and r is the radius of revolution. Notice that as the ball spins more rapidly, v increases, or alternately, T decreases. Either way, greater rate of spin requires more acceleration, and, hence, more force to keep the water on the ball. What provides this force? In the case of a tennis ball, it would be the force of cohesion keeping the water on the surface of the ball. Our experience tells as that at low rotation speed, water will remain on the ball, but as the speed of rotation increases, cohesion is insufficient to keep water on the tennis ball, so the water tends to leave the ball's surface. This equation conforms to that expectation.

This principle of centripetal force and acceleration is found in many applications. A good example of this is tires on a car while undergoing a turn. Frictional force provides the force that compels the vehicle to turn. If the tires encounter slick pavement, there may not be enough friction to provide the force necessary to make the turn, and the car will skid. For a weight spun on the end of a string, it is tension in the string that provides the centripetal force. In each case, there is no "magical" force that arises to produce circular motion. Instead, there must be some physical force, such as adhesion, friction, or tension, that provides the necessary force.

Let us turn to the spinning earth. How much centripetal acceleration is required to keep water or any other object on the earth's surface from sailing off in obedience to Newton's first law of motion? The greatest need will be on the earth's equator. There, the radius will be the earth's radius, 6.38×10^6 m. The period of rotation is 86,400 seconds, the number of seconds in a day.[2] Putting these values into the above equation, we get 0.034 m/s^2. This is 0.0034 times the measured acceleration of gravity $(9.8$ m/s$^2)$, or 0.34% the acceleration of gravity. Of course, it is gravity that provides this centripetal acceleration. Therefore, the weight of an object on the earth's equator is reduced by 0.34% from what it would be in the absence of rotation. It is gravity that keeps objects on the earth's surface, the same force that would keep water on the earth's surface even if the earth didn't rotate. Hence, this objection raised by flat-earthers is easily explained. And all those videos on the Internet showing water slinging off a spinning ball are concocted to mislead and fool those who know nothing about physics. But this is common among flat-earther videos — they make poor analogies and fail to quantify their claims. If they did quantify their claims, as I have here, it would demonstrate that the claims are bogus.

---

2. Technically, we ought to use the sidereal day, which is about 236 seconds less, but the difference doesn't matter much — only 0.27%.

Fact or Theory?

Of course, this brings up the subject of gravity, something that many flat-earthers object to. Most flat-earthers deny that gravity exists. When asked about this, the astronomer Neil DeGrasse Tyson famously dropped a microphone to demonstrate that gravity does exist. Flat-earthers have had a field day with that video. The problem is that flat-earthers haven't been very clear on what they mean by rejecting gravity. Of course, most objects tend to fall downward, as when Tyson dropped the microphone. This is the *phenomenon* that we call gravity. When flat-earthers say that they don't believe in gravity, they aren't denying this phenomenon. What they mean is that they reject the conventional theory of gravity. However, I suspect that most flat-earthers don't really understand what the conventional theory of gravity is, so how can they so easily reject it? Flat-earthers often dismiss gravity by saying that "it's just a theory and has never been proven." Such a statement reveals an all too common misunderstanding of theories and what constitutes proof in science. I will attempt a brief explanation here.

Contrary to common misconception, a theory is not an unproven idea that is the opposite of a fact. Rather, a theory is a well-developed idea that has much empirical support. That is, we use facts either to support or to disprove a theory (hence, facts and theories can't be opposites). For example, anyone who has studied music has studied music theory, even if the word "theory" wasn't used. Music theory involves the basics of how music works — elements such as key signatures, time signatures, notation, dynamics, and rhythmic notation. No one would seriously suggest that music theory isn't tested, doesn't work, or isn't true. In similar manner, in science, a theory is a tested idea that explains much physical phenomena. To be a good theory, a theory must explain what we already know, but must anticipate some things that we don't yet know. That is, a theory must have explanatory power and predictive power.

This predictive power is what we call proof in science. We reason that if a theory is true, then we can predict the outcome of new experiments or observations. If we perform those experiments or observations and the results match our predictions, we say that the theory is *proved*. However, rather than saying the theory is *proved*, it might be better to say that the theory is *confirmed*. You see, there may be other explanations that we haven't thought of yet that may equally explain the experimental or observational results. While our theory may explain the phenomena so far considered, further experimental results or observations may contradict the theory that we thought was true, leading us to the conclusion that the theory is wrong. We then say that the theory is disproved, and we cast about for one of those other explanations (new theories) that explain both the old results and the new results, and the process continues. Hence, we can never be certain that our theories are true, though we can determine whether they are false.

This standard of proof is a bit different from what most people think of as being proof. Most people think that proof means that something is absolutely, positively true. However, it never occurs to most people just how one goes about proving propositions. Furthermore, this isn't what proof means in science. In science, proof means that observations and experimental results agree with our predictions from our theory, giving us confidence that our theory is likely true. It's this misunderstanding of science that leads people to mistaken beliefs about what science is, how it operates, and what is deemed proven in science. How do flat-earthers think that one could go about proving a theory of gravity? They never seem to say. Nevertheless, in the next section, I will explain how Newton's theory of gravity came to be proved in the scientific sense.

Gravity

If flat-earthers don't believe in gravity, how do they explain the phenomenon that we call gravity? There are two different suggestions that flat-earthers have proposed. One camp says that gravity is a result of buoyant forces, while another camp claims that what we call gravity is a result of electromagnetic effects. However, this amounts to hand-waving, since flat-earthers offer no detailed explanations of how buoyancy or electromagnetism might work to do this. Hence, neither one of these ideas amounts to theories. At the second Flat Earth International Conference in 2018, the buoyancy idea seemed to be dominant. In the conventional understanding of physics, gravity is a fundamental force, while buoyancy is a consequence of gravity. Apparently, many flat-earthers want to reverse this, assuming that buoyancy is fundamental, resulting in gravity being a consequence of buoyancy. I suppose that one could work out how this might work, but until one does this (works out a theory), there is nothing to discuss.

Meanwhile, flat-earthers throw up silly objections, such as asking how gravity simultaneously can hold objects onto the earth's surface and cause the moon to orbit. I call this a silly objection because, as with any force, gravity can operate in a static situation (things sitting on the earth's surface) or a dynamic situation (orbital motion, such as with the moon). Furthermore, as I've already demonstrated, absent a centripetal force, the moon would move in a straight line, causing it to depart, never to return. It was Isaac Newton's great insight to posit that the same force that holds objects onto the earth is the same force that provides the centripetal force that compels the moon to remain in orbit around the earth.

How did Newton do this? To get there, let me state Newton's third law of motion and his law of gravity. Newton's third law of motion states:

> For every action, there is an equal and opposite reaction.

This means that whenever an object produces a force on another object, the second object acts on the first object with the same force, but in the opposite direction. Examples abound. If you push or pull on an object, you can feel the object push or pull back against your effort. When you sit on a chair, you exert your weight on the chair. But the chair also pushes back against you with a force equal to your weight. If it didn't push back, you could sit motionless in the chair indefinitely without becoming fatigued. Therefore, when the earth's gravity acts on you, pulling you downward, you pull upward on the earth. Why doesn't the earth move noticeably? While the force of gravity may be the same on either object, the acceleration won't be the same. Newton's second law of motion tells us that acceleration is inversely proportional to mass. Since the earth has 10^{22} times as much mass as a person, the earth accelerates 10^{-22} as much as a person does. This is undetectable.

Newton's law of gravity states:

> Every object in the universe attracts every other object in the universe with a force directly proportional to the masses of the bodies and inversely proportional to the square of the distances between them.

We can write this in equation form as

$$F = \frac{Gm_1m_2}{r^2}$$

where F is the force of gravity, m_1 and m_2 are the masses of the two bodies, and r is the distance between the center of masses of the two bodies. G is the constant of gravity; its value depends upon which units one chooses for force, mass, and distance. When using the standard SI units[3] of newtons for force, kilograms for mass, and meters of distance, G has the value of 6.67 x 10^{-11} Nm²/kg². How did Newton discover this law? Let m_1 be the mass of an object on the earth and m_2 be the mass of the earth. It is a matter of experiment to determine that an object's weight (the force of gravity) is directly proportional to the object's mass. Therefore, the mass of the object must appear in the numerator of the equation. However, Newton's third law means that the situation is reflexive. Therefore, if the mass of one object involved in a gravitational reaction must appear in the numerator, then the mass of the other object involved in a gravitational reaction must appear in the numerator as well.

This takes care of the numerator, but what about the denominator? Obviously, the farther away an object is, the less its gravity ought to be. Therefore, the force of gravity ought to be inversely proportional to some power of the distance, placing the distance in the denominator. However, what exponent should the distance have? How did Newton realize that the exponent was two? To answer that question, Newton used the equation for centripetal acceleration required to keep the moon in orbit around the earth. The sidereal month, the orbital period with the respect to the stars, is the moon's true, dynamic orbital period. Since ancient times, people had measured the sidereal month to be 27.3 days. About 75 years before Newton's work, the famous Danish astronomer Tycho Brahe had measured the distance to the moon. Tycho did this by measuring the moon's *diurnal parallax*. Diurnal parallax is the apparent shift in the moon's position throughout the night as our position changes on the rotating earth. As I discussed in chapter 3, throughout the night, the

---

3. SI is the abbreviation of *Système International*, the name for the form of metric units used in science.

moon moves along a portion of its orbit, so diurnal parallax manifests itself as a slight wobble in the moon's observed motion. Tycho was a keen observer, and he apparently was the first to observe diurnal parallax. From the baseline of our daily motion, which requires knowing the earth's size, Tycho determined the moon's distance close to the modern value. Time delay of electromagnetic radiation bounced off the lunar surface is the basis of the modern measured moon distance. This once was done with radar, but now it is done with lasers reflecting off mirrors left on the lunar surface by the Apollo astronauts. By the way, these distance measurements of 240,000 miles are in stark contrast to the 3,000 miles often claimed as the distance to the moon by flat-earthers. How did Tycho know the earth's size? As I discussed in chapter 1, Eratosthenes measured the earth's circumference around 200 B.C.

The sidereal month is 27.3 x 86,400 = 2.36 x 10^6 seconds. The distance between the earth and moon is 3.84 x 10^8 m. Putting this into one of the equations for centripetal acceleration:

$$a_c = \frac{4\pi^2 \, (3.84 \; x \; 10^8 \; m)}{(2.36 \; x \; 10^6 \; s)^2} = 0.0027 \text{ m/s2}$$

This acceleration is 1/3600 the measured acceleration of gravity at the earth's surface. Combining the moon's distance from Tycho and the earth's radius from Eratosthenes, Newton realized that on the earth's surface, we are 60 times closer to the earth's center than the moon is. The relationship between 60 and 3600 is a squared one. This is how Newton determined that gravity acted with the inverse square of the distance, thus completing his law of gravity. If you are not impressed with this reasoning, then you must not have understood it.

This was an impressive result, but could Newton test it? Yes. A couple of decades before Newton was born, Johannes Kepler had worked out an empirical relationship between the orbital periods and orbital sizes of the planets. He found that the squares of the orbital periods were proportional to the cubes of the orbital sizes. If we express the orbital period, T, in years and the orbital size, r, in *astronomical units* (the astronomical unit is the average distance of the earth from the sun), Kepler's third law of planetary motion can be expressed:

Planet	T (years)	r (AU)	S (years)
Mercury	0.24085	0.3871	0.3173
Venus	0.61521	0.7233	1.5987
earth	1	1	------
Mars	1.88089	1.5237	2.1354
Jupiter	11.8653	5.2037	1.2775
Saturn	29.6501	9.5803	1.0921

$$T^2 \propto r^3$$

The table gives the orbital periods and sizes of the planets known at the time of Kepler. You can confirm that these numbers conform to the above relationship. Newton was easily able to derive this equation by inserting the equation for centripetal acceleration into Newton's second law of motion and equating with his law of gravity: a

$$m_1 a_c = \frac{m_1 4\pi^2 r}{T^2} = \frac{Gm_1 m_2}{r^2}$$

where m_1 is the mass of a planet and m_2 is the mass of the sun. This easily reduces to

$$T^2 = \frac{4\pi^2}{Gm_2} r^3$$

Inspection shows that this has the same functional dependence as Kepler's third law of planetary motion, the square of the orbital period is proportional to the cube of the orbital size. The constant of proportionality is different here because the units used are different (SI vs. AUs and years). If the units of Newton's generalized form of Kepler's third law are converted to those of Kepler's version of his third law, the constant of proportionality is unity as well. It is relatively straightforward to derive Kepler's other two laws of planetary motion, that the planets orbit the sun on elliptical orbits with the sun at one focus (first law), and that the radius vector of a planetary orbit sweeps out equal areas in equal intervals of time (second law). When Newton derived this, Jupiter had four known natural satellites, and Saturn one. The motions of all five objects conformed to Newton's description. By the time Newton published his results in the *Principia*, astronomers had discovered four additional satellites of Saturn, and they conformed to Newton's description, too. Edmund Halley showed that comets obeyed Newton's theory as well, even though comet orbits, being highly elliptical, are very different from planetary orbits. This theory allowed Halley to predict the return of a comet that he had observed 75 years later. Of course, Halley didn't live to see the return of his comet, but its return bore testimony to the success of Newton's theory. Eventually, the discovery of two additional planets, along with their satellites, and many asteroids, or minor planets, showed that their motions obeyed Newton's description as well. Since the time of Newton, astronomers have discovered many thousands of binary stars. They, too, conform to Newton's laws of motion and law of gravity. With its explanatory and predictive power, Newton's well-established and proven scientific theory is now called the "law of gravity."

You may wonder how Kepler knew the orbital sizes and periods of the planets. Copernicus found these three decades before Kepler was born. Not only did Copernicus argue for the heliocentric theory, he apparently was the first to work out the consequences of that model to find the orbital parameters of the five planets then known (the five naked-eye planets in terms of the earth's orbital size and distance). How did Copernicus do this? The *sidereal period* is the orbital period of a planet with respect to the stars. The sidereal period is the true orbital period, and so it is the period we must use in dynamical equations, such as the generalized form of Kepler's third law of planetary motion. Since the earth is orbiting the sun, we do not directly observe the *sidereal periods* of the planets. Instead, we observe the *synodic period* of a planet, the orbital period of a planet as seen from the earth with respect to the sun. The synodic periods of the planets had been known since ancient times. How did Copernicus figure out the sidereal periods of the planets? Consider two planets, A and B, as in the figure. Planet A orbits on a smaller orbit, while planet B orbits on a larger orbit. At position 1, planet A and planet B are lined up on the same side of the sun. Planet A travels more quickly than planet B, and it has less distance to travel to complete one orbit, so it will return to position 1 before planet B will. However, planet B will have moved forward on its orbit, so planet A must travel an additional distance in its orbit to once again catch up with planet B at position 2. Let a planet's sidereal period be T years and let its synodic period be S years. Since the earth completes one orbit per year, then in S years, the earth will complete S trips around the sun. The other planet will complete S/T trips around the sun.

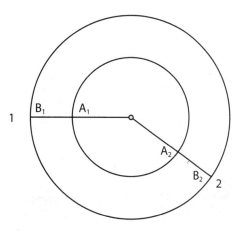

Synodic and Sidereal periods.

Let us first consider an *inferior planet*, a planet that orbits the sun closer than the earth does (Mercury and Venus). In this case, the earth will be planet B, and the inferior planet will be planet A. Since during its synodic period the inferior planet has made one more trip around the sun than the earth has,

$$S + 1 = \frac{S}{T}$$

which simplifies to

$$\frac{1}{T} = 1 + \frac{1}{S}$$

What about a *superior planet*, a planet with a larger orbit than the earth's orbit? In this case, the earth is planet A and the superior planet is planet B, and it is the earth that gains a lap. Therefore, the relationship is

$$S = \frac{S}{T} + 1$$

which reduces to

$$\frac{1}{T} = 1 - \frac{1}{S}$$

Both the synodic and sidereal periods of the five naked-eye planets are given in the table. With a calculator, the reader can confirm the values of sidereal periods of the planets given the synodic periods of the planets.

How did Copernicus determine the distances of the planets from the sun? The figure shows the situation of an inferior planet. As seen from the earth, an inferior planet has a point of greatest elongation from the sun as indicated at point P, with the earth at point E and the sun at point S. The three points form the triangle EPS. At greatest elongation from the sun, the line between the earth and the planet is tangent to the circle representing the inferior planet's orbit. Therefore, there is a right angle at point P. The hypotenuse is one AU, while the side opposite E is the radius of the inferior planet's orbit. The average angle of greatest elongation from the sun for both Mercury and Venus had been known since ancient times. From trigonometry, the radius of the inferior planet's orbit (in AUs) is the sine of the angle of greatest elongation from the sun.

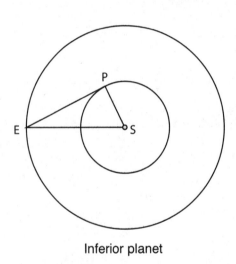

Inferior planet

The situation for a superior planet is different. In the figure, a superior planet is at point P, the earth is at point E, and the sun is at point S. Notice that the superior planet and the earth are lined up on the same side of the sun. We call this situation *opposition* because the superior planet appears opposite the sun in the sky, and thus is up all night. When the earth has reached point E′ and the superior planet has reached P′, we say the planet has reached *quadrature* because the angle between the

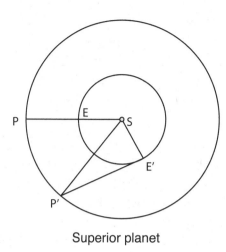

Superior planet

planet and the sun measured at the earth, P′E′S, is 90 degrees. The average length of time to go from opposition to quadrature for the three naked-eye superior planets was measured by ancient astronomers. Since we know the sidereal periods of the superior planet and the earth, we can calculate the angles PSP′ and ESE′, and their difference is the angle P′SE′. The line P′E′ is tangent to the earth's orbit, so the angle P′E′S is 90 degrees. The leg of the right triangle SE′ is the radius of the earth's orbit, 1.0 AU. Therefore, the hypotenuse SP′ is the radius of the superior planet's orbit, r, and is given by

$$r = \frac{1}{\cos(\text{SE}′\text{P}′)}$$

I have gone into some detail, but anyone with a good high school math background can follow it. The point is, Newton's work on his law of gravity drew upon the work of countless people going back two millennia earlier, and it shows a well-developed, consistent pattern of explaining what we see.

Let me illustrate this a different way. The length of time between the March equinox and the September equinox is about a week longer than the length of time between the September equinox and the March equinox (anyone can check this by counting the number of days between successive equinoxes). Observationally, this is because the sun appears to move along the ecliptic at a non-uniform rate. More specifically, the sun appears to move more rapidly along the ecliptic between the September equinox and the March equinox than it does between the March equinox and the September equinox. Why is that? In the flat-earth model, it just does. But in the conventional understanding of things, it is a consequence of

Kepler's first and second laws of planetary motion. The earth's orbit is an ellipse (Kepler's first law), with perihelion (the point of closest approach to the sun) occurring about two weeks after the December solstice, and aphelion occurring about two weeks after the June solstice. How do we know that the earth moves on an elliptical orbit? One evidence is that the sun appears largest on the date of perihelion and appears smallest on the date of aphelion. The earth moves more rapidly when near perihelion than when near aphelion, which results in the sun appearing to move along the ecliptic most rapidly when the earth is at perihelion. Kepler's second law (the law of equal areas) proscribes very precisely how the earth's motion changes. This predicted time-varying apparent motion of the sun exactly matches what we observe. Newton went on to use his theory of gravity to derive Kepler's laws of planetary motion (including Kepler's third law).

If one comprehends what I have written here, there are only three possible conclusions one could reach. One possibility is that this is all a remarkable coincidence. The synodic periods of the five naked-eye planets, when converted to sidereal periods within the heliocentric model, as well as the timings of their greatest elongations, oppositions, and quadratures, conform excellently with Newton's law of gravity that varies with the inverse square of the distance. But it's all just a coincidence, because there is no reality behind the heliocentric theory and gravity which compels the planets to orbit the sun. It's just a coincidence that the earth's orbit beautifully conforms to the predictions of this theory. Furthermore, it merely is happenstance that the moon conforms to this, as well as the natural satellites of the other planets. For that matter, it is by chance that the other planets, satellites, asteroids, and comets discovered since Newton's time all follow his law of gravity. Binary stars, two stars observed orbiting one another, of which there are many thousands, conform to Newton's theory in some monumental coincidence.

A second possibility is that all this is not coincidence, but rather is the result of a carefully developed strategy of faked data. Of course, much of these data have been known for two millennia or more, and thus occurs in many extant old references, information that supposedly was manufactured long before someone as clever as Newton came along to synthesize it into an elegant, simple, but false, theory of gravity.

Furthermore, much of these data, such as the synodic periods and the time required for the superior planets to go from opposition to quadrature, could be remeasured today for anyone who wishes to take the time to do so.

The third possibility is that all of what I have presented here is a good description of how the world works. If that is the case, then we have very good evidence that this model of a solar system where gravity plays a critical role in the motion and stability of orbiting bodies is true. If one wishes to replace this elegant description, then one must do just that — replace it with a better model. However, thus far, flat-earthers seem to have no understanding of the observed motions of the planets. Their entire opinion on the planets is an assertion that the planets are not what astronomers claim that the planets are. No reasons for this are given. No alternative model for what the planets are is given. The flat-earthers' case here amounts to monumental denial.

The Foucault Pendulum

In 1851, the French physicist Léon Foucault gave the first direct evidence of the earth's rotation. Foucault used a pendulum consisting of a large mass suspended by a long wire. With a Foucault pendulum, the mass is pulled to one side of its equilibrium position and released. As with any pendulum, gravity pulls the mass back to its equilibrium position, the mass overshoots, the mass swings on the other side to the same distance from where it was released, and the cycle continues. Since the only net torque or force acting on the pendulum is gravity, conservation of momentum constrains the pendulum to swing in the same plane. If a pendulum operates on a platform that is rotated about a vertical axis, an observer not on the rotating platform will see that the pendulum's plane of swing does not change. However, to an observer on the rotating platform, the plane of the pendulum's swing will appear to rotate in the direction opposite to the platform's rotation. We call this effect *precession*.

Since the earth is not a platform but is a spinning ball with gravity locally directed toward the earth's center, the Foucault pendulum's behavior on the earth is a bit more complicated. At the earth's North Pole and South Pole, the situation is indistinguishable from the platform example — a Foucault pendulum will be observed to rotate with the earth's sidereal period (23 hours, 56 minutes, 4 seconds). However, at the earth's equator, the plane of swing of a Foucault pendulum does not rotate. Effectively, its precession period there is infinite. It is beyond the scope of this book to derive this result, but the period of the plane of the swing of a Foucault pendulum, T, is given by

$$T = \frac{T_0}{\sin \varphi}$$

where T_0 is the earth's sidereal period and φ is the latitude. Foucault demonstrated the first of these pendula at Paris Observatory in 1851, followed by a more public demonstration shortly thereafter. A reproduction of the original Foucault pendulum is still in operation in the Pantheon.

I have performed this experiment myself many times. The Department of Physics and Astronomy at Clemson University is in Kinnard Hall. Between Kinnard Hall and Martin Hall, there is a Foucault pendulum that extends through four floors encased in a tube with a window on each floor so that the pendulum is visible. On the basement level, there is a large glass window where one can see the swinging suspended mass with a circle marked in degrees below the pendulum. A point on the bottom of the mass indicates the angle at any given time. By noting the time and the angle over several days, one can determine that the period of rotation is a little more than 42 hours, just as the equation above predicts.

How do flat-earthers respond to the Foucault pendulum? Many don't. Among the flat-earthers who do, the most common response is that some Foucault pendula don't precess, while other Foucault pendula precess backwards. This merely repeats the claims of flat-earthers going back to Rowbotham, but there never is any evidence given for these claims. Some flat-earthers respond by pointing out that Foucault pendula often have a device underneath that imparts a small kick to the swinging mass via electromagnetic induction. They insist that it is this device that causes the precession of a Foucault pendulum. It is true that many Foucault pendula have such a device, but their purpose isn't so nefarious. Due to wind resistance and friction in the wire, a Foucault pendulum eventually will stop swinging. The electronic device merely provides a small amount of energy each swing to overcome friction. Weights on a pendulum clock do the same thing. Care must be taken that the electronic device does not impart a bias into the swing of the pendulum. Furthermore, these devices merely eliminate the need to restart a Foucault pendulum each day or even more than once per day.

While many Foucault pendula have such a device, some do not. For instance, the Foucault pendulum in the science building on the campus of Grace College in Winona Lake, Indiana, has no such device. On September 22, 2018, I was on the Grace College campus and conducted a simple experiment. Since the pendulum has no inducing device, it wasn't swinging when I arrived. The pendulum spans four floors, and the bob is very heavy. I tried lifting the bob. I did raise the bob a short distance as tension was reduced in the cable, but I wasn't able to fully lift the bob. I pulled the bob aside and released it. I then made note of the angle of the plane of the swing and left for about 45 minutes. Upon my return, the pendulum's plane of swing had obviously moved. The plane had moved in the clockwise direction (the expected direction) and at a rate consistent with the expected precession period of a little more than 36½ hours. Obviously, an electronic device was not at work here. When I pointed these facts out to some flat-earthers, they didn't have much to say.

The Coriolis Effect

The Coriolis effect is similar to the Foucault pendulum. The Coriolis effect occurs in a rotating reference frame. Consider a spinning merry-go-round. If a person on the merry-go-round rolls a ball along a radius of the spinning merry-go-round, he will observe that the ball veers to one side. However, from the perspective of a stationary observer not on the merry-go-round, the ball will move in a straight line. The difference is a consequence of the spinning frame of reference experiencing a centripetal acceleration, while the stationary frame of reference is not accelerating. An *inertial frame of reference* is a reference frame that is not accelerating. In an inertial frame, Newton's laws of motion hold. However, in an accelerating, *non-inertial* frame of reference, Newton's laws of motions don't hold. Within a non-inertial frame, one must invent fictitious forces to explain what is observed, such as *centrifugal force*. Centrifugal force does not exist — it is a term people use to describe the effects of a non-inertial system, such as a car rounding a curve. This thinking has led to the term

Coriolis *force*. However, since this isn't a force, physicists prefer to call this the Coriolis effect.

The Coriolis effect is a result of a rotating spherical earth. The earth's circumference is nearly 25,000 miles, or almost exactly 40,000 km. Dividing by 24 hours, the rotational speed of an object on the earth's equator is 1,040 mph or 1,670 km/hr toward the east. On the other hand, an object at one of the poles isn't moving at all because it is located on the axis of rotation. Objects at various latitudes in between are moving at different rates toward the east. Suppose that an object, say a large air mass, leaves the equator traveling northward. As it does, it will continue moving eastward with its speed of 1,040 mph. However, it will soon find itself traveling over a portion of the earth that isn't moving eastward as fast as it is. Therefore, from the perspective of the ground, the air mass will appear to curve toward the east. That is, the air mass will appear to deflect to the right. Now consider an air mass in the Northern Hemisphere traveling southward toward the equator. It will be moving eastward at a slower rate than the surface it is moving over, so it will lag with respect to the surface. Therefore, the air mass will appear to curve to the right as well. In the Southern Hemisphere, the directions are reversed, with air masses appearing to veer to the left.

The Coriolis effect has a profound influence on weather and climate. Due to solar heating, air tends to rise in the tropics, requiring replacement of air at surface level. Replacement air from the north moving southward into the tropics veers rightward toward the west. Meanwhile, replacement air from the south moving northward veers leftward, also toward the west. This explains the trade winds found in the tropics, the prevailing winds being east to west. The air that rises in the tropics moves away from the tropics at high altitude and descends in temperate latitudes (all the while veering eastward). Some of the down-drafting air returns to the tropics, but some moves away from the tropics. In the Northern Hemisphere, the Coriolis effect deflects this northward moving air to the right toward the east. In the Southern Hemisphere, the Coriolis effect deflects the southward moving air to the left, again toward the east. Therefore, in the temperate latitudes, the prevailing winds are west to east.

There is a similar process at high latitudes. Therefore, at high latitudes, the prevailing winds are again east to west, as in the tropics. The prevailing winds at different latitudes drive ocean currents. The currents, in turn, are subject to the Coriolis effect, in addition to the effect of wind direction at different latitudes. The result is that there is a gyre of circulating currents in the oceans. In the north Atlantic and north Pacific, the currents move clockwise, while in the south Atlantic, south Pacific, and Indian Ocean, the currents move counterclockwise.

The spiraling nature of high-pressure and low-pressure systems in the atmosphere are also the result of the Coriolis effect. At the earth's surface, air is driven radially away from high-pressure systems. But the Coriolis effect deflects that motion rightward (clockwise) in the Northern Hemisphere and leftward (counterclockwise) in the Southern Hemisphere. Similarly, at surface level, air is compelled to move radially inward in a low-pressure system. In the Northern Hemisphere, the Coriolis effect deflects the inward motion of air in a low-pressure system to the right (counterclockwise), while the direction is reversed in the Southern Hemisphere. Therefore, large storms, such as hurricanes and winter storms, turn counterclockwise in the Northern Hemisphere and clockwise in the Southern Hemisphere. Smaller systems, such as tornadoes, usually turn the same direction as large storm systems.

However, the oft-repeated statement about emptying sinks and tubs spinning counterclockwise in the Northern Hemisphere and clockwise in the Southern Hemisphere isn't always true. The reason is that the Coriolis effect is very feeble and only shows up over large distances, and tubs and sinks are too small for this to matter very much. It is far more likely that the act of releasing the drain will introduce a more significant movement of water that dictates the direction of spin. Only if all other factors are eliminated will the Coriolis effect be the factor in determining direction of spin. I usually can impart whatever direction of spin I want by swirling the water in one direction before releasing the drain. Having said that, all other effects being equal, drains in the Northern Hemisphere have a slight tendency to spin counterclockwise, and drains in the Southern Hemisphere have a slight tendency to spin clockwise.

The Coriolis effect is an effective demonstration that the earth is a spinning ball. I have yet to see a flat-earther even acknowledge that the Coriolis effect is real, let alone explain it in terms of a flat, stationary earth. The usual response of flat-earthers is to assert that the Coriolis is not real, and throw up objections to it, such as we don't have to correct for it while walking or driving a car. We don't have to, of course, because over very small distances, such as those involved in walking or driving moment by moment, the Coriolis effect is very feeble. When driving or walking, we constantly correct for all sorts of things, such as differences in pavement and slight irregularities in height. We do this so instinctively that we generally aren't aware of them. These slight corrections swamp any correction necessary for the Coriolis effect.

It is ironic that the first person to discuss the Coriolis effect was a geocentrist. Giovanni Battista Riccioli published *Almagestum Novum (New Almagest)* in 1651. This exhaustive discussion of astronomy as it existed at that time included 126 arguments concerning the earth's motion, with 49 supporting the earth's motion and 77 against. One of Riccioli's arguments against the earth's rotation was that if a cannon were fired north or south, the cannon ball would miss its target due to different rotation speeds. Since this wasn't observed, Riccioli included this as an argument against the earth moving. The problem with Riccioli's argument is that the range of cannons at that time was limited so that the amount of deflection was very small, a matter of inches. The horizontal spread in the trajectories of cannon balls due to wind and other irregularities easily dwarfs this. Riccioli was the last prominent geocentrist. It also is important to note that Riccioli did not believe the earth was flat. Furthermore, he supported a modified version of the Tychonic model rather than the Ptolemaic model.

Let me quantify the Coriolis effect. In the figure, R is the earth's radius. Point E on the earth's equator travels on a circle of circumference $2\pi R$ over 24 hours. Division of these two quantities yields the rotational speed of 1,040 mph. Now consider the point P on the earth's surface at latitude φ. Each day, P will move through a circle of radius r around the point Q. Therefore, the line segment QP has length r. Notice that being closer to the earth's rotation axis, $r < R$. Since P is on the earth's surface, it is at distance R from the earth's center, C, so the line CP has length R. The triangle QPC is a right triangle, with CP being the hypotenuse. The lines QP and CE are parallel and are cut by the transversal CP, so the interior angle at vertex P is φ. Therefore,

$$r = R \cos \varphi$$

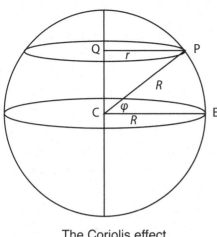

The Coriolis effect

To find the rotation speed, we can multiply by 2π and divide by 24 hours, but we already did this for φ equal to zero (the equator), so the speed of rotation at any latitude is $(\cos \varphi)$ 1,040 mph. To generalize this, let v_e be the speed of rotation at the earth's equator. Then the speed of rotation at any latitude, v, is

$$v = v_e \cos \varphi$$

Notice that motion in the east-west direction introduces no change in latitude, so there is no Coriolis effect when traveling east or west. We can evaluate the change in velocity, Δv, one would experience when moving in the north-south direction by taking the differential of the above equation:

$$\Delta v = v_e \sin \varphi \, \Delta \varphi$$

Let us evaluate this for someone at latitude 40 degrees north walking northward with a stride of three feet. Taking v_e = 1,040 mph and φ equal to 40 degrees, $v_e \sin \varphi$ = 668 mph. As discussed in chapter 5, most flat-earthers seem to accept Gleason's 1892 New Standard Map of the World. Since this map appears to adopt the standard relationship of 69 statute miles per degree of latitude, I will do likewise. Therefore, when taking a three-foot step, a person traverses 8.4×10^{-6} degree of latitude. But for use in this equation, we must convert to radians by dividing by 57.3 to get 1.5×10^{-7} radians. Therefore, the person taking this step will land their foot in a region that is moving eastward 10^{-4} mph slower than his other foot. Obviously, this difference in speed is impossible to notice. What little correction necessary for this is more than swamped by the many other corrections that our minds make as we walk.

What about a car that is traveling northward at 60 mph? In one second, the car will travel 88 feet, nearly 30 times farther than the example of a person walking. Therefore, during one second, the car will encounter pavement that is moving eastward at a rate that is 0.003 mph slower than the car is moving eastward. Again, this difference is not noticeable. The driver of a car continually uses the steering wheel to correct for many factors, such as irregularities in the pavement that completely swamp this meager correction.

What about airplanes? Other than the Concorde, which is no longer flying, commercial aircraft have a maximum speed of about 600 mph or less. Since this is ten times faster than 60 mph, then an aircraft flying northward at 600 mph is encountering land that is moving eastward 0.03 mph slower than the airplane is moving eastward. Again, this small difference is dwarfed by the continual corrections made by the pilot or autopilot. Even an airplane traveling northward at Mach 3 would encounter a differential eastward speed of only 0.1 mph.

What about bullets fired from rifles? Flat-earthers frequently claim that no correction is *ever* made in shooting at targets. The M1 Garand rifle has a muzzle velocity of 2800 ft/s, but that velocity slows to 2300 ft/s after 200 yards. Consider a target 400 yards away, near the limiting range of the M1. If we take 2300 ft/s as the average velocity over the 400 yards, the bullet travels for 0.52 seconds. If the bullet travels due north at 40 degrees north latitude, the target will be moving 0.040 mph more slowly to the east. Multiplying this speed differential by 0.52 seconds and converting hours to seconds and miles to feet, the bullet will deflect by 0.030 feet = 0.36 inches. This deflection will easily be less than typical wind velocity and deviations caused by irregularities in the bullet. Hence, the correction for the Coriolis effect is not necessary for most rifle shots.

However, the situation is very different for large guns, such as artillery or guns aboard naval vessels. Here, the range can be many miles. The Army Field Manual indicates that for artillery, corrections for the Coriolis effect must be made. For instance, the 1945 *Army Field Manual* says the following:

> **Rotation of earth.** The rotation of the earth affects the location of the point of impact of the projectile in range and direction. The magnitude of these effects depends upon the latitude of the gun position, the direction of fire, and the range to the target. [p. 4]

Corrections for Rotation of the Earth. The firing tables for certain long-range weapons give the range and deflection effects of rotation of the earth. These effects may be combined with the effects due to nonstandard conditions of weather and material, and the corrections applied in the same manner. For heavy artillery, rotation of earth effects always should be considered and applied as additional range and deflection corrections. The latitude of the piece is obtained from a map. [p. 142]

There are many other editions of the *Army Field Manual*, and all of them say much the same thing. Therefore, it is easy to refute the common claim of flat-earthers that no correction is ever made in firing guns.

Flights Between the East and West Coasts

One of the more bizarre claims of flat-earthers involves flights between the east and west coasts of the United States. The typical passenger jet cruises between 460 and 575 mph. However, as computed in the previous section, at 40 degrees latitude, the earth is rotating more than 650 mph toward the east. Therefore, many flat-earthers reason, a passenger jet flying from San Francisco to New York cannot overtake the eastward rotation of the earth and, hence, should lose ground the entire time while flying eastward (this is proof numbers 25 and 26 in Dubay's *200 Proofs*[4]). On the other hand, a flight from New York to San Francisco ought to be very short because the speed ought to be the sum of the plane's speed and the earth's rotation. For that matter, many flat-earthers reason that helicopters or hot-air balloons in New York could hover for three hours while they wait for the earth's rotation to carry them over San Francisco (technically, the latitude of San Francisco is a little south of New York's latitude, the helicopter would set down north of San Francisco, but you get the idea). This is Dubay's proof number 21 in his *200 Proofs*. Flat-earthers also argue that planes cannot land on runways with north-south orientation on a rotating spherical earth for the same reason—the runway is moving hundreds of mph east with respect to the plane (this is Dubay's proof number 27 in his *200 Proofs*[5]). Ergo, flat-earthers conclude, the earth must not rotate.

---

4. Dubay, *200 Proofs Earth Is Not a Spinning Globe*, p. 4.
5. Ibid., p. 5–6.

Obviously, there is a flaw in this reasoning, but what is it? Recall from Newton's first law of motion that an object in motion will remain in straight-line motion unless acted upon by a net force. Suppose that a plane is sitting on the ground at an airport that, due to the earth's rotation, is moving eastward at 650 mph. Since the plane is sitting on the ground, it is moving with the same speed eastward that the runway is moving. As the plane accelerates along the runway, its airfoil generates lift that at some speed overcomes the downward force of gravity (weight) on the plane, allowing the plane to become airborne. The vertical and oppositely directed forces of lift and weight are the only significant forces acting on the plane. The only force acting on the plane horizontally is the thrust provided by the engines. At first, the thrust allows the plane to gain speed, but the plane soon attains a cruising speed, which is constant. This constant speed is achieved when the thrust equals the wind resistance on the plane. At no time is there any force directed to change the plane's 650 mph eastward motion due to the earth's rotation. Therefore, by Newton's second law of motion, the plane continues to move eastward 650 mph just as the land beneath it is moving 650 mph eastward.

The error in reasoning on the part of flat-earthers is that they assume that when an object becomes detached from a moving object, the detached object will magically stop moving. However, this would violate Newton's first law of motion. A way to see that this is not the case is by conducting an easy experiment aboard one of the planes in question. Suppose that you are aboard a plane cruising at 550 mph. Try tossing a small object, such as a coin, into the air so that it travels upward two feet. In the ¼ second it takes the object to move upward the two feet, the plane will have moved forward 200 feet. If a hovering helicopter is detached from the earth's rotational motion the instant that it leaves the ground, then the coin will become detached from the plane's forward motion as soon as it is flipped. This would render the coin a dangerous hazard to people near the back of the plane. If this is the way the world worked, it would be impossible for flight attendants to pour any drinks. Since this is obviously not the case, this is not how the world works, and so this objection to a spinning spherical earth is nonsense.

The origin of this improper thinking can be traced back to chapter 3 of Samuel Rowbotham's book *Zetetic Astronomy*. The chapter began with a discussion of the classic question of dropping an object from the top of the mast of a ship. Everyone agrees that if the ship is moored at port, the mass will fall vertically so that it strikes the deck at the base of the mast. However, what happens when the ship is moving? Aristotle thought that the object would be left behind by the ship's motion, and thus it would not land on the deck by the base of the mast. This thinking held sway for nearly two millennia. It was Galileo who argued four centuries ago that the object would continue moving forward and land on the deck at the base of the mast. Therefore, the result is the same whether the ship is stationary or moving at a constant rate. The reason for this result is momentum. And Rowbotham agreed with this result, but he incorrectly stated the reason. He said that the object is acted upon by two forces acting at right angles: the downward force of gravity and the horizontal force of momentum. But momentum is not a force. Force is the time rate of change of momentum. Since there is no horizontal force, the momentum is conserved, and the object continues to move horizontally. According to Rowbotham, it was the combination of these two forces that compelled the object to move diagonally, and thus keep up with the ship. But this description of the motion is incorrect too, because while the horizontal motion is linear in time, the vertical motion is quadratic in time because there *is* a constant force in the vertical direction. Therefore, the correct description of the motion is part of a parabola, not a diagonal line.

This improper understanding of physics set the stage for Rowbotham's next mistake. He then considered an object launched vertically upward from the top of the mast as the ship was moving. Rowbotham concluded that as the object rose, it would maintain its horizontal motion as before. Though he didn't state it, I suppose that his reasoning was again that the "force" of momentum was responsible. And again, he incorrectly argued that the path the object followed would be diagonal when, in reality, the path is part of a parabola. But Rowbotham claimed that when the ball reached its maximum height, "the two forces will have been expended,"[6] but he didn't explain why. It isn't clear what two forces Rowbotham was talking about. One must have been the horizontal "force" of momentum, but what was the second force? It couldn't be gravity, because then

---

6. Parallax (pseudonym of Samuel Birley Rowbotham), *Zetetic Astronomy* (London, England: Simpkin, Marshall, and Co., 1881), p. 65.

the object wouldn't fall downward. Perhaps Rowbotham thought that by throwing the ball upward, this "force" of momentum was at work in the vertical direction, too. At any rate, Rowbotham concluded that after reaching its maximum height, the object would fall vertically with no horizontal motion, and thus the object might miss the ship entirely as the ship continued moving away.

In the physics lab at the university where I taught, we had a piece of equipment that demonstrated how wrong Rowbotham was about this. It was a small cart with a spring-loaded gun that fired a steel ball vertically upward. If you launched the ball while the cart was stationary, the ball traveled upward vertically a short distance before falling back down vertically, whereupon it landed at the launch point on the cart. When you repeated the experiment while the cart was rolling at a constant rate, the ball again traveled upward and back down, whereupon it again landed at the launch point on the cart. From the reference frame of the moving cart, the ball moved entirely in the vertical direction. But from observers who were at rest (my students), the ball moved along a parabolic path.

Airplanes didn't yet exist in Rowbotham's lifetime, but unfortunately, his poor understanding of physics lives on. Modern flat-earthers have merely updated Rowbotham's miserable discussion of motion and applied it to modern aircraft.

Leaving the Atmosphere and Moon Behind

Related to this is another misunderstanding. Flat-earthers sometimes object that if the earth were rotating or moving through space, the earth's atmosphere would be left behind. Or if the earth were orbiting the sun, the moon would be left behind. For that matter, the sun is moving about 250 km/s roughly in the direction of the bright star Vega. In recent years, there have been videos on the Internet illustrating the motion of the earth and other planets as they travel with the sun through space — the combined motion are helixes. To flat-earthers, this is poppycock, because they can't see how the earth could keep up with all this motion.

This sort of objection isn't new, because Aristotle and others in the ancient world who opposed the heliocentric model employed it, as did people for the next millennium and a half. They said that if the earth moved, the atmosphere would be left behind, as well as the moon. However, as described above, Galileo uncovered the true nature of relative motion. Furthermore, when he looked at Jupiter through the telescope, he discovered four previously unknown natural satellites, or moons, orbiting it. Everyone agreed that Jupiter moved because one could easily see that it changed position in the sky. Therefore, if Aristotle were right about relative motion, Jupiter's four satellites ought to be left behind as Jupiter moved. But they weren't. Instead, they keep up with Jupiter as Jupiter moves. Therefore, this objection to the earth moving is baseless.

However, flat-earthers seem to be ignorant of these facts. It's sad. Even flat-earthers must admit that Jupiter moves. And even a small telescope will reveal the motion of Jupiter's satellites from night to night.

Water on a Spherical Earth

Many flat-earth arguments are straw-man arguments. A case in point are the many diagrams showing water running off the sides of a spherical earth. For instance, this is illustrated in Dubay's *200 Proofs*[7] and in his *The Flat-Earth Conspiracy*.[8] The obvious argument is that if the earth were a sphere, then water would run off it. Of course, the response to this lame argument is that gravity holds water on the earth. Flat-earthers immediately scoff at that answer, disparagingly referring to gravity as some "magic" force. Flat-earthers don't seem to realize that the supposed downward force of gravity that leads one to think water would fall off a spherical earth is imposed from the flat-earth model. In the flat-earth model, gravity works downward, a direction that is the same for all locations on the earth, and perhaps beyond the earth as well. However, within the spherical-earth model, where Newton's law of gravity operates, gravity is directed in the radial direction toward the earth's center. Flat-earthers are free to doubt that this works, but to impose their version of how gravity works onto the spherical earth where gravity doesn't work their way is a slight-of-hand trick that makes this a straw-man argument. To expose a flaw in the spherical-earth model, one must demonstrate a problem within that model, not by importing an element from the flat-earth model that is incompatible with the spherical-earth model.

---

7. Dubay, *200 Proofs Earth Is Not a Spinning Globe*, p. . 38.
8. Dubay, *The Flat Earth Conspiracy*, p. 29.

This is ironic because in his presentation at the second Flat Earth International Conference in 2018, "Testing the Globe: A Zetetic Investigation," Rob Skiba cautioned non-flat-earthers about the same sort of thing. Skiba began his talk with a dozen cautions under the heading of "Debunking Flat Earth 101." Number six on the list was "You can't just insert the flat earth into the Copernican model of the universe."[9] But apparently, it's okay for flat-earthers to do so.

A similar sort of argument is employed by flat-earthers with the concept of level. The appropriate definition of level from Merriam-Webster is

> a line or surface that cuts perpendicularly all plumb lines that it meets and hence would everywhere coincide with a surface of still water.[10]

As mentioned above, in the flat-earth model, the downward direction at any location is parallel to the downward direction at any other location. Consequently, the level line is the same direction everywhere or the level plane is the same plane everywhere. However, in the spherical-earth model, the direction of a plumb line is radially toward the earth's center. Therefore, the direction of plumb is not the same at every location on earth. Furthermore, at any point on the earth's surface, the line or plane defining level is tangent to the earth's surface at that point. Consequently, the level line or plane is not parallel to the level line or plane at other locations. On a local scale, the deviation of the level line or plane at different locations is not appreciable. Flat-earthers extrapolate this indistinguishability of level on the local scale to the nonlocal scale. That is, they impose the concept of level in the flat-earth model onto the spherical-earth model to get absurd results. But, as before, this is a straw-man argument. If one wishes to demonstrate the absurdity of a proposition, one must do so within the definition of that proposition, not by importing a concept that is foreign to that proposition.

Apparently to gain badly sought attention, a flat-earther that goes by the name D. Marble (his first name is Darryle) has taken to carrying a spirit level with him on flights. Once the planes achieve cruising altitude,

---

9. https://www.youtube.com/watch?v=g9R-YWnBxhI.
10. https://www.merriam-webster.com/dictionary/level.

D. Marble uses his spirit level to gauge whether the planes are flying level, which they are. D. Marble reasons that if the earth is spherical, then the planes must deviate from level as they make their way along an arc on the earth's surface. Since D. Marble finds no deviation from level, he erroneously concludes that the earth must be flat. Of course, D. Marble's unusual behavior doesn't go unnoticed by fellow passengers, which gives him the opportunity to share the gospel of flat earth with others. As before, the flaw in his little "experiment" is that D. Marble has imported his flat-earth concept of gravity into the spherical-earth model. Hence, this is a straw-man argument.

Flat-earthers apply this shoddy reasoning to rivers as well. This is the argument of proofs 3–5 of Dubay's *200 Proofs*.[11] The claim is made that over the course of long rivers, the rivers must ascend to overcome the hill that lies between their headwaters and eventual mouths. Again, this is a problem only if one assumes that gravity operates in one direction at all locations. Of course, on the spherical earth, the direction of gravity is always along a radius. Therefore, elevation is determined from how high above the earth's center a location is. More properly, elevation is determined from mean sea level. Due to the earth's rotation, there is a slinging effect so that the earth's diameter through its equator is a few miles greater (out of 8,000 miles) than it is through its poles, technically rendering the earth's surface an oblate spheroid. Being a fluid, the water in the world's oceans find, and hence define, the level to which all rivers will descend.[12] The headwaters of all rivers that drain into the ocean are higher than sea level. Furthermore, the gradients of all these rivers are downward toward their mouths. Therefore, this is a straw-man argument.

In his *200 Proofs*, Dubay attempted to quantify the supposed problem for the spherical earth, and he botched the numbers terribly. Dubay wrote that "the Mississippi River in its 3,000 miles would have to ascend 11 miles before reaching the Gulf of Mexico."[13] This exaggerates the length of the Mississippi River because its length is closer to 2,300 miles, and this is the distance along the river's meanders, not the straight-line distance, which is even less. Perhaps Dubay might

---

11. Dubay, *200 Proofs Earth Is Not a Spinning Globe*, p. 1.

12. Of course, there are few exceptions, such as the Jordan River, that end in inland seas.

13. Dubay, *200 Proofs Earth Is Not a Spinning Globe*, p. 1.

have considered the course of the Missouri River because its length to where it joins the Mississippi River is much longer than the Mississippi River alone. However, assuming the 3,000-mile figure to be correct, the 11-mile figure is incorrect. Using the eight inches per mile squared approximation, 3,000 miles yields 1,100 miles, not 11 miles. It appears that Dubay incorrectly computed this drop by using 300 miles rather than 3,000 miles. And this isn't even the proper formula to use because it is an approximation. The correct formula yields a different answer, but far more than 11 miles. Dubay also stated that "the Nile River flows for a thousand miles with a fall of only one foot."[14] I cannot verify that statistic. I find it difficult to believe. The Nile River's discharge is about 300 million cubic meters per day. It would be difficult to sustain a flow rate of that magnitude with such a low gradient. Spot-checking elevations along the Nile River with Google Earth produces no portions that would match this description. This figure appears in proof 4 of Carpenter's book, suggesting that Dubay merely copied it without any attempt at verification.

Canals, Railways, Bridges, and Tunnels

Another variation on this theme is the claim that canals, railways, bridges, and tunnels are not constructed with an allowance for the earth's curvature. For instance, proof number 7 of Dubay's *200 Proofs* states:

> Surveyors, engineers and architects are never required to factor the supposed curvature of the Earth into their projects. Canals, railways, bridges and tunnels for example are always cut and laid horizontally, often over hundreds of miles without any allowance for curvature.[15]

This statement is bolstered by further examples in Dubay's proofs 8–12, three of which are testimonials from engineers to this effect. Those testifying were flat-earthers, and their words appeared in flat-earth publications more than a century ago.

These statements are correct. However, that does not mean that the earth is flat. Rather, it means that it isn't necessary to correct for the

14. Ibid., p. 1.
15. Ibid., p. 2.

earth's curvature. Suppose that you are laying a straight (no deviation to the right or left) section of railroad track over one mile. Due to the earth's curvature, one end of the track will lie eight inches below a level line as defined on the other end of the track. A straight line drawn from one end of the track to the other will make an angle of less than one arcminute from the level line defined at the other end of the track. A spirit level cannot measure a deviation this small. Variations in elevation of the terrain are far larger than this. To assure proper drainage, rail beds are generally elevated above the local terrain. Therefore, there is much removing and filling of material in constructing a rail bed. If it is desired to keep the track level over the course, a theodolite is used, but over far less than the entire mile's distance. Furthermore, spirit levels may be used to ensure that each rail is laid level, but as already pointed out, spirit levels cannot detect the deviation that the earth's curvature introduces. Therefore, railways, highways, bridges, and tunnels are constructed using a locally defined level along the entire length. That is, the level from one end of a long section of track is not exported to the other end. Besides not making any sense, it isn't practical.

The same is true of canals. For instance, the 120-mile-long Suez Canal connects two bodies of water that are at sea level. All that was necessary to construct the canal was to excavate a channel deep enough to accommodate the required depth below sea level. This was done by surveying from either end of the intended route. Following this technique, the canal follows the arc of the earth. In all these examples, flat-earthers have once again sneaked into the spherical earth their concept of gravity from a flat-earth model. However, if one properly applies gravity as it operates on the spherical earth, there is no problem.

There are projects that require allowance for the earth's curvature during construction. The Laser Interferometer Gravitational-Wave Observatory (LIGO) consists of two nearly identical facilities, one in Hanford, Washington, and the other in Livingston, Louisiana. Both facilities consist of two pipes arranged in an L-shape. The length of each pipe is 4 km (2.5 miles). The pipes contain an ultra-high vacuum (less than 10^{-12} atmosphere) through which a laser beam passes. The earth's curvature over the length of the pipes is a little more than four feet. This is nearly the diameter of the pipes (1.3 meters = 4.3 feet). If the pipes were constructed using conventional techniques of conforming to local level along their courses, the curvature in the pipes would obstruct much of the beams. Therefore, each pipe is constructed so that one end is a little more than four feet higher above mean sea level than the other end is. Therefore, the LIGO construction proves that the earth is curved. However, since LIGO was financed by the National Science Foundation and is operated by Caltech and MIT, flat-earthers probably will dismiss this as part of some great conspiracy.

Another example of straight construction over long distances are light pipes (Krause-Ogle boxes) that were used in above-ground nuclear tests. The light pipes were used to film the detonation of nuclear devices. The cameras were located miles from the detonation sight, so the light pipes had to be constructed straight without any deviation for the earth's curvature, much as the pipes with LIGO.

Diving Airplanes

Yet another variation on this theme involves airplanes. The claim is made that for an airplane to maintain a constant elevation over a spherical earth, the pilot must continually dip the nose of his airplane, or else the plane would gain altitude. In proof number 15 of his *200 Proofs*, Dubay stated that a plane cruising at 500 mph "would have to constantly dip their nose downwards and descend 2,777 feet (over half a mile) every minute!"[16] This claim makes no sense. A plane traveling at 500 mph travels 8.33 miles in one minute. Applying the eight inches per mile squared approximation, the earth's curvature would cause the earth's surface to fall away 46 feet in that one minute, not 2,777 feet. During that one minute, the plane moves forward 44,000 feet, so 46 feet is a very modest one part in a thousand, which is hardly noticeable. But the plane doesn't even dive that modest amount, as we shall soon see.

Where did Dubay get this grossly erroneous conclusion? He computed the amount of the earth's curvature over 500 miles (167,000 feet), how far the plane would travel in an hour, and divided by 60 to get 2,777 feet per minute (about a half-mile). Notice that the ratio of the drop to the total distance is about one part in 16, quite a bit more than one part in a thousand as when one considers an interval of one minute. Why

16. Dubay, *200 Proofs Earth Is Not a Spinning Globe*, p. 3.

the large discrepancy? It is due to an accumulated squared relationship, something that Dubay obviously fails to grasp the significance of. Doing the calculation over ever-smaller intervals of time may help resolve this paradox. Let us repeat the calculation over one second of flight. In one second, the plane travels 733 feet (0.139 miles). The amount of curvature over 733 feet is 0.15 inches (0.013 feet). Compared to the distance traveled, this drop is less than one part in 56,000. Accounting for round-off error, the ratio of the discrepancy changes by a factor of 60 each time, the number of seconds in a minute, and the number of minutes in an hour. If we repeated the calculation for 1/60 of a second, the ratio of the drop to the distance traveled would be approximately one part in 3.5 million.

With such discordant results, something must be amiss in this approach. Notice that as we repeat the calculation for ever-smaller time intervals, the amount that the plane must "dive" diminishes. An airplane doesn't fly an hour all at once, or even a minute, or even a second. A plane flies moment by moment, and those moments accumulate into seconds, minutes, and hours. It is this accumulation that causes the erroneous amounts of dives supposedly required by the airplane. As we reduce the time interval considered, the amount of "dive" diminishes, eventually becoming zero in the instantaneous situation.

But the plane doesn't need to dive at all to maintain level flight. Level flight means keeping the same altitude above mean sea level. As the plane moves forward, mean sea level gradually curves beneath the plane (not abruptly, as the above calculations would suggest). Therefore, as the plane maintains constant altitude over a spherical earth, the plane follows the curvature of the earth. Once again, hiding in this argument put forth by flat-earthers is the importation of their notion of gravity, a notion that is foreign to the spherical earth. Therefore, this, too, is a straw-man argument.

How Do Rockets Work in Space?

As we shall see in chapter 8, flat-earthers deny that we have ventured into space. They reason that this is impossible because the dome covering would prevent orbital motion. I discuss some of the arguments that flat-earthers have with space travel in chapter 8, but here I will discuss one physical objection that they have. Flat-earthers claim that rockets can't work in space because space is a vacuum, and rockets require air to push against to work. This is a failure to comprehend Newton's third law of motion. A good demonstration of Newton's third law of motion is to stand with your toes two feet from a wall. Place your hands on the wall and bring your face almost in contact with the wall. If you quickly remove your hands, it is impossible to right yourself. Instead, you will fall into the wall. Now try pushing against the wall. You will find that as you push on the wall, the wall will push back on you with an opposite and equal force, and you will right yourself.

A rocket operates by pushing matter out a nozzle. As the nozzle pushes against the ejected matter, the ejected matter pushes back with an opposite and equal force. This is Newton's third law of motion. The nozzle is attached to the rocket, so since a force is acting on the nozzle, both the nozzle and rocket are accelerated in a direction opposite to the direction of the ejected matter. Notice that there is no need of air for this to operate. What is confusing to some people is that jet engines operate by a similar principle. One difference is that air (containing oxygen) for combustion of the fuel is inserted on the front of a jet engine; operating in a vacuum, a rocket engine must provide its own oxygen as well as fuel. Another difference is that the ejected exhaust of a jet engine does push against air behind the engine. The action-reaction pair of forces is transferred to the jet engine, adding some additional thrust that would not be there in a vacuum. However, the jet engine and the plane it is attached to must force themselves through air in front of the plane, producing a retarding force on the plane. Therefore, any small gain in thrust by acting in the air is cancelled by overcoming air in its way. When this is accounted for, the action-reaction pair of forces of Newton's third law of motion is what is responsible for the acceleration of a jet. Hence, this objection to rockets operating in space is baseless.

Flat-Earthers Don't Understand Physics

If it isn't obvious already, flat-earthers fail to comprehend physics. And it's not just restricted to the topics discussed in this chapter. As I showed in chapter 2, atmospheric refraction due to temperature inversions explains how distant objects beyond the earth's curvature can sometimes be seen.

This, too, relies upon knowledge of physics to understand. There are other examples scattered throughout many chapters of this book. Just because some people fail to understand something doesn't mean that it isn't true.

Chapter 7

Geocentrism and Flat Earth

Geocentrism is the belief that the earth is the center of the universe. This contrasts with *heliocentrism*, which is the belief that the earth is one of eight planets that orbit the sun. For much of history, geocentrism was the dominant model. However, during the 17th century, the geocentric model was abandoned in favor of the heliocentric model. Though most people assume that this question was settled long ago, the late 20th century saw a revival of interest in the geocentric model. However, unlike the dominant geocentric cosmology of the past, the Ptolemaic model, the modern geocentric theory is the Tychonic model, with the other planets orbiting the sun, but with the sun, in turn, orbiting the earth and carrying the other planets along with its motion. This amounts to a coordinate transformation from the sun to the earth. The modern geocentric movement has two camps — those who think the earth spins once each day, and those who don't. There are some very highly educated people who are geocentrists today, including physicists and at least one person with a PhD in astronomy. Geocentrists use physical arguments, but their main motivation seems to be their belief that the Bible teaches that the earth does not move. And this movement has not appeared to have any flat-earthers in its midst.

It should be obvious that flat-earthers must be geocentrists. However, one ought not confuse the "traditional," or Tychonic, geocentrists described above with the flat-earth movement. It is ironic, however, that after the Tychonic geocentrists had labored for decades, the sudden rise in the flat-earth movement has resulted in there probably being more flat-earth geocentrists today than there are geocentrists who believe the earth is a sphere. To add insult to injury, the flat-earthers use many of the arguments, both physical and biblical, that they borrowed from the Tychonic geocentrists. However, it is doubtful that any flat-earthers understand the physical arguments as well as most Tychonic geocentrists do.

For decades, Gerardus Bouw has been the primary proponent of geocentrism. Bouw, who has a PhD in astronomy, is not a flat-earther, and he has written little on the flat-earth movement. In recent years, Robert Sungenis has arisen as the best-known advocate of geocentrism. Sungenis, who lacks the academic credentials of Bouw, has spoken and written on geocentrism. In 2014, Sungenis coproduced *The Principle*, a documentary that promoted geocentrism. The movie generated much controversy because two scientists featured, Lawrence Krauss and Michio Kaku, and the narrator Kate Mulgrew said that they were duped into participating in the project and were not aware of the true purpose of the movie. Sungenis has critiqued flat earth in a book, *Flat Earth/Flat Wrong: An Historical, Biblical and Scientific Analysis*. Interestingly, at the second Flat Earth International Conference in 2018, Robert Sungenis and Rob Skiba debated whether the Bible teaches that the earth is flat. Since both participants were geocentrists, that aspect of their beliefs wasn't an issue.

It is not my intent here to offer a complete rebuttal to geocentrism. Rather, I intend to respond to some of the claims made by flat-earthers on this front. I will begin this chapter with a discussion of motion and some of the scientific experiments that geocentrists claim prove that the earth doesn't move. Later in the chapter, I will examine a few of the Bible passages that flat-earthers claim teach that the earth does not move. Again, there is much overlap with the traditional geocentrists because flat-earthers have borrowed heavily from the geocentrists. However, it is not my intent here to critique fully the geocentric movement that teaches the earth is a globe.

Motion

Motion is a tricky concept. The only motion that we can measure is relative motion. For instance, if we walk or drive about, we perceive that we are moving with respect to the earth. We see birds and planes fly with respect to the earth, provided that we aren't moving ourselves. But even then, we can account for our motion to determine how birds and planes move with respect to the earth. But if I'm moving with respect to the earth, could I say that I'm not moving and it's the earth that is moving? Before you dismiss this as obviously wrong, consider what nearly everyone who has driven a vehicle with a manual transmission has experienced. Suppose you are stopped at a traffic light on a street with a slope and multiple lanes. Now suppose that you are distracted by something inside the vehicle, such as tuning the radio. If a vehicle next to you slowly ascends the hill and you notice this with your peripheral vision, you immediately interpret this as your foot has slipped off the brake, and your vehicle is rolling. Not wishing to cause a collision, you quickly press hard on the brake and look up, only to realize that it was the vehicle next to you, not you who was moving. This has happened to me more than once.

If we are so easily fooled by relative motion, perhaps it isn't so easy to determine who is moving and who is not. It seems more likely that I am moving rather than the rest of the world that is moving, but can I be certain about that? People generally have assumed and continue to assume that there is some absolute standard of rest against which all motion can be measured. But what is that standard? Alas, science (and more particularly, physics) can't answer that question. Instead, we must make some sort of assumption about this. Some critics claim that this is a metaphysical assumption, and, hence, is outside the bounds of science. However, every system of thought must begin with a few axioms, definitions, and postulates from which conclusions can be reached. For instance, in geometry, we begin with the assumption of points, lines, and planes, plus a few other assumptions generally shared with other systems of mathematics (postulates, axioms, and definitions). Science is a bit different from mathematics in that our conclusions are informed by observations of the world. But neither mathematics, science, nor philosophy is possible without a few underlying assumptions. For physics, one assumption may be about what is truly at rest. But even more basic than that, we must assume that the physical world exists, that the physical world is not an illusion. In analogy to the three things assumed in geometry, physicists assume that space, time, and matter exist. Physicists define many properties of space, time, and matter, but they never really define exactly what those quantities are. Again, we must start a system somewhere.

The classic experiment with regard to the question of what is moving is a pail of water that is suspended by a wound rope that is allowed to unwind, thus spinning the pail. Eventually, friction between the bucket and water causes the water to spin, too. As the water spins, its surface develops a concavity. How does the water know that it is spinning and that it ought to develop this concavity in response? The assumption made in physics is that the matter of the universe is at rest with respect to space. Nearly all matter individually is in motion, but if all matter collectively is at rest with respect to space, then the average of a great deal of matter would effectively define the standard of the rest. We call this Mach's principle, named for Ernst Mach, who wrote about this more than a century ago, though he wasn't the first person to do so. The original form of Mach's principle appealed to the distant stars as a standard whereby to gauge motion. Our understanding of cosmology has changed a bit since then, so today we'd prefer the average of many distant galaxies and quasars or the cosmic microwave background (CMB) as the standard of rest. But keep in mind that this is a convention that conforms to much of what we know of physics. Also keep in mind that this is an assumption that makes physics as we know it possible. In a very real sense, we don't know what the absolute standard of rest is. However, physics works very well with the assumption of Mach's principle, giving us confidence that it is correct.

Since all we can ever measure is relative motion, in many respects, we are free to use whatever standard of rest we wish. For instance, I believe that it is the earth that rotates each day, producing sunrise and sunset. However, sunrise and sunset could be explained by a stationary earth around which the sun and everything else spins once per day. Therefore, in a very real sense, the sun does rise and set each day. I'm not appealing merely to appearance or saying that sunrise and sunset are phenomenological. I'm saying that in a very real sense, the sun does move in the sky each day. But that doesn't mean that I'm denying that the earth spins each day. If you think that I am engaging in double speak here, then you have failed to grasp my discussion of motion. And this is the crux of the matter. Tychonic geocentrists frequently speak of the fact that all we can observe, and measure, is relative motion. Thus, they conclude that the concept of absolute motion isn't really a scientific matter, but a question of metaphysics. But then somewhere along the line, geocentrists change tack and claim that they can scientifically prove that the earth doesn't move. This is inconsistent. How can they scientifically prove something that at the outset they claim isn't a scientific question?

The Experiments

By the 19th century, considerable physical evidence had accumulated that indicated that light is a wave phenomenon. A wave is a periodic vibration in a medium. So, what is the medium of light? It can pass through transparent things, such as air, water, and glass, but it also can pass through a vacuum. No other wave does that. Therefore, physicists deduced that space must be filled with a medium. Physicists called this medium the *luminiferous aether*, often referred to simply as the aether, and sometimes spelled "ether." The aether had some peculiar properties. It didn't seem to have mass,[1] but it had incredible strength and elasticity, seeing that it was capable of immediately closing in behind objects as they moved. And the aether didn't seem to interact with matter in any way.

Physicists developed theories about how the aether worked, and they devised experiments that would test those theories. The most famous of these experiments was the Michaelson-Morley experiment in 1887. This experiment used a Michaelson interferometer (figure). A Michaelson interferometer uses a monochromatic (having a very narrow range in wavelength) light source. Light passes through a beam splitter, a piece of partially silvered flat glass oriented at 45 degrees to the original light beam's path, splitting the beam into two beams. Beam 1 passes through the glass, while beam 2 reflects off the glass so that it travels along a path that is at a right angle to the original beam and beam 1. These two beams travel along their separate arms before reflecting off a mirror at the end of either arm to send the beams back to the beam splitter. Upon return to the beam splitter, part of beam 1 is reflected off the glass to the observer at point O. Meanwhile, part of beam 2 passes through the glass to reach point

---

1. In contrast, some modern Tychonic geocentrists think that the aether has incredibly high density, and, hence, has mass.

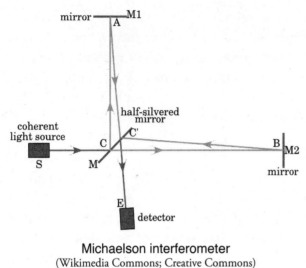

Michaelson interferometer
(Wikimedia Commons; Creative Commons)

O. Thus, a portion of the split beams are recombined at point O. If there is any path difference between the two beams, the light from the two beams will interfere with one another at point O. This interference produces an interference pattern of dark and light fringes. These fringes are small, so they are viewed with a magnifier.

The interferometer in the Michaelson-Morley experiment was situated with one beam in the direction of the earth's orbital motion around the sun and the other arm perpendicular to that motion. Because of the earth's motion, the two light beams would not traverse the same distance, so the light beams would produce an interference pattern. However, there was a complication. A path difference of just a fraction of the wavelength of light, about one ten thousandths of an inch for visible light, would produce an interference pattern. Since it was impossible to construct a Michaelson interferometer with two arms so precisely the same length, even a stationary device would produce an interference pattern. To solve this problem, Michaelson and Morley rotated their device 90 degrees so that the beam that originally was aligned with the earth's motion was now perpendicular, while the beam that originally was perpendicular to the earth's motion was now in the same direction as the earth's motion. This ought to produce an interference pattern that was different from the original alignment, but the patterns were identical.

What does this null result mean? One possibility is the one favored by all modern geocentrists, that the earth is not moving. However, at the time, few scientists, if any, seriously considered this because there was direct evidence that the earth was moving (aberration of starlight, annual parallax, and annual variations in the Doppler motions of stars).

Indeed, the Michaelson-Morley experiment wasn't intended as a test of whether the earth was moving. Rather, it was a test of a particular theory of the aether. This experiment and others eliminated different versions of the aether. The best conclusion was that the aether, at least as understood by 19th-century classical physics, did not exist. Over the next two decades, physicists struggled with modifications of the aether to account for the experimental results while still providing a framework for some medium that light traveled in. Most notable was the work of Hendrik Lorentz, George Fitzgerald, Henri Poincaré, and Joseph Larmor. Their work presaged some of the results of Albert Einstein's special theory of relativity, such as length contraction, time dilation, and mass increase with increasing velocity.

The New Aether

The situation changed dramatically with the publication of Einstein's theory of special relativity in 1905. Rather than concentrating on the aether, Einstein took the result of the Michaelson-Morley experiment as axiomatic. In Newtonian physics, it is axiomatic that space and time are absolutes. That is, all observers will measure the same distances between locations in the universe, and they will measure the same time intervals between events. However, velocities that we measure will depend upon how fast we are traveling. A person at rest with respect to the earth may measure an automobile's speed to be 45 mph, but a person overtaking that car while traveling at 60 mph will measure the other car's speed as 15 mph. Similarly, in classical physics, how fast light travels will depend upon how fast one is traveling, as well as the velocity of the source of light. It was this difference in the speed of light that the Michaelson-Morley experiment was designed to measure, but the result was that the speed of light was the same regardless of our motion. Einstein took the invariance of the speed of light as an axiom and worked out the consequences.

What were those consequences? Part of this was the Lorentz-Fitzgerald contraction already worked out in terms of a modified aether theory. However, that modification required several *ad hoc* assumptions that seemed to have no real basis. Furthermore, Einstein's solution sidestepped the aether because it didn't rely upon any medium for light to travel through. That is, Einstein's special theory of relativity did not appear to require the existence of the aether. The same year that Einstein published his special theory of relativity he also published his explanation of the photoelectric effect. This built upon Max Planck's explanation of black-body radiation published five years earlier. Both explanations posited that light was a particle. Unlike waves, particles don't require a medium to travel. These two developments probably led to the conclusion by Einstein and other physicists at the time that there was no aether.

The idea that light was a particle was a return to the dominant theory of light prior to the 19th century. However, this was not a complete return because there was considerable evidence that light had a wave property as well. In classical physics, this made no sense because particles and waves were distinctly different things. To add to the mix, accumulated experimental evidence suggested that entities that had been viewed as small particles, such as electrons, also had a wave nature. These paradoxes were resolved in the development of the wave-particle duality of quantum mechanics. In quantum mechanics, waves and particles can be described as different aspects of the same thing. As it turns out, this is a very powerful theory with much experimental evidence in its favor. Quantum mechanics and modern relativity theory are the twin pillars of what we now call modern physics. This contrasts with classical physics. It's not that classical physics is wrong; rather, modern physics applies in the general case, whereas classical physics is more restricted in where it can be used. In many instances, the predictions of modern physics are indistinguishable from those of classical physics. Since classical physics is easier to use, it is best to express our understanding in terms of classical physics when the circumstances allow it.

As brilliant as special relativity was, people realized right away that it was incomplete. There was a need to formulate a more general theory, which is what led Einstein to publish general relativity a decade after special relativity. General relativity provides a more fundamental approach to gravity than Newton's theory. It also relates time to the three usual spatial dimensions. Physicists now began to speak of a four-dimensional space-time, usually referred to as space. They generally speak of space-time as a fabric because of this mathematical description of space. Essentially, this makes space a thing. We may not know what space is, but we know much about its properties. This may seem strange, but there are many things that physicists know a lot about, yet don't know what they are — time, matter, energy.

But notice that in general relativity, space is a thing. Einstein was much impressed with Mach's principle, and he wanted to incorporate it into general relativity, though he never quite accomplished that. However, the two are compatible. And Mach's principle suggests that there is a preferred standard of rest defined by the matter of the universe. After he published his paper on general relativity, Einstein came to realize that space itself could be a sort of aether. Therefore, Einstein walked back his earlier pronouncement that he had eliminated the aether. Rather, he had replaced the aether of classical physics with an aether of modern physics.

Besides four-dimensional space-time, there is at least one other candidate for the aether. The first half of the 19th century had seen many experimental results that demonstrated the intimate relationship between electricity and magnetism. Up to this time, electricity and magnetism were viewed as different phenomena, but these experiments led to their unification into a single theory. This unification was propounded by four elegant equations worked out by James Clerk Maxwell in the second half of the 19th century. Simultaneous solution of the four equations results in the propagation of a wave in electric and magnetic fields that travels at the speed measured for light. Maxwell did not consider this a coincidence. That theory was soon developed to the point that we now call light and other related waves electromagnetic radiation. This is probably the best candidate for the medium of light. Note that it is very different from the classical aether of the 19th century.

Supposed Biblical Support for Geocentrism

In chapters 10 and 11, I discuss the supposed biblical argument for the earth being flat. There I mention a list of 240+ supposed flat-earth Bible verses.[2] One heading on that list is Earth Is Fixed and Immovable. That list includes verses that geocentrists have used for a long time. For instance, one verse on the list is 1 Chronicles 16:30, which reads:

> Tremble before him, all the earth;
> yes, the world is established; it shall never be moved.

---

2. An internet search for "240+ flat-earth verses" will usually produce many results for this list. One such site is https://www.flatearthdoctrine.com/flat-earth-scriptures.

Another is Psalm 93:1:

> The LORD reigns; he is robed in majesty;
> the LORD is robed; he has put on strength as his belt.
> Yes, the world is established; it shall never be moved.

Yet another is Psalm 96:10:

> Say among the nations, "The LORD reigns!
> Yes, the world is established; it shall never be moved;
> he will judge the peoples with equity."

And another is Psalm 104:5:

> He set the earth on its foundations,
> so that it should never be moved.

All four verses clearly and emphatically state that the earth shall never be moved. Therefore, by the literal hermeneutic, the earth must be stationary. But let us consider Psalm 16:8:

> I have set the LORD always before me:
> because he is at my right hand, I shall not be moved[3] (KJV).

Here, David is speaking of himself. If one is consistent in the literal hermeneutic, David must have remained stationary the remainder of his life. No one would insist that is the case, so the meaning of the word "moved" here must mean something less than the completely literal sense. Indeed, we use the word "move" in this manner quite frequently, such as saying, "Your argument doesn't move me," meaning that an argument isn't persuasive, and so it hasn't moved a person from their opinion. Obviously, this example is meant in a figurative sense. There are many other examples of how we use the words "move" and "moved" in a far less than literal sense. Lest there be any doubt, the same Hebrew verb translated "moved" is used in all five of these verses. It is grossly inconsistent to insist on a hyper-literal meaning in four of the verses, only to bail out on the fifth verse, insisting that it isn't to be taken quite so literally.

---

3. In this book, I have normally quoted the ESV. However, here I quote from the KJV because the ESV uses the word "shaken" here rather than "moved." That is the only difference in the reading of Psalm 16:8 in the two versions.

What is the proper meaning of these four verses? The emphasis is on the fact that God has created the earth. And God created the earth with purpose. God's plan and purpose will not be thwarted, so earth will endure for as long as he sustains it. Indeed, this is expressed in Isaiah 45:18:

> For thus says the LORD,
>   who created the heavens
>   (he is God!),
> who formed the earth and made it
>   (he established it;
> he did not create it empty,
>   he formed it to be inhabited!):
> "I am the LORD, and there is no other."

Interestingly, the abovementioned list includes this verse as well, though this verse nowhere states that the earth is immovable. Why is it included on the list? It probably was flagged by the similar language of God forming and establishing the earth, and the compiler of the list merely assumed that this verse went on to say that the earth is immovable without reading further to see if it did.

This list rounds out with four more verses. One verse is Psalm 33:9:

> For he spoke, and it came to be;
>   he commanded, and it stood firm.

There is hardly anything geocentric in this verse, so it isn't clear why it was included.

Another verse on the list is Psalm 119:89–90:

> Forever, O LORD, your word
>   is firmly fixed in the heavens.
> Your faithfulness endures to all generations;
>   you have established the earth, and it stands fast.

Again, there is hardly anything geocentric in this verse, so it isn't clear why it is on the list.

Another verse on the list is Isaiah 14:7:

> The whole earth is at rest and quiet;
> they break forth into singing.

Really? The context of this verse is the prophesied taunt of Israel by the king of Babylon. The oppression of Babylon will be lifted (v. 4b–6) so that the people of the earth will be at rest and peace. Therefore, the rest here is not lack of motion on the part of the earth, but that various people in the earth will be free of fear of conquest.

The list concludes with Zechariah 1:11:

> And they answered the angel of the LORD who was standing among the myrtle trees, and said, "We have patrolled the earth, and behold, all the earth remains at rest."

Apparently, the compiler of the list thinks that this verse means that the earth is at rest as opposed to motion. However, like Isaiah 14:7, this verse obviously refers to the people of the earth living in peace. Clearly, none of the nine passages listed under this heading teach that the earth is fixed and immovable.

Another listing of verses from the 240+ flat-earth verses is under the heading Earthquakes Shake Earth and Does Not Move. The verses under this heading are 2 Samuel 22:8, Isaiah 13:13, and Revelation 6:12–13. Since Psalm 18 almost completely duplicates 2 Samuel 22:2–51, one ought to include Psalm 18:7 in this list as well. However, while all these verses mention the earth quaking, none of them state that the earth does not move. Whoever compiled this list, as well as the people who have repeated and embellished the list, obviously did not check these verses carefully.

Another heading, "Be Still and Know that I Am God," has but one verse — Psalm 46:10:

> Be still, and know that I am God.
> I will be exalted among the nations,
> I will be exalted in the earth!

The heading accurately describes what this verse says, but this verse hardly promotes anything remotely related to geocentrism or flat earth. It is a mystery why anyone would think this verse promotes flat earth.

Another heading is "Sun Moves, Not the Earth." Under this heading, there are 53 verses, far too numerous to discuss individually here. Most of these verses mention sunrise or sunset. However, a few listed passages use sunrise or sunset to refer euphemistically to directions of east or west. Of course, this makes those passages nonliteral references to sunrise or sunset. As I discussed above, this means nothing, because motion can be a tricky thing. Other astronomers and I speak today of sunrise and sunset. We also speak of the moon, planets, and stars rising and setting. In a very real sense, all these astronomical bodies rise and set. However, we also understand that it is the earth's rotation that causes this motion. There is nothing in these verses that compels one to believe that the Bible is geocentric or that the earth does not spin or that the earth is flat.

Furthermore, there is an inconsistency here. The flat-earth model today is one in which the sun moves in a circle around the sky. In this model, the sun doesn't pass below the horizon. Hence, in the modern flat-earth model, the sun neither rises nor sets. To explain the phenomenon of sunrise and sunset, flat-earthers appeal to flimflam about perspective merely causing the sun to *appear* to rise and set. Many critics of geocentrism say that sunrise and sunset are phenomenological. That is, the sun passes above or below the horizon due to the earth's rotation, causing the sun to *appear* to rise and set. Modern (non-flat-earth) geocentrists respond that the statements of the Bible are absolute, not of mere appearance. This puts flat-earthers in a bind. They insist on a hyper-literal interpretation of Scripture, but the moment they appeal to the appearance of sunrise or sunset with the sun not actually rising or setting, they have made a radical departure from their literal interpretation. Flat-earthers can't have it both ways.

Let me close this section with one verse the flat-earthers don't like to discuss — Psalm 99:1. In the King James Version, it reads:

> The LORD reigneth; let the people tremble: he sitteth between the cherubims; let the earth be moved.

Notice that this verse clearly states that the earth moves. No wonder flat-earthers never mention this verse. Please don't misunderstand — I'm not claiming that this verse proves heliocentrism. Far from it. Rather, I'm using it to point out that a hyper-literal approach to interpreting anything, but especially Scripture, can get one into trouble. Other verses noted above say that the earth doesn't move, but this verse says the earth does move, so how can one rectify this inconsistency? Context is king. And the context of this and other verses is not whether the earth literally moves, in the sense of changing location. When taken properly in context, these verses aren't teaching cosmology.

Joshua's Long Day

Probably the most important biblical passage to geocentrists is the account of the battle of Gibeon in Joshua 10:1–28.[4] Indeed, this always has been exhibit A in arguing for geocentrism, for people point out that in Joshua 10:12–14, Joshua commanded the sun (and moon) to stand still, not the earth. For instance, this was the biblical response to Galileo (though most of the case against Galileo came from Aristotle and Ptolemy). And as I pointed out in chapter 1, Luther allegedly cited this argument in response to Copernicus (though his first argument was that Copernicus was attempting to upset the established [Aristotelian and Ptolemaic] science of astronomy). In handling this objection to the earth rotating, most Christians argue that Joshua was speaking phenomenologically. That is, Joshua was using the language of appearance. In this sense, the sun appears to rise, move across the sky, and set, even though this apparent motion is caused by the earth's rotation. Therefore, if the earth's rotation stopped during the battle of Gibeon, then the sun would have appeared to stop in the sky. This is the way we speak today. Astronomers regularly speak of the sun rising and setting, as well as the moon and other astronomical bodies rising and setting, though I'm sure that none of them think that it is the sun, moon, and stars that are moving to cause these phenomena.

While this may be a satisfactory answer, perhaps a better answer is in the nature of motion itself. As I discussed above, motion is a tricky thing. All we can measure is relative motion. The concept of absolute motion requires knowledge of an absolute standard of rest. In physics, we assume that Mach's principle properly describes that absolute standard of rest.

---

4. I have discussed this passage previously, though not in the context of geocentrism. D. Faulkner, *The Created Cosmos: What the Bible Reveals About Astronomy* (Green Forest, AR: Master Books, 2016), p. 115–123.

But note that this is an *assumption*. Change the assumption, if even for just a moment, and the description changes. I can say that in a very real sense, the earth's rotation is what causes the apparent motion of the sun each day. But in another very real sense, I can say that the sun moves each day. Both are accurate statements. Both are true statements. There is no contradiction, because the two statements are made from different frames of reference. However, keep in mind that in physics, it does matter what the absolute standard is. For instance, the laws of physics are equivalent in inertial reference frames, that is, reference frames that aren't accelerating. In non-inertial (accelerating) reference frames, the laws of physics must be modified to describe observations. Physicists prefer to work with inertial frames of reference.

There is at least one verse in the Bible that expresses this relative motion in a surprising manner. Acts 27 gives the account of Paul's shipwreck while en route to Rome. In the Greek, verse 27 states that land approached the ship. In Young's Literal Translation (YLT), Acts 27:27 reads:

> And when the fourteenth night came — we being borne up and down in the Adria — toward the middle of the night the sailors were supposing that some country drew nigh to them.

Notice that the country (land) drew nigh to the ship, not that the ship drew nigh to the land. Most English translations scrap this literal reading in favor of the more familiar wording that the ship drew nigh to the land. However, there are a few exceptions, such as the Darby Translation, the Lexham English Bible, and the 1599 Geneva Bible. The latter two have footnotes that clarify that it was the ship that drew nigh to land. Was Luke, the author of the Book of Acts, teaching a ship-centric model here? Hardly, Luke merely was giving an alternate description — that from the perspective of someone on the ship, the land appeared to approach. As I said, motion can be a tricky thing.

We are given a very bare description and no physical explanation of what happened in Joshua 10:12–14. Whatever the nature of the cosmology and the miracle it required, it is a true description that the sun did stop for about a day. The only way that one can conclude that this passage teaches geocentrism is first to assume geocentrism. But that amounts to reading geocentrism into this passage. That is eisegesis, not exegesis.

Conclusion

Again, this chapter is not meant to be an exhaustive treatment of geocentrism. Rather, here I have demonstrated the vacancy of the flat-earth version of geocentrism. Many of the Bible verses which are claimed to teach geocentrism clearly do not. For more information on how flat-earthers treat the Bible, see chapters 10 and 11.

Chapter 8

NASA and Flat Earth

If the earth is a flat disk covered by a dome that contains all astronomical bodies, then the moon cannot orbit the earth. Nor can satellites orbit the earth. Therefore, there are no satellites. There are no astronauts. We haven't been to the moon. Then what about all those images from space, such as the International Space Station (ISS) and the photos and videos of astronauts on the moon in the late 1960s and early 1970s? Obviously, they all were faked. NASA is a sham organization that has lied about everything it supposedly has done. Flat-earthers spend considerable time and effort attempting to debunk all things from NASA and arguing against NASA.

What's In a Name?

Take NASA's name, for instance. Flat-earthers claim that in Hebrew, the word "NASA" means to deceive. Hence, this proves that from its founding, NASA admitted in plain sight that it deceives people. Only on the campy 1960s "Batman" TV show would such an outrageous clue make any sense. There are several Hebrew words in the Bible that are translated as "deceive" or some derivative thereof. The intended Hebrew word here is *nasha'*, which appears 16 times in the Old Testament. Twelve times *nasha'* is translated "deceive" or "deceived" (2 Kings 18:29, 19:10; 2 Chronicles 32:15; Isaiah 19:13, 36:14, 37:10; Jeremiah 4:10 [twice for emphasis so that it is translated "greatly deceived"], 29:8, 37:9, 49:16; Obadiah 1:3, 7). In its first appearance (Genesis 3:13), it is translated as "beguiled." However, in Psalm 55:15, *nasha'* is translated "seize," and in

Jeremiah 32:9, it is translated as "utterly." Why the difference in these two verses? It's probably because of the semantic range of the word and the nuance of context. In either case, the meaning clearly isn't to deceive.

But is there a similarity between NASA and *nasha'*, and if so, does it imply a connection between the two? Most people say the acronym NASA yet have no idea what NASA stands for (National Aeronautics and Space Administration). Unlike other government agencies, such as the FBI and CIA, we tend to pronounce NASA as a word rather than saying the letters that spell it out. This has lent to thinking of NASA as a word rather than initials for a government agency. Notice that this has led to pronouncing the first letter *A* in NASA as a short *a* and the second letter *A* as a short *e*. We pronounce the two consonants as we normally do, with the accent on the first syllable. However, compare that to how the Hebrew word *nasha'* is pronounced. The first consonant is pronounced the same way that we say our letter *n*. But the second consonant is pronounced as "sh." Furthermore, both *a*'s are pronounced as we would say "awe." Finally, the accent is on the second syllable, not the first. If most people heard the Hebrew word *nasha'* properly pronounced, they wouldn't make any association with NASA. Therefore, the flat-earther claim that NASA means to deceive in Hebrew is a specious argument.

Orbiting in the Thermosphere

One of the complaints lodged by flat-earthers is that satellites in low-earth orbit would travel through what astronomers call the thermosphere, where the temperature typically exceeds 2,000 degrees C. Since this is above the melting points of many substances, such as metals, that satellites are made of, flat-earthers argue that if satellites were real, they would be destroyed by the heat where they supposedly orbit.

At first glance, this seems like a reasonable objection, but with closer scrutiny, it falls apart. Do flat-earthers think that there is a thermosphere and that the temperature in the thermosphere is so high? Flat-earthers never comment on whether they believe that these temperatures exist at high altitude. Why should they believe that the thermosphere exists? Who has told us that there is a thermosphere and its temperature is so high? Why, it's the same scientists who supposedly have lied about so many other things, such as that there are satellites. So why should flat-earthers believe what they otherwise consider to be unreliable sources about this matter? And look at the name — thermo*sphere*. Many flat-earthers use the term "thermosphere" in this argument with no sense of irony. Flat-earthers probably don't believe that either the thermosphere or its high temperatures exist, so raising this objection makes about as much sense as the Sadducees, who didn't believe in the Resurrection, asking Jesus a hypothetical question about the Resurrection (Matthew 22:23–28). Apparently, flat-earthers hold scientists in such contempt that they think scientists are stupid enough to create a fake structure for the earth's atmosphere that makes it impossible for fake satellites to orbit. That doesn't make any sense.

But the greatest problem here is that flat-earthers have confused temperature with heat. They aren't the same thing. We all learned in grade-school science that heat is a form of energy. We also learned that when an object is heated, the particles making up the object move more quickly. Any moving object contains kinetic energy, the energy of motion. The kinetic energy of the random motion of many particles on the microscopic scale is the phenomenon of heat. This understanding comes from the kinetic theory of heat, a very robust, well-tested theory in physics. Temperature is a measure of the average kinetic energy of the particles involved. On the other hand, heat is the sum of the kinetic energy of all the particles making up an object. We can relate heat and temperature by multiplying the average heat per particle (which temperature is a measure of) by the number of particles to find the heat.

In a gas, such as in the thermosphere, we can find the heat density by multiplying the average kinetic energy per particle by the density of the gas. And this is where the confusion of flat-earthers comes in. The thermosphere is very rarified, making it a very hard vacuum. At the altitude of low-earth orbit, the density of the gas is 10^{-11}–10^{-12} kg/m³. The density of air at sea level is a little more than 1.22 kg/m³, so the density of the thermosphere is between one hundred billionth and one trillionth of the density of the air we breathe. The air around us has a temperature of about 300 K. The temperature of the thermosphere is typically 2,500 K, nearly ten times greater than the air temperature we experience. Since temperature is a measure of the average kinetic energy of particles, then the gas particles in the thermosphere have average kinetic energy nearly ten times greater than the average kinetic energy of the air particles around us. However, since the density of air near the ground is 10–12 orders of magnitude greater than the density of gas in the thermosphere, the energy density of the air around is 10–100 billion times greater than the gas in the thermosphere. Therefore, while the thermosphere is at high temperature, there is very little heat in the thermosphere. This is a paradox only to those who don't understand the difference between heat and temperature.

We can look at this another way. If an object cooler than air temperature is immersed in air around us, the object is warmed by collisions with the particles of air. As air molecules collide with the object, they transfer some of their kinetic energy (heat) to the object. Each collision delivers a microscopic amount of heat, but the collisions are so numerous and frequent that they represent a large heat gain. This process continues until the object reaches the same temperature as the air. At that point, half the collisions heat the object, while the other half cool the object, so there is no heat gain, and, hence, no further change in temperature. The presence or absence of the sun changes this. If an object is lit by bright sunshine, the object may rise to a temperature greater than the air temperature, whereupon the object loses heat to the air. On the other hand, if it is night and the sky is clear, the object will emit infrared (IR) radiation, often cooling it below the air temperature. The air will heat the object as before, but there will be a temperature differential. If the temperature of the object cools below the dewpoint, dew or frost forms.

What happens to an orbiting spacecraft? When above the sunlit side of the earth, sunlight will heat the spacecraft, but only on the side that is facing the sun. At the same time, the spacecraft will cool by emitting IR radiation. The sunlit side of the spacecraft can get very warm, but the dark side remains cool. The dark side of a satellite can have a temperature far below freezing. When the spacecraft enters the earth's shadow (every low-earth orbit satellite spends nearly half the time there), both sides of the spacecraft cool. What about the heating effect of the gas particles? The gas is so rarefied that collisions with the spacecraft rarely happen. Each collision will deliver a microscopic amount of heat, but there are so few collisions that the amount of heat gain is swamped by the much larger heat loss due to IR emission. Therefore, satellites orbiting in the thermosphere are in no danger of melting. This is a bogus argument on the part of flat-earthers.

Van Allen Belts

Flat-earthers frequently bring up the Van Allen belts around the earth as proof that we never sent astronauts to the moon. Flat-earthers generally term the Van Allen belts as "deadly," and so claim that the Apollo astronauts could not have survived a journey through the Van Allen belts. What are the Van Allen belts? The Van Allen belts are fast-moving charged particles (mostly protons, electrons, and helium nuclei) trapped by the earth's magnetic field. The inner belt extends from a few hundred miles to a few thousand miles above the earth's surface. Beyond the inner belt there is a safe zone with an outer belt from about 8,000 miles to nearly 40,000 miles above the earth's surface. The outer belt consists mostly of electrons. Both belts are toroidal-shaped with a tilt to the earth's equator. The inner belt comes closest to the earth over the South Atlantic Ocean, a region called the South Atlantic Anomaly.

Exposure to fast-moving charged particles pose a risk to living things, but how significant is the risk? Contrary to the misconception of flat-earthers, the risk is cumulative, so a single exposure to the belts is not deadly. There are several ways to ameliorate the risk. One way is to avoid the belts. Astronauts in low-earth orbit effectively do this by orbiting below the inner belt. The trajectories to the moon of the Apollo missions were chosen carefully to avoid maximum exposure. The paths took the Apollo astronauts through the least dangerous part of the inner belt and avoided the outer belt altogether by passing above or below it. And the Apollo astronauts traveled most quickly (25,000 mph) through the inner belt, thus reducing the length of time spent there. Finally, the skin and instruments lining the walls of the Command Module of the Apollo spacecraft offered some shielding. Ironically, the earth's magnetic field that creates the Van Allen belts also shields the earth from fast-moving charged particles from the sun. But once past the outer belt, the Apollo astronauts were left unprotected from those particles. These particles from the sun proved to be a greater risk than the Van Allen belts. All the manned missions to the moon carried dosimeters to assess the exposure during the trip. The measurements showed acceptable risks, much less than the maximum annual exposure deemed acceptable for people who work with radioactivity.

Part of the confusion about the Van Allen belts comes from discussions of possible future manned missions to the moon and the risks the belts could pose for those missions. Our society has changed from the heyday of the Apollo program a half-century ago. We seem far more squeamish today about the risk the belts could pose to humans than we did back then. That attitude in the 1960s was that the Van Allen belts were just one of the risks that Apollo astronauts took when they accepted the job. We now seem to think that we need to agonize over any risk, no matter how small that risk may be. However, a more realistic concern is the effect that radiation exposure has on modern electronics. Far more electronic devices today are digital and much more compact than they were a half-century ago. With the larger analog devices back then, there was far less risk of damage. Furthermore, the far greater reliance of missions on such devices today could prove disastrous if there were a failure of one of the components due to radiation damage. Since this potential difficulty did not exist in the Apollo program, concern about future manned missions to the moon hardly proves that there were no manned missions in the past.

Loss of Technology That Took Us to the Moon

Flat-earthers sometimes seize upon news stories relating that we have somehow lost the plans for the Apollo spacecraft and the Saturn V rocket (the rocket that launched Apollo astronauts to the moon). They intone how could this happen, if we really went to the moon? To anyone who has worked at a vast agency or bureaucracy, the answer is easy. For people who have no knowledge of how such large projects work, it is easy to think that meticulous records are kept. But when you have huge numbers of people and large amounts of money and effort spent on a project, it is very easy for the paperwork to be left behind and forgotten when the project is completed. But for the Apollo program, there were even more factors. There was urgency to get the project completed. While there were overall plans for the hardware involved, those plans were very fluid. Many decisions to alter the plans were made on the fly. With important deadlines to meet, the documentation of those changes was often left unattended. NASA contracted the actual construction of the components to different private companies. Many of the necessitated changes to the construction remained undocumented within those companies. There were so few Apollo spacecraft constructed, and with modifications made to the spacecraft throughout the Apollo program, each unit amounted to a custom job. When the Apollo program ended, the engineers that worked out the many details quickly disbanded, and its members dispersed to many other projects. Many of the manufacturing plants closed or were redirected to other projects. Molds for parts and other materials no longer deemed necessary were discarded. Many companies involved with the Apollo program closed or merged with other companies. Given these considerations, it isn't at all surprising that no one seems to know where, or even, if, all the detailed plans for the Apollo spacecraft exist today.

These stories about the loss of the plans for the Apollo spacecraft began circulating about 25 years after the conclusion of the Apollo program. It never seems to occur to the critics that if we desired to return to the moon, would we want to do so with plans that are now 50 years old? Imagine manufacturing automobiles today with the specifications and designs used 50 years ago. At the very least, such cars would fail emissions, fuel economy, and safety standards that exist today, making such automobile manufacture infeasible. This is why when Volkswagen introduced the new Beetle in 1997, it was very different from the original Beetle. Most people are not content with the way houses were built 50 years ago (many of them are too small to suit most people's tastes). We certainly aren't content with the way television and other entertainment was delivered a half-century ago. It is folly to think that we would return to the moon today using 50-year-old plans.

Loss of Apollo Mission Telemetry

Related to the above topic, flat-earthers have capitalized on the missing Apollo 11 telemetry tapes. The live broadcast from the lunar surface on the evening of July 20, 1969, featured ghostly images of the astronauts. People just assumed that the live feed was as good as the image could be. Almost no one knew that the Apollo 11 carried a superb camera that produced very high-quality video. That video was downloaded at tracking stations and recorded to one-inch-wide tapes for backup in case the live feed failed. While the video from the moon was high quality, the format of the video was completely incompatible with television broadcast. Therefore, the live video was converted to a format compatible with television. The conversion amounted to a television camera focused on a screen displaying the high-quality video coming from the moon. It was this conversion that produced the serious downgrade in quality.

Shortly after the year 2000, a team of enthusiasts realized the possibility of digitally processing the original tapes to provide the first clear video of the historic Apollo 11 moonwalk. All they needed was those tapes. What had happened to the tapes? Once recorded, the tapes were sent to the Goddard Space Flight Center in Greenbelt, Maryland, from which the tapes eventually were shipped to the Washington National Records Center (WNRC) in Suitland, Maryland. Currently, the WNRC has 789,000 square feet (18 acres) of space and is capable of containing 3.9 million cubic feet of records.[1] A diligent search was launched for the tapes, but they were never found. The questions raised over this failure to find the tapes resulted in an official report.[2] Of course, flat-earthers have spun this as part of a nefarious plot. According to the flat-earthers, the original video tapes never existed because the Apollo 11 was staged. Furthermore, flat-earthers argue, if such high-resolution tapes ever existed, NASA knows that flat-earthers could easily use the video to prove that the event was staged. Therefore, the need to concoct the story of the lost tapes.

This argument from the flat-earthers gives far too much credit to bureaucracy. There were many thousands of magnetic tapes used in the Apollo program. The original tapes went through several sets of hands. By the time that the tapes arrived at the WNRC, it is likely that the person handling the tapes had no idea what he or she had. All the people directly involved with recording, handling, transferring, and storing the tapes have long since retired. Many are deceased. Those yet alive probably have faulty memories of their actions, if they remember them at all. What about records of the tapes? Again, recordkeeping in such a vast bureaucracy isn't nearly as good as many people seem to think.

---

1. I keep imagining the vast warehouse at the end of the *Raiders of the Lost Ark*, the first Indiana Jones movie.
2. https://www.hq.nasa.gov/alsj/a11/Apollo_11_TV_Tapes_Report.pdf.

What happened to the tapes? One theory is that the tapes may have been recycled. That happened a lot back then. Tapes were expensive, and if the information on a tape was deemed no longer necessary, it often was taped over.[3] It's entirely conceivable that a person asked to retrieve some tapes for recycling may have not known the historic nature of the data on tapes he had selected. The tapes may still exist, if not at the WNRC, perhaps somewhere else. If the tapes ever do show up, it may not be easy finding a machine capable of playing the tapes — that is very old technology now. Furthermore, tapes degrade with time, so we don't know what condition the tapes are in. In hindsight, this has been a tragedy of errors. However, hindsight, as they say, is always 20-20.

Are All Astronauts Freemasons?

If there are no astronauts, then what about all those people who claimed to have gone into space? The number is in the hundreds. Twelve men have said that they even walked on the moon, and another 12 claimed to have orbited the moon. Are all these people lying? According to flat-earthers, yes. Why would all these astronauts lie about such a thing? The stock answer is that *all* astronauts are Freemasons. Since flat-earthers believe that Freemasonry is at the center of the vast conspiracy to convince people that the earth is a sphere, this explanation makes sense to them. But have *all* astronauts been Freemasons? Flat-earthers typically reply with evidence that *some* astronauts have been Freemasons. For instance, at least one official photograph of the Apollo 11 crew shows a masonic ring on Buzz Aldrin's ring finger of his left hand. And Freemason publications have proudly proclaimed that the second man on the moon was one of their members. There are other examples of astronauts who indeed have been Freemasons. This is indisputable.

But does this prove that *all* astronauts have been Freemasons? After all, the claim by flat-earthers is that *all* astronauts have been Freemasons, as if being a Freemason is a prerequisite to becoming an astronaut. Demonstrating that *some* astronauts have been Freemasons does not prove that *all* astronauts have been Freemasons. It is incredibly poor

---

3. Having recorded quite a bit of programming from TV with VHS, I recall on several occasions recording over something that I didn't want to lose. And I had only a few VHS tapes to manage.

logic to suggest otherwise. Given the large number of astronauts, people that are relatively accomplished in their achievements, it would be very strange if *no* astronauts were Freemasons. There is no evidence that Neil Armstrong, the *first* man on the moon, was a Freemason. If Armstrong were a Mason, why would Freemasons have made such a big deal about the *second* man on the moon being one of their members? Wouldn't it be more impressive to claim the first man on the moon as a member? When confronted with this question, some flat-earthers respond with the claim that some astronauts choose to keep their Freemason membership secret. Apparently, in the weird logic of flat-earthism, no evidence of being a Freemason and even a denial of being a Freemason constitutes evidence of being a Freemason. It is impossible to refute such bogus logic.

By the way, the belief that NASA faked the Apollo moon landings has been around longer than the modern flat-earth movement. A few cranks were claiming we didn't go to the moon shortly after the Apollo 11 mission in 1969. However, those ideas didn't get much attention until after the Fox Network broadcast a documentary about this conspiracy theory in 2001. The Apollo moon landing hoax theory focused on the idea that NASA faked merely the moon landings. Proponents of this theory seemed to accept that there were satellites and that astronauts had orbited the earth. But now flat-earthers have hijacked the moon-landing conspiracy and have combined it with their denial of spaceflight to promote their peculiar cosmology.

Faked Moon Landing Photos

One of the major stock in trade of flat-earthers and others who don't believe that we've landed on the moon is the many supposed faked photos of lunar landings. There are so many examples of these that I can't take the time and space here to discuss them all. However, I will discuss a sampling of them. Consider the meme reproduced here. The text in the meme suggests that in the photograph, the Lunar Excursion Module (LEM) is making its final descent onto the lunar surface. Of course, this raises the obvious problem: if the LEM is about to land, who was already on the surface to take a photo of the LEM's descent? We are supposed to believe that the clever people at NASA were too dense to anticipate this problem. The answer to this is easy. This isn't a photo of the Apollo 12 LEM making its final descent. Here is the original photo, from which this very poor-quality blowup in the meme was obviously made. Notice in the original photograph and in the meme the moon's curvature. The moon's curvature indicates that this photo was taken from considerable height above the moon. Also, notice the craters on the lunar surface. Some of those craters are several miles across, which also indicates considerable height above the moon. This photo was taken out of a window of the Command Module (CM) by Dick Gordon, the CM pilot shortly after the LEM separated from the CM. The LEM, carrying Pete Conrad and Alan Bean, would

Faked moon landing meme

Actual Apollo 12 photo

soon begin its descent to the lunar surface. This photograph has not been altered, other than cropping and blowing up, but it has been greatly misinterpreted by those trying to prove that NASA faked the Apollo missions.

This is another meme with the same message. You can see the LEM as before, with the same claim that this photo was taken just before the

HERE IS A PICTURE OF JUST BEFORE NASA LANDED ON THE MOON.

THE ONLY PROBLEM IS....WHO TOOK THE PICTURE?

mematic.net

Another faked moon landing meme

LEM touched down, again asking the provocative question of who was already on the lunar surface to take the photograph. This one is even easier to debunk. The moon's curvature is more noticeable and the large crater to the left is readily identifiable. It is the crater Eratosthenes. Since the diameter of Eratosthenes is more than 35 miles, this photograph was obviously taken from considerable altitude. At first, I thought that this photograph might have been taken from the CM shortly after the LEM had separated, just like the last example. However, a quick search produced this photograph of Eratosthenes.

Eratosthenes

Careful examination of the orientation of the photograph and the shadows on the lunar surface reveals that this is the same photograph. Except that the LEM is missing from the original. Obviously, someone has altered this photograph, but it wasn't NASA. Apparently, someone inserted the LEM in this photograph to produce a meme that supposedly demonstrates that NASA faked the Apollo missions. But how does a faked photograph prove that NASA fakes photographs? If anything, this doctored photograph is evidence of the lies of people who claim that NASA lies.

What would motivate a person to create such a false meme? The only reason that comes to mind is that this is a prank. If so, then the person who created this meme knew what he was doing and must be having great delight that so many people so readily accepted this meme as genuine evidence that NASA lies. This sort of thing is not difficult to debunk. It is sad that flat-earthers so readily accept such a poor argument simply because they want NASA to be such an evil agency. If flat-earthers would exercise just a little of the skepticism that they have for NASA on the arguments for flat earth, they might come to realize that they have been duped.

This next meme shows a photograph of Buzz Aldrin descending the ladder of the LEM to step out on the lunar surface. The upper part of the meme shows a photograph of the moon with the location of the Apollo 11 landing site marked. The meme further states that the moon

Another faked moon landing meme

Another faked moon landing meme

keeps one face toward the earth (due to synchronous rotation, as discussed in chapter 5). Since the Apollo 11 landing site is near the center of the side of the moon that we perpetually see, the earth ought to be high overhead from that site. Therefore, the meme asks how the earth could be so low in the sky, just above the horizon. This appears to be a very good question. Of course, the implication is that all of this is faked, and NASA placed the earth in the sky, but that it never occurred to the clever people at NASA that the situation that they faked is impossible. That doesn't make sense.

Before answering this question, consider the next meme. It shows the same photo, along with some sort of enhancement, indicating that the photograph has been altered to put the moon there. Again, the implication is that NASA faked the photograph but goofed in one major detail.

Buzz Aldrin descending

Except that NASA didn't fake the photograph. Here is the original photograph from NASA of Buzz Aldrin descending. The only difference is that the earth isn't present in the sky near the horizon. That is because the earth was high overhead at the time. If

NASA didn't fake the photograph, who did? Obviously, once again, it was the person who created the meme. Again, this person had to know he was faking the photo, so what was his motivation? Again, the most obvious answer is that he did this as a joke to see how many people he could sucker into believing this was proof that NASA fakes everything.

These memes from the Internet weren't difficult to refute. Admittedly, some of the other memes are a bit more difficult to debunk, but suffice it to say that the only trickery going on here is on the part of those who want to discredit NASA. It is ironic that flat-earthers are unwilling to consider anything that NASA says because they are convinced that NASA lies about everything. But how do flat-earthers know that NASA lies about everything? Because they've listened to liars telling them that NASA lies about everything. It really is quite sad, because many of the people flat-earthers unquestionably follow are playing them for fools.

The Changing Size of North America

Flat-earthers frequently criticize NASA by displaying images of the earth taken from space showing surface features having various sizes. For instance, the most common examples are images taken at different times with the earth's size about the same but North America appearing in different sizes in the images, such as in this meme. Flat-earthers argue that since North America obviously has a fixed size, if North America

has different sizes in the images, it must be that NASA has faked the images. At first glance, this appears to be a good argument — why would North America have different sizes in different images when the earth is the same size in each image? But think about this for a minute. The clever people at NASA supposedly went to great trouble to produce these computer-generated images, but no one on the team noticed that North America kept changing size? That doesn't make sense.

In search of a more plausible answer, I took these two photographs of a 12-inch-diameter globe using a Nikon D3200 camera. For the photograph on the left, I used an AF-S DX NIKKOR 55-200mm f/4-5.6G ED VR II lens zoomed in all the way. I adjusted the distance so that the globe nearly filled the frame vertically. The distance required to do this was 16½ feet from the globe's center. For the image on the right, I used an AF-P DX NIKKOR 18-55mm f/3.5-5.6G lens, the standard lens that comes with the camera. I zoomed that lens all the way out, which allowed me to get as close as possible to the globe while matching the size of the globe in the image on the left. The distance required to do that was 16 inches from the globe's center. Therefore, the photograph on the left was taken at a distance more than 12 times greater than the photograph on the right, though the globe appears about the same size. For both photographs, the camera was on a tripod adjusted so that the lens was on a horizontal line passing through the center of the globe.

Notice that North America appears much larger in the photograph on the right than it does in the photograph on the left. How is that

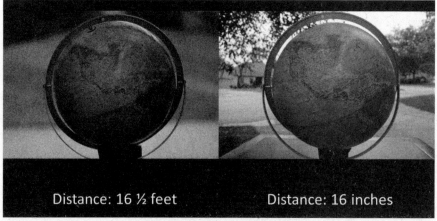

Distance: 16 ½ feet   Distance: 16 inches

A globe from different distances

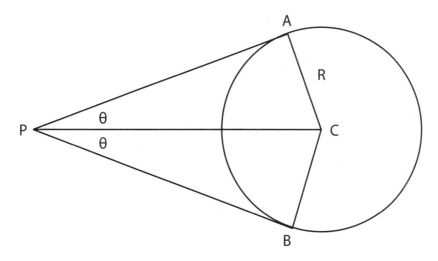

Drawing of a globe cap

possible? The accompanying figure illustrates the situation. The circle represents the globe. The point *P* represents the location of the camera lens at the distance *PC* from the center of the globe. The lines *PA* and *PB* are tangent to the globe. Notice that points on the circle to the right of points *A* and *B* are blocked from view at point *P*. The only points on the circle visible from point *P* are those points between points *A* and *B* on the left side of the circle. That is, less than half the circumference of the circle is visible from point *P*. This is a two-dimensional representation. In three dimensions, the portion of the globe visible at point *P* will be the spherical cap inscribed by a cone with its apex at point *P* having apex angle of *2θ* and bounded top and bottom by the lines *PA* and *PB*. The result is that less than half of the globe's surface is visible. Notice that as the distance *PC* increases, the amount of area visible increases. At very great distance, the amount of area ought to approach the entire half of the globe facing the point *P*.

Let me quantify this. The lines *CA* and *CB* are radii of the globe. Let that radius be *R*. The triangles *PAC* and *PBC* are congruent right triangles. Hence,

$$sin\ \theta = \frac{R}{PC}$$

Since the globe is 12 inches in diameter, R = 6 inches. In the photograph on the left, the distance PC = 16½ feet = 198 inches. Therefore, in the photograph on the left, θ = 1.7 degrees. The area of a spherical cap is

$$A = 2\pi R^2 \,(1 - \cos\,\theta)$$

where θ is the complement of θ. It may be more instructive to determine how much of the hemisphere facing point P is visible. The area of a hemisphere is $2\pi R^2$, so the fraction of how much of the hemisphere facing the camera that is visible is given by $(1 - \cos\,\theta)$. For the photograph on the left, that fraction is 0.97. Therefore, 97 percent of the hemisphere facing the camera is visible. The situation is different for the photograph on the right. For that view, the distance PC = 16 inches, resulting in θ = 22 degrees. The amount of the hemisphere facing the camera that is visible is only 63 percent.

Taking the ratio of those two percentages, it follows that the photograph on the left shows 155 percent more surface area of the globe than the photograph on the right does. How can this be, given that the globe in either photograph appears to be about the same size? The answer is that the globe is not the same size in the two photographs. Rather, the *portion* of the globe that is visible appears to be the same size. Remember that what we see is a spherical cap that encompasses less than half the surface of the globe. And the sizes of the spherical caps visible in the two photographs is different. The problem is that since what we see appears as circles about the same size, our minds incorrectly assume that we are seeing the entire half of the globe in either photograph.

Examining the two photos demonstrates that far more area is visible in the left photograph than in the right photograph. In the left photograph, all of North America is visible, including Alaska, part of the Bering Sea, and part of Siberia. But in the right photograph, only a portion of eastern Alaska is visible, with none of the Bering Sea and Siberia visible. In the photograph on the left, we can see the North Pole, all of Greenland, with ocean east of Greenland, as well as Iceland, and parts of Europe, such as the British Isles. But in the right photograph, only part of Greenland is visible, but none of the oceans beyond or any of Europe are visible. In the left photograph, one can see part of Africa, but none of Africa is visible in the right photograph. In the left photograph, one can see South America, except for the extreme southern tip. One also can see the South Atlantic Ocean east of South America. But in the right photograph, much of southern South America is obscured, as is most of the South Atlantic Ocean. Along the bottom of the left photograph, one can see far south of the Tropic of Capricorn, but in the right photograph, very little south of the Tropic of Capricorn is visible. Continuing around, on the left side of the left photograph, one can see the Hawaiian Islands, as well as the entire word "ocean" labeling the Pacific Ocean. But in the right photograph, the Hawaiian Islands are not visible, nor are the first two letters of "ocean."

Since the globes in the two photographs *appear* to have the same size, but the photograph on the left contains more surface area of the globe than the photograph on the right, the surface features in the left photograph must appear shrunk compared to those same features in the photograph on the right. This explains why North America appears smaller in the photograph on the left than in the photograph on the right. I have not employed a trick here. The only trick is in our minds when we see the portions of the globe that are visible presented as the same size and we *assume* that we are seeing the entire half of the globe on the same scale. However, when we view a globe from different distances, the portion of the globe that we see is different.

In similar manner, the satellite photographs that show varying sizes of terrestrial features at different times come from different spacecraft orbiting at different distances from the earth. Therefore, rather than proving that these photographs have been faked, the changing size of earth's features proves that the photographs are not faked because they show exactly what we expect to see if the earth is a globe photographed from different distances.

Conclusion

There are far more images ostensibly from NASA out there on the Internet that supposedly demonstrate that NASA fakes everything. There are even more videos that attempt much the same. Obviously, a book cannot refute the videos, nor can a reasonable-length treatment of the false claims of flat-earthers on this front be exhaustive. However, the sample presented here demonstrates how shoddy these attempts are.

There is a documentary called *A Funny Thing Happened on the Way to the Moon*. A portion of that documentary features a discussion between the ground crew and astronauts aboard an Apollo spacecraft on the way to the moon. The narrator of the documentary claims that the conversation between Houston and the astronauts reveals how they planned to fake a live broadcast of the earth from space. Apparently, many people watching the documentary find this part of it compelling. However, if one ignores what the narrator says and listens to what the NASA personnel say, one easily sees that this is not the case. That is, the narrator is lying to the audience. I am amazed that *anyone* finds this documentary convincing. I suspect that the makers of the documentary put this together as a prank. It makes a good study on how propaganda works.

Chapter 9

Miscellaneous Claims about Flat Earth

The Shape of the Sun and Moon

In support of their model, flat-earthers make many odd claims. For instance, flat-earthers generally believe that the sun and moon are round disks rather than spheres. This is odd, because most ancient civilizations thought that the sun and moon were spheres, even if they may have thought that the earth was flat. Why do modern flat-earthers think that the sun and moon are flat, too? That isn't clear. It could be that they fear the argument by analogy that the ancient Greeks used (as discussed in chapter 1). That is, since the moon and sun are spherical, the earth must be spherical, too. This is, at best, a weak argument, so there is no need to fear it. Or perhaps modern flat-earthers think that the argument by analogy is rigorous, reasoning that since the earth is flat, the sun and moon must be flat, too. But, again, that puts them at odds with many ancient flat-earth civilizations. More likely, modern flat-earthers have adopted the idea that the sun and moon are flat because Samuel Rowbotham, the founder of the modern flat-earth movement in the 19th century, taught that the sun and moon were flat.

As discussed in chapter 5, there are several observations that indicate that the sun and moon are spheres. Let us examine another one here. The sun always appears round in the sky.[1] A spherical sun always appears

---

1. The only exception is when the sun is very low in the sky. When so low in the sky, differential refraction can flatten the sun's image, making it appear slightly wider than it is tall.

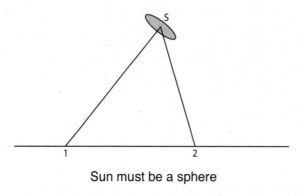

Sun must be a sphere

round, regardless of its location in the sky. But what if the sun were a disk? See the figure. A disk can appear round, but only if viewed from a point on the axis of the disk, the axis being a line perpendicular to the plane of the disk and passing through the disk's center. This is the case for an observer at point 1 in the figure. But what about an observer not at point 1, say at point 2? It is easy to see that to a person at point 2, the sun would appear as an ellipse, not a circle. But the situation gets worse. Throughout the day, the sun's position changes. To maintain its round shape, the sun must pivot to keep the observer on the axis of the disk. However, this would be the situation for only one unique place on earth. For all other locations, the sun would always appear elliptical, with the most radical departures from circularity at the greatest distances from the favored location. Furthermore, the elliptical shape would vary throughout the day as the sun pivoted to keep the favored location so favored. However, this is not what we observe — the sun always appears round. The only shape that maintains a constant round shape regardless of orientation is a sphere. Therefore, the sun must be a sphere.

A similar argument applies to the moon. While a full moon looks round, we can't always see the moon's limb on the dark portion of the moon. This is particularly true at quarter phases (when we see half of the moon lit) and gibbous phases (where more than half of the moon appears lit). However, at crescent phases, we often can see the dark portion of the moon,[2] which clearly reveals that the moon appears round.

---

2. This phenomenon is called *earthshine*. As seen from the moon, the earth goes through phases that are shifted by 180 degrees from lunar phases. That is, when the moon is in the crescent phase, the earth, as seen on the moon, is nearly full. Being four times larger, the earth has 16 times the surface area of the moon. In addition, the earth reflects light better than the moon does, so the "full earth" is more than 30 times brighter than the full moon. Hence, when the moon is a crescent, the dark portion of the lunar landscape is flooded with bright light from the earth, making it visible on earth.

At any rate, flat-earthers don't dispute that the moon appears round, because they generally claim that the moon is a flat disk. However, a disk-shaped moon would appear circular only to observers that view the moon along the axis of its disk. As the disk-shaped moon moves across the sky throughout the night, a disk-shaped moon would maintain its circular appearance only if its axis retained this orientation for the observer. That is, to appear as a circle, the disk must pivot as it moves across the sky. However, for observers at other locations, the moon will not appear as a circle. How much the moon would deviate from a circle depends upon how far apart the different observers are, as well as the details of which flat-earth model one adopts.

Let me illustrate this with an example. In the quantitative flat-earth models that I have seen, the moon's disk is 32 miles across and 3,000 miles above the earth's surface. On April 30, 2018, the moon was full. When full, the moon is up all night. At local midnight, the full moon on that date was directly overhead (at the *zenith*) for observers at a latitude of 10 degrees north of the equator (this is called the *sublunar point*). Suppose that at local midnight, a person on the same meridian of longitude as the sublunar point, but at latitude 53.5 degrees north (the latitude of Belfast), sees a round moon. To see the moon as round, the observer at this latitude must be on the axis of the moon's disk (see the figure). There are 69 statute miles per degree of latitude, so the observer at 53.5 degrees north latitude must be about 3,000 miles from the point where the moon is directly overhead. Hence, the moon, the observer at 53.5 north latitude, and the sublunar point form a 45-45-90 triangle, with the right angle at the sublunar point.

Now consider a second observer on the same meridian but at 33.5 south latitude, 3,000 miles south of the sublunar point. This second observer, the moon, and the sublunar point will form another triangle congruent with the first triangle, again with the right angle at

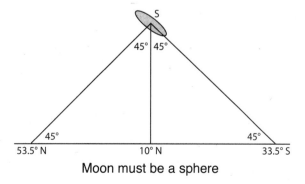

Moon must be a sphere

the sublunar point. Therefore, the two observers and the moon will form another 45-45-90 triangle similar to the other two triangles, but with the right angle at the moon. Since the moon's disk is perpendicular to the leg of the first observer, the second observer, who lies along the other leg, will view the moon's disk from its edge. Therefore, to the second observer, the moon will appear as a line. People farther south will see the backside of the moon's disk. This obviously is not the case, so the flat-earth model cannot be correct. This argument about the moon's apparent shape in the flat-earth model also applies to the sun.

This isn't a problem with the conventional understanding of cosmology. If the moon is a sphere 240,000 miles away, then the parallax effect of looking at the moon from different parts of the earth will be minimal. The widest possible separation would be 8,000 miles. This results in a maximum angle equal to the arctangent of 8,000/240,000, which is 1.9 degrees. This would allow us to peek around the limb of the moon a little. This is an example of diurnal libration. I discussed librations in latitude and longitude in chapter 5. These two librations are greater than diurnal libration.

One of the arguments flat-earthers advance against the moon being spherical is the way that the moon reflects the sun's light. They reason that if the moon is illuminated by the sun, then there ought to be a bright spot in the center of the full moon. Since the full moon appears uniformly lit, flat-earthers conclude that the moon must not be a sphere reflecting the sun's light. In this argument, flat-earthers assume that the moon acts as a mirrored ball, similar to the decorative gazing balls people sometimes place in their yards. We astronomers are partly to blame for this misunderstanding because we often describe the moon as reflecting the sun's light. More properly, we ought to say that the moon's surface scatters light from the sun. Most surfaces are rough to the extent that light bounces off in all directions, thus scattering the light. This is why we generally don't see our reflections on most surfaces, including flat ones, such as walls.

What is required for a surface to truly reflect light? First, the surface must be smooth. Glass panes are smooth, and so they reflect a small percent of the light that falls on them. Light passing through the glass is usually much brighter than the reflected light, so we don't notice the reflected light. However, if one side of the pane has much greater illumination than the other side, one can easily see reflections on the lit side. For instance, during the day, it is difficult to view the inside of a room from outside a window because so much light is reflected off the sunlit side of the panes. On the other hand, it is easy to look out the window from the room. But at night, for a well-lit room, the situation is reversed — one can easily see their reflection in a window while inside the room, making it difficult to look out the window at night (and making it easy for neighbors to see in). A second factor that aids in reflection is to coat the smooth surface with a reflective substance, such as a metal. This is why highly polished, smooth metal surfaces, such as chrome, reflect well. This also is why we coat mirrors with a metallic film. A mirrored ball, such as a gazing ball, forms an image of the sun, making a bright spot at its center. However, the lunar surface is very rugged, so it doesn't have a smooth surface. Furthermore, the lunar surface doesn't have a reflective coating. Therefore, the lunar surface appears uniformly illuminated when full.

To illustrate this, I took the accompanying photograph. The photograph shows four croquet balls with a foam rubber ball in the middle. The croquet balls are smooth and have a glossy finish. Even though the croquet balls are scuffed from much use, they reflect light reasonably well (and scatter light, too). The scene was illuminated by a floodlight, and I took the photograph as close to the beam of light as I could without blocking it with my shadow. Notice that each croquet ball has a bright spot near its center. These are images of the floodlight as described above. However, notice that the foam rubber ball is uniformly illuminated. This is because it has a rough, unreflective surface. The moon has a similar appearance because its surface is rough and nonreflective, too.

Four croquet balls and one rubber ball in the middle

How Far Away Is the Sun?

Crepuscular rays, or sunbeams, are rays of sunlight between gaps in clouds that appear to radiate from the point in the sky where the sun is located. Flat-earthers often produce photographs of crepuscular rays in support of their model. The illustration here is from Dubay's proof number 125.[3] Flat-earthers argue that since these rays converge on the sun, it proves that the sun is only a short distance above the clouds. The word "converge" is key because such photos are the result of convergence due to perspective. Parallel lines appear to converge in the distance (at the vanishing point) as a matter of perspective. One example of this phenomenon is the rails of a straight section of train track on level ground. The rails appear to converge on the horizon. Of course, this is an aspect of perspective,

Sunray triangle

as the rails don't actually intersect. Another example of convergence is the top and bottom of a rectangular side of a building. The top and bottom are parallel, but they appear to converge in the distance. The difference between this example and the rails of a train track is that the edges of a building are usually truncated long before reaching the vanishing point. If the sun is very far away, then its rays are virtually traveling parallel to one another. Therefore, the sun's rays will appear to converge on the sun as a matter of perspective because the sun is very far away. In other words, the convergence of the sun's rays proves exactly the opposite of what flat-earthers claim it does. That is, the sun is very far away.

Of course, how far away is the sun if the flat-earthers are correct about this argument? It would be just a matter of a short distance from

---

3 Dubay, *200 Proofs Earth Is Not a Spinning Globe*, p. 24.

the clouds to the sun. After all, Dubay wrote in his proof number 125 that the sun is "relatively close to Earth just above the clouds."[4] Indeed, some flat-earthers have produced photographs in which some clouds appear to be in front of the sun, while other clouds appear to be behind the sun. This introduces at least two very large problems. First, the flat-earth model most flat-earthers, including Dubay, profess is that the sun is a disk 32 miles in diameter and only 3,000 miles above the earth. But that doesn't square with the claims that the sun's rays prove that the sun is just above the clouds. Second, if the sun is so close to the earth's surface, then it is impossible for observers separated by some considerable distance, such as between the east and west coasts of the United States, to see the sun at the same time.

What about those images that supposedly show some clouds in front of the sun but with some clouds behind the sun? This image from Christianflatearthministry.org is a good illustration. Sure enough, it appears as if some clouds are in front and some clouds are behind, placing the sun in the midst of the clouds. These photos are usually taken late in the day with the sun low in the sky. That brings up an interesting question of what someone some distance away where the sun is high in the sky would see. If the sun is a disk that appears round to the first observer, wouldn't the sun appear as a flat ellipse to the second observer?

But let's get back to the question at hand. Clouds have different thickness, with some clouds appearing very opaque, and others appearing

4. Ibid., p. 24.

less opaque. The camera has a linear response with an upper limit to its response. Once that limit is reached, no more response is possible. A thin cloud in front of the sun may not attenuate the sun's light to below the saturation level, so the cloud will not show up in front of the sun in the photograph. This will give the impression that the cloud is behind the sun. But at the same time, a thicker cloud may decrease the sun's light below the saturation point, showing the part of the sun behind the cloud dimmer, and, hence, giving the correct impression that the cloud is in front of the sun. On the other hand, the eye responds logarithmically to light, giving it much more dynamic range than cameras have. Therefore, it is very rare for the eye to see this effect of clouds appearing to be behind the sun.

Geosynchronous Satellites

According to flat-earthers, there are no satellites. If there are no satellites, then there can be no satellite communication. If there is no satellite communication, then what are all those satellite dishes doing in people's yards or attached to their homes? If the earth is flat, those dishes can't be picking up TV transmissions from satellites. In proof number 169 of his *200 Proofs*, Dubay sums up the flat-earth position very well:

> So-called "satellite" TV dishes are almost always positioned at a 45 degree angle towards the nearest ground-based repeater tower. If TV antennae were actually picking up signals from satellites 100+ miles in space, most TV dishes should be pointing more or less straight up to the sky. The fact that "satellite" dishes are never pointing straight up and almost always positioned at a 45 degree angle proves they are picking up ground-based tower signals and not "outer-space satellites."[5]

Let's see how many false statements Dubay has committed here. First, except for locations on the earth's equator, communication satellites that carry TV transmissions are never directly overhead. Satellites orbit with a period determined by the size of their orbits, measured from the earth's center. Low-earth orbit satellites have orbital periods of about 90 minutes, and at any given location on the earth, they aren't above the hori-

---

5. Dubay, *200 Proofs Earth Is Not a Spinning Globe*, p. 33.

zon during most orbits. And even for those orbits when they are above the horizon, it is only for a few minutes once each orbit. Obviously, this will not do for effective transmission. Increasing the orbital size increases the orbital period. It is advantageous to place a satellite in an orbit so that it orbits once each day as the earth rotates. We call such a satellite a *geosynchronous satellite*. How large must the orbit be for a satellite to be geosynchronous? Putting one day into Newton's generalized form of Kepler's third law from chapter 6, the orbital size of a geosynchronous satellite is about 42,000 km = 26,000 miles. But this is the distance from the earth's center. Since the earth's radius is 4,000 miles, a geosynchronous satellite is 22,000 miles above the earth's surface. So much for Dubay's claim that communication satellites are 100+ miles above the earth. Technically, 22,000 miles is 100+ miles, but his using the ridiculously low value of 100 miles demonstrates that Dubay has no idea what he is talking about.

This orbit must be in the same plane as the earth's equator. If it is not, then its orbit is inclined at an angle to the earth's equator, with the satellite crossing the equatorial plane twice a day. While a satellite in such an orbit would perpetually be above nearly half the earth's surface, it would bob up and down once each day, making it impossible for a stationary dish to continually point at the satellite. Only if the satellite is precisely in the equatorial plane will the satellite not bob up and down.

Where will the satellite's location be in the sky? It is preferred that satellites orbit above nearly the same meridian of longitude as the receiving dish. Therefore, satellite dishes are generally oriented toward the south, with some deviation to the east or west. As discussed in chapter 4, we can extend the earth's equatorial plane into the sky to define the celestial equator. Looking southward from a given location, the celestial equator will make an angle with the horizon that is equal to the complement of the latitude of the location. However, due to a parallax effect, the satellite will appear slightly lower than the celestial equator.

To evaluate this, I will do a calculation for my latitude 40 degrees north. In the figure, the earth is represented by a circle with center C. My location is point P, so that the line segment *CP* is 4,000 miles long, the earth's radius. The satellite is located at point E. Hence, the line segment *CE* is the satellite's distance from the earth's center, 26,000 miles (note

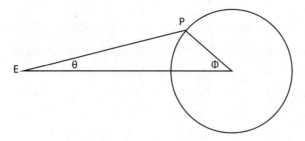

Altitude of a geosynchronous satellite

that the diagram is not to scale). The equatorial plane is perpendicular to the page passing through the line segment CE. The line segment PE is the line of sight from my location to the geosynchronous satellite. The three line segments form the triangle CPE. The angle θ at vertex E is how far below the celestial equator the satellite will appear. The only known angle is φ (my latitude) at vertex C, but its two adjacent sides are known. Applying the law of cosines, we can find the unknown side *PE*:

$$PE = \sqrt{(CE)^2 + (CP)^2 - 2(CE)(CP)\cos\phi}$$

Putting in the values, *PE* is a little less than 23,100 miles. Now applying the law of sines:

$$\sin\theta = \frac{CP\sin\varphi}{PE}$$

Again, putting in the appropriate values results in θ being a little more than six degrees. Since my latitude is 40 degrees, looking south, the celestial equator will make an angle of 50 degrees to the horizon. Since the satellite is six degrees lower in the sky, the satellite's altitude will be 44 degrees, within one degree of the angle that Dubay estimated is the angle that satellite dishes make with the horizon. Therefore, rather than proving that satellite dishes cannot be receiving transmissions from satellites, Dubay's own observation, when properly understood, proves that they can.

But Dubay also claimed that satellite dishes are oriented toward the nearest "ground-based repeater tower."[6] It isn't clear what sort of tower Dubay intended, but other flat-earthers have embellished this to be cell

6. Dubay, *200 Proofs Earth Is Not a Spinning Globe*, p. 33.

phone towers. It doesn't matter, because from any location, the nearest communication tower of any kind is unlikely to be toward the south. Instead, the direction toward the nearest tower could be any direction. By simply observing many satellite dishes in use, one can easily see that all satellite dishes in northern temperate latitudes generally face south. Furthermore, by pointing roughly 45 degrees upward, one cannot receive transmission from a tower unless the tower were very close (a matter of hundreds of feet away at most). Instead, if the signal were coming from a tower, the dish would be oriented almost horizontally. Incidentally, some newer, smaller satellite dishes are oriented much lower in the sky, almost horizontally. This is because the receiver is mounted much lower, making the reflected signal to deviate downward toward the receiver.

Clearly, these claims by flat-earthers about satellite dishes are wrong.

What Are Satellites?

With the naked eye, we can see man-made satellites orbiting the earth. Satellites have no bright lights aboard. Instead, we see satellites from the sunlight that they reflect. Hence, satellites are visible in the evening sky for about an hour and again in the early morning before dawn. For most of the night in between, satellites are in the shadow of the earth, so they are not visible. We are more apt to see satellites during the summer than in winter because the sun's light shines over the polar regions in summer, extending the time that we can see satellites. Most satellites orbit from west to east, the direction that the earth is rotating, so sometimes in the evening we can see satellites disappear into the earth's shadow. Conversely, in the morning, satellites sometimes emerge from the earth's shadow. Some satellites tumble, which causes them to dim and brighten alternately. The brightest satellite is the International Space Station (ISS). It rivals Venus in brightness, the brightest appearing object in the sky after the sun and moon. Large reflective surfaces, such as solar panels, occasionally cause a glint, or flare, of brightness, as sunlight reflecting directly off their surfaces passes over the earth on a narrow path. I once saw a flare from the wings of the space shuttle. The most famous flares are those due to the 66 Iridium satellites in low-earth orbit. These Iridium flares are very bright, even being visible in daylight, but only lasting a second or so.

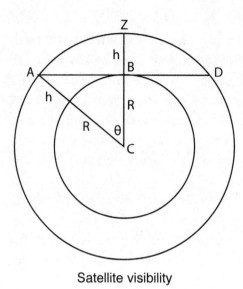

Satellite visibility

Traveling a little more than 17,000 mph, it takes a few minutes for a satellite to traverse the sky. The duration depends upon several factors, the most important being how close to the zenith the satellite passes. See the accompanying figure. The observer is at point B at radius R from the earth's center, C. Suppose a satellite passes directly overhead with height h (note that the figure is not to scale). The satellite will rise at point A, pass the zenith at point Z, and set at point D. The triangle ABC has a right angle at B. The length of the line segment AB is the distance, d, between the observer and where the satellite is when it rises. The angle, θ, at vertex C is

$$\theta = \cos^{-1}\left(\frac{R}{R+h}\right)$$

To find the distance that the satellite travels in its orbit along the arclength AZ, we must convert θ to radians and multiply by the radius of its orbit:

$$AC = \left(\frac{\theta}{57.3}\right) \times (R+h)$$

With these values, the arclength is 1,610 miles. But this is only half the observed path, from rising to zenith. We must double this to find the total distance the satellite travels from rising to setting. Assuming an orbital speed of 17,000 mph, the length of visibility is about 11 minutes. There are other factors that would alter this result. A higher satellite will be visible longer due to increasing the distance AB, but also because the satellite will move more slowly. However, with increasing distance above the earth, the satellite will be fainter. The rotational motion of the observer would increase the time for a satellite traveling east to west. But other factors would decrease the time of visibility. A satellite will rarely pass through the zenith, the situation of maximum transit time. When near points A and D, the satellite will be farther away, and, hence, will be fainter. Furthermore, near points A and D, a satellite is more likely to be lost from view due to absorption by its light passing through so much atmosphere. The earth's shadow will render the satellite invisible for at least part of the track. Therefore, one would typically expect a satellite to be visible for something less than 11 minutes. Over the years, I have seen hundreds, perhaps thousands, of satellites. From my observations, satellites are typically visible for 5–6 minutes or less.

Notice that because of perspective, satellites appear to move most quickly near the zenith and most slowly when they approach the horizon. This and the other aspects discussed here conform to what we see in the sky. This gives us confidence that there really are artificial satellites orbiting the earth.

How do flat-earthers explain these satellite phenomena? Some of them double down, insisting that since satellites don't exist, and since they haven't seen any satellites, then there is nothing to explain. Their unwillingness to even look for satellites is very revealing as to how skewed their worldview is. Other flat-earthers take a slightly more rational approach, claiming that what we think are satellites are drones. That is, every evening and morning, vast fleets of drones are dispatched to continue to fool those of us who believe that there are artificial satellites. Flat-earthers must not have worked out the details of this answer. For instance, people have seen satellites pass over since the first satellites in 1957, decades before drones existed.

Furthermore, one readily can use software on the Internet to compute when a satellite is due to pass over, and, hence, be visible. This depends upon one's latitude and longitude. If what we see truly are satellites orbiting a few hundred miles above us, then for two observers a mile or so apart, the time and the path in the sky that the satellite will be visible will be very similar. For instance, it takes an object traveling at 17,000 mph only 0.2 second to travel one mile, so if I see a satellite pass exactly through my zenith, an observer one mile to the east will see it pass through his zenith just 0.2 second later. But if we are seeing drones

rather than satellites, then two people a mile or two apart will see very different things. How high are these drones? Assume for the moment that
the drones are 1,000 feet high. If one of these drones is directly overhead
for me, then to be directly overhead for another observer one mile to the
east, the drone must travel to the second location in 0.2 seconds. This
would require a speed of 17,000 mph, about 23 times the speed of sound.
Yet, there is no sonic boom. Furthermore, after traveling that one mile,
the drone would make an angle of $\varphi = \tan^{-1}(1{,}000/5{,}280) = 11$ degrees
with the horizon. That is, the drone that passed overhead at this speed
would appear only 11 degrees above the horizon only 0.2 second later.
This doesn't conform to any behavior of satellites that we see. Therefore,
this explanation will not suffice. One could quibble about the height of
the drones. Making the drones lower only makes the situation worse.
Only very high drones will make this work. If one does enough calculations, one will see that only if the drones are as high as satellites are and
moving with the speeds of satellites will this explanation work. But then
the drones would be satellites. As I said, flat-earthers have spent no time
working out these sorts of details, opting instead to assert that drones
would work, but showing no plausible model for them.

There is another possibility. It could be that the drones are a few hundred feet high and work for each location. That is, I see the movement
and lights of one drone, while the observer a mile east sees a different
drone. This might work for just two observers a mile apart. But what
about the possibility of thousands of observers over a large area? Wouldn't
that require many thousands of drones? And what about two observers
not that far apart, say two neighbors separated by a few hundred feet?
Unless the drones were very high, we wouldn't see the drones follow the
same path across the sky. But if we make the drones too high, it produces
the same problem encountered with the first proposal. Furthermore, if
we make the drones high enough, eventually different observers could
see not only the drones meant for them, but also drones meant for other
people a short distance away.

With all the potential viewers of satellites on clear evenings and
mornings, this would require not just thousands, but probably tens of
thousands, if not millions, of drones. Given the conspiratorial bent that
so many flat-earthers have, their response would probably be that when

people use their cell phones or computers to find out what satellites are up on a given evening, Big Brother intercepts their requests, which leads to the dispatching of the appropriate drones to entertain and fool the observers. However, just like drones, people saw satellites in the sky long before there were apps to tell them where and when the satellites would be visible. I've *never* used an app or computer program to predict satellite visibility, but I've managed to see hundreds, if not thousands, of satellites. And what about people who see a satellite and *then* use an app to identify what satellite it was? One can't say that Big Brother dispatched the satellite in response to a query in an app.

The only reasonable conclusion is that flat-earthers don't have *any* explanation for the observation of satellites. That doesn't absolutely prove that satellites are real, but until someone can develop an alternate explanation that works, then the conventional understanding remains the only explanation that makes sense.

Polar Flights

One of the arguments that many people who believe the earth is spherical use against the flat earth is polar flights. For instance, if one flies from the United States to Asia, most flights travel far to the north over Alaska or even north of Alaska into the Arctic. On a globe, it is easy to see why this is the case, because a great circle arc[7] is the shortest distance between two points on a sphere, and great circle arcs between two widely separated points in the Northern Hemisphere pass close or through the Arctic. Flat-earthers respond that this works on a flat earth, too. This isn't surprising, because the flat-earth model is a sort of projection of the spherical earth onto a plane parallel to the equator. While the flat-earth map is a good projection in latitude, the distortion in longitude increases with increasing distance from the pole. However, for projecting flight paths between many Northern Hemisphere cities, the flat-earth map works reasonably well, so that it does nearly as good of a job as a globe does. The flat-earth map certainly works better to show these long-distance routes than the common Mercator map of the earth does. Therefore, this is not a good argument against the flat earth.

---

7. A great circle arc is the intersection of a surface of a sphere and a plane that passes through the center of the sphere. By way of example, the equator and meridians of longitude are great circle arcs, while parallels of latitude are not.

However, flat-earthers claim a similar argument for flight paths between widely separated cities in the Southern Hemisphere. More specifically, what do flights look like between cities in southern South America, southern Africa, and Australia (and New Zealand)? If the earth is a globe, then routes between these continents ought to be along great circle arcs that pass close to the Antarctic, though, given the distribution of land masses in the Southern Hemisphere, none of the flights would pass over Antarctica. But if the earth is flat, these flights would be impossibly long. How do flat-earthers respond to this problem? Their claim is that there are no direct flights between airports far south of the earth's equator. Indeed, if one searches for flights on U.S. carriers, there are no direct flights between airports in the Southern Hemisphere. For instance, if one wishes to book a flight on a U.S. carrier between southern Africa and southern South America, one must fly from the first continent to North America first before boarding another flight for the other continent. On the flat-earth map, this is nearly a straight line. Therefore, flat-earthers claim that this proves that the earth is flat and not a globe. Similar things are true if one wishes to fly between Australia/New Zealand and southern South America or between Australia/New Zealand and southern Africa.

Before one rashly concludes that the earth must be flat, there is more to consider. If one checks flights of flag carrier airlines in the Southern Hemisphere, one will discover that there are many direct flights between airports on different continents in the Southern Hemisphere. For instance, Qantas Airlines (Australia) has regular nonstop service between Australian cities and airports in southern Africa and southern South America, as does Air New Zealand. Similarly, both LATAM Chile and South African Airways have direct flights to the other Southern Hemisphere continents. These flights follow great circle arc routes that carry them close to Antarctica, as expected if the earth is a globe. However, these routes not only don't make sense on a flat earth, but are so long as to be impossible, at least within the time to complete the flights and without refueling along the way. Why don't U.S. airlines have regularly scheduled direct service between Southern Hemisphere airports? U.S. carriers are in the business of transporting passengers and goods between U.S. cities and between U.S. cities and foreign cities. That is, U.S. carriers are not in the business of flying between two foreign destinations. International agreements probably prevent that in most cases.

This argument pursued by flat-earthers is based upon incomplete information. Using U.S. carriers, it is very easy to show that no direct flights exist between Southern Hemisphere airports, but instead one must travel between these destinations by routes that might make more sense if the earth were flat. However, as anyone easily can demonstrate by searching for flights on appropriate flag carrier airlines, there are many nonstop flights between cities on different continents in the Southern Hemisphere. It isn't clear if the originators of this false argument for a flat earth knew better and concocted it as a joke, or if the originators themselves were fooled in their zeal to promote flat earth.

Captain Cook's Exploration of Antarctica

The first people to venture south of the Antarctic Circle was the crew on Captain James Cook's second voyage in 1772–1775. Flat-earthers frequently claim that Cook traveled 60,000 miles while circumnavigating Antarctica. This distance is more than twice the circumference of the spherical earth, but, given Antarctica's high latitude on the spherical earth, the distance around Antarctica would be far less. Flat-earthers point out that this distance is what one would expect if Antarctica were an ice wall at the edge of a round, but flat, earth. Therefore, flat-earthers conclude, this is evidence that their model is correct. This argument contains a kernel of truth, but we must delve into the history of Captain Cook's voyage to sort this out.

Since antiquity, many people believed that there was a vast continent at the bottom (southern) part of the earth. This continent came to be called Terra Australis. This argument in itself is evidence that people in the ancient world thought that the earth was spherical. The reasoning was that with so much land in the Northern Hemisphere, there must be a large land mass in the Southern Hemisphere to balance it. Europeans discovered Australia and New Zealand in the 17th century, and many came to think that these lands were part of Terra Australis. Cook circumnavigated New Zealand on his first voyage (1768–1771), demonstrating that it was not part of a continent. Cook also mapped the east coast of Australia on that voyage, but, by that time, many

Europeans appeared to think it unlikely that Australia was part of the hypothetical Terra Australis. If there were any doubts, on his second voyage, Cook sailed southward from England to near the Antarctic and then proceeded eastward well south of Australia. Cook wintered in New Zealand and then explored eastward near the Antarctic Circle before turning northward near South America to complete a large loop in the southern Pacific Ocean to spend the second winter in New Zealand. After the second winter, Cook sailed eastward below South America, completing his circumnavigation of Antarctica and returning to England.

Cook's deepest penetration into the Antarctic was a little more than 71 degrees south latitude, about 4½ degrees south of the Antarctic Circle. There the crew turned back because they encountered solid sea ice. On other forays into the Antarctic on the second voyage, the crew encountered pack ice and adverse weather. It is important to note that at no time did they spot land — that would not come until early in the 19th century. Nor did they see a continual "ice wall" as flat-earthers repeatedly claim. As for the 60,000-mile claim, that was the distance traveled during the *entire* three-year voyage, including the trip to and from England, as well as two large loops in the south Pacific and much backtracking. Hence, the total distance traveled in circumnavigating Antarctica was far less than the 60,000-mile total distance and more in line with the distance expected on a spherical earth. That is, contrary to claims made by flat-earthers, Cook's second voyage confirms the globe-earth model and disproves the flat-earth model.

Nikola Tesla

Flat-earthers frequently claim the eccentric physicist Nikola Tesla believed that the earth is flat. As proof of this, they offer this quote from Tesla:

> Earth is a realm, it is not a planet. It is not an object, therefore, it has no edge. Earth would be more easily defined as a system environment. Earth is also a machine, it is a Tesla coil. The sun and the moon are powered wirelessly with electromagnetic field (the Aether). This field also suspends the celestial spheres with electromag levitation. Electromag lev-

itation disproves gravity because the only force you need to counter is the electromagnetic force, not gravity. Though free to think and act, we are held together, like the stars in the firmament, with ties inseparable.[8]

This quote sounds very convincing that Tesla believed that the earth is flat. Except that Tesla only wrote the last sentence. The rest of this quote comes from Darrell Fox, a flat-earther. The source of this merged quote appears to be from Santos Bonacci's Facebook page on January 11, 2016. Though Bonacci properly split what Fox wrote and what Tesla wrote into two paragraphs, each with an appended attribution at their ends, many flat-earthers so wanted to claim Tesla as one of their own that they overlooked the authorship of the two paragraphs and merged them into one paragraph attributed entirely to Tesla. Since then, this fake quote has morphed into several different versions. For instance, at least one version rewrote the one sentence of Tesla's to read, "The stars are attached to the firmament."[9] To get Tesla's original 19-word sentence down to these seven words, flat-earthers had to delete 15 words and add three new words. Everyone ought to recognize that such a mangled quote isn't a quote at all.

Some might argue that since Tesla mentioned the "the stars in the firmament," then Tesla entertained at least some of the flat-earth cosmology, but this is not the case. In Tesla's day, the King James Version (KJV) was the overwhelmingly popular version of the Bible. The KJV places astronomical bodies, including the stars, in the "firmament of heaven" (Genesis 1:14, 15, 17). Hence, it was common in Tesla's lifetime, as it is today, to speak of the stars being in the firmament. Furthermore, notice that Tesla used the stars in the firmament in a simile about human interaction. Indeed, these words from Tesla come from an article he wrote for the June 1900 issue of *The Century Magazine* entitled "The Problem of Increasing Human Energy, with Special References to the Harnessing of the Sun's Energy." Lest there be any doubt as to whether Tesla was a flat-earther, in this very article Tesla referred to the earth as a "globe" 12 times. For instance, one sentence reads:

---

8. https://www.quora.com/Did-Tesla-really-say-that-the-Earth-was-flat.
9. https://www.youtube.com/watch?v=92DodP2H_Ag.

> It is a well-known fact that the interior portions of the globe are very hot, the temperature rising, as observations show, with the approach to the center at the rate of approximately 1 degree C. for every hundred feet of depth.[10]

Therefore, despite all those T-shirts and bumper stickers that flat-earthers display about Tesla, Tesla was not a flat-earther.

Auguste Piccard

Auguste Piccard was a Swiss physicist. On May 31, 1931, he and Paul Kipfer used a balloon to ascend to nearly 52,000 feet to study cosmic rays. By far, this was the highest altitude that anyone had yet achieved. The August 1931 issue of *Popular Science* briefly reported on this balloon voyage. The article contained this interesting description:

> Through portholes, the observers saw the earth through copper-colored, then bluish, haze. It seemed a flat disk with upturned edge. At the ten mile level the sky appeared a deep, dark blue.

Flat-earthers have had a field day repeating this statement, arguing that this proves that the earth is flat. To be such a silver bullet requires that Piccard himself was a flat-earther, but there is no evidence that he was. So, what do we make of this statement? Note that in the original article these words are not in quotes. In the article, the only words in quotes are those referring to "blue air." Here is that reference:

> The explorers trapped samples of the upper air, "blue air," as Piccard reported it to appear, in cylinders.[11]

The fact that the author of the article thought it important to put Piccard's description of what the air at ten miles high looked like indicates that the "flat disk with upturned edge" were not the words of Piccard, but instead were the words of the article author. It is unknown what the author of the article meant.

---

10. https://teslaresearch.jimdo.com/articles-interviews/the-problem-of-increasing-human-energy-with-special-reference-to-the-harnessing-of-the-sun-s-energy-by-nikola-tesla-century-illustrated-magazine-june-1900/.

11. http://blog.modernmechanix.com/ten-miles-high-in-an-air-tight-ball/.

When flat-earthers promote this claim, they ignore the testimony of the many thousands of people who have seen the earth's curvature from high altitude. At 35,000 feet, where most airliners typically fly, the earth's curvature begins to become visible. However, the earth's curvature at that altitude is barely noticeable, and it requires having a wide field of view, something difficult to achieve in the relatively small windows of commercial aircraft. At 50,000 feet, the earth's curvature is much more obvious, and at 60,000 feet, it is difficult not to see.[12] Unfortunately, commercial aircraft normally cannot fly that high. For instance, the Boeing 747 has a ceiling of 45,000 feet, and the Boeing 777 has a ceiling of 43,000 feet. On the other hand, the Concorde typically flew at 60,000 feet, and passengers consistently reported that they could see the earth's curvature from that altitude. Some military aircraft fly high enough to see the earth's curvature. The B-52 typically flies at 50,000 feet. The ceiling of the F-16 and F-18 is 50,000 feet. The B-1 ceiling is 60,000 feet, and the B-70 ceiling was 77,000 feet. The SR-71 could reach 85,000 feet. The pilots and crew of these planes report seeing the earth's curvature when operating at such altitudes. For instance, I recently spoke to a retired Air Force navigator. She confirmed that aboard a B-52 she regularly saw the earth's curvature. It is dishonest for flat-earthers to repeatedly reference the questionable text from the *Popular Science* article from nearly a century ago, while simultaneously ignoring the testimonies of the many thousands of people who have flown at the same or even higher elevations.

Neil DeGrasse Tyson and the Earth's Shape

There is even a better example of how flat-earthers take the quotes of people and twist them to mean something other than what they clearly mean. Neil DeGrasse Tyson is a well-known astronomer, who is frequently invited to interview on a wide range of topics related to astronomy. In one interview, Tyson was asked about something he had written about the earth's shape. In this interview, Tyson likened the earth to being pear-shaped. Flat-earthers have had a field day repeating this clip, accompanied by an illustration of a pear with a map of the earth

---

12. D.K. Lynch, *Applied Optics*, 2008, 47, no. 34:H39–H43.

superimposed on it. Exactly what the many flat-earth memes prompted by this is supposed to mean is not clear. I must conclude that either the makers of these memes are very confused about what Tyson said, or they intentionally choose to misrepresent what Tyson said.[13]

At one point in the interview, Tyson said, "Cosmically speaking, we're practically a perfect sphere."[14] That one statement is very clear, and it contradicts what flat-earthers claim Tyson said. Tyson prefaced this comment with several things. For instance, Tyson pointed out that many globes representing the earth have mountains sticking up higher than surrounding terrain, but this isn't correct. The deepest part of the ocean (Mariana Trench) is 36,000 feet below sea level, while the highest point above sea level is 29,000 feet above sea level. That is a difference of 65,000 feet, about 12 miles. But the earth is 8,000 miles in diameter. The difference in height between those two extremes is 0.15% of the earth's diameter. And since those extremes are not next to one another, all the relief on such globes is even less than this. If a relief globe were done to true scale, you could not feel mountain ranges, such as the Himalayas or Andes sticking up above surrounding terrain. Consider Hawaii's Mauna Kea. Most of Mauna Kea is below the ocean. The height from its under-water base to the summit of Mauna Kea is 33,000 feet, making it the highest mountain on earth. But that bump, if scaled properly on a globe, would be a mere 0.08% of the earth's diameter. With the hand or eye, this would be utterly indistinguishable from a perfectly smooth sphere.

Tyson also pointed out that more important than this is that the earth is slightly oblate, meaning that the earth's diameter is greater through the equator than through the poles. How oblate is the earth? The equatorial diameter is 7,926.4 miles, while the polar diameter is 7,899.8 miles, a difference of 26.6 miles. This is a difference of 0.3%. This is a little more than twice the maximum difference in altitude from sea level on the earth's surface. This too, would be impossible for the eye or the hand on a properly scaled globe to detect. As Tyson pointed out, the equatorial

---

13. Even before seizing upon Tyson's interview, flat-earthers used the descriptions of the earth's shape as an oblate spheroid with an additional slight bulge in the Southern Hemisphere (likened to a pear-shape) as supposed proof of something nefarious. See Dubay's proof 188, Dubay, *200 Proofs Earth Is Not a Spinning Globe*, p. 36.
14. This quote appears at the 3:36 point in this video: https://www.youtube.com/watch?v=SoCKapivHGM.

bulge makes a 20,000-foot-tall mountain in Ecuador the most distant point on the earth's surface from the earth's center.

Finally, Tyson mentioned that the earth is slightly bulged below the earth's equator. This was the context of the pear-shape comment, for a pear is bulged below its equator, but by far more than the earth is. The earth's pear-like bulge is extremely small, much less than the irregularities discussed above. Those other departures from a perfect sphere are not readily noticeable, rendering this even smaller departure undetectable by normal means. Remember that in this interview, Tyson said, "Cosmically speaking, we're practically a perfect sphere." It is dishonest for flat-earthers to keep repeating this misrepresentation of what Tyson said. Flat-earthers ought to exercise more caution in repeating what they heard. Before they uncritically repeat things, they ought to check for context and facts.

NASA Reference Publication 1207

Some flat-earthers quote from a 1988 NASA publication, "Derivation and Definition of a Linear Aircraft Model."[15] The paper begins with this statement:

> This report documents the derivation and definition of a
> linear aircraft model for a rigid aircraft of constant mass flying
> over a flat, nonrotating earth.

The second paragraph following starts with an almost identical sentence. Many flat-earthers present these two statements from this report as an explicit admission from NASA that the earth truly is nonrotating and flat. But think this through for just a moment. If NASA is this evil, deceitful agency that has been the chief culprit in promoting the lie that the earth is a spinning globe, why would it admit the truth so readily? This makes no sense. Hence, could there be a better explanation of this reference to a flat, nonrotating earth?

Having taught physics at the university level for more than a quarter-century, I'm very familiar with the way that physicists go about their work. It is customary at the beginning of a calculation to list all the assumptions being made in the derivation. Many of these assumptions are

---

15. https://www.nasa.gov/centers/dryden/pdf/88104main_H-1391.pdf.

simplifying assumptions. For instance, it is common when considering the trajectories of falling bodies or projectiles to ignore the effect of wind resistance, leaving the downward force of gravity as the only significant force. Indeed, when the speeds achieved are modest, experiments show that this is a good assumption. However, when large velocities are involved, this is not a good assumption, and much more complicated modeling of wind resistance must be factored in. If, in the case of modest velocities, the more complicated formulation is used, the results will not be significantly different from the simple assumption of ignoring wind resistance.

Similarly, when considering the motion of objects on flat surfaces, physicists often ignore the role of friction between the body and the plane surface. This is a particularly good assumption if the body in question is moving on wheels with little friction, or if the surfaces in contact are well-lubricated. Experiments again show that when friction is minimal, the predicted results agree well with the observed results. However, when friction is a significant factor, assuming that there is no friction doesn't work very well, so one must include friction, but the computation in this case is much more complicated.

Another simplifying assumption is to treat real objects with physical extent as point masses. This avoids the complication of torques applying rotational velocity to objects. An example is a ball that is thrown, kicked, or batted. If the amount of rotational motion imparted to the object is minimal, then the only acceleration on the object will be translational motion due to forces (no rotation due to torques). Once again, experiments show that in many, but not all, cases, this simplifying assumption is justified, for the calculated and observed results are very similar. However, there are situations where rotational motion must be taken into account, but this complicates the matter.

In similar manner, the statement quoted above lists four simplifying assumptions about airplanes that the researchers who produced this report made. First, the researchers assumed that the airplane is rigid. Generally, this is a good assumption, but it isn't strictly true. As with any physical structure, airplanes are subject to flexure. While sitting in a window seat during takeoff, I've watched the wingtips of the planes rise a foot or more as the wings began producing lift for the planes to become airborne. Furthermore, the control surfaces on airplanes, the ailerons, elevators, spoilers, and rudders, are not rigid surfaces. However, these departures from rigidity are so minor as to be insignificant.

Second, the researchers assumed that the airplane has constant mass. But this isn't true either. Real airplanes consume fuel. The stored fuel can represent a large portion of the takeoff weight of an airplane, but as the flight progresses, the amount of stored fuel diminishes, and so the plane's mass decreases. However, moment by moment, the mass of the airplane doesn't change significantly. Therefore, the assumption of the airplane having constant mass is a good assumption when considering relatively short time durations during flight.

Third, the researchers assumed that the earth was flat. What does this mean? It probably doesn't refer to the earth in its entirety, but rather to the ground over which the airplane is flying. In the idealized condition that they were considering, the vertical distance between the airplane and the ground was constant. That is, that airplane was flying over an area where there were no hills or valleys.

Fourth, the researchers assumed that the earth isn't rotating. Undoubtedly, this must refer to ignoring the Coriolis effect. As shown in chapter 6, the Coriolis effect is subtle and has minimal influence on airplanes. Much as when driving a car, an airplane's motion is continually altered by the pilot or the autopilot. The Coriolis effect is very small compared to the many other factors, such as turbulence through which the airplane flies.

Therefore, the assumption of a flat, nonrotating earth in this NASA document doesn't mean what many flat-earthers think that it means.

What Is in a Number?

Flat-earthers are fond of pointing out that in the conventional understanding of the world, the earth orbits the sun at a speed of 66,600 mph. If you don't see the significance of that number, be patient. The approximation for the curvature per mile on the spherical earth discussed in chapter 2 is eight inches per mile squared. But if we convert that eight inches to feet, it comes out to 0.666 feet. Do you see it now? Okay, one more — flat-earthers point out that the earth's tilt is 66.6 degrees. By now, it ought to be obvious what is going on here — flat-earthers see the number 666, the number of the beast in Revelation

13:8. Flat-earthers intone that the conspirators foisting the lie that the earth is a sphere on the world are mocking us by creating a false model that flouts the number 666 in plain sight, thus proving that there is such a conspiracy.

Let's unpack this. Does the earth orbit the sun at a speed of 66,600 mph? The radius of the earth's orbit, the AU, is 9.2956 x 10⁷ miles. Multiplying by 2π gives the circumference. To find the average orbital speed, we must divide by the sidereal year, the dynamic orbital period of the earth, 365.25636 days, and divide by 24 hours. This yields an average speed of 66,627 mph. This is close to 66,600, and, when expressed at three significant figures, it is 66,600 mph. But it isn't 666. Does the earth curve 0.666 feet over the first mile of distance? The earth's mean radius is 3,958.8 miles. Using the approximation from chapter 2, this yields a drop of 0.66687 feet over the first mile. If one truncates this to three significant figures, then it is 0.666 feet, but if one rounds to three significant figures, it is 0.667 feet. Close, but even if it were 0.666 feet, 0.666 is not 666. Finally, is the earth's tilt 66.6 degrees? No, the current value for the earth's tilt is 24.43689 degrees. If one takes the complement of this angle and rounds to three significant figures, the value is 66.6 degrees. For instance, this is the latitude (expressed to three significant figures) of the Arctic and Antarctic Circles. However, this is not the *tilt* of the earth's axis, as flat-earthers typically claim. To claim that this is the tilt is sloppy at best and ignorant or dishonest at worst. At any rate, 66.6 is not 666.

Besides misunderstanding the earth's tilt, rounding or truncating these three numbers, and ignoring the placement of the decimal points to get 666, there is a more fundamental problem. All these number manipulations are dependent upon the units of measure used. While this flimflam may make sense to some who use English units of measure, to most of the world that uses metric, this is nonsense. In metric, the earth's orbital speed is 107,200 km/hr. Expressed in metric, the earth curves 7.84 cm in the first kilometer. Of course, these two numbers mean nothing to most people. While most of the world uses degrees to measure angles, that is not the only way to measure angles. For instance, in mathematics and physics, radian measure is more useful. Expressed in radian measure, the earth's tilt is 0.4090509 (its complement is 1.161745). Again, these numbers bear no special significance.

Therefore, the manipulation of these numbers hardly proves the existence of some grand, evil conspiracy. About all that it proves is that some flat-earthers have far too much time on their hands, and that many flat-earthers are willing to believe almost anything that they think promotes their view of the world.

Bizarre

One of the more bizarre arguments for flat earth is the repetition of a newspaper account from the April 21, 1900, *Cook County Herald.* Here is the newspaper article in its entirety:

SAYS EARTH IS ROUND
AND HE MAY BE THROWN INTO PRISON

Sad Condition of Affairs In England —
Sir John Gorst Accused of Intention
to Teach False Precepts — City of Portsmouth Excited.

It is painful to read that Sir John Gorst, the head of the British educational department, is in serious trouble and has been threatened by Mr. Ebenezer Breach and other taxpayers of the city of Portsmouth, in the kingdom of England, with prosecution under the "imposters' act." It seems that the Schools of Portsmouth have been teaching the damnable and heretical doctrine that the earth is a sphere. Sir John's attention has been called to this dissemination of seditious and treasonable doctrine, but he has refused to correct the abuse. Ebenezer and his friends know, of course, that the earth is as flat as a pancake.

They have been patient with Sir John, and day after day have allowed the false teaching regarding the shape of the earth to go on, but can stand it no longer, they say, to see their children corrupted with this most "heretical doctrine," as the complainants call it in this protest. Sir John Gorst has many political enemies, and even his political friends do not always agree with him; but the depth of his depravity was not known until he was unmasked by Mr. Ebenezer Breach and his friends. Sir John may cavort about parliament and deceive some people, but when he runs up against a body of respectable British taxpayers, the bulwarks of the throne and the guardians of the constitution, it is another matter.

Such new fangled ideas as that of the earth being a sphere he may impose upon the frivolous persons who riot in the ungodly city of London, but not upon the taxpayers of Southampton. Ebenezer and his friends mean business, and have served formal notice upon the Portsmouth school board that the teaching that the earth is a sphere "cannot be allowed to continue under any circumstances, plea or explanation whatever," and that it must be abandoned for schism by the law provided. After having stamped out the dastardly doctrine in the schools of Southampton, the committee announce that they will next go up to London and bring the London school board before the courts, being well advised and informed that the same doctrine regarding the shape of the earth is also taught in the London schools.

Sir John, meantime, is to be brought to court and prosecuted under the "imposters' act" aforesaid. Now, the "imposters' act" is a part of the British constitution, probably—no one knows what is, and what is not a part of that nebulous thing—and provides certain pains and penalties, such as forfeiture of estate and burning at the stake, if recalcitrant. Ebenezer and his friends are worthy and reputable citizens and mean business. If necessary they will light the fires of Smithfield again for the wicked Sir John. At last accounts, Sir John was still at large, and so was Ebenezer.[16]

It's not clear how this newspaper story is evidence that the earth is flat. When I ask those promoting this argument about this, the typical answer is that it allegedly shows that belief that the earth is flat was widespread as late as 1900. Let us investigate the details of this story.

Who was Sir John Gorst? Gorst was a British politician who served in various capacities, including as a member of Parliament. He was Vice

---

16. https://chroniclingamerica.loc.gov/lccn/sn90060625/1900-04-21/ed-1/seq-1/.

President of the Committee on Education 1895–1902, though the committee was reorganized in 1900. Therefore, if there were a complaint lodged against teaching something in British schools in 1900, Gorst likely would have been the person ultimately held responsible. But who was Ebenezer Breach? Though not well-known today, in the late 19th and early 20th century, Breach was a British flat-earth gadfly. Apparently, in 1899, Breach embarked on an overseas trip. There were interviews with Breach printed in the September 12, 1899, *Arizona Republic* and the September 19, 1899, *Los Angeles Herald*. The same year, a British astronomical journal contained this note about Breach:[17]

> The following paragraph has been sent me by a correspondent. It is a cutting from some newspaper, but has no name or date attached:
>
> The Flat Earth Man
Transvaal Folk recognize his Merit
>
> The patience and long-suffering of Mr. Ebenezer Breach, the philosopher who maintains that the Earth is flat, have at length had their reward. He has received a letter from Johannesburg announcing that he has been elected "Grand Master of the Ancient Order of Unshaven Boers."
>
> But previous to his taking office he has to fulfill two conditions — the first that he shall don the regalia of the order, namely, yellow breeches and red embroidery; and the second that he shall apply to the magistrates for a certificate of identification.
>
> Armed with the letter he yesterday appeared before the Portsmouth [England] magistrates, and asked them to sign a document which read: "this is proof that Ebenezer Breach is a resident and burgess of the borough of Portsmouth."
>
> The bench told him that he should have put his photograph on the document, in case they probably might have signed it.

---

17. Anonymous, *The Observatory*, 1899, 22:456.

Mr. Breach tried to argue that point, but in the end he withdrew, declaring that he would comply with the suggestion and apply again.

It may be remembered that some time ago Mr. Breach wrote to Sir John Gorst threatening to put in force against him an old statute which is said to have made it illegal to teach in schools that the Earth is round. To this letter he has not had a reply.

The letter mentioned at the end of this note almost certainly refers to the same incident cited above from the *Cook County Herald*. Where and what was this newspaper? The Cook County in question is in the northeastern corner of Minnesota. The *Cook County Herald* was published 1893–1907 in Grand Marais, the county seat. It was preceded by the *Cook County Pioneer*, which was renamed the *Cook County Herald* upon sale to a new owner in 1893. In 1907, that owner sold the newspaper to a competitor, the *Grand Marais News*, and the combined newspaper was rechristened the *Cook County News Herald*, which continues to publish more than a century later. Even today, this region of Minnesota is sparsely populated, but Cook County's population in 1900 was 810. Obviously, the newspaper then and now serves an area larger than Cook County.

This appears to be the only newspaper account of this story. One must wonder why this story did not appear in British newspapers at the time, and why it failed to make it to major U.S. newspapers, showing up instead in this very minor newspaper. This is particularly strange since the *Cook County Herald* concentrated on news of local interest. If one examines a copy of this issue of the newspaper, one will see that this story was accompanied by some other strange stories from other distant places. In the 19th century, it was common for newspapers to add short articles as a sort of gag that weren't intended to be taken as serious reporting to help fill the allotted pages of an issue. This practice was in decline by 1900. This article was almost certainly an embellishment of the account of Breach sending his letter to Gorst. It's sad that a modern flat-earther stumbled upon this article, whereupon it quickly and uncritically spread throughout the flat-earth community.

Chapter 10

Does the Bible Teach Flat Earth?

Introduction

As discussed in chapter 1, belief that the earth is flat has rapidly grown of late, largely through dissemination via countless Internet sites and the influence of social media. Unfortunately, many Christians have fallen prey to this, misled into believing that the Bible teaches the earth is flat and that, until five centuries ago, the church likewise taught that the earth is flat. In this chapter, I will examine some of the biblical passages that supposedly teach that the earth is flat, and I will show that, in fact, they do not. But before doing so, I must respond to two false assumptions mentioned above — that the church historically taught that the earth is flat and that this changed 500 years ago. Some of what I write here will necessarily overlap with my discussion in chapter 1.

As the medieval scholar Jeffrey Burton Russell ably demonstrated,[1] contrary to common misconception, the medieval church did not teach that the earth was flat. Thomas Aquinas introduced Aristotelian thought into medieval church teaching. Writing in the mid-fourth century B.C., Aristotle clearly taught that the earth was spherical. In the early second century B.C., Eratosthenes accurately measured the circumference of the spherical earth. Claudius Ptolemy's *Almagest*, from the early second century A.D., provided a useful model for calculating the positions of heavenly bodies. While this model was geocentric, it did not

---

1. Jeffrey Burton Russell, *Inventing the Flat Earth: Columbus and Modern Historians* (New York: Praeger, 1991).

promote a flat earth, but instead was based upon a spherical earth. The works of Aristotle, Eratosthenes, and Ptolemy were all widely available and discussed in the mid- and late-medieval period, and continued to be through the transition to the Renaissance. Given the clear record of history, why is it so commonly believed today that most people, and especially the church, thought that the earth was flat?

This misconception is easily traced to the writings of 19th-century skeptics. John William Draper and Andrew Dickson White, who invented the conflict thesis, are worthy of note. The conflict thesis holds that religion in general, and Christianity in particular, held back progress. The contention of the conflict thesis was that medieval Europe was gripped with superstition (Christianity) that prevented intellectual advancement, and it was only after man's reason reasserted itself during the Renaissance that man slowly became unshackled from religious dogma, bringing about the Enlightenment. It is true that four centuries ago, the Roman Catholic Church opposed Galileo's teaching of the heliocentric theory. According to the conflict thesis, it was the alleged geocentric teaching of the Bible that caused the Roman Catholic Church to oppose Galileo. However, the historical record demonstrates that it was the teachings of Aristotle and Ptolemy that played the major role in that conflict. That is, the Galileo affair was a battle between *two scientific theories* — geocentrism and heliocentrism — with the Bible playing a very minor role. Hence, the conflict thesis reinterpreted the Galileo affair into something that it was not.

The promoters of the conflict thesis also retold the story of Christopher Columbus. Most people today persist in the belief that at the time of Columbus, nearly everyone thought that the earth was flat. According to the story, Columbus was one of the few people who thought the earth was spherical, so he understood that on a spherical earth, one could sail westward from Europe to reach India and China. Supposedly, Columbus had to argue against strong objections coming from those who thought that the earth was flat to get support for his expedition. Finally, according to the story, Columbus managed to complete a voyage to the New World, and when he returned to Europe, people realized that Columbus was right — the world was round and not flat. Really? How did sailing from Europe to the Caribbean and back to Europe prove that the world was spherical? It didn't. The truth is that no one told Columbus he could not reach the Far East by sailing west. Everyone knew that it was possible because everyone knew that the earth was spherical. The problem was that the earth was very large. Most people understood that the distance westward from Europe to the Far East was far greater than going eastward (a look at any globe proves this). The question was not how possible it was to reach the Far East by going westward, but rather how feasible it was. The belief was that the ocean between Europe and Asia was vast, with little or no land in between. At the time of Columbus, voyages over open water were very risky, and ships rarely sailed more than three days out of the sight of land. A voyage westward across the ocean to Asia would have required months, with no opportunity for resupply or rescue along the way if problems developed.

The facts of history refute the commonly held story about Christopher Columbus. Much of the work supporting a flat earth today uncritically repeats and builds upon this false view. The flat-earth movement began in the mid-19th century, the same time that the conflict thesis was being developed. While the skeptics were ridiculing the Bible for allegedly teaching that the earth is flat, a few Christians foolishly accepted this false claim. Undoubtedly, the recent surge of interest in the flat earth among Christians has been fueled by the (false) belief that the Bible teaches that the earth is flat. Those who have enlisted in the flat-earth movement of late are apparently ignorant of the fact that those who promoted the conflict thesis made the same arguments to discredit the Bible. This could be ironic, or perhaps it is not. It is possible that some people promoting the flat earth today are doing so to discredit the Bible and Christianity all over again. If so, then Christians who have been misled into believing that the earth is flat have foolishly fallen into the trap. Let us examine the Scriptures to see what they say. We shall find that promoters of the flat earth do not handle them any better than they handle history.

There are various lists of Bible verses that supposedly teach that the earth is flat. The most exhaustive list circulating today claims 240+ such verses.[2] In this chapter, I will discuss many of these verses.

---

2. There is no definitive reference for this, for much flat-earth material exists on the Internet. A search for "240+ flat-earth Bible verses" will produce several hits. For instance, one website that has this list is https://www.flatearthdoctrine.com/flat-earth-scriptures.

Isaiah 40:22

Everyone seems to agree that a key verse with regard to the earth's shape is Isaiah 40:22. That verse reads:

> It is he who sits above the circle of the earth,
> and its inhabitants are like grasshoppers;
> who stretches out the heavens like a curtain,
> and spreads them like a tent to dwell in.

Many Christian authors claim that the Hebrew word for circle here (*hug*) refers to the earth being a globe. Notice the parallel structure here. The first half of the verse describes the roundness of the earth, followed by a simile about the inhabitants of the earth. The second half of the verse describes the stretching of the heavens (probably a reference to what God did on day two of the creation week), followed by a simile about the heavens. Everyone agrees that the heavens appear to have curvature, whether a dome or a sphere around the earth. Could this parallelism subtly indicate that as one is spherical the other is spherical, too? Perhaps that is reading too much into this verse.

The Hebrew word *hug* is used only two other times in the Old Testament. One appearance is in Proverbs 8:27:

> When he established the heavens, I was there;
> when he drew a circle on the face of the deep.

(The "I" here is a personification of wisdom.) The only other time that this word appears in the Old Testament is Job 22:14:

> Thick clouds veil him, so that he does not see,
> and he walks on the vault of heaven.

Note that in the King James Version, this word is rendered "circuit." Also note that if one goes with "vault" as a good translation of *hug* as the English Standard Version does, a vault is a two-dimensional surface that is curved in a third dimension. This is an apt description of the surface of a sphere, as a vault is generally hemispherical. No wonder flat-earthers generally don't mention Job 22:14, because that might lead to the conclusion that Isaiah 40:22 really does describe the earth being spherical.

The Hebrew word *hug* derives from the word *chuwg*, which appears only once in the Old Testament, in Job 26:10:

> He has inscribed a circle on the face of the waters
> at the boundary between light and darkness.

This obviously is a reference to the creation of light on day one. On a spherical earth, the division between night and day is always a circle. Therefore, this verse appears to be consistent with a spherical earth, too.

How do flat-earthers respond to this? First, they respond that the division between night and day would be a circle on a flat earth, too. But, more importantly, they say that the Hebrew word *hug* must mean a circle, not a globe. Their evidence is that the prophet Isaiah used a word meaning "ball" elsewhere, so if Isaiah had meant to convey that the earth was spherical, he would have used this word in Isaiah 40:22. The verse in question is Isaiah 22:18:

> And whirl you around and around, and throw you like
> a ball into a wide land. There you shall die, and there shall
> be your glorious chariots, you shame of your master's house.

The Hebrew word translated "ball" here is *kaddur*. It occurs two other times in the Old Testament. One occurrence is in Isaiah 29:3:

> And I will encamp against you all around,
> and will besiege you with towers
> and I will raise siegeworks against you.

Obviously, the meaning here isn't a ball, but a circle. The other time *kaddur* appears is Ezekiel 24:5:

> Take the choicest one of the flock;
> pile the logs under it;
> boil it well;
> seethe also its bones in it.

Here, *kaddur* is translated "pile." Note that in the English Standard Version, a footnote on the word "logs" indicates that the Hebrew word used there literally means "bones." The important thing to recognize is that the Hebrew word *kaddur* can be translated several ways, such as ball, circle, and a pile, or heap. Therefore, the insistence that *kaddur* is *the* appropriate Hebrew word for "ball" is unwarranted. In English, most people don't think of the word "round" to be restricted to two dimensions. Many people speak of the earth being round when they mean that the earth is a globe. But flat-earthers speak of the earth being round, too. That is, roundness applies to either a circle or a sphere (topologically, a sphere is merely a three-dimensional circle).[3] An honest assessment of Isaiah 40:22 is that its meaning is ambiguous enough that one cannot conclusively say it indicates whether the earth is a sphere.

Does the Bible Teach That the Earth Has an Edge?

Nearly everyone understands that a sphere does not have an edge. Indeed, we can travel indefinitely around a sphere and never reach a boundary or edge. On the other hand, if the earth is flat, it must have an edge somewhere, unless the earth is an infinite plane. However, few people today suggest the latter, and no one in the ancient world did. Bible skeptics are fond of pointing out that the phrase "four corners of the earth" appears three times in the Bible. Surely, the skeptics claim, this must refer to a flat, square earth — thus proving that the Bible teaches a flat earth. At the very least, they reason, this shows that the Bible writers believed one of the flat-earth cosmologies of the ancient world, thus proving that the Bible is not inspired, but that the people who wrote the Bible merely reflected the worldview of their times. There are examples of flat-earth cosmologies from the ancient world, but they always consisted of a flat, *round* earth. A circle was considered a much more perfect shape than a square, so none of the ancient flat-earth cosmologies involved a square earth. The argument is often made that the Bible reflects the cosmology of the ancient world. If a square flat earth were the cosmology of the Bible, then it would have been at odds with every other ancient flat-earth cosmology. Therefore, this attempt by the skeptics to claim that the Bible teaches a flat earth does not square with the facts of history.

If the verses that mention the earth's four corners do not refer to a flat earth, then to what do they refer? Let me begin with Revelation 7:1,

---

3. Some flat-earthers that I've encountered insist that the word "round" applies only to circles, not spheres.

which speaks of four angels standing on the four corners of the earth and restraining the four winds of the earth. Even the most ardent students of hyper-literal interpretation of the Bible acknowledge the frequent poetic elements and the use of imagery in the Book of Revelation. This extends to the many occasions where numbers appear in the Book of Revelation. In this one verse, the number four appears three times. In each usage, the things mentioned are intimately tied together, so there is a one-to-one correspondence between each of the three groups of four.

The four winds refer to the four directions from which winds can come: north, south, east, and west. We often use this nomenclature today, such as saying that the wind is "out of the west." The repetition of the number four ("four angels . . . four corners . . . four winds") ties each angel and each corner with one of the four compass directions. There-fore, there is no warrant to interpret these four corners as literal corners of a flat, square earth, particularly when it does not match any cosmol-ogy. Hence, the phrase "four corners of the earth" probably refers to the four cardinal directions, north, south, east, and west.

However, there is another likely meaning. The phrase "four corners of the earth" was probably an idiom in the Apostle John's time, much as it is in English today, referring to every distant location on the earth. This is the meaning from the context of Revelation 20:7–8, the other occurrence of the phrase "four corners of the earth" in the Book of Revelation (the King James Version has the word *quarter* here rather than *corner*, though the Greek word is the same in both Revelation 7:1 and 20:7–8). Idioms in one language can be difficult to translate into another language because a literal translation may be meaningless in the target language (imagine how a literal translation of our English idiom "You're pulling my leg!" would be understood in other languages). It is probable that the English idiomatic understanding of "the four corners of the earth," referring to the remotest parts of the earth, stems from Revelation 20:7–8. From an evaluation of its context, we may conclude that this is also the meaning of "the four corners of the earth" in Isaiah 11:12, the third appearance of this phrase in the Bible. It's use there is generally understood to be idiomatic.

Bible skeptics frequently use these three verses to argue that Scrip-ture teaches that the earth is flat. While some promoters of the flat earth use these three verses, many do not. Why? They probably realize that a square earth with corners does not agree with their model of a *round*, flat earth.[4] This is a notable omission. How would Christians who believe in a flat earth because they earnestly believe that is what the Bible teaches handle these three verses? They likely would interpret them much as I have. However, once one admits that some biblical passages which supposedly teach a flat earth are idiomatic, it is difficult to claim that similar passages are not also idiomatic. For instance, the phrase "ends of the earth" appears 28 times in the King James Version, and, if taken very literally, suggest that the earth has an edge, which would rule out a spherical earth.

However, critical evaluation of each of these 28 instances of the phrase "ends of the earth" in their respective contexts shows plainly that this phrase, too, is an idiomatic expression. For example, in 12 of the 28 occurrences, the Hebrew word *'epes* ("extremity, end") used in construct with *'eres* ("earth"), evidences that the biblical authors intend this phrase as a reference to the uttermost reaches of the inhabitable world. The fact that this phrase is sometimes used to speak not of the distant parts of the earth itself, but rather of the people who inhabit these remote places (e.g., Psalm 67:7, 98:3; Isaiah 45:22) argues strongly against this phrase being used to indicate that the earth has a physical edge.

To see this, let us examine two of these verses in greater detail. Psalm 67:7 reads:

> God shall bless us;
> let all the ends of the earth fear him!

Notice that this verse states that the ends of the earth fear God. How is that possible? Geography can't fear. Is it possible that this is nonliteral? If so, one must question whether the other occurrences of the "ends of the earth" ought to be taken so literally, too. The phrase "ends of the earth" here must refer to people, not real estate. Much of Hebrew poetry works off parallels and contrasts. We have a parallel here between the first and

---

4. However, within the flat-earth movement, there are those who do believe that the earth is both round and square. In 1893, Orlando Ferguson produced the map shown in the figure here. Ferguson's map has a flat, yet round earth. However, the flat earth is modified as an inverse toroid.

Orlando Ferguson's square, round earth map mentioned in the footnote. Despite Ferguson's claim, he was not a professor. Notice the very literal basis for this map from Revelation 7:1.

second lines of the verse. The first line states that God shall bless people. The parallel structure works only if the second line restates that thought. Hence, it must refer to people, too.

Consider Isaiah 45:22. It reads:

> Turn to me and be saved,
> all the ends of the earth!
> For I am God, and there is no other.

Here God directs His command to turn to Him and be saved. What is the subject of this imperative statement? "All the ends of the earth." Can the physical earth, or a portion thereof, turn to God and be saved? The obvious answer again is no. Hence, the phrase "ends of the earth" here refers to people. In both verses, the people are scattered across the earth. Some of the other appearances of the phrase "ends of the earth" in the Bible aren't so clear that they refer to people living in the remotest parts of the earth. But neither is there any reason that those passages refer to a physical edge of the earth. Hence, the phrase "ends of the earth" likely is an idiomatic expression.

Job 38:14

One of the verses that contains the phrase "ends of the earth" is Job 38:13. That verse is followed by Job 38:14:

> It is turned as clay to the seal; and they stand as a garment (KJV).

Flat-earthers frequently point out that this verse refers to God creating the earth. Furthermore, they argue, clay seals were flat, so this must mean that the earth is flat. This is wrong on both points. First, many of the seals in Job's time were cylinders that were rolled onto clay to make an impression, thus changing the clay tremendously from something amorphous into lettering or a symbol. Some commentaries state that this rolling action is indicative of the earth's rotation, implying exactly the opposite of what flat-earthers claim. However, this interpretation may be just as biased as the claims of flat-earthers. Second, this verse isn't referring to the creation of the earth. The context is Job 38:12–15:

Hast thou commanded the morning since thy days; and caused the dayspring to know his place;

That it might take hold of the ends of the earth, that the wicked might be shaken out of it?

It is turned as clay to the seal; and they stand as a garment.

And from the wicked their light is withholden, and the high arm shall be broken (KJV).

Notice that in context, the first verse of this passage establishes sunrise, which God ordains and controls, as the subject. Verse 14 contains two similes, each with pronouns that refer to what preceded the verse. Simile is a poetic device, so one must be very careful in interpreting Job 38:14, for a simile generally has one essential point of comparison. In no way does this passage appear to be discussing creation. Rather, the first simile in verse 14 seems to indicate how the coming of dawn transforms the earth. One could argue that the rolling of a cylindrical seal over clay is similar to how morning light rolls over the landscape, transforming it. However, even that may be a stretch. And it doesn't address whether the earth is flat or a sphere because this simile, if so applied, works in either model.

Only if one already views the earth as being flat would one interpret this verse to mean that the earth is flat. Hence, this verse hardly proves that the earth is flat.

Do Heights in the Bible Teach the Earth Is Flat?

Perhaps the most bizarre argument that the Bible teaches a flat earth relies on Daniel 4:11, which reads:

The tree grew and became strong, and its top reached to heaven, and it was visible to the end of the whole earth.

This description is repeated almost word for word in Daniel 4:20. Both skeptics and the flat-earthers reason that on a spherical earth, it would not be possible for a tree to be visible from the entire earth, but such a tree could be visible anywhere on a flat earth. But what is the context of these verses? The fourth chapter of Daniel is the account of Nebuchadnezzar's second dream. Verse 5 directly quotes the words of Nebuchadnezzar stating that he had a dream. Verses 10–17 quote Nebuchadnezzar describing the content of his dream. Note that this is a *dream*. With their wild and fantastic elements, dreams are hardly statements about reality, let alone cosmology. It is remarkable that *anyone* would construe the content of a pagan king's dream recorded in Scripture as evidence that the Bible teaches that the earth is flat.[5] Verses 19–27 contain Daniel's interpretation of Nebuchadnezzar's dream, and verses 28–37 recount the fulfillment of the dream. Key to the dream's interpretation is the identification of Nebuchadnezzar with the tree in his dream (verses 20–22). Immediately, one ought to see that since the tree *represents* Nebuchadnezzar, it is *not* a literal tree (though, being in a dream, the tree wouldn't be literal anyway). Furthermore, the literal fulfillment of the dream does not involve a tree in any way, reinforcing the nonliteral nature of the tree. Even if the dream correctly reflected the cosmology of Nebuchadnezzar (assuming he thought that the earth was flat), it hardly constitutes evidence that the Bible teaches the earth is flat. Rather, the Bible merely records the thinking of Nebuchadnezzar.

The same sort of reasoning is used to argue that Matthew 4:8 teaches a flat earth. Matthew 4:1–11 gives an account of the temptation of Jesus. The temptation began in the wilderness after Jesus had fasted for 40 days and nights. Satan first tempted Jesus to change stones into bread to satisfy Jesus' hunger (Matthew 4:3). Presumably, this was while still in the wilderness. Next, the devil took Jesus to the pinnacle of the temple in Jerusalem and suggested that Jesus cast himself down (Matthew 4:5). Note that there was considerable distance between the wilderness and the temple (at least 50 miles). Did Satan instantly and literally transport Jesus from the wilderness to Jerusalem? Or did Satan present this view to Jesus while still in the wilderness, perhaps in a vision? Matthew 4:8 records the third temptation:

> Again, the devil took him to a very high mountain and
> showed him all the kingdoms of the world and their glory.

---

5. While I recognize the doctrine of biblical inerrancy, it is necessary to understand that the property of inerrancy extends only to the accuracy of Scripture's record and not the accuracy of the things recorded. In other words, Scripture does, with relative frequency, faithfully record inaccuracies and lies contained in the speech of the individuals it quotes. Thus, while inerrancy ensures that the details of Nebuchadnezzar's dream are accurately represented in the biblical text, such does not guarantee (or even imply) that what Nebuchadnezzar saw in his dream was an accurate reflection of reality.

Those who wish to argue for a biblical flat earth point out that all the kingdoms of the earth would be visible from a tall mountain only if the earth is flat. However, if this mountain of Matthew 4:8 with its view of the entire earth is literal, then where is it? Those who pursue this line of reasoning have never determined the location of this hypothetical mountain. If this mountain is hypothetical even on a flat earth, then this verse hardly constitutes proof that the Bible teaches the earth is flat. But does this verse truly imply the visibility of the entire earth from the peak of this mountain?

The other two synoptic Gospels also record the temptation of Christ (Mark 1:12–13; Luke 4:1–13), though Mark's account has no details. The details of Luke's account match many of the details of Matthew's record, but there are differences. For instance, the second and third temptations are switched. This is not a difficulty if one allows that either or both accounts of the temptation of Christ are treated thematically rather than chronologically. Those who claim the Bible teaches a flat earth concentrate on Matthew's account but largely ignore Luke's gospel in this matter. Notice the differences between Matthew 4:8 (above) and Luke 4:5:

> And the devil took him up and showed him all the kingdoms of the world in a moment of time.

Notice that no mountain is mentioned, but merely that the devil took Jesus "up" (earlier English translations based upon the *Textus Receptus* do have the word *mountain*, but the Greek word for *mountain* does not appear in earlier manuscripts, so its inclusion in the *Textus Receptus* probably came from an addition from a copier who was knowledgeable of Matthew's parallel account). This is a relatively minor point, but it may have some bearing on whether the mountain that Matthew recorded was literally a tall mountain from which all the world's kingdoms could be viewed. One more detail in Luke's Gospel sheds light on this question. Luke stated that the devil showed Jesus all the kingdoms of the world "in an instant of time." The emphasis is not on where Jesus was, but what Jesus saw. This was not a grand panorama that took some time to absorb. Rather, the glory of all the world's empires was shown to Jesus all at once. This sounds more like a vision rather than a vista. There may not have been a mountain involved, but, more likely, it probably refers to a high, desolate spot, probably in the wilderness, where the third temptation, and its attendant vision, occurred. No wonder those who promote the flat earth normally concentrate on Matthew 4:8 while ignoring Luke 4:5. As mentioned above, one might incorrectly infer from Matthew 4:8 that there actually is a mountain so high that the earth's entire surface is visible from it, but by interpreting Scripture in terms of Scripture, one can see that this is incorrect. But that still leaves the location of this hypothetical mountain. Since such a mountain doesn't exist on earth, it is silly to insist that Matthew's account requires that the earth be flat.

In similar vein, flat-earthers claim that Revelation 1:7 indicates that the earth is flat. That verse reads:

> Behold, he is coming with the clouds, and every eye will
> see him, even those who pierced him, and all tribes of the
> earth will wail on account of him. Even so. Amen.

Flat-earthers argue that only if the earth is flat can "every eye" see Jesus. Keep in mind that this is a prophetic passage, so one must be very careful in determining exactly what this means. Since it is a future event, we have difficulty anticipating how this will be fulfilled. Notice that the "every eye" specifically includes "those who pierced" Jesus. Who pierced Jesus? Quite literally, it was one of the Roman soldiers who crucified Jesus (John 19:34–37). I suspect that that soldier has been dead for nearly 2,000 years, so how could he see Jesus in this prophetic passage? In both John 19:37 and Revelation 1:7, the Apostle John quoted from Malachi 12:10 about the people of Israel looking on the one that *they* (plural) pierced (Jesus). Many commentaries on the Book of Revelation opine that this refers to Israel in the future. Since the Jews did not literally pierce Jesus, this introduces a nonliteral hermeneutic, at least for Revelation 1:7. Obviously, this is a problem for flat-earthers. Instead of offering a slam dunk that the earth is flat, this verse merely raises more doubts about their approach.

Is the Firmament a Dome over the Earth?

The cosmology of the flat earth holds that a dome covers a circular, flat earth, with its edge resting on the earth beyond the ice wall of

Antarctica. The stars are affixed to this dome, while in most versions, the sun and moon are above the earth but beneath the dome. Some have called this a snow globe cosmology because of its resemblance to a snow globe. Supposedly, this is the cosmology that the Bible teaches. Ironically, skeptics make the same argument, but their intent is to discredit the Bible. Few flat-earthers appear to be aware of this fact or the irony. Let us examine the Scriptures that supposedly support this cosmology.

Key in this discussion is the *firmament*. The Hebrew word *rāqîa'* is translated as *firmament* in the King James Version. It appears a total of 17 times in the Old Testament, with over half of the occurrences (nine times) in chapter 1 of Genesis alone. It is necessary to discuss all 17 uses of the word *rāqîa'* to determine its likely meaning. But, first, it is important to study its etymology. The word is a noun that derives from the Hebrew root *raqa'*, meaning to stamp out. An example of this action is to stamp or pound a metal into thin sheets. This is a common practice with gold, because gold is so malleable. For instance, *raqa'* is the verb that is translated "hammered out" in Exodus 39:3:

> And they hammered out gold leaf, and he cut it into
> threads to work into the blue and purple and the scarlet yarns,
> and into the fine twined linen, in skilled design.

Gilding is the process of attaching gold leaf to objects, giving the impression that the objects are pure gold. For instance, the verb *raqa'* is used in Isaiah 40:19 to refer to a goldsmith overlaying an idol with gold. The King James Version renders this as "spreadeth." The ark of the covenant was gilded with gold leaf over acacia wood (Exodus 25:10–11). I must note that the verb *raqa'* isn't used here in reference to the ark of the covenant, but the process of overlaying with gold, as in Isaiah 40:19, is the process described. Gold leaf can be pounded or rolled so thin that bright light can be seen through it. The same verb is used in Job 37:18 in reference to spreading out the skies. From this meaning of this word, we can deduce that the *rāqîa'* is something that has been pounded or stretched out.

Unfortunately, some people reason that since the Hebrew verb *raqa'* is an action that sometimes is done to a metal, the thing being stretched out must have some physical property in common with metals. For instance, the verb *raqa'* is applied to bronze in Numbers 16:39 and to silver in Jeremiah 10:9. Furthermore, they reason that since metals are often hard, the intended property of the *rāqîa'* must be hardness. This certainly is the sense of the archaic English word *firmament*, which has a common root with the word "firm." However, is this the intended meaning? Not all metals are hard. For instance, gold is very soft, yet gold is the object of the verb *raqa'* in two verses. The Hebrew verb *raqa'* occurs 11 times in the Old Testament, of which I've listed only 5. What of the other 6 appearances? Twice *raqa'* refers to stamping of the feet on the ground (Ezekiel 6:11, 25:6), and a third implies this action (2 Samuel 22:43). The three other times *raqa'* appears, it refers to God stretching out the earth (Psalm 136:6; Isaiah 42:5, 44:24).

In any language, when a noun is created from a verb, as is the case with *rāqîa'*, it is the action of the verb that gives the meaning to the noun, not some property of what, in some cases, may be the object of the verb. For instance, consider the English verb *expand*. This verb, imported from French, came first, and then later the noun *expanse* developed. An expanse is something that has been expanded. In the meaning of the noun *expanse*, there is no hint of any property of something that has been expanded. Rather, the meaning of *expanse* is derived entirely from the action of the verb *expand*. In similar manner, it ought to be obvious that the meaning of the Hebrew noun *rāqîa'* comes from the action of the Hebrew verb *raqa'*, not from some property of what is sometimes the object of the verb.

Given these considerations, it is questionable that *rāqîa'*, by necessity, must be something that is hard. It is more likely that the intended meaning of *rāqîa'* is related to the process of stamping out, not a physical property of the thing subjected to the process. The process has the effect of spreading out a substance or possibly making the substance thin. This is why many more modern translations of the Bible render *raqa'* as *expanse* rather than *firmament*.

Lest anyone think that this is a modern imposition, consider the words of John Calvin:

> The work of the second day is to provide an empty space
> around the circumference of the earth, that heaven and earth

may not be mixed together. For since the proverb, "to mingle heaven and earth," denotes the extreme of disorder, this distinction ought to be regarded as of great importance. Moreover, the word *rakia* comprehends not only the whole region of the air, but whatever is open above us: as the word heaven is sometimes understood by the Latins. Thus the arrangement, as well of the heavens as of the lower atmosphere, is called *rakia* without discrimination between them, but sometimes the word signifies both together sometimes one part only, as will appear more plainly in our progress. I know not why the Greeks have chosen to render the word *stereoma*, which the Latins have imitated in the term, *firmamentum*; for literally it means expanse.[6]

Martin Luther shared in this opinion. For instance, Luther wrote the following about day two of creation:

The unformed mass of mist, which was created on the first day out of nothing, God seizes with the Word and gives the command that it should extend itself outward in the manner of a sphere. The Hebrew word *rāqîa* denotes "something spread out," from the verb *raqa'*, which means "to expand" or "fold out." The heaven was made in this manner, that the unformed mass extended itself outward as the bladder of a pig extends itself outward in circular form when it is inflated — if I may be permitted to make use of a coarse comparison in order to make the process clear.[7]

Notice that Luther described the *rāqîa'* as a "sphere," not a dome, as the modern flat-earthers insist. Luther thought of the *rāqîa'* as a crystalline sphere to which the stars were attached. Where did he get this idea? As we shall see, it came from ancient Greek cosmology, with which he was very familiar from his extensive education. However, the important thing is that Luther and other important church leaders never thought that the

---

6. *Genesis*, translated and edited by J. King (Carlisle, PA: Banner of Truth Trust, 1965), p. 78–79.

7. *Luther's Works Volume 1: Lectures on Genesis Chapters 1–5*, translated by G. Schick, edited by J. Pelikan (St. Louis, MO: Concordia, 1958), p. 24.

earth was flat with a dome over it. Most of them thought that the earth was a sphere with a celestial *sphere* around it.

Three centuries ago, Matthew Henry wrote about day four of the creation week:

> We have here an account of the second day's work, the creation of the firmament, in which observe, 1. The command of God concerning it: Let there be a firmament, an expansion, so the Hebrew word signifies, like a sheet spread, or a curtain drawn out. This includes all that is visible above the earth, between it and the third heavens: the air, its higher, middle, and lower, regions — the celestial globe, and all the spheres and orbs of light above: it reaches as high as the place where the stars are fixed, for that is called here the firmament of heaven (v. 14, v. 15), and as low as the place where the birds fly, for that also is called the firmament of heaven, v. 20.[8]

Thus, Henry thought that the *rāqîaʿ* is best translated as "expanse." Writing in the 19th century, Browne obviously agreed, for he wrote this about *rāqîaʿ* in Genesis 1:6:

> The original sense of the word has been much debated, but is of little consequence; for the sacred writer would use the common language of his people, and not go out of his way to devise one which would be philosophically accurate. The verb, from which the substantive is derived, signifies (1) to beat or stamp upon, Ezek. vi. 11, xxv. 6; (2) to spread abroad by stamping, 2 S. xii. 43; (3) to beat out metal into thin plates, or gold into gold leaf, Ex. xxxix. 3, Num. xvi. 38, Isai. xl. 19; (4) to spread forth, extend, stretch out, Job xxxvii. 18, Ps. cxxxvi. 6, Is. xlii. 5, xliv. 24. The most probable meaning of the substantive therefore is *the expanse or the expansion*. The LXX rendered it *firmament* (see Quarry "on Genesis," p. 79); and hence it has been argued that Moses taught the sky to be a hard, metallic vault, in which the sun and stars were fixed; but

---

8. M. Henry, *Matthew Henry's Commentary on the Whole Bible, Volume 1: Genesis to Deuteronomy* (Old Tappan, NJ: Flemming H. Revell), p. 5.

the most learned modern commentators, including Gesenius, Kalisch, &c., believe the true etymology of the word to shew that expanse, not *firmament*, is the right translation.[9]

More recently, Matthews has written:

> The "expanse" is the atmosphere that distinguishes the surface waters of the earth (i.e., "the waters below") from the atmospheric water or clouds (i.e., "the waters above"). The Hebrew term *rāqîaʿ* ("expanse") may be used for something that is beaten out or spread out like a covering (e.g., Job 37:18; Ezek 1:22–26; 10:1). The stars are depicted as the brightness of the *rāqîaʿ* (Dan 12:3). The atmosphere then is depicted as a canopy or dome spread out over the earth. There is no indication, however, that the author conceived of it as a solid mass, a "firmament" (AV) that supported a body of waters above it. The "expanse" describes both the place in which the luminaries were set (vv. 14–15,17) and the sky where the birds are observed (v. 20). Thus Genesis' description of the "expanse" is phenomenological — to the observer on earth, the sun and stars appear to sit in the skies while at the same time birds glide through the atmosphere, piercing the skies. In the Old Testament elsewhere there is evidence that the Hebrews understood that clouds produced rain and thus, from a phenomenological perspective, "water" can be described as belonging to the upper atmosphere.[10]

Indeed, this phenomenological use, or the language of appearance, is in much use today. For instance, the sky gives the appearance of being a dome. That is why a dome is used in planetariums to give a good representation of what the night sky looks like. The dome of a planetarium is tangible, making it quite literal, but it is hardly a literal representation of the real sky (which isn't a dome, though it appears that way). Furthermore, astronomers use the concept of the celestial sphere

---

9. E.H. Browne, *Genesis; or, the First Book of Moses. With a Commentary* (New York: Scribner, Armstrong & Company, 1873), p. 33.

10. K.A. Matthews, *The New American Commentary, Volume 11 Genesis 1–11:16*, E.R. Clendenen, editor (Nashville, TN: Broadman and Holman, 1996), p. 150.

(only half of which is visible at a time from the earth's surface, giving the appearance of a dome). The celestial sphere is a very useful concept, though I doubt that anyone today thinks that this correctly represents cosmology.

How did so many people come to think that the Bible teaches a flat-earth cosmology with a dome? As discussed in chapter 1, that view was developed by Bible skeptics in the 19th century to discredit Scripture and Christianity. It isn't coincidental that the flat-earth movement was born at this time. Apparently, Rowbotham and other flat-earthers of the time foolishly believed this false charge and readily adopted this belief as a badge of honor. Bible scholars largely saw the folly of this and ignored this false claim. Things began to change with the publication of two papers by Paul Seely in the early 1990s.[11] In these two papers, Seely appeared to argue that since Moses was a product of the Ancient Near East (ANE), then he naturally would have written Genesis in a way that reflected ANE cosmology.[12] To be fair to Seely, he later responded to criticisms of his papers in the creation science literature, stating that he didn't think that the Bible teaches that the earth is flat with a dome over it, but that Bible writers must have thought this, so this cosmology is reflected in how and what they wrote. Is this confusing? Yes. This is so muddled that it is no wonder that nearly no one else sees this distinction. Seely accepted a 19th-century skeptics' argument undermining the Bible, yet he claims that this doesn't threaten the doctrine of the inspiration and authority of Scripture. Unfortunately, others, such as John Walton and Michael Heiser, have taken their lead from Seely and gone further. Today's flat-earthers commonly refer to one of Heiser's diagrams of the supposed biblical cosmology to prove that the Bible teaches that the earth is flat. Heiser has responded that while this is the cosmology of the Bible, he doesn't think that the earth is flat, but he still believes in the authority of Scripture.[13]

---

11. P.S. Seely, "The Firmament and the Water Above, Part I: The Meaning of raqia' in Gen 1:6–8," *The Westminster Theological Journal*, 1991, 53:227–40, and P.S. Seely, "The Firmament and the Waters Above, Part II: The Meaning of 'The Water Above the Firmament' in Gen 1:6–8," *The Westminster Theological Journal*, 1992, 54:31–46.

12. For instance, Acts 7:22 tells us that Moses was educated in all the wisdom of the Egyptians.

13. http://drmsh.com/christians-who-believe-the-earth-is-really-flat-does-it-get-any-dumber-than-this/

Did the ancient Hebrews believe that the earth was flat and covered by a dome? Perhaps, but we don't know for sure because we don't have any truly ancient Hebrew works on cosmology.[14] The Old Testament narrative and prophets end in the late fifth century B.C., about 75 years prior to Aristotle writing *On the Heavens*, in which he clearly taught that the earth is a globe. Shortly thereafter, Alexander the Great's conquest brought Greek thought, including cosmology, to the ANE. During the intertestamental period, much of the world around the Hebrews came to adopt the concept of a spherical earth. Therefore, if we were to adopt the thesis of Seely, then the New Testament writers certainly believed that the earth is spherical. But does it really matter what cosmology the ancient Hebrews might have had? If one believes that the Bible is the product of men, then it certainly does matter. But if the Bible is God's inspired word for mankind, then what the ancient Hebrews thought about cosmology doesn't matter. An objective examination of Scripture shows that, unlike so many other ancient texts, the Bible doesn't clearly teach whether the earth is flat or a sphere. Or if there is a dome over the earth. This demonstrates the wisdom of God, something that I will explain in more detail shortly.

So, what is the *rāqîaʿ*? Certainly, it must have meant something to the ancient Hebrews. They may indeed have thought that the *rāqîaʿ* was a dome over the earth, but that doesn't mean that is what the *rāqîaʿ* is. And it must mean something to us today (at the risk of interpreting the *rāqîaʿ* in terms of our modern cosmology). No matter how anyone may view it, the *rāqîaʿ* must have some objective meaning. It is best to turn to Scripture to learn the most likely meaning of *rāqîaʿ*.

The first use of the word *rāqîaʿ* in the Bible is probably helpful in deciphering its meaning. This is found in Genesis 1:6, the beginning of the day two creation account. The day two creation account begins with God's declaration that there be a *rāqîaʿ* to divide the waters from the waters. The next verse tells us that God made the *rāqîaʿ* and divided the waters that were below the *rāqîaʿ* from the waters that were above the *rāqîaʿ*. Thus, the word *rāqîaʿ* appears three times in this verse. Before

---

14. One could argue for the pseudepigraphic *Book of Enoch*, probably written during the intertestamental period. While this book isn't about cosmology primarily, it does describe the earth being flat, with the sun traveling below the earth each night. I discuss the *Book of Enoch* in chapter 12.

declaring an end to day two in Genesis 1:8, God called the *rāqîa'* "heaven." Therefore, the Hebrew word *rāqîa'* appears five times in the day two account.

There are several observations that we can make from this passage. First, the waters that God divided were the waters mentioned in Genesis 1:2. The waters that God separated below probably refer to surface water (mostly oceans) on the earth. But what are the waters above the *rāqîa*? How we answer that question will depend upon what we understand the *rāqîa'* is. Notice that God equated the *rāqîa'* with heaven. The Hebrew word *šāmayim* is translated as "heaven" most of the more than 400 times it occurs in the Old Testament, as it is here.

Interpreting Scripture in terms of Scripture, we find reinforcement of the equation of the *rāqîa'* with heaven. At least 11 verses in the Old Testament speak of God stretching out the heavens (Job 9:8; Psalm 104:2; Isaiah 40:22, 42:5, 44:24, 45:12, 48:13, 51:13; Jeremiah 10:12, 51:15; Zechariah 12:1). On day two, God made the *rāqîa'*, something that is spread or stretched out. Furthermore, on day two, God called the *rāqîa'* heaven. The stretching of the heavens probably refers to when God made the *rāqîa'*.

Heaven is generally understood as being above us. Depending on the context, the word can refer to that which is immediately above us, where flying birds, clouds, and rain are. It also can refer to the realm of astronomical bodies. Finally, it often refers to the abode of God. "Heaven" has all these meanings, both in modern use and in the Bible. Does the *rāqîa'* refer to all of these meanings, or just some of those meanings? The other appearances of the word *rāqîa'* in the Genesis 1 creation account can help in answering this question. The next use of the word *rāqîa'* is in the day four account of creation (Genesis 1:14–19), where it appears three times. Each time it appears in conjunction with the Hebrew word *šāmayim*. The best way to express this relationship in English is with a noun modified by a prepositional phrase, "expanse of heaven." This construction emphasizes, lest there be any doubt, that the thing mentioned in the day four account is the thing that God made on day two. In Genesis 1:14, God commanded that there be luminaries in the firmament of heaven. Genesis 1:15 expands that command so that the luminaries are not only lights in the firmament of heaven but on the earth as well. Genesis 1:17–18 states that God made the lights and *set* them in the firmament of heaven. It is clear here that the lights are the heavenly bodies, the greater and lesser lights, and the stars also (Genesis 1:16). Therefore, the firmament of heaven (the *rāqîaʿ*) is where God placed the heavenly, or astronomical, bodies. Today, we would call this *outer space*, or simply *space*.

As an aside, some flat-earthers appear to make a distinction here that is unwarranted. They argue that the stars are embedded in a dome above the earth (the *rāqîaʿ*), but they hold that the sun and moon (the greater and lesser lights) are *below* the dome while still above the earth (this conforms to most flat-earth cosmologies today). This requires artificially distinguishing the stars from the greater and lesser lights in Genesis 1:17, so that it is only the greater and lesser lights that are placed in (that is, *inside*) the *rāqîaʿ* in Genesis 1:17, while the stars are effectively placed *on* the surface of the *rāqîaʿ*. Flat-earthers who pursue this distinction suggest that the phrase "in the firmament of heaven" of Genesis 1:17 (and possibly Genesis 1:14–15 as well) ought to be understood as "*inside* the firmament of heaven." That is, God placed the sun and moon inside the firmament, much as one might place an object inside a container, such as a box. The box does not indicate the object's location but merely contains the object. However, the Hebrew text (and even the English text) does not permit this. The masculine plural pronoun of verse 17 refers back to the sun, moon, and stars collectively, and the verse does not distinguish as to their placement. The most natural understanding of the day four creation account is that all heavenly bodies are located in the *rāqîaʿ*. Again, today we call this space.

How far down to the earth does the *rāqîaʿ* extend? The final use of the word in Genesis 1, in the day five creation account, is helpful in answering that question. In describing the creation of flying things, Genesis 1:20 uses the phrase "expanse of heaven" to describe where they fly. While this phrase is the same as its three appearances in the day four account, the wording before that phrase is different. The Hebrew literally states that the birds were to fly "upon the face of the expanse of heaven." The Hebrew word usually translated as "face" in Genesis 1:2 appears in this verse. However, I'm not aware of any English translation that renders that word as "face" in Genesis 1:20, though some, such as the Geneva

Bible and the New American Standard Bible, use the word "face" in a footnote. This could mean that the birds fly on this side of the firmament of heaven or in the near side of the firmament of heaven. If the former, then the *rāqîaʿ* may not extend down to where the birds fly. If the latter, it may include where birds fly. Either way, the *rāqîaʿ* would appear to include what we today would call outer space and much, if not all, of earth's atmosphere. Keep in mind that the distinction between the earth's atmosphere and outer space is of modern origin. Furthermore, even in today's parlance, there is no clear delineation as to where the atmosphere ends and space begins. Neither the modern understanding nor the ancient one is necessarily right or wrong; they are just different.

The next use of the word *rāqîaʿ* (the tenth time in the Old Testament) does not occur until Psalm 19:1. The meaning there is consistent with what I have concluded from Genesis 1. The comparative parallelism of the two statements of Psalm 19:1 indicate that the *rāqîaʿ* and the *šāmayim* are the same thing, something that Genesis 1:8 already equated. Furthermore, Psalm 19:4b–6 describes the motion of the sun in the heavens (equivalent to the *rāqîaʿ*), further enforcing the understanding gleaned from Genesis 1.

What about the remaining seven times that the Hebrew word *rāqîaʿ* appears in the Old Testament outside of Genesis 1 and Psalm 19? The word appears one more time in Psalms, in Psalm 150:1, which reads, in the King James Version,

> Praise ye the LORD. Praise God in his sanctuary:
> praise him in the firmament of his power.

Because word order is different in different languages, some passages, such as this one, can be tricky to translate. The KJV translators attempted to follow Hebrew word order in this verse. Consequently, the final two words, "his power," clearly refer to God, though this is a bit awkward in English. The English Standard Version (ESV) changed the word order slightly so that the final phrase reads, "his mighty heavens." That is, the word *mighty*, a synonym for *power*, modifies the *rāqîaʿ*, rather than being descriptive of God (also notice that the ESV translated *rāqîaʿ* "heavens" here, perhaps based upon God calling the *rāqîaʿ* "heaven" in Genesis 1:8). This translation shifts the meaning, but is that difference in meaning consequential? God made the expanse, so if the expanse is mighty, God is even mightier yet. However, the KJV is probably the correct translation, though the word order is awkward. In the New English Translation, the second part of this verse reads "Praise him in the sky, which testifies to his strength!" This wording, while different from the KJV, more clearly gets across the meaning intended by the KVJ. Furthermore, this reading is consistent with the very clear meaning of Psalm 19:1, as well as Genesis 1:5.

The word *rāqîaʻ* appears once in the Book of Daniel. The context is established in Daniel 12:1–2 as the eschaton, when the resurrection of the dead will occur, some to eternal life and others to eternal punishment. In the KJV, Daniel 12:3 reads:

> And they that be wise shall shine as the brightness of the firmament;
> and they that turn many to righteousness as the stars for ever and ever.

Notice the parallelism contained in these two similes separated by a semi-icolon and the conjunction *and*. Clearly, the "wise" of the first simile and "they that turn many to righteousness" of the second simile are the same people, forcing at least a rough equivalence between the things that they are compared to. The first simile says that the wise will shine like the brightness of the *rāqîaʻ*. In the second simile, the words *shine* and *brightness* are omitted; but those words are understood, which further enforces the parallelism. Indeed, the people who turn many to righteousness are likened to the stars which shine brightly. Furthermore, from the day four creation account of Genesis 1, we know that the stars are located in the *rāqîaʻ*. Therefore, the *rāqîaʻ* of Daniel 12:3 clearly refers to the same thing found in Genesis 1 and Psalm 19:1.

The final five appearances of the word *rāqîaʻ* are in Ezekiel, four times in the first chapter and once in chapter 10. Ezekiel 1:1–3 sets the scene: Ezekiel was with other exiles along the Chebar Canal (or river) when the heavens opened, and he beheld a vision. The indication is that Ezekiel's companions did not see the vision, but that he alone did. Did God transport Ezekiel to heaven, where he literally saw the things of his vision? Or did God reveal these things in a vision while Ezekiel was still in Babylon physically, much as what one might experience in a dream? We do not know for certain, but, given the description, the latter would seem more likely. Furthermore, the vision of Ezekiel 11 is clearly of the latter type (Ezekiel 11:1, 24).

The first things that Ezekiel saw were four living creatures that resembled men, but each had four faces. Each creature had feet and wings and a wheel. The creatures moved about together, and as they moved, the wheels went with them. Ezekiel described the creatures as bright and colorful (Ezekiel 1:7, 13, 16). Throughout Ezekiel's description of his vision, he repeatedly used the words *like* and *likeness*, words that indicate the use of simile. Clearly, Ezekiel had difficulty describing the indescribable, so he expressed what he saw in terms of things familiar to him. As such, it is improper to take these comparisons entirely literally, because, by definition, a simile is nonliteral. In Ezekiel 1:22, the prophet recorded that above the heads of the four creatures, there was something *like* a *rāqîaʿ*. Again, notice the use of simile: Ezekiel did not say that it *was* a *rāqîaʿ*, but that it was *like* a *rāqîaʿ*. On the other hand, what God made on day two was not *like* a *rāqîaʿ*; it *was* a *rāqîaʿ*. Given the difficulty that Ezekiel had in describing what he saw, we cannot be sure exactly what this expanse was. One possibility is that it was merely an expanse, or gap, between the four creatures and what was above. What was above? Ezekiel 1:23 describes the four creature's wings *under* the expanse. Ezekiel 1:25 records that a voice came from *above* the expanse, and Ezekiel 1:26 states that there was something *like* a throne *above* the expanse. From Ezekiel 1:28, we know that this is the throne of God. Therefore, this gap could have been between the creatures and the throne of God.

However, there is another possibility. Ezekiel 1:22 compares the appearance of this expanse to a "crystal." The King James Version uses the phrase "terrible crystal." Unfortunately, the word *terrible* has changed meaning in the past four centuries. Its original meaning is best rendered today as *awesome* or *awe-inspiring*.[15] Indeed, several modern English translations use the word "awesome." (Interestingly, the Geneva Bible, which predates the King James Version, uses the word "wonderful,"

---

15. Even the word "awful" has changed meaning. Originally, it had a positive connotation, meaning awe-inspiring. However, "awful" now has a negative connotation in the sense of being horrible or disgusting.

which still reads well today.) What does it mean to be a crystal? One must be careful, because the modern and ancient definitions are different. In the ancient world, a crystal was any substance that was solid and transparent. Examples include glass, quartz, rock salt, diamond, and other precious stones that transmit light. Except for glass, these crystals had naturally occurring facets. However, glass, particularly lead glass, can be cut to produce facets. Today, we define a crystal as a substance having an orderly array of atoms or molecules. This orderly array is responsible for the natural cleavage along facets of crystals (following the ancient definition). Nearly all solid substances have a crystal structure,[16] so most crystals (in the modern sense) are not transparent. It is important that we understand the word in the ancient sense, not the modern sense. The word translated "crystal" here elsewhere in the Old Testament is translated as "ice." In the ancient sense, ice would have been considered a crystal because it was hard and transparent. In the modern sense, ice is a crystal, too, because it has a hexagonal crystal structure. Whether in the modern sense or in the ancient sense, should we view this expanse that Ezekiel described as a literal crystal? Probably not. Ezekiel compared what he saw to an expanse, but he furthermore compared its appearance to a crystal, the emphasis being on the light that it gave off. That is, it shined, glowed, sparkled, or had a hue like a crystal. We might describe what Ezekiel saw as an aura.

A later vision commences in Ezekiel 8, with Ezekiel being a part of that vision. Ezekiel 10:1 mentions a *rāqîaʿ* above the heads of the cherubim with what appeared to be a throne above. If this sounds similar to Ezekiel 1, it is. The description of the cherubim in Ezekiel 10:9–14 is similar to the description of the four living creatures in Ezekiel 1:5–21. Indeed, Ezekiel twice states that these cherubim were the same as the four living creatures that he saw in his vision by the Chebar Canal (Ezekiel 10:15, 20–22). To reiterate, the *rāqîaʿ* of Ezekiel chapters 1 and 10 is not the *rāqîaʿ* found elsewhere in the Old Testament. It is an error to blithely equate these two very different meanings.

Both skeptics and flat-earthers alike miss this point. Absent this distinction, it is very easy to think that the thing Ezekiel described as being

---

16. Glass is the major exception. Glass is termed as an amorphous solid because it has no orderly array of atoms, molecules, or units as nearly all solids do.

like a *rāqîa'* is the same as the *rāqîa'* God made on day two, and, hence, derive properties of the Genesis 1 *rāqîa'* from the *rāqîa'* described in Ezekiel. With the many similarities between the visions of Ezekiel briefly discussed above and the Apostle John's description of part of his vision in Revelation 4:6–8, the problem is compounded by gleaning properties of the day two *rāqîa'* from what the Book of Revelation tells us. For instance, Revelation 4:6a states that before God's throne, there was a sea of glass, like crystal. Assuming that this sea of glass is below God's throne, and noting that Ezekiel mentioned God's throne above an expanse (Ezekiel 1:26, 10:1), one might conclude that Ezekiel's expanse and John's sea of glass are the same thing, viewed from opposite sides. However, if one equates every mention of the *rāqîa'* in the Old Testament, then it follows that John's sea of glass is the *rāqîa'* that God made on day two. To many who espouse the snow globe earth, this is perfectly in line with Isaiah 66:1, which says the heaven is God's throne and the earth is his footstool. That is, in the snow globe model, God sits immediately above the dome over the flat earth.

For those who insist on taking *everything* in the Bible as *woodenly literal*, this is fraught with problems. For instance, Isaiah 66:1 states that heaven *is* God's throne, but Ezekiel and John made it clear that God's throne *is in* heaven. Both cannot be true literally. Furthermore, God is spirit (John 4:24), and, hence, does not possess a physical body. The many instances of anthropomorphisms in the Bible, suggesting such things as God having hands (Psalm 8:3; Isaiah 66:2) or eyes (Proverbs 15:2), are clearly not literal. So, does God literally place his feet on the footstool? There also is an inconsistency in the flat-earth argument here. Flat-earthers believe that the firmament is a transparent dome over the earth, and, hence, is curved. Flat-earthers further insist that no body of water is curved, but rather all seas have flat surfaces. But John described a sea of glass, which, by every other use, must be flat, so why is this one curved?

The flat-earthers use one more verse which does not contain the word *rāqîa'*, but the verb it derives from. It is Job 37:18, where Elihu asked Job,

> Hast thou with him spread *out* the sky, which is strong,
> and as a molten looking glass? (KJV).

There are several reasons why one must be careful in gleaning the meaning of this verse. First, this one verse is within a textual unit (Job 37:14–18) which poetically uses weather phenomena to illustrate the overwhelming power and wisdom of God — so teaching cosmology is not the point. Second, these are the words of Elihu, not God. While the Bible is inspired, not everything recorded in the Bible is necessarily true. This is a truthful record of what Elihu said because God saw fit to preserve Elihu's speech, but that does not mean that Elihu was speaking infallibly. Therefore, if Elihu's words contain cosmological information, it merely reflects his understanding and not necessarily reality. Third, the Book of Job contains language and idioms that are unique to it, and many are difficult to translate. Also, Job, being ancient Hebrew poetry, evidences many examples of imagery and phenomenological language. Job 37:18 contains a particularly challenging case of imagery.

Notice that the word *sky* appears in this verse rather than *firmament*. This is because the Hebrew word *rāqîaʿ* is not in the text, but rather *šeḥāqîm* (the plural of *šaḥaq*) is used. What does this Hebrew word mean? It appears in its various forms 21 times in the Old Testament. Five times it appears in the Book of Job, as it does in Job 37:18. In the other four occurrences in Job, the King James Version translates *šeḥāqîm* as "clouds" (Job 35:5, 36:28, 37:21, 38:37). Note that one of these other four verses (Job 37:21) is within the immediate literary context of Elihu's speech. Furthermore, within that same context, Elihu uses two other Hebrew words to describe clouds (*ʿānān* in 37:15 and *ʿāb* in 37:16). Therefore, *šeḥāqîm* in Job 37:18 likely ought to be translated "clouds" as well. Accordingly, Elihu here is not even addressing cosmology; if anything, he is commenting on weather phenomena.

What about the term "looking glass"? This is an archaic term for a mirror, and so more modern translations render it as such. The word "molten" is a bit misleading, because today we might think of this as being in a hot, liquid state. In ancient times, mirrors were made of polished metal, typically bronze. Mirrors were manufactured by casting them, so when cast, they were molten, but when in use, they were solidified. The terminology here probably refers to how the mirror was manufactured, so today it would be best translated as a "cast mirror" (as in many modern Bible translations).

What of the phrase "which is strong?" The King James Version has it modifying the word *sky* (or, as we have seen, the word which ought to be translated "clouds"). However, in the Hebrew text, the phrase underlying the translation ("which is strong") modifies the word translated "looking glass/mirror," not the sky. As such, Elihu is not saying that the sky (or clouds) is strong, but rather he is comparing it *in appearance* to a strong (firm or hard) mirror. This makes sense, for even today we refer to severely overcast conditions as a "leaden sky." Clearly, Elihu is not talking about a solid dome over the earth, but rather is referring to a particularly gloomy, cloudy sky.

There is at least one other verse that flat-earthers use to argue that there is a dome over the earth, Amos 9:6, which reads:

> Who builds his upper chambers in the heavens
> and founds his vault upon the earth;
> who calls for the waters of the sea
> and pours them out upon the surface of the earth —
> the LORD is his name.

The Hebrew word translated "vault" here in the English Standard Version (as in the New American Standard Bible) is *aguddah*, though translations vary on how they translate this word. This word appears only four times in the Old Testament. The first time, in Exodus 12:22, it is translated as a bunch (of hyssop). The second time, in 2 Samuel 2:25, *aguddah* refers to a troop, or band (of men). These two uses imply things bound together, hyssop in the first case being a literal binding, while men in the second use is more metaphorical. The third use, in Isaiah 58:6, refers to a heavy burden. Some translations render this as a band (of a yoke). In this latter sense, one can see how the use sort of relates to the first two uses. But then in Amos 9:6, *aguddah* doesn't seem to have any relation to the previous three uses. This is why translators are puzzled as to how to translate this word in Amos 9:6. Wycliffe, whose translation predated the King James Version by more than two centuries, translated it "burden." That is a very literal translation. Interestingly, the Geneva Bible that predates the KJV by a few years translated *aguddah* in Amos 9:6 as "globe of elements." The KJV went with "troop," as it reads in 2 Samuel 2:25. Young's Literal Translation went with "troop" as well in Amos 9:6. Both the KJV and YLT translations of *aguddah* in Amos 9:6 are very literal, though those translations don't make a lot of sense. Therefore, the use here must be nonliteral. That is, whatever it is talking about must have some relation to a binding, though it's not all clear what this metaphorical use means. Perhaps it is an idiom lost to us. Again, translators are all over the place. Some modern translations render *aggudah* in Amos 9:6 as a vault. Obviously, they are motivated by the belief that this is how the ancient Hebrews viewed cosmology and/or this is the cosmology that the Bible teaches. On the other hand, the Geneva Bible translators seem to have been influenced by the belief that the heavens are a sphere. One cannot dismiss that translation merely because one doesn't agree with it. Proving one's point by insisting on a particular translation of Amos 9:6 amounts to begging the question. This is clearly what the flat-earthers are doing here. Furthermore, for flat-earthers to get a dome or vault out of Amos 9:6, they must depart from their self-professed literal hermeneutic, because *aguddah* doesn't mean either a vault or a dome. This is inconsistent.

The discussion of the Hebrew word *rāqîaʿ* has been very long, perhaps long enough to be a chapter unto itself. However, the meaning of this word is pivotal to the flat-earth position, so it warrants a thorough discussion. An objective study reveals that the word *rāqîaʿ* is best translated as "expanse." Hence, flat-earthers are victims of a poor translation of this word.

Windows of Heaven

Related to the flat-earth argument for the firmament is the phrase "windows of heaven." This phrase occurs twice in the Flood account (Genesis 7:11 and 8:2). In the first instance, the windows of heaven being opened is one of the two sources of the Flood mentioned, the other being "all the fountains of the great deep" being broken up. In the second instance, both the fountains of the deep and the windows of heaven were stopped. Flat-earthers often go in different directions at this point. Some flat-earthers believe that at the time of the Flood, openings in the hard dome allowed water from above the dome to pour onto the earth. This is similar to the canopy model that was once popular among recent creationists but is not so popular now. One difference is that the canopy wasn't above a hard dome over the earth but was a layer of water in some form above the earth's atmosphere. Another difference is that flat-earthers generally think that some of the water is still above the dome, whereas in the canopy model, that water is no longer above the earth. Other flat-earthers believe that rainwater still comes from this source above the dome. Apparently, they have been influenced by the likes of Michael Heiser, who teaches that this is what the ancient Hebrews thought. It may be that some ancient Hebrews thought this, but, as mentioned before, it hardly follows that this is what the Bible teaches. Yet many flat-earthers draw this conclusion, not realizing that this claim about the Bible originated with 19th-century critics.

There are other variations among flat-earthers on the windows of heaven. This is an example of a hyper-literal approach to Scripture. Flat-earthers (and others) fail to recognize that the "windows of heaven" is a figure of speech, a figure of speech occasionally employed in English today. This figure of speech occurs at least three more times in the Old Testament. Two occurrences are in 2 Kings 7. The context is Ben-hadad's siege of Samaria (2 Kings 6:24–33). Conditions were dire, but Elisha prophesied that within 24 hours, the siege would be lifted, and flour and grain would sell for a cheap price. Whereupon 2 Kings 7:2 records:

> Then the captain on whose hand the king leaned said to the man of God, "If the LORD himself should make windows in heaven, could this thing be?" But he said, "You shall see it with your own eyes, but you shall not eat of it."

The second mention of the "windows of heaven" in this chapter is in verse 19, where the words of the official are repeated. Notice that the use of this phrase here is in the context not of water falling, but rather the blessing of food falling. It's not as if God needed to open a window to make either grain or rain fall. This is an idiomatic expression. This phrase and its idiomatic use are found again in Malachi 3:10:

> Bring the full tithe into the storehouse, that there may be food in my house. And thereby put me to the test, says the LORD of hosts, if I will not open the windows of heaven for you and pour down for you a blessing until there is no more need.

In some translations, the phrase "windows of heaven" appears one other time, in Isaiah 24:18. However, in this instance, another Hebrew word for heaven is used instead of *šāmayim*. While this is not word for word the same as in the other four instances, the wording is similar enough to assume that the same meaning is intended. It, too, appears to be idiomatic. Only with a hyper-literal hermeneutic can one conclude that there are physical windows in heaven.

Chapter 11

How Did a Domed, Flat-Earth Cosmology Get Imported into the Bible?

Introduction

From the brief survey of relevant Old Testament passages in Chapter 10, we saw that there is no clear evidence that the *rāqîa'* is a solid dome over the earth. Rather, the *rāqîa'* is likely what we today would call space and much of the earth's atmosphere. Furthermore, biblical passages that supposedly indicate the earth is flat do no such thing. This being the case, why do flat-earthers and skeptics alike think that the *rāqîa'* is a hard dome surrounding a flat earth? The development of that false idea has a long history, which I can only briefly summarize here.

The Influence of Ancient Greek Cosmology

The Septuagint was a third-century B.C. translation of the Old Testament from Hebrew to Greek. The need for this translation was that many Jews of the time no longer could speak or read Hebrew. This was particularly true of Jews of the Diaspora, of which many were living in Alexandria, Egypt, where the Septuagint translation was done. Alexandria was a major Greek city and was a center of Greek learning and culture. Consequently, the people of Alexandria, including its Jews, were heavily hellenized. Therefore, the Jews of Alexandria were familiar with the then-current science.

The Greek cosmology of the time held to a spherical earth concentric within a much larger solid, transparent sphere on which the stars were affixed (the celestial sphere). The sun, moon, and five naked-eye planets moved on smaller spheres within the celestial sphere. The Greek word *stereoma*, referring to something hard, was used to describe the celestial sphere. Since hellenized Jews of the time were aware of this cosmology, it is no accident that the Septuagint translated the *rāqîaʿ* as *stereoma*, apparently in an attempt to accommodate the cosmology of their day. Aside from some mentions in the *Book of Enoch* (the subject of chapter 12), the earliest known Jewish writings that address cosmology are from the medieval period, and they reflect medieval cosmology described above. Therefore, we have no knowledge of what specific cosmology the ancient Hebrews believed. However, the Greek word that the Septuagint translators chose is a strong clue as to what at least hellenized Jews of the ancient world thought. It likely was a spherical earth centered in the celestial sphere. This is very different from a vaulted dome over a flat earth that flat-earthers promote and the supposed cosmology of the Bible that liberal theologians promote.

Flat-earthers sometimes appeal to the *Book of Enoch* and Josephus as expositions of what the ancient Hebrews thought about cosmology. I discuss the pseudepigraphic *Book of Enoch* in the next chapter. While cosmology does not seem to the be the purpose of the *Book of Enoch*, as I point out in the next chapter, it does seem to endorse something like the flat-earth cosmology of today, but with some important differences. It isn't known how popular the cosmology of the *Book of Enoch* was among Jews two thousand years ago. As for Josephus, he wrote very little about cosmology. According to William Whiston's 1737 translation, in book 1, chapter 1 of *Antiquities of the Jews*, Josephus wrote the following about days two, three, and four of the creation week:

> After this, on the second day, he placed the heaven over the whole world, and separated it from the other parts, and he determined it should stand by itself. He also placed a crystalline [firmament] round it, and put it together in a manner agreeable to the earth, and fitted it for giving moisture and rain, and for affording the advantage of dews. On the third day he appointed the dry land to appear, with the sea itself round about it; and on the very same day he made the plants

and the seeds to spring out of the earth. On the fourth day he adorned the heaven with the sun, the moon, and the other stars, and appointed them their motions and courses, that the vicissitudes of the seasons might be clearly signified. [brackets in the original][1]

This is sparse. However, notice that Josephus seems to separate "the heaven over the whole world" and the "crystalline [firmament] round it." This deviates from what the day two account reveals, for Genesis 1:6–8 makes it very clear that God made the *rāqîaʿ* and equated it with heaven. That is, at least in the day two account, the *rāqîaʿ* and heaven are the same thing. Therefore, Josephus' separation of the two is unwarranted. Flat-earthers like to mingle the two, particularly Josephus' statement that the crystalline firmament and heaven were put "together in a manner agreeable to the earth, and fitted it for giving moisture and rain, and for affording the advantage of dews." Flat-earthers want to merge this function into one entity, with the waters above being part of the rain cycle, particularly at the time of the Flood. But this isn't necessarily what Josephus said. However, most important is that Josephus wrote that God placed the crystalline firmament *round* the earth, not *above* the earth. This terminology doesn't make sense if the earth is flat with a dome over it. However, this makes sense in terms of the dominant Greek cosmology of his day, a spherical earth surrounded by a firm celestial sphere(s) on which the astronomical bodies were affixed.

Several centuries after the translation of the Septuagint, Jerome translated both the Old Testament and the New Testament into Latin. Jerome selected the Latin word *firmamentum* to translate *rāqîaʿ*, a word analogous to the Greek word *stereoma*. The hard, transparent celestial-sphere model of the ancient Greeks was still the dominant cosmology in Jerome's day. Therefore, he both accommodated that cosmology and endorsed the Septuagint's reading on the matter. Much later, translators of early English versions of the Bible merely transliterated Jerome's choice into English as *firmament*, perhaps because they also believed this ancient Greek cosmology, or perhaps because they didn't

---

1. *The Works of Josephus*, translated by W. Whiston (Peabody, MA: Hendrickson Publishers, 1987), p. 29.

know what to do with the Hebrew word *rāqîaʿ*. This has caused problems ever since because people recognize the word "firm" within that word and assume that the *rāqîaʿ* must be something hard. However, as we have already seen, rather than referring to something necessarily hard, the word *rāqîaʿ* probably refers to something that has been spread out. This is why many modern English translations render the *rāqîaʿ* as "expanse." This is a good translation because it gets to the heart of what the likely intended meaning of *rāqîaʿ* is. Some modern translations render *rāqîaʿ* as "sky." This, too, is a good translation, because the sky that we see above us encompasses the likely meaning of the *rāqîaʿ*, as discussed previously.

We can reach three broad conclusions. First, the Bible does not explicitly teach any cosmology of man. Rather, one may piece together certain passages to sort out what possible cosmology may be there, but one must be careful not to read into these passages interpretations coming from external sources. Our approach ought to be *exegesis*, taking from Scripture what the likely meaning is, rather than *eisegesis*, reading a meaning into Scripture. As we shall see, an eisegetical approach is what led to the mistaken belief that the Bible teaches a solid dome over the earth. I recognize that I am not immune to this difficulty, but at least acknowledging the temptation to interpret Scripture through the lens of external factors makes it possible to be on guard. Let me emphasize again that the Bible does not explicitly endorse any cosmology of man. This is a good thing, and it is consistent with God's wisdom. If God had endorsed in Scripture an ancient cosmology, those who believed some other ancient cosmology would have dismissed the Bible on the basis that the Bible's cosmology was wrong. Certainly, modern man would make that argument because modern cosmologies differ from all ancient cosmologies. But what if God had endorsed the modern cosmology? Then people up to relatively recent times would have dismissed the Bible, because, in their minds, it taught the wrong cosmology.

Second, while not an inspired source, Josephus does frequently reflect the thinking of Jews in the first century A.D. Josephus lived in Israel, not Alexandria, but his writings show evidence of hellenization. Since his sect was the only one to survive the persecution and destruction that came in A.D. 70, his work came to be recognized as representing the Jews of his time. However, Josephus misrepresented the ideas of the other sects and presented his own sect in the best possible light. This sort of misrepresentation extended even to his presentation of the religious beliefs of the other sects. Thus, we must be very careful in using Josephus. With that caveat, what do Josephus' writings reveal about cosmology among at least some of the ancient Jews? As I have already shown, Josephus' account of day two of creation is consistent with the Greek cosmology of his day, but not the domed-vault cosmology.

Third, the cosmology of the West throughout the medieval period was that of the ancient Greeks, not a domed vault over a flat earth. It was within this cosmology that the second century A.D. astronomer Claudius Ptolemy developed his model to explain the motions of the planets. The Ptolemaic model was overturned (along with the other elements of ancient Greek cosmology) only four centuries ago in favor of more modern cosmologies, such as the heliocentric theory.

The Influence of 19th-Century Skeptics

If the domed vault is not the cosmology of the Bible, how did so many people come to think that it was? This idea came about as the result of three developments in the 19th century. First, modern archaeology began in earnest in the 19th century. Interpretations of early excavations in the Near East indicated a domed-vault cosmology, from which archaeologists and historians erroneously concluded that this was *the* Ancient Near Eastern cosmology.

Second, the documentary hypothesis proposed that the Pentateuch was written much later than the time of Moses (and many of its proponents doubt if Moses even existed!). According to the documentary hypothesis, four different documents arose in the first half of the first millennium B.C., and those sources were redacted much later during the intertestamental period. Supposedly, the Jews picked up much of their cosmology, cosmogony, and early history from Ancient Near Eastern cultures, and these are reflected in both the creation and Flood accounts of Genesis. Therefore, it became fashionable to interpret biblical passages in terms of the supposed-dominant domed-vault cosmology.

Third, the conflict thesis claimed that Christianity had held back development of thought throughout the Middle Ages, and it was not until man allegedly was freed from the strictures of the Bible during the Renaissance that man's reason enabled a renewal in learning. Part of the case made against Christianity as part of the conflict thesis was that the church and the Bible taught that the earth was flat and was surrounded by a domed vault. As demonstrated elsewhere, the church never taught that the earth is flat. Such a blatant lie ought to call into question the claim about the domed vault being the biblical cosmology as well. The Flammarion engraving is a very famous depiction of the domed vault over the flat earth. (See a picture of the engraving in chapter 1.) Most people think that this is a medieval piece of artwork, but it dates from the 1880s. One is hard-pressed to find *any* medieval depictions of the supposed vaulted-dome/flat-earth cosmology of the Bible because this was not believed in the Middle Ages. The influence of the Flammarion engraving as used by promoters of the conflict thesis cannot be overestimated. This one depiction appears to have, more than anything else, promoted the false notion that medieval cosmology was a domed vault over a flat earth.

The domed vault was not even the dominant cosmology in the Ancient Near East. Later excavations and studies revealed a plethora of Ancient Near Eastern cosmologies.[2] If one wishes to interpret the cosmology of the Bible in terms of the cosmology of the Ancient Near East, then one must first decide which cosmology to use. Unfortunately, many Bible scholars today have been deceived by the conflict thesis into thinking that the Bible's cosmology is that of a domed vault over a flat earth, which has led to many depictions of a flat earth from the late 20th and 21st centuries with a domed vault above supported by pillars.[3] However, such depictions began to appear in the 19th century after the damage done by the conflict thesis. This line of thinking has gained much traction in recent years. For instance, the New International Version (NIV) of the Bible, first released in 1984, originally translated the *rāqîaʿ* as "sky," but the updated edition published in 2011 translated it as "vault." Again, this false understanding of biblical cosmology by some Bible scholars (scholars who, by and large, have been deceived by the conflict thesis) is relatively recent.

---

2. For instance, see Wayne Horowitz, *Mesopotamian Cosmic Geography* (Warsaw, IN: Eisenbrauns, 1998).

3. If the earth were supported by pillars, it would contradict Job 26:7, which tells us that God hung the earth on *nothing*.

Compounding the problem, Christians who endorse the flat earth use depictions by contemporary theologians who wrongly portray biblical cosmology as a flat earth under a domed vault as evidence of what the Bible teaches. Therefore, they are victims of the conflict thesis twice, once in embracing a flat earth, and once again in accepting the false domed-vault cosmology. Again, this concept of biblical cosmology did not come from ancient sources, but rather arose in the 19th century as an attempt to discredit the Bible. Those who support the flat earth, believing that this is what the Bible teaches, have fallen into a trap. Ironically, while apparently motivated to defend the Bible, they have been tricked into using the same false arguments that skeptics use.

Does the Earth Have Pillars?

Flat-earthers frequently tie in biblical mentions of the earth having pillars to the earth being flat. There are three such passages — 1 Samuel 2:8, Job 9:6, and Psalm 75:3. Notice that the second and third verses come from the poetic books. But also notice that the first verse comes from Hannah's song of thanksgiving (1 Samuel 2:1–10), making it a poetic passage as well. As mentioned before, the poetic books have many instances of non-literal usage of language. Hence, one must exercise caution in determining the meaning of such passages. To insist on a very literal interpretation of poetic passages is to mishandle Scripture, particularly when a teaching gleaned that way is not supported elsewhere in the Bible. For instance, the first verse listed here, 1 Samuel 2:8, reads:

> He raises up the poor from the dust;
> he lifts the needy from the ash heap
> to make them sit with princes
> and inherit a seat of honor.
> For the pillars of the earth are the LORD's,
> and on them he has set the world.

Every commentary on 1 Samuel and the notes of all reference Bibles indicate that the use of the phrase "pillars of the earth" here is figurative. It is interesting that this passage also includes the previously discussed phrase "ends of the earth," for verse 10 reads:

> The adversaries of the LORD shall be broken to pieces;
> against them he will thunder in heaven.
> The LORD will judge the ends of the earth;
> he will give strength to his king
> and exalt the horn of his anointed.

This is another example of how the "ends of the earth" doesn't refer to a literal end of the earth. As previously discussed with other passages that use this phrase, if it were literal, then it would mean that God will judge real estate. That is absurd, for it clearly refers to God judging *people*. For that matter, verse 10 contains another idiomatic expression, "horn." This refers to the horn of an animal, such as a ram, or to a musical instrument, such as a shofar, made from the horn of a ram. This idiom refers to one's strength. I doubt that anyone, including the most hyper-literal of flat-earthers, would think otherwise.

The list of 240+ supposed flat-earth Bible verses includes Job 26:7 with these three verses under the heading "Earth Has Pillars and Hangs on Nothing." But this would seem to contradict the three verses that mention the earth having pillars if those verses are taken so literally. The usual response that flat-earthers have to this objection is that there is a difference between being supported below by pillars and being suspended above by a cable or rope. In an engineering sense, this is true, because the former is under compression, while the latter is under tension, and the reaction of materials under these different conditions is different. Is such a difference warranted by the words used? The Hebrew word translated "hang" in Job 26:7 occurs 27 other times in the Old Testament, and each time it is translated as "hang." For instance, it is the word used many times in the Book of Esther to refer to executing someone on a gallows. The same word is used to refer to the hanging of bodies from trees as a reminder after people were executed by some other means. This word is used in Deuteronomy 21:22–23 in regulating that a body couldn't remain hanging after sunset.[4] The word is also used to describe Absalom's predicament of hanging by his head in a tree in 2 Samuel 18:10. The word is also used to refer to the hanging of inanimate objects, such as in Psalm 137:2. Therefore, it seems reasonable that this word probably refers to supporting something from above rather than from below.

---

4. The Apostle Paul quoted from this passage in Galatians 3:13.

However, does this mean that Job's words in Job 26:7 were parsed very carefully so that he was making a distinction between the earth not being supported from above, while simultaneously believing that the earth was supported from below? If so, then it guts the entire meaning of the verse. There is wonder and majesty in God hanging the earth on nothing, but what is the point if that merely means that God provided for support underneath instead?

But I digress. The earth having pillars refers to God making the earth stable. Related to the earth having pillars, flat-earthers sometimes mention passages that say that the earth has a foundation. For instance, Psalm 104:5 reads:

> He set the earth on its foundations,
> so that it should never be moved.

But Psalm 82:5 says:

> They have neither knowledge nor understanding,
> they walk about in darkness;
> all the foundations of the earth are shaken.

Well, which is it? A hyper-literal hermeneutic leads to problems with these two verses, but recognizing the nonliteral nature of many of the poetic passages resolves this problem.

Speaking of the earth being moved, that is expressed in the second pillar passage listed above, Job 9:6, which reads:

> Who shakes the earth out of its place,
> and its pillars tremble.

Therefore, we have here both the earth and its pillars shaking. But contrast this with the next pillar verse, Psalm 75:3:

> When the earth totters, and all its inhabitants,
> it is I who keep steady its pillars.

So, here the earth moves, but the pillars remain steady.

These considerations illustrate the thicket that one becomes entangled in when taking a hyper-literal approach to the poetic books of Scripture.

Clearly, the earth having pillars is a figurative expression. And insisting that the earth rests upon pillars would contradict Job 26:7, which states that God hangs the earth upon nothing.

Words for Earth and World

The first appearance of the word "earth" in the Bible is in Genesis 1:1 and following in the creation account. The Hebrew word used here is *'ereṣ*, which occurs more than 2,500 times in the Old Testament. Most often, *'ereṣ* is translated as "land," with "earth" being the second most common translation (together they account for nearly 90 percent of the occurrences). In context, *'ereṣ* can mean many different things. For instance, it can refer to a part of the earth (e.g., Genesis 19:28) or to the territory of a nation (e.g., Genesis 10:10). It also can refer to the inhabitants of the earth (e.g., 1 Kings 2:2). Or *'ereṣ* can mean "soil" (e.g., Genesis 1:11–12). It also can refer to the entire earth (e.g., Genesis 22:18). This is especially true when *'ereṣ* is used in contrast with heaven. There are other nuances to the meaning of *'ereṣ*, but these few meanings ought to give you the general idea of the broad range of meanings the word can have.

What is the meaning of *'ereṣ* when it first appears, in Genesis 1:1–2? Given that the first appearance is in contrast with heaven, it must mean the entire earth.[5] This establishes the context of Genesis 1:2, where it also must mean the entire earth. However, the third occurrence of *'ereṣ* is in Genesis 1:10, where it is clearly defined to refer to the land mass of the earth. This context continues in Genesis 1:10–11, where *'ereṣ* refers to the land mass, or more specifically, the soil covering the land mass. However, there is no clear indication of the (entire) earth's shape in Genesis 1, or, for that matter, in many other passages.

A different Hebrew word with similar meaning to *'ereṣ* is *tēbēl*. Occurring 36 times, *tēbēl* is usually translated as "world." The *Theological Wordbook of the Old Testament (TWOT)* says that *tēbēl* is used in three basic situations. Those three situations are:

---

5. There are some liberal Bible scholars who claim that the earth of the Genesis 1 creation account refers only to a part of the earth, such as the Garden of Eden or even the Promised land. However, this is without foundation, as it is a desperate attempt to salvage the Bible in the face of the supposed billions of years age of the earth and the attendant assumption of evolution.

1. The noun is employed to represent the global mass called earth, including the atmosphere or heavens
2. Is sometimes limited to "countries" or "the inhabitable world
3. May also refer to the inhabitants living upon the whole earth

TWOT concludes its discussion of *tēbēl* with:

> In several passages the sense of tēbēl as the global earth in combination with its inhabitants is clearly observed. Everything belongs to Yahweh as his creation (Ps 50:12). Yahweh alone controls this world (Job 34:13; Nah 1:5) and his power is over all the earth which always responds to his presence (Job 37:12; Ps 97:4).[6]

Notice the overlap with the meaning of *'ereṣ*, so that in many respects, the two words may be used interchangeably. Indeed, in some of the poetic and prophetic books, the two words are used in parallel structure as is the common feature of the poetic and prophetic books. For instance, Psalm 89:11 reads:

> The heavens are yours; the earth also is yours;
> the world and all that is in it, you have founded them.

This would seem to conform to situation number 1 of the *TWOT* quoted above. But notice something very important: in giving the meaning of *tēbēl*, the *TWOT* twice describes the earth as being global. While I would not endorse everything that the three authors of the *TWOT* have written or said, they were eminent Hebrew scholars. Flat-earthers frequently claim that Hebrew scholars claim that the Bible teaches that the earth is flat, yet these three Hebrew scholars obviously did not see it that way.

Above I quoted Psalm 89:11 from the English Standard Version. Most English translations render *tēbēl* simply as "world," but that originally wasn't the case in English translations. For instance, in the Coverdale Bible (1535), the first English translation of the entire Bible, it reads (it is Psalm 88 because the chapter divisions are slightly different from modern Bibles):

---

6. R.L. Harris, G.L. Archer, B.K Waltke, *Theological Wordbook of the Old Testament* (Chicago, IL: Moody Press, 1980), p. 359.

> The heaues are thine, the earth is thine:
> thou hast layed the foundacio of the roude worlde and all
> that therin is. [7]

Notice the archaic spelling, but that Coverdale translated *tēbēl* as "round world." In the 1539 Great Bible, the same verse reads:

> The heauens are thyne, the earth also is thyne:
> thou hast layed the foundacyon of the rounde worlde, and
> all that therin is.[8]

The Great Bible was the first Bible authorized for use in the Church of England. Miles Coverdale prepared it, mostly from William Tyndale's work, who was executed in 1536. The Bishop's Bible (1568) reads:

> The heauens are thine, the earth also is thine:
> thou hast layde the foundation of the rounde worlde, and
> of all the plentie that is therin.[9]

The roundness of the earth similarly appears in early English versions of Proverbs 8:31, though the Hebrew word there is *'ereṣ*, not *tēbēl*. Early English translations rendered *'ereṣ* as "world," while later English versions more consistently translated it as "earth."

The King James Version (1611) was largely an update of the Bishop's Bible, so why was the word "round" deleted in Psalm 89:11? It may be the influence of the Geneva Bible, perhaps the first English translation (1560) to delete mention of the world being round in this verse. Where did the early English translators get the idea that they ought to translate Psalm 89:11 with an explicit mention of the world being round? They largely worked from the Latin Vulgate. The appropriate passage in the Vulgate is (Psalm 88:12):

> Tui sunt cæli, et tua est terra: orbem terræ,
> et plenitudinem ejus tu fundasti.

---

7. https://www.originalbibles.com/Zip/Zippy.php?../SpecialBibles/Zip1/Coverdale1535.zip?Coverdale1535_Part244.pdf.

8. https://www.originalbibles.com/the-great-bible-1540-original-pdf/.

9. https://www.originalbibles.com/bishops-bible-1568-pdf/.

I have never formally studied Latin, but even I can spot *orbem*, the Latin word from which we get the word "orb." Translate.google.com rendered this as:

> The heavens and the earth is round world,
> and all that you have established.

Why did Jerome translate Psalm 89:11 into Latin this way? Perhaps he had a good understanding of the Hebrew word *tēbēl* (Jerome knew at least some Hebrew). At any rate, the fact that the Vulgate remained the standard Bible in the West for the next millennium ought to put to rest the false notion that the church always taught that the earth was flat.

Some flat-earthers have seized upon the reading of 2 Samuel 11:11 in the 1537 Matthew Bible as evidence that the Bible teaches the earth is flat. In the King James Version, this verse reads:

> And Uriah said unto David, The ark, and Israel, and Judah, abide in tents; and my lord Joab, and the servants of my lord, are encamped *in the open fields*; shall I then go into mine house, to eat and to drink, and to lie with my wife? as thou livest, and as thy soul liveth, I will not do this thing. (emphasis added)

However, in the Matthew Bible, instead of the phrase "in the open fields," "on the flatt erthe" appears. Why the difference? That isn't clear, for almost no other English translation reads this way. Most importantly, the Hebrew word here is not *ʾereṣ*, but instead is *sadeh*. This word appears 333 times in the Old Testament. Its meaning is "field" or "land." As such, it can have some overlap with *ʾereṣ*. But unlike *ʾereṣ*, which can refer to the entire earth, *sadeh* never refers to the whole earth. Rather, *sadeh* always refers to a portion of the earth. The form of *sadeh* in 2 Samuel 11:11 is *hassadeh*, which occurs 131 times in the Old Testament. It translates well as a prepositional phrase. Examples are found in Genesis 2:5 (twice), 19, 20, 3:1, 14, and 18, where the word is translated similarly.

The Hebrew rendered as "open" here is *paneh*. This word appears 2,128 times in the Old Testament, and it has a very wide range of possible meanings. One meaning is "open," as here. Another possible meaning is "face," so this could be translated here as "face of the earth" or "face of the ground." Normally, people select a reasonably flat area to pitch a tent, for sleeping on a slope is uncomfortable. Hence, ground suitable for camping is usually reasonably flat. Hence, the Matthew Bible translation of 2 Samuel 11:11 is an acceptable translation. However, insisting that this means that the entire earth is flat is unwarranted because the Hebrew word *sadeh* never refers to the entire earth. Therefore, one could reach the conclusion that 2 Samuel 11:11 teaches that the earth is flat only if one presupposes that the earth is flat. This is proof-texting at its worst.

Stars Falling from Heaven

Flat-earthers use other verses that by their own admission don't explicitly teach that the earth is flat. However, flat-earthers claim that these passages are more properly understood within the flat-earth model, and, hence, imply that the earth is flat. An example of this is the passages that mention the stars falling. For instance, in Matthew 24:29, Jesus said,

> Immediately after the tribulation of those days the sun will be darkened, and the moon will not give its light, and the stars will fall from heaven, and the powers of the heavens will be shaken.

A parallel verse is Mark 13:25:

> And the stars will be falling from heaven, and the powers in the heavens will be shaken.

Flat-earthers argue that since these verses speak of the stars falling, then this is literally what the stars will do. They also assume that these stars will fall *to the earth*, something these two verses do not specifically state. This idea will be examined below. Flat-earthers intone that this is impossible if the conventional understanding of cosmology is true. According to conventional cosmology, the stars are much larger and more massive than the earth, and the stars are very far away. Therefore, stars (as understood in the modern sense) can't fall to the earth. Flat-earthers conclude that, on the other hand, this is quite plausible in the flat-earth model, where the stars are much closer and smaller than generally thought and are attached to a dome over the flat, disk-shaped earth. Hence, flat-earthers believe that these verses imply that the earth is flat.

Let us examine what these verses likely mean. These verses are part of Jesus' apocalyptic statements that deal with astronomical bodies (Matthew 24:29–31; Mark 13:24–27). Interestingly, the parallel passage from the other synoptic Gospel, Luke 21:25–28, doesn't mention the stars.

Before examining those other passages, perhaps I ought to better explain what the flat-earthers who espouse a biblical approach think of stars. Many flat-earthers think that stars are angels, and, hence, modern astronomers are completely wrong about the nature of stars. The equation of angels with stars is not unique to flat-earthers, for many Christians equate the two, at least in some cases. There are several biblical passages that suggest this equation. For instance, in Job 38:7, God asks Job in the context of creation if he were there

> when the morning stars sang together
> and all the sons of God shouted for joy.

Most people think that the morning stars and the sons of God of these parallel lines are angelic beings. Revelation 1:20 identifies the seven stars in Jesus' right hand in Revelation 1:16 as the angels of the seven churches in Asia (Revelation 1:4). Some passages use the phrase "host of heaven" to refer to stars (e.g., Deuteronomy 4:19; 2 Kings 23:5; Isaiah 34:4; Jeremiah 33:22; Acts 7:42). On the other hand, some passages use the phrase "host of heaven" to refer to angels (cf. 1 Kings 22:19; Luke 2:13–14). However, does it follow that stars and angels must be the same thing in every context? Hardly. How can we tell which meaning is intended? As usual, context is key. The word "heaven" is used more than one way in Scripture, such as the abode of God, the astronomical realm, and the atmospheric realm. When "heaven" in "host of heaven" is the abode of God, angels are probably intended, while when "heaven" in the "host of heaven" is the astronomical realm, stars are almost certainly intended.

What does it mean for the stars to fall in Matthew 24:29? The Greek word translated "will fall" in Matthew 24:29 is πεσοῦνται (*pesountai*). Technically, πεσοῦνται is an indicative mood, future tense, middle or passive voice, and third person verb. The English verb "will be falling" in Mark 13:25 is in the future progressive tense, a different tense than the "will fall" of Matthew's account. Why the difference? This is because Mark used a slightly different Greek word, the present tense, active, masculine, plural, nominative participle πίπτοντες (*piptontes*). Both Greek words derive from the root πίπτω (*piptó*), meaning "to fall." And this is how this word and its related forms are usually translated the many times that they appear in the New Testament, such as with both the rain and the house in the parable of the two builders in Matthew 7:24–27 and the seed in the parable of the sower in Matthew 13:1–23. Therefore, Matthew 24:29 and Mark 13:25 are good translations.

But does this require that the stars must physically fall to the earth? First, notice that where the stars fall is not identified in these verses, so it is an assumption that the stars will fall to the earth. But, more to the point, must we understand that this falling is to be taken so literally? For instance, the English word "fall" has nonliteral meanings. Consider Edward Gibbon's *Decline and Fall of the Roman Empire* or William Shirer's *The Rise and Fall of the Third Reich*. In either case, neither the rise nor the fall are to be taken literally. And such nonliteral usages of the Greek word translated "fall" appear in the New Testament. One example is Revelation 2:5, where in addressing the church at Ephesus, the Apostle John wrote:

> Remember therefore from where you have fallen; repent,
> and do the works you did at first. If not, I will come to you
> and remove your lampstand from its place, unless you repent.

Clearly, the word "fallen" here is not literal. The Greek word here is πέπτωκας (*peptōkas*), again from πίπτω. When the Apostle Paul wrote in 1 Corinthians 13:8 that love never ends, or fails, he used the Greek word πίπτει (*piptei*), likewise from πίπτω. One could translate that as "love never falls," which is clearly a nonliteral usage of the word "fall." However, the exact same Greek word literally means "to fall" in Matthew 17:15 and Mark 5:22. The point is, the Greek word translated "fall" in the New Testament often means literally to fall, but in some passages, the same Greek word doesn't literally mean to fall, but instead means to fail, or cease.

Given this information, how can we know if the description of stars falling in Matthew 24:29 and Mark 13:25 are literal or nonliteral? It is important to interpret Scripture with Scripture. Matthew 24:29 is more detailed than Mark 13:25, and it includes four elements:

1. The sun will be darkened.
2. The moon will not give its light.
3. The stars will fall from heaven.
4. The powers of the heavens will be shaken.

Some of these elements are found in various Old Testament passages. Before deciding whether these Old Testament passages are talking about the same thing, let us explore how many of these elements are present in each passage. For instance, Isaiah 13:10 contains elements one and two, but rather than element three, it says something slightly different about the stars:

> For the stars of the heavens and their constellations
> will not give their light;
> the sun will be dark at its rising,
> and the moon will not shed its light.

That is, the stars are described as withdrawing their light, much as the light of the sun and moon will also be dimmed.

While it uses different terminology from the Gospel accounts of Jesus' words, Isaiah 24:23 seems to refer to the first two elements:

> Then the moon will be confounded
> and the sun ashamed,
> for the LORD of hosts reigns
> on Mount Zion and in Jerusalem,
> and his glory will be before his elders.

It would be absurd to suggest that the moon will literally be confounded and that the sun will literally be ashamed (though the hyper-literal hermeneutic of flat-earthers might demand that). Some may object that within the context of Isaiah 24:23 (Isaiah 24:21–23), verse 21 reads,

> On that day the LORD will punish
> the host of heaven, in heaven,
> and the kings of the earth, on the earth,

leading to the conclusion that verse 23 doesn't literally refer to the sun and moon. However, given that verse 22 seems to describe the punishment of the host of heaven and the kings of the earth (declared in verse 21), and then verse 23 moves on to focus on the glory of the Lord and His reign, the most likely meaning of the passage is that the glory of the sun and moon will be nothing compared to the glory of the Lord.

Hence, Isaiah 24:23 is likely referring to the sun and moon being dimmed — or at least dim in comparison to God's glory.

Joel 2:10 mentions the first, second, and fourth elements, and, as with Isaiah 13:10, the stars are said to dim:

> The earth quakes before them;
> the heavens tremble.
> The sun and the moon are darkened,
> and the stars withdraw their shining.

Amos 8:9 appears to include the first element:

> "And on that day," declares the Lord GOD,
> "I will make the sun go down at noon
> and darken the earth in broad daylight."

Ezekiel 32:7–8 includes elements one and two, but as with Isaiah 13:10 and Joel 2:10, element three may be expressed as the stars dimming:

> When I blot you out, I will cover the heavens
> and make their stars dark;
> I will cover the sun with a cloud,
> and the moon shall not give its light.
> All the bright lights of heaven
> will I make dark over you,
> and put darkness on your land,
> declares the Lord GOD.

Joel 3:15 includes the second and third elements, but, as with Isaiah 13:10, Ezekiel 32:7–8, and Joel 2:10, the third element may be expressed as a dimming of the stars:

> The sun and the moon are darkened,
> and the stars withdraw their shining.

Finally, Joel 2:30–31 includes elements one and four, but something different is said about the moon:

> And I will show wonders in the heavens and on the earth,
> blood and fire and columns of smoke. The sun shall be turned
> to darkness, and the moon to blood, before the great and awe-
> some day of the Lord comes.

What does it mean that the moon will be turned to blood? Contrary to common belief, this does not necessarily mean that the moon will turn red. I have argued elsewhere that this likely refers to the dimming of the moon.[10] This understanding unifies Joel 2:30–31 (as well as Acts 2:20 and Revelation 6:12 that also mention the moon turning to blood) with the darkening of the moon in Isaiah 13:10, 24:23; Ezekiel 32:7–8; Joel 2:10; and Joel 3:15. Hence, Joel 2:30–31 likely contains the second element as well.

Some may object that this understanding of the moon turning to blood in Joel 2:30–31 is too far of a stretch. Some might even opine that when Joel referred to blood, he literally meant blood. Of course, few people would insist on such an extreme literalism. It is important to keep in mind that the prophetic books contain many examples of symbolism, allusions, similes, metaphors, and poetic devices. It would be very boring to say the same thing the same way every time. A hyper-literal approach to these passages would result in the conclusion that each passage is referring to its own unique event or events rather than the same event or events.

For example, consider Isaiah 13:10 and Amos 8:9. Isaiah 13:10 says that the sun will be dark at its rising, but Amos 8:9 says that the sun will go down at noon. Taken very literally, these cannot be the same events. For one thing, the rising of the sun and noon are roughly six hours apart. More importantly, Isaiah 13:10 has the darkened sun rising, while Amos 8:9 says that the sun will unexpectedly set (not dim) at noon. For that matter, Ezekiel 32:7–8 states that God will cover the sun with a cloud. That is, if Ezekiel 32:7–8 is taken literally, the sun neither inexplicably dims nor abruptly sets very early, but is merely covered by a cloud. But

---

10. Danny R. Faulkner, *The Created Cosmos: What the Bible Reveals About Astronomy* (Green Forest, AR: Master Books), p. 170–173.

that is hardly apocalyptic, because the sun is blocked on any overcast day. Nearly everyone would agree that these verses are not to be taken quite so literally, and many believe they refer to the same event. Admittedly, Ezekiel 32 is a prophecy against Egypt, and there is debate about whether this has been fulfilled already or if it awaits a future final judgment, and if it has been fulfilled, if Ezekiel 32:7–8 is an example of a prophecy that had an immediate fulfillment and will have a later fulfillment as well. Therefore, there is some doubt as to whether Ezekiel 32:7–8 ought to be included in this discussion.

Since each of these apocalyptic passages contain some of the four elements in Jesus' statement in Matthew 24:29, but none of them state that the stars will fall, perhaps we ought to collate Jesus' words about the stars falling with the dimming of the stars in Isaiah 13:10; Ezekiel 32:7–8; Joel 2:10; and Joel 3:18. The one explicit Old Testament passage that mentions the stars falling may be the key passage to consider. Isaiah 34:4 states the following:

> All the host of heaven shall rot away,
> and the skies roll up like a scroll.
> All their host shall fall,
> as leaves fall from the vine,
> like leaves falling from the fig tree.

Many assume that "the host of heaven" is the stars.[11] Notice that only one of four elements of Matthew 24:29 appears here. Also notice that the English verb "fall" occurs three times in Isaiah 34:4. However, the New American Standard Bible doesn't use the word "fall," but rather it translates the Hebrew verb as "wither." Why the difference? The Hebrew verb used here is a *Qal yiqtol* (sometimes called an "imperfect") verb from the root *nbl*. This verb appears at least 25 times in the Old Testament. It normally is translated as "fade" or "wither." *HALOT*[12] gives

---

11. However, according to Gary Smith, *Isaiah 1–39: An Exegetical and Theological Exposition of Holy Scripture* (Nashville, TN: B&H Publishing Group, 2007), p. 575: "These heavenly 'hosts' (NIV 'stars') could refer to (a) the physical stars and planets that will become dim; (b) the destruction of the pagan gods that were represented by these heavenly hosts; (c) an army of heavenly beings; or possibly (d) all of the above factors are included in one holistic view of the celestial world."

12. L. Koehler and W. Baumgartner *The Hebrew and Aramaic Lexicon of the Old Testament* (Boston, MA: Brill, 2001).

the meaning as "to wither, decay; to crumble away." "Fall" is not even a recognized proper meaning.[13] Why, then, is this Hebrew word translated as "fall" here? The Septuagint translators (as well as the subsequent KJV translators) might have chosen to translate this word as *piptó* based on the theological influence of other passages, even though it is not the best translation, at least in a literal sense. Perhaps people in the past had no problem in understanding that the word "fall" has many nonliteral meanings. Interestingly, the Vulgate didn't translate these verbs as "fall," but as "flow away" and "fade," which is closer to the primary meaning of the Hebrew verb used.

It is important to note the parallel structure found in lines one and three of Isaiah 34:4. The first line says that the "host of heaven" will "rot away." The New American Standard Bible says that the "host of heaven" "will wear away," while the King James Version states that the "host of heaven" "shall be dissolved." All are good translations of the Hebrew verb used there. This verb rarely means "to fall." If the meaning of the third line is that the host of heaven will literally fall, then this parallelism is destroyed.

Lines four and five are similes with dependent clauses that are compared to the withering of the stars. The stars are compared to the withering of leaves on a vine (presumably a grapevine) and the withering of *something* on a fig tree. Why do I say "something" here? While the subject of the dependent clause in line four (leaves) is in the Hebrew text, the subject of the dependent clause in line five is *not* in the Hebrew text. Since the subject of the dependent clause is absent in the Hebrew, it is left unstated, but probably meant to be implied from the text. But it is very important in English, so it is the sense of the translators what subject to provide. The translators of the English Standard Version quoted above provided "leaves" as the subject in the dependent clause in line five. The King James Version provides the subject "fig," but it is in italics to indicate that the word is absent in the Hebrew. Likewise, the New American

---

13. Although some lexicons have "fall" as a minority meaning. F. Brown, S. Driver, and C. Briggs *The Brown-Driver Briggs Hebrew and English Lexicon* (Peabody, MA: Hendrickson, 1996) has "sink or drop down" (from exhaustion or discouragement) as its first definition. "Wither and fall, fade" is its second definition. NIDOTTE *New International Dictionary of Old Testament Theology and Exegesis*, W.A. VanGemeren, editor (Grand Rapids, MI: Zondervan, 1997) defines it as "wither, fade, decay, languish, fall."

Standard Bible inserted the impersonal pronoun "one" in italics in the dependent clause in the fifth line. Since leaves are clearly not figs, all these translations cannot be right. "One" reads awkwardly in English. Perhaps the Geneva Bible offered the cleverest and most accurate solution to this difficulty, for it inserted the impersonal pronoun "it." That leaves the subject of the dependent clause in the fifth line unidentified, which, by its absence in the Hebrew, is unidentified. By the way, the Vulgate solved this problem by combining the fourth and fifth lines into a single line, "like the fading leaf of the vineyard and of the fig tree," thus implying the use of "leaf" in both lines. Does it matter whether the subject of the fifth line is leaves or figs? So far, no, but it might matter elsewhere, as we shall soon see.

Given these facts, and the context of comparing the action of leaves on a vine or to leaves (or fruit) on a fig tree, "wither" is probably a much more appropriate translation than "fall" in Isaiah 34:4. This collation with other Old Testament apocalyptic passages of astronomical interest strongly argue that Matthew 24:29 and Mark 13:25 refer to the stars dimming, not that the stars will literally fall to the earth.

However, Christians hold to differing views on what the Bible means when it speaks of the stars falling, and yet none of the popular understandings require or imply a flat earth in any way. For example, some Christians view these statements as being symbolic. From their perspective, these types of passages are not to be understood in a literal fashion, but they represent a symbolic way of describing catastrophic events, such as the collapse of a nation or final judgment. Others believe that the stars and other heavenly bodies should be viewed in a metaphorical sense. In this view, these heavenly bodies represent angelic powers opposed to God who have been, or will be, defeated. The language about them falling or being cast down is understood as God humiliating these principalities and powers by stripping them of the authority and position that he had previously given them. Yet others understand the passages to be speaking of objects literally falling to the earth, but that they are not stars, but merely asteroids and/or meteors.

There is one other New Testament passage that is potentially problematic for this interpretation about collating these different passages. Revelation 6:12–14 reads:

When he opened the sixth seal, I looked, and behold, there was a great earthquake, and the sun became black as sackcloth, the full moon became like blood, and the stars of the sky fell to the earth as the fig tree sheds its winter fruit when shaken by a gale. The sky vanished like a scroll that is being rolled up, and every mountain and island was removed from its place.

This is the one biblical passage that states clearly of stars falling to earth. Taken at face value, one might understand this to be a literal falling of the stars to the earth. However, the comparison to the Old Testament passages discussed above are striking. Since the sun here is described as turning dark, it is likely that the moon becoming like blood is a reference to the moon's dimming as well. If so, then the first three of the four elements of Matthew 24:29 are present here. But one could argue from the full context (Revelation 6:12–17) that the fourth element is present as well.

But the comparison to Isaiah 34:4 is even more striking. John's likening of the vanishing of the sky to the rolling up of a scroll appears to be an allusion to Isaiah 34:4. This imagery appears nowhere else in Scripture, suggesting that John had Isaiah 34:4 in mind when he wrote Revelation 6:13. Furthermore, John's simile of the stars falling as a fig tree sheds its unripe fruit appears to come from Isaiah 34:4 as well. Except that we've seen it isn't clear that Isaiah 34:4 mentions the fruit of the fig tree at all, and that Isaiah 34:4 doesn't use the word "fall" to describe the stars, leaves, or even figs. How do we resolve this issue?

There are at least two ways to solve this dilemma. Many commentators believe that the falling of the stars in Revelation 6:13 refers to an exceptional meteor shower. Flat-earthers are likely to strenuously object that Revelation 6:13 says that the stars will fall, not meteors. However, this is to commit the fallacy of equivocation. The word "meteor" in the modern sense dates to the Elizabethan era, only four centuries ago. Prior to that, meteors were known as *falling stars*, a term, along with *shooting stars*, that is in common use today. Until the invention of the telescope four centuries ago, any point-like luminous objects in the sky, including meteors and planets, were considered stars. Therefore, it is quite proper to consider that Revelation 6:13 may refer to an exceptional meteor shower.

However, this introduces the problem of collating with the Old Testament passages that tell of the dimming of the stars. Even a huge meteor storm would not affect the stars: they would presumably remain visible. One could argue that there are two physically separate, but possibly synchronized, events: a huge meteor storm *and* supernatural dimming of the stars. While many commentators have no problem with this solution, I find it wanting because it seems to multiply effects unnecessarily.[14]

The other way to resolve this dilemma is to realize that, being prophetic, the Book of Revelation has much imagery and symbolism, so one must be careful in employing hyper-literalism in deducing its meaning. For instance, the Book of Revelation mentions stars in several places where almost no one thinks that literal stars are intended. For instance, in John's vision of Jesus (Revelation 1:9–3:22), seven stars are mentioned (Revelation 1:16, 20, 2:1, 3:1). Jesus Himself identifies the seven stars as the angels of the seven churches (Revelation 1:20). Lest a flat-earther go hyper-literal here and insist that stars are literally angels and angels are literally stars, Jesus here also identifies the seven lampstands as the seven churches. Clearly, churches aren't literal lampstands. Speaking of angels, most commentators think that the stars of Revelation 12:4 are the angels who, depending on one's eschatology, either fell with Satan or will eventually be cast down to the earth with him. Revelation 12:1 mentions a sign in the sky of a woman with a crown of 12 stars. Almost no one believes that these are literal stars, but opinions vary widely as to whether these 12 stars refer to the 12 tribes of Israel or something else. About the only exception to this are people who thought that the sign of Revelation 12:1–6 would be fulfilled with a solar/planetary/stellar alignment on September 23, 2017, but since that date passed without incident, that isn't likely.[15] Finally, Revelation 2:28 and Revelation 22:16 refer to Jesus as the "morning star," but we know that Jesus Christ is not literally a star. There are many other examples of nonliteral things in the Book of Revelation, but the examples here of stars that are not to be taken literally ought to demonstrate the problems that may arise

---

14. Although one could argue that the dimming of the sun and moon would allow for any meteors to stand out even more brilliantly in the sky, especially if they were meteorites hitting the earth or exploding in the earth's atmosphere.

15. For more discussion about this, see https://answersingenesis.org/astronomy/stars/reflections-september-23-2017.

when mentions of stars elsewhere in the Book of Revelation are taken in a hyper-literal way. In conformity with Old Testament passages, perhaps Revelation 6:13 refers to the dimming of stars, a conclusion that I have reached elsewhere.[16]

Here I have examined Isaiah 34:4, Matthew 24:29, Mark 13:25, and Revelation 6:12, the only four verses in the Bible that speak of the stars falling.[17] Clearly, these prophetic passages are apocalyptic, which calls for their interpretation in terms of other similar passages. Collation of the relevant biblical passages, along with careful study of the Hebrew and Greek words used in these passages, indicate that in most cases, they likely don't refer to a literal fall of literal stars (as understood in the modern sense) to the earth. Rather, I consider it most likely that the stars are prophesied to dim, along with the sun and moon. This dimming will be perplexing, or else what kind of sign would that be?

Flat-earthers promote a strictly literal understanding of the Bible. However, one does not have to look far in Scripture to see that such a hyper-literal hermeneutic is fraught with problems. And even the most literal of flat-earthers eventually jettison their hyper-literal hermeneutic. On the evening before His crucifixion, Jesus told His disciples that He was the true vine and they were the branches (John 15:1–11). Clearly, this is not literally true but is a metaphor. Jesus also said that He was the good shepherd (John 10:11–17), though there is no record that He tended any literal sheep. But Jesus also said that He was the door of the sheepfold (John 10:7–10). Can one be a literal shepherd while simultaneously being a literal door to a literal sheepfold? Jesus also claimed to be the bread of life (John 6:35–51). Is this literally true? Jesus told the woman at the well about living water (John 4:10). Judging by her response, the woman at the well took this literally because she didn't understand the metaphorical nature of this living water (John 4:11–12, 15). This metaphorical term was used in the Old Testament (Jeremiah 2:13, 17:13; Zechariah 14:8). Such nonliteral use is common in the prophetic books

---

16. Danny R. Faulkner, *The Created Cosmos: What the Bible Reveals About Astronomy* (Green Forest, AR: Master Books), p. 179–182.

17. Revelation 8:10–11 is another such passage, but only mentions a single "star" falling. This is probably describing a meteorite since it produces a physiological effect upon the waters of the earth. What the nature of that effect is (radiation, heavy metal, or chemical poisoning) is not explicitly stated, but the passage definitely mentions a cause-and-effect relationship.

of the Old Testament. Since the Apostle John frequently used metaphors in his gospel, he certainly was acquainted with their use. And since the Apostle John alluded to Old Testament prophetic passages in the Book of Revelation, he certainly was aware of the use of metaphor in prophecy. Therefore, it comes as no surprise that John would use metaphors, symbolism, and other literary devices in the Book of Revelation, which, after all, is prophetic, too.

Flat-earthers chide creation organizations, such as Answers in Genesis, for not taking Scripture literally. However, we've never made the claim that we think that everything in the Bible should be understood in a strictly literal sense. We believe that the Bible is inspired by God, and, hence, is authoritative and without error. This means that when the Bible gives an historical account, that history is true. The nature of historical narrative is that it is factual, and apart from idioms and figures of speech, is largely, but not entirely, literal. However, poetic and prophetic passages are a very different genre from historical narrative in that they use much imagery, metaphors, similes, and other literary devices. It really isn't very difficult to distinguish between these different genres. Unfortunately, flat-earthers appear to have great difficulty seeing the difference. Perhaps they are motivated by fear, fear that if they accede that there is *anything* nonliteral in the Bible, then it opens the door to all sorts of figurative interpretation of Scripture. But we ought not to be motivated by fear, but by desire for truth. Otherwise, we are not rightly handling the Word of Truth (2 Timothy 2:15).

But there may be a more insidious motive underlying the flat-earth movement. It may be that much of the flat-earth movement was spawned as a subtle attack on creation ministries, such as Answers in Genesis, and upon the authority of Scripture itself. By promoting a hyper-literal approach to Scripture, when many parts of the Bible clearly are not meant to be understood in this manner, this ultimately undermines confidence in Scripture. I fear that many flat-earthers who profess salvation through the Lord Jesus Christ will fall away if they come to realize that the earth isn't flat after all. It's no accident that the claim "the Bible teaches the earth is flat" first arose among 19th-century skeptics. Many professing Christians who have fallen into belief that the earth is flat may be unwittingly doing the devil's work in this area.

Miscellaneous Bible Verses Improperly Used

The number of verses claimed to teach that the earth is flat varies from source to source. Some lists claim 40. Others claim 60. The most common claim is that 200 verses or more than 200 verses teach that the earth is flat.[18] For instance, as I'm writing this, I have before me a copy of a meme with the provocative title "200+ Flat Earth Bible Verses." Another list before me is entitled "240+ Flat Earth Doctrine Scriptural Proofs." The list of supposed flat-earth verses seems to continue to grow. One would think that among those verses would be at least a few verses that read something to the effect, "the earth is flat," but none of them do. Instead, to reach the conclusion that these verses teach that the earth is flat, one must employ understanding of those verses unique to flat-earthers and Bible critics.

Many of these lists amount to false advertising. For instance, the first passage on the two lists before me is Genesis 1:1–19 under the heading "Earth Created Before the Sun." Sure enough, if one reads that passage, one sees that God created the earth at the very beginning, but that God didn't make the sun (along with other astronomical bodies) until day four, three days after God created the earth. But how does one conclude from this passage that the earth is flat? One can't. I've been in the biblical creation movement for decades. All the biblical creationists that I know believe that the earth came before the sun solely based upon this very passage. But none of them believe that the earth is flat, and they would be puzzled that anyone else would believe the earth is flat based upon this passage.

The next verse on these two lists is Genesis 2:1. The heading before this verse on the 200+ list is "Universe is Complete." Okay, that's what Genesis 2:1 says, but how does that address the earth's shape? It doesn't. The heading on the 240+ list is "Universe Is Complete, NOT Ever Expanding." This heading isn't necessarily true, for expansion of the universe is not incompatible with the universe being complete. Furthermore, Genesis 2:1 doesn't state anything about expansion, so, at best, this

---

18. The "Square and Stationary Earth" map of Orlando Ferguson previously mentioned in a footnote in this chapter claims "Four hundred passages in the Bible that condemn the globe theory, or the flying earth, and none sustain it." I don't know if Ferguson's list of 400 passages survives.

is an inference, and a shaky inference at that. I know many creationists who don't believe that the universe is expanding, but I've not heard any of them use Genesis 2:1 as a proof text. And all of them would be surprised to learn that anyone saw flat earth in Genesis 2:1, or any other part of the Bible.

The greatest number of supposed biblical passages that support the flat-earth model are under the heading "Sun Moves, Not the Earth." These are verses that geocentrists use, some of which I discussed in chapter 7. The modern geocentric movement has been around for decades, far longer than the modern flat-earth movement. The geocentrists do not think that the earth is flat, and they strongly disagree that these passages teach flat earth.

The heading with the third greatest number of Bible verses listed is "Earth Has a Face (A Geometrical Flat Surface)." This list leads off with Genesis 1:29, 4:14, 6:1, 7, 7:3, 4, 8:9, and 11:8, 9. The phrase in these verses is "face of the earth." Flat-earthers argue that the word "face" must be a flat, two-dimensional entity, such as the face of a watch.[19] The word "face" can mean that, but it can mean many other things as well. For instance, human faces, from which the word "face" probably arises, are not flat. The word "surface" comes from the same root, and it often has the connotation of a curved, two-dimensional entity. The only requirement for a literal face or surface is that they be two-dimensional spaces. Hence, there is no requirement that the phrase "face of the earth" must mean that the earth is flat. Furthermore, the Hebrew word translated "face" here is *paneh* that I discussed above. As previously pointed out, this Hebrew word has a very broad range of meanings, even greater than the English word "face." As with so many flat-earth arguments, if one already believes that the earth is flat, there is nothing in these passages that would contradict that belief. But if one already believes that the earth is a sphere, there is nothing in these passages that would contradict that belief either. That is, there is nothing in these verses that demands, or even hints, the earth be flat.

Under the heading of "Waters Have a Face (A Geometrical Flat Surface)," there are three verses, Genesis 1:2, Genesis 7:18, and Job 38:30.

---

19. This example is not the least bit subtle, for watch faces are generally round and flat, just like the flat-earth model.

Each of these three verses uses the Hebrew word *paneh* again. However, the Hebrew word *paneh* is also used in Genesis 1:20 to describe where the birds fly. The Hebrew phrase there is *paneh rāqîaʿ šāmayim*. The King James Version translates this as "the open firmament of heaven." One might better translate the phrase as "the *face* of the firmament of heaven." Young's Literal Translation has "face" here. The Geneva Bible reads the same as the King James Version, though it has this alternate reading in a footnote. The New American Standard Bible has "open expanse of the heavens," but has in a footnote that "open" literally ought to be "on the face of." Flat-earthers insist that the firmament of heaven is a dome, but that can't be if the word *paneh* must refer to a flat, planar surface. Clearly, the flat-earthers' claim about the Hebrew word *paneh* is not true.

The list of 240+ verses has the heading "Breadth, Spread Out FLAT, of the Earth" with four verses listed. The first, Genesis 13:17, reads in the English Standard Version:

> Arise, walk through the length and the breadth of the land, for I will give it to you.

The Hebrew word translated "breadth" here is *rochab*, meaning "breadth" or "width." This is how the word is translated most of the 101 times it occurs in the Old Testament. What about the land described here as having breadth? The Hebrew word used is *ʾereṣ*. Since *ʾereṣ* is often translated as "earth," flat-earthers who think this verse proves the earth is flat must think that the entire earth is the intended meaning in Genesis 13:17. However, every translation that I know translates this as "land." Why is that? It is because the context is not the entire earth, but the land that God had promised to Abram.

Isaiah 8:8, the third verse under this heading, has similar meaning. Both *rochab* and *ʾereṣ* are used. The context is the fall of the northern kingdom to the Assyrians, so the breadth of the land here refers to the northern kingdom. The fact that flat-earthers would use these two verses to support their cosmology indicates how careless they are in treating Scripture to find support of their cosmology.

Job 38:18, the second verse under this heading, reads in the English Standard Version:

> Have you comprehended the expanse of the earth?
> Declare, if you know all this.

Most English translations have "breadth" here rather than "expanse." The Hebrew word is a cognate of *rochab*. The context here is probably the earth in its entirety. The meaning is the size of the earth. Again, there is no hint of the earth being flat.

The fourth verse under this heading is Revelation 20:9, which reads in the English Standard Version:

> And they marched up over the broad plain of the earth
> and surrounded the camp of the saints and the beloved city,
> but fire came down from heaven and consumed them.

Instead of "the broad plain of the earth," the King James Version reads, "the breadth of the earth." The Greek word in question here is *platos*. Flat-earthers point out that we get the English word "plate" from this Greek word. Since a plate is something that is flat, flat-earthers insist that this must be the meaning of the Greek word *platos*. But is it? The word *platos* appears three other times in the New Testament (Ephesians 3:18; Revelation 21:16 [twice]). In all three verses, it is usually translated as "breadth." The root Greek word is *platus*, which has the meaning of wide, or a street. The one time that this root occurs in the New Testament is Matthew 7:13, where Jesus described the gate that leads to destruction as being wide. There are other related Greek words. For instance, the feminine form of *platus* is *plateia*, meaning street. This is how *plateia* is translated the nine times that it occurs in the New Testament (Matthew 6:5, 12:19; Luke 10:10, 13:26, 14:21, Acts 5:15; Revelation 11:8, 21:21, 22:2). While the English word "plate" has come to mean something flat, flat-earthers are wrong in claiming that the meaning of the Greek word *platos* from which it derives means flat. Flat-earthers have imposed on the Greek word the meaning of an English word derived from the Greek word. This is not how etymology works.

Four passages are listed under the heading, "Earth's Measurements Unknown." The first passage, Job 38:4–5, reads:

> Where were you when I laid the foundation of the earth?
> Tell me, if you have understanding.

> Who determined its measurements — surely you know!
> Or who stretched the line upon it?

Notice that these rhetorical questions don't tell us that the earth's measurements are unknown or unknowable. Rather, the rhetorical questions, which are directed at Job, tell us that it was God who created the earth. As the maker of the earth, God certainly determined the earth's size, just as any builder lays out the size of an edifice he is building. Again, there is nothing in this passage that even hints that we can't measure the earth's size.

The second verse under this heading is Job 38:18:

> Have you comprehended the expanse of the earth?
> Declare, if you know all this.

Flat-earthers seem to believe that this verse means that Job could not know the earth's size, and presumably no one else can either. However, this may not be the meaning at all. Here is how Young's Literal Translation renders this verse:

> Thou hast understanding, Even unto the broad places of earth! Declare — if thou hast known it all.

This reads differently from how less-literal translations (including the King James Version) read. Rather than stating man cannot know the earth's size, it suggests that a mere man can't fathom all that the earth encompasses. Given the size of the earth, this is true. I can't even fathom all that is in the county where I live.

The third verse under this heading is Jeremiah 31:37:

> Thus says the LORD:
> "If the heavens above can be measured,
> and the foundations of the earth below can be explored,
> then I will cast off all the offspring of Israel
> for all that they have done,
> declares the LORD."

Notice that it is the *heavens* that cannot be measured here, not the earth. As an astronomer, I know that while we can measure distances in the universe with some accuracy, we have no idea how large the universe is. Secular astronomers are unsure if the universe is finite or infinite. In this sense, we can't measure the heavens. However, this verse doesn't say that we can't measure the earth's size. Rather, it says that we can't explore "the foundations of the earth below." While we know the earth's size accurately, and we have some knowledge of the earth's interior, there is much about the earth's interior that we don't know. We haven't even explored much of the near interior. I've done a fair amount of spelunking, cave exploring. I've been in a few places where no one else has been before. Yet, man knows of only a tiny fraction of all the caves that likely exist under the earth, nor will we ever know about most of them. So, quite literally, we can't explore all the earth below.

The final verse under this heading is Proverbs 25:3:

> As the heavens for height, and the earth for depth,
> so the heart of kings is unsearchable.

Notice that this verse doesn't speak of the earth being unmeasurable, but that the earth's depths (and the heavens' height) are unsearchable. This verse is problematic, for the heart of kings are compared to the heavens above and the earth below, something, as the three previous passages discussed here, which is compared to God's wisdom and power. Why the shift here? The context is Proverbs 25:2–7, which is a comparison between the ways of God and the ways of rulers. The passage seems to say that just as God's ways are difficult for men to comprehend, it is often difficult for the governed to understand the ways of those who govern.

At any rate, the four passages under this heading fail to deliver because they do not tell us that the earth is immeasurable.

Under the heading of "Creation Worshippers" are Deuteronomy 4:19, 17:3; 2 Kings 23:5; and Jeremiah 8:2. These four verses warn of the dire consequences of worshiping astronomical bodies. Again, these verses hardly teach that the earth is flat, so why do flat-earthers think that these verses are relevant? It's probably because flat-earthers claim that heliocentrism was inspired by sun worship. Therefore, in the minds of flat-earthers, belief that the earth orbits the sun amounts to sun worship. Except that I don't know any sun worshipers, though I know many heliocentrists. This is the genetic fallacy — even if we grant that the heliocentric theory had pagan roots (though it doesn't), that doesn't mean that the theory must be wrong. Furthermore, flat-earthers have confused geocentrism with belief in flat earth. The two are very different ideas. All flat-earthers are geocentrists, but not all geocentrists are flat-earthers.

Jeremiah 42:5 and Revelation 3:14, 19:11, 21:5, and 22:6 are listed under the heading of "God's Word Is ALWAYS Faithful and True." This heading is true, though the passages listed there are taken a bit out of context. There are better Bible passages to support this point, such as 2 Peter 1:20–21. But what do any verses that teach the truth and authority of Scripture have to do with the earth's shape? No such passage teaches that the earth is flat. Here, flat-earthers commit the informal fallacy of begging the question. They reason that since they think the Bible teaches that the earth is flat, any verse that upholds the truth and authority of Scripture also teaches that the earth is flat.

There are other biblical passages under these headings. I discuss many of these in other places, such as chapter 7, where I discuss geocentrism.

Science Falsely So Called

Flat-earthers frequently quote the King James Version of 1 Timothy 6:20–21a with the Apostle Paul's warning:

> O Timothy, keep that which is committed to thy trust, avoiding profane and vain babblings, and oppositions of science falsely so called:
> Which some professing have erred concerning the faith.

Their argument is that this passage is warning, at least in part, against belief that the earth is a globe. Since belief that the earth is spherical largely comes from science, they reason that we ought to reject science on this matter. Instead, their "true science" demonstrates that the earth is flat. The greatest problem with using this passage this way is that it isn't talking about science as we know it today. Until 180 years ago, what we call "science" today was called "natural philosophy." And what we call "scientists" today were called "natural philosophers." It was William Whewell who suggested this change by appropriating the word "science," and his suggestion quickly caught on. Previously, the word "science" had referred to any pursuit of knowledge not generally thought of as an art.

That is why one of the largest schools on almost any university campus is the College of Arts and Sciences. Many of the departments included in a College of Arts and Sciences are neither an art nor a science in the modern sense; however, all these departments were either arts or sciences in the original sense.

At the time of the translation of the King James Version four centuries ago, no one would have understood 1 Timothy 6:20 to refer to natural philosophy, but instead they would have understood that it meant knowledge falsely so called. Consequently, nearly every modern translation of the Bible has the word "knowledge" in 1 Timothy 6:20 rather than "science." Even the English Revised Version (ERV) made this change. The New Testament of the ERV was published in 1881, less than 50 years after the meaning of the word "science" had changed. Therefore, this argument is specious. But even more important is the context of 1 Timothy. In this epistle, the Apostle Paul warned Timothy about false teachers that had crept into the church (1 Timothy 1:3–7, 6:3–5). It is generally thought that this false teaching was gnosticism. One of the tenets of gnosticism was that special knowledge led to salvation or to a higher level of spirituality. It was probably this false notion of knowledge that Paul was referring to.

Does the Moon Have Its Own Light?

Flat-earthers frequently claim that the Bible says the moon has its own light, so the moon cannot reflect the light of the sun. Flat-earthers offer several verses in support of their contention. One verse is Genesis 1:16:

> And God made the two great lights — the greater light to rule the day and the lesser light to rule the night — and the stars.

I suppose that the reasoning is that since God made the lesser light (the moon), then the lesser light must have its own unique light source. But this imposes a meaning foreign to this verse. All that the verse requires is that there be a lesser light without regard to the light's source. We regularly employ lights that have no source of light in themselves. For instance, I frequently open blinds to allow light from windows to illuminate rooms in my home. The source of the light is the sun, even if the sun's light does not directly shine into the rooms. Similarly, skylights allow the light of day into a room. We call a skylight a skylight, even though it has no light source of its own. Photographers and videographers frequently use reflectors as a source of light, even though the reflectors merely reflect light from another source (the sun, if outdoors).

Flat-earthers impose their meaning on the other verses that they quote on the moon's source of light (Isaiah 30:26; Jeremiah 31:35), or the moon withholding its light in apocalyptic passages (Isaiah 13:10; Ezekiel 32:7; Matthew 24:29; Mark 13:24), or no need of the moon's light in the future state (Isaiah 60:19–20; Revelation 21:23). Again, there is no requirement in these passages that the moon have its own light source, so flat-earthers impose their model onto these passages.

Arguments from Silence

Flat-earthers frequently engage in a variation of the informal fallacy of argument from silence. An argument from silence is concluding that something doesn't exist based upon lack of explicit mention of that something existing. An example of this fallacious reasoning comes from the encounter of Balaam with the angel of the Lord in Numbers 22:22–35. There is no indication from the account that Balaam was astonished that his donkey spoke. Indeed, the account records that Balaam engaged in a brief conversation with his donkey. Some people gather from this conversation that Balaam was not astonished, but this conclusion is based upon the assumption that the account includes all details. It could be that Balaam was astonished, but that once he recovered from his initial surprise, he answered the donkey's questions. That is, the account of Balaam and his donkey does not necessarily include everything that happened.

Flat-earthers frequently challenge those who don't agree with them to produce one verse, just one verse, that states that the earth is a globe that orbits the sun. This demand includes much — both the earth being a sphere, as well as the heliocentric model (recall that flat-earthers seem to conflate these two separate ideas all the time). Alas, no such verse exists. But it hardly follows that the earth is flat and remains motionless. Both sides can play this game. I can demand one verse, just one verse, that states that the earth is flat. At this point, most flat-earthers respond with the 240+ verses that supposedly teach that the earth is flat. But to truly qualify as teaching that the earth is flat, wouldn't that require that a verse say something like, "The earth is flat"? Of course, no such verse exists. Therefore, the earth must not be flat. See, isn't that easy? The problem is, flat-earthers begin by believing that the earth is flat, read biblical passages in a way that they think is consistent with the earth being flat (that is eisegesis), and so, in their minds, those verses say that the earth is flat. Except that objective analysis of all 240+ verses reaches a very different conclusion about them.

Another form of this argument from silence comes from some flat-earthers who demand a biblical reference for planets in the Bible. The ready conclusion is that since planets aren't mentioned in the Bible, then planets must not exist. It's not clear what is meant by this claim. Does it mean that planets, such as Venus, Mars, Jupiter, and Saturn, don't exist? Clearly, they do exist, because we readily can see them in the sky — they appear as bright stars (the fifth naked-eye planet, Mercury, is more difficult to see). Or does this claim mean that the planets exist, but not as we know them today, large spheres that orbit the sun as the earth orbits the sun? More likely, the latter, but given the gross ignorance of astronomy that flat-earthers have, one must wonder.

Technically, it is possible that the planet Saturn is mentioned in Acts 7:42–43. The "star of your god Rephan," may refer to Saturn (this verse is a quote from the Septuagint's reading of Amos 5:25–27). Don't forget that in many ancient cultures, the planets were embodiments of deities. But the term for planets is found explicitly in Jude 13, where it warns of unbelievers that have sneaked into the church:

> Wild waves of the sea, casting up the foam of their own shame; wandering stars, for whom the gloom of utter darkness has been reserved forever.

The Greek term translated "wandering stars" is *asteres planētai,* the ancient Greek term that has been shortened and handed down to us as "planets." The planets are wandering stars in the sense that, while they look like stars, unlike the stars that remain relatively fixed with respect to one another, the planets appear to move among the stars. Originally, this term also applied to the sun and moon, because, though they look very different from stars, they, too, appear to move among the stars.

The term *asteres planētai* also applied to comets and meteors. However, once the heliocentric model came into favor four centuries ago, the term "planet" assumed its modern definition. What does *asteres planētai* mean in Jude 13? We don't know for certain. Most commentaries favor the understanding that it refers to meteors. Since the word for planets, *asteres planētai*, does show up in the New Testament, does that mean that flat-earthers will accept their reality? Probably not.

Conclusion

Here I have examined many of the biblical passages flat-earthers generally use to claim the Bible teaches the earth is flat. There are other passages flat-earthers occasionally use. However, the frequency of use of those passages is far less than the verses I discussed here. Furthermore, those remaining verses generally require the assumption the earth is flat to begin with. Once these more important, frequently cited passages are dismissed as teaching a flat earth, the remaining few verses probably do not matter. **Clearly, the Bible does not teach that the earth is flat.** It was Bible skeptics who introduced this false claim in the 19th century. It is a shame that professed Bible-believers have recently embraced this false argument and have gone on to promote the flat earth. When combined with its many scientific and observational problems, the flat-earth theory is disproven.

Chapter 12

The Book of Enoch *and Flat Earth*

Introduction

In the previous chapter, I discussed a few of the biblical passages that, according to some people, teach that the earth is flat. There I made the point that the Bible doesn't endorse any cosmology, but instead gives only bare details regarding cosmology that could be understood several ways. For instance, Genesis 1:1 states that in the beginning God created heaven and earth. The day two account (Genesis 1:6–8) tells us that God made the *rāqîa* (firmament or expanse or sky), and that God called it "heaven." On day four (Genesis 1:16–19), God made the luminaries (astronomical bodies) that he placed in the *rāqîa*. These statements briefly describe God's creative acts during creation week, but they hardly teach any particular cosmology, such as geocentrism or heliocentrism, whether the earth is flat or a sphere, or whether the universe is expanding or static. God exemplified His wisdom in not endorsing any of man's cosmologies in His Word. If God had done otherwise, it would have needlessly exposed the Bible to ridicule in nearly every age, for man's cosmologies have changed continually over time.

Nevertheless, throughout the ages, people have chosen to understand these verses from the creation account, as well as other verses throughout the Bible, in terms of the cosmology of their day. Examples include the Septuagint's translation of *rāqîa* as *stereoma* and Thomas Aquinas' endorsement of the Ptolemaic model. The first example ultimately led to the poor translation of *rāqîa* as "firmament," which, in turn, led to much

Figure 1

confusion (including the flat-earth movement today). The second example resulted in the Galileo affair. Even today, we live with the consequences of both mistakes. This should be a lesson to all of us not to read into Scripture (eisegesis) our preferred cosmology. However, flat-earthers have failed to learn this lesson because they insist that their understanding of biblical passages teach that the earth is flat.

Where do flat-earthers get this notion? Contrary to common misconception, for the two millennia of the Christian age, the church did not teach that the earth is flat. Depictions of an enclosed dome over a flat earth (figure 1) supposedly taught in the Bible did not start appearing until the 19th century. But it was Bible critics, not Christians, who introduced these diagrams. Only in recent decades have Christians fallen for this lame attack on the authority of Scripture and have foolishly begun reproducing these figures as if this is what the Bible taught all along. Unfortunately, some Christians of late have swallowed this *faux* history (and much more false history) and have begun proclaiming flat earth as truth in a misguided attempt to defend the Bible.

The *Book of Enoch*

Some flat-earthers have appealed to the *Book of Enoch* to support their argument that the Bible teaches that the earth is flat. What is the *Book of Enoch*? As the name suggests, this ancient book (sometimes referred to as 1 Enoch) was ostensibly penned by Enoch, the great-grandfather of Noah. However, most scholars believe the *Book of Enoch* was written in the second or first centuries B.C., not three millennia earlier when Enoch most likely lived. Therefore, the book is pseudepigraphic. Neither Jews nor Christians have considered the *Book of Enoch* to be part of the canon, though some smaller sects (especially in Ethiopia) have given it some status. To the non-Christian, the *Book of Enoch* is just another ancient manuscript on par with the Bible. However, to the Christian, the *Book of Enoch* is in a totally different category from Scripture, though it may be of some value as a window to what *some* ancient Jews thought. Some Christians who teach that the earth is flat split the difference, treating the *Book of Enoch* as a sort of commentary on the Bible. But the *Book of Enoch* doesn't claim to be a commentary, but instead comes across as a revelation, at least implying the claim that it is an inspired text. Still, other Christian flat-earthers seem to treat the *Book of Enoch* as inspired text.

Several defenses are put forth for holding the *Book of Enoch* in such high regard. One defense is that it was included with the Qumran scrolls. However, all this proves is that for whatever reason, the Qumran sect liked it. Another defense is that the New Testament writer Jude (v. 14–15) quoted from it. But this quote is only one sentence from a very lengthy book. Nor is the *Book of Enoch* alone in being quoted in the New Testament. In Titus 1:12, the Apostle Paul quoted a single line from Epimenides, a sixth-century-B.C. Greek poet. In Acts 17:28, Paul also quoted from Epimenides, as well as Aratus, a third-century-B.C. Greek poet. But no one seriously suggests that any writings of Epimenides or Aratus are on par with the Bible. Clearly, the mere quotation of a single line from ancient extrabiblical sources does not impart special status to those texts to interpret Scripture.

Does the *Book of Enoch* teach that the earth is flat? Let us examine some of its passages that supposedly do. I will quote from M. Knibb's 1978 translation, with notes by Andy McCracken.[1] Enoch 18:1–5 reads:

> And I saw the storehouses of all the winds, and I saw how with them He has adorned all creation, and I saw the foundations of the Earth.
>
> And I saw the cornerstone of the Earth. And I saw the four winds which support the Earth and the sky.
>
> And I saw how the winds stretch out the height of Heaven, and how they position themselves between Heaven and Earth; they are the Pillars of Heaven.
>
> And I saw the winds which turn the sky and cause the disc of the Sun and all the stars to set.

---

1. http://scriptural-truth.com/images/BookOfEnoch.pdf.

> And I saw the winds on the Earth which support the
> clouds and I saw the paths of the Angels. I saw at the end of
> the Earth; the firmament of Heaven above.

This passage contains some words and phrases that are found in the Bible, such as "four winds" and "foundations of the earth," albeit put together a little differently, and with additional information. For instance, the phrase "disc of the sun" appears nowhere in the Bible. One could read the last verse quoted above as the firmament (dome, if one insists that is what "firmament" means) resting upon the "ends of the earth," which is consistent with the flat-earth model promoted today. Or perhaps not. The meaning is ambiguous.

Rob Skiba, a prominent flat-earth proponent today, prefers the 1917 R.H. Charles translation of the *Book of Enoch*.[2] As to be expected, there are some differences in translation. For instance, in verse 3, the Charles translation has "the vaults of heaven" as opposed to "the height of Heaven," as in the Knibb translation quoted here. Furthermore, in verse 4, the Charles translation has "the circumference of the sun" instead of "the disc of the sun," as the Knibb translation has. The latter variation appears inconsequential, but flat-earthers would probably insist that the "vaults of heaven" is a better translation because it more explicitly conforms to their cosmology. Or does it? The dominant modern flat-earth cosmology has *a single* dome or vault over the round, flat earth. If that is the correct cosmology, why is the plural "vaults" used here?

Why are there differences in the translations? Some differences can be attributed to textual variants.[3] However, some differences in translation could be due to differences in the sense of the translators. For

---

2. R. Skiba, *Genesis and the Synchronized, Biblically Endorsed, Extra-Biblical Texts* (King's Gate Media, 2013). Not only does this book include Genesis and the *Book of Enoch*, but it also includes the *Book of Jubilees* and the *Book of Jasher*. The *Book of Jasher* is popular with flat-earthers because it is mentioned in Joshua 10:13 (as well as 2 Samuel 1:18). While the *Book of Jubilees* and the *Book of Enoch* date from the intertestamental period, the *Book of Jasher* first appeared in 1625. The original *Book of Jasher*, or, more properly, the *scroll of the upright*, since Jasher is an English transliteration of the Hebrew word for "upright," is lost. The fact that Skiba's text of the *Book of Jasher* is that of an 1840 English translation printed by a Mormon publishing house in 1887 does not appear to faze Skiba.

3. The more copies we have of ancient texts, the more textual variants exist. The best example is the New Testament, of which many ancient and early medieval copies exist, and there are many textual variants among them. Fortunately, none of the textual variants affect essential doctrines.

instance, Charles could have been influenced more by the notion that arose in the 19th century that the cosmology of *all* Ancient Near Eastern sources was a flat, round earth with a dome over it. That is, Charles' translation of the *Book of Enoch* may reflect that cosmology because he *assumed* that cosmology.

But Enoch 18:1–5 conveys some information that most flat-earthers would disagree with. For instance, it attributes the motion of the sun and the stars across the sky to winds. Do flat-earthers today believe this? I have yet to encounter that claim in material promoting the flat earth. This passage credits the winds with stretching out the height of heaven, and it identifies the winds as the pillars of heaven. Again, I have yet to encounter this teaching in flat-earth material.

Speaking of "pillars of heaven," that phrase from Enoch 18:3 is found once in the Bible. Job 26:11 reads:

> The pillars of heaven tremble
> and are astounded at his rebuke.

Forget for a moment what the *Book of Enoch* says — what are the pillars of heaven in Job 26:11? That isn't clear at all. First, note that God isn't speaking in Job 26, but rather it is the beginning of Job's long response (Job 26–31) to Bildad's comments in Job 25. Therefore, the thoughts expressed here are those of Job and may not necessarily reflect God's truth. Furthermore, since Job is a poetic book, we ought to be very careful about reading this too literally. The trembling here may refer to physical shaking (some commentators think the pillars here refer to mountains, which certainly appear to hold up the sky), so one could argue that this refers to some physical shaking, such as an earthquake.

But what about the second part of this verse? It says the pillars of heaven are astounded at His (God's) rebuke. Can inanimate objects be astounded? Obviously not, so perhaps the trembling in the first part of the verse does not refer to literal trembling. Carefully note that I am not saying that because one part of one verse in Scripture is nonliteral that we are free to assert a nonliteral interpretation anywhere else in the Bible as we please. Rather, the tight structure of individual verses, with the hallmark parallelism and contrasts found within a single verse in ancient Hebrew poetry, indicates looking at the entire verse coherently. To argue

that part of a single verse in Hebrew poetry is to be taken very literally, while its parallel expression is not, is to destroy this characteristic of
ancient Hebrew poetry. Returning to this passage in the *Book of Enoch*, it
contains enough poetic elements to warrant questioning whether any of
this passage teaches that the earth is flat.

Continuing, Enoch 18:6–12 reads:

> And I went towards the south, and it was burning day and
> night, where there were seven mountains of precious stones,
> three towards the east and three towards the south.
>
> And those towards the east were of coloured stone, and
> one was of pearl, and one of healing stone; and those towards
> the south, of red stone.
>
> And the middle one reached to Heaven, like the throne
> of the Lord, of stibium, and the top of the throne was of
> sapphire.
>
> And I saw a burning fire, and what was in all the mountains.
>
> And I saw a place there, beyond the great earth; there the
> waters gathered together.
>
> And I saw a deep chasm of the earth, with pillars of heav-
> enly fire, and I saw among them fiery pillars of Heaven, which
> were falling, and as regards both height and depth, they were
> immeasurable.
>
> And beyond this chasm, I saw a place, and it had neither
> the sky above it, nor the foundation of earth below it; there
> was no water on it, and no birds, but it was a desert place.

The last verse is interesting. Similarly, Enoch 21:1–2 reads:

> And I went round to a place where nothing was made.
>
> And I saw a terrible thing, neither the High Heaven nor
> the firm ground, but a desert place, prepared and terrible.

Apparently, flat-earthers interpret these two passages as referring to what
lies beyond the dome that covers the earth. According to the dominant
flat-earth model today, the dome rests on the ice wall we call Antarctica. This place is described in Enoch 18:6, 9 as burning, though Antarctica is the coldest place on earth. Enoch 18:6–8 further mentions seven

mountains there, with three toward the east and three toward the south with one central mountain (these mountains appear again in Enoch 24). These directions are a bit ambiguous in the flat-earth model, so it is difficult to reconcile that model with the description of Enoch 18:6. I don't know what to make of these passages from the *Book of Enoch*. But then again, I don't have to worry about that because I don't consider the *Book of Enoch* to be authoritative. Nor should we be bound to interpret Scripture in terms of an interpretation of these few verses in the *Book of Enoch*.

Enoch 23:1–4 (the entire chapter) reads:

> And from there I went to another place, towards the west, to the ends of the Earth.
>
> And I saw a fire that burnt and ran, without resting or ceasing from running, by day or by night, but continued in exactly the same way.
>
> And I asked saying: "What is this which has no rest?"
>
> Then Raguel, one of the Holy Angels, who was with me, answered me, and said to me: "This burning fire, whose course you saw towards the west, is the fire of all the Lights of Heaven."

Or consider Enoch 35:1:

> And from there I went towards the west, to the ends of the Earth, and I saw there, as I saw in the east, three open Gates — as many Gates and as many outlets.

Apparently, in the cosmology of the *Book of Enoch*, one can reach the earth's edge by traveling eastward or westward. However, this is very different from the cosmology of the modern flat-earth movement. In the modern flat-earth cosmology, one can travel indefinitely eastward or westward without ever reaching the edge. Instead, one simply goes around the world. At least this is the stock answer flat-earthers give to those who don't believe that the earth is flat, haven't studied the modern flat-earth model much, and ask how it is possible to circumnavigate the flat earth. Once again, the cosmology of the *Book of Enoch* doesn't conform to the cosmology of the modern flat-earth movement.

But Enoch 34:1 is even more problematic. It reads:

> And from there I went towards the north, to the ends of
> the Earth, and there I saw a great and glorious wonder at the
> ends of the whole Earth.

That is, according to the *Book of Enoch*, one can travel northward to reach
the earth's edge. But in the modern flat-earth model, the North Pole
is the center of the earth. Therefore, one cannot reach the earth's edge
by traveling northward. Only by traveling southward can one reach the
earth's edge.

Consider Enoch 33:1–2, which reads:

> And from there I went to the ends of the earth, and I saw
> there large animals, each different from the other, and also
> birds, which differed in form, beauty, and call — each differ-
> ent from the other.
>
> And to the east of these animals, I saw the ends of the
> Earth, on which Heaven rests, and the open Gates of Heaven.

Setting aside the objection that according to the modern flat-earth model
one cannot reach the earth's edge by traveling eastward, this passage
from the *Book of Enoch* does appear to teach a cosmology akin to that of
21st-century flat-earthers, for it speaks of heaven resting on the ends of
the earth.

Enoch 72:1–4 reads:

> The Book of the Revolutions of the Lights of Heaven. Each
> as it is; according to their classes, according to their period
> of rule and their times, according to their names and places
> of origin, and according to their months. That Uriel, the
> Holy Angel who was with me, and is their leader, showed to
> me. And he showed me all their regulations, exactly as they
> are, for each year of the world and for ever, until the new cre-
> ation shall be made which will last forever.
>
> And this is the First Law of the Lights. The light called the
> Sun; its rising is in the Gates of Heaven that are towards the
> east, and its setting is in the western Gates of Heaven.

And I saw six Gates from which the Sun rises, and six Gates in which the Sun sets, and the Moon also rises and sets in those Gates, and the leaders of the stars together with those whom they lead. There are six in the east and six in the west, all exactly in place, one next to the other; and there are many windows to the south and the north of those Gates.

And first there rises the greater light, named the Sun, and its disc is like the disc of Heaven, and the whole of it is full of a fire which gives light and warmth.

Flat-earthers may prefer an older translation of the *Book of Enoch* (such as Charles'), where in the last verse above, rather than "disc," it is translated "circumference." For them, this is close enough to the word "circuit," as it appears in Psalm 19:4b–6:

In them he has set a tent for the sun,
which comes out like a bridegroom leaving his chamber,
and, like a strong man, runs its course with joy.
Its rising is from the end of the heavens,
and its circuit to the end of them,
and there is nothing hidden from its heat.

Some flat-earthers assume that the psalmist David had read the *Book of Enoch* and go on to suggest that Psalm 19 may be an echo of the *Book of Enoch*. Never mind that the *Book of Enoch* was written nearly 1,000 years after David lived. It is far more likely that the writer(s) of the *Book of Enoch* echoed Psalm 19 here.

Enoch 74 contains a similar description of the moon and its motion. These discussions of the sun and moon, as well as the sun's description in Psalm 19, are interpreted in terms of the flat-earth model as clearly teaching the earth is flat. But do they? They are vague enough to be interpreted in terms of a geocentric spherical earth. Indeed, geocentrists have made this argument about Psalm 19 for years, long before the recent rise of the flat-earth phenomenon. And those who believe in a spherical earth in a heliocentric cosmology have, too. So, does the *Book of Enoch* teach that the earth is flat? Enoch 21 and Enoch 33 appear to do so, though the other passages often claimed do not make that case so clearly.

Parts of the *Book of Enoch* Flat-Earthers Don't Talk About

However, flat-earthers who use the *Book of Enoch* in support of their cosmology are selective in what the *Book of Enoch* teaches. I have given some
examples already, but there are more. For instance, most flat-earthers
claim that the sun neither rises nor sets. Rather, they claim, the sun
only *appears* to set as a matter of perspective. Indeed, if the sky merely
spins about the center of a round, flat earth (the North Pole) as flat-
earthers maintain, then the sun is continually above the horizon. Flat-
earthers insist that the sun ceases to shine for us at night because the sun
is a downward-directed spotlight. When the sun moves far enough away
that we are no longer in the spotlight, it gets dark. Why does the sun set
each evening and rise each morning? Flat-earthers respond with flimflam
about perspective somehow making the sun only appear to set and rise.

Besides the fact that this explanation doesn't really work, there is a
problem related to the *Book of Enoch* on this matter. You see, the *Book
of Enoch* describes the sun rising through a gate, or portal, in the east
in the morning and setting through another gate in the west in the
evening. Above, I quoted Enoch 72:1–4, but consider the next verse,
Enoch 72:5:

> The wind blows the chariots on which it ascends, and
> the Sun goes down in the sky and returns through the north
> in order to reach the east, and is led so that it comes to the
> appropriate Gate and shines in the sky.

That is, the sun passes below the horizon in the west, loops under the
northern horizon, and then rises in the east the next morning. This
explanation is repeated in Enoch 78:5. Apart from the gates, this description is very similar to the conventional (spherical earth) explanation of
the sun's daily motion in the sky. Enoch 72 says that there are six gates
from which the sun rises and six gates in which it sets. Which gates the
sun uses depends upon the time of year, as the azimuth of the rising and
setting sun changes seasonally. The moon rises and sets through the same
gates as the sun. Enoch 36 describes special gates in the eastern sky that
the sun rises through, as well as many smaller gates that the stars rise
through. Enoch 33:3 similarly details the rising of the stars:

> And I saw how the stars of Heaven come out, and
> counted the Gates out of which they come, and wrote down
> all their outlets, for each one, individually, according to their
> number. And their names, according to their constellations,
> their positions, their times, and their months, as the Angel
> Uriel, who was with me, showed me.

None of this conforms to the flat-earth model in discussion today because they teach that, like the sun, the moon and stars do not rise or set.

Enoch 33–36 describes 12 gates, 3 in each of the cardinal directions. Winds blow from each of these gates. Enoch 76 gives more detail of these winds. Four of the winds are good, but eight are bad. I seriously doubt that flat-earthers accept these teachings, altogether ignoring them instead.

But the very existence of these three gates at the edge of the earth in the four cardinal directions is problematic for the modern flat-earth cosmology. The North Pole is at the center of the modern flat-earth model. At the North Pole, all directions are south, so there are no cardinal directions at the North Pole. The only way that gates at the ends of the earth in the four cardinal directions make sense is if the observer (the writer of this portion of the *Book of Enoch*) is at the earth's center, which is *not* at the North Pole. Only then can there be gates at the edge of the earth in each of the four cardinal directions. Gates in the four cardinal directions only make sense if the location of reference is at the earth's center. However, from other locations on the earth's surface, those gates would not have the same orientations in the four cardinal directions. Indeed, in answering the question of how people can circumnavigate the earth if it is flat, flat-earthers claim that circumnavigation in one direction (either east or west) makes a circuit around the North Pole. But if one can continually circle the flat earth in either the east or west direction, never reaching the earth's edge, then neither east nor west intersect the dome at the earth's edge. Therefore, there can be no gates at the edge of the earth in those directions. Again, the cosmology of the *Book of Enoch* conflicts with the flat-earth cosmology of today.

At least one other astronomical teaching found in the *Book of Enoch* clearly contradicts the flat-earth cosmology of today. Enoch 78 talks about light transferring from the sun to the moon. This is consistent with the conventional understanding that the moon shines by reflecting the sun's light, indicating that the author of this portion of the *Book of Enoch* properly understood the moon's light. Indeed, the changing amount of the lit half of the moon that is visible as it orbits the earth with respect to the sun (the synodic month) explains lunar phases. The curved terminator (the division between light and dark on the moon) shows that the moon is a sphere. But modern flat-earthers insist the moon is a flat disk, not a sphere. Furthermore, they claim that the moon shines by its own light, not by reflecting the light of the sun. Also, notice that flat-earthers don't offer any explanation for lunar phases. They seem to be confident of what doesn't cause lunar phases, but they seem to have no curiosity as to the true cause.

Conclusion

Flat-earthers have a peculiar relationship with the *Book of Enoch*. Non-Christian flat-earthers view the Bible and the *Book of Enoch* as having equal authority. Christian promoters of flat-earth must do careful choreography to accept the *Book of Enoch* to the extent of using it to interpret Scripture, while simultaneously giving lip service to the fact that the *Book of Enoch* falls far short of biblical authority.

Some passages of the *Book of Enoch* that supposedly teach that the earth is flat are ambiguous. However, a few passages do appear to indicate that the writer(s) of the *Book of Enoch* believed the earth is flat. However, other cosmological details of the *Book of Enoch* clearly contradict the preferred cosmology of modern flat-earth proponents. This selective reading of the *Book of Enoch* is misleading at best.

The *Book of Enoch* often appears in popular literature related to a different subject. Many flat-earth adherents, such as Rob Skiba, have used the *Book of Enoch* to promote strange theories about the *Nephilim*. Some of these authors have written entire books speculating about the *Nephilim*, and how they might connect to supposed conspiracies in our day. This is strange, considering that this word appears only three times in the Old Testament (once in Genesis 6:4 and twice in Numbers 13:33). Each time, the King James Version translates *Nephilim* as "giants." Another Hebrew word for giants, *rephaim*, occurs 25 times in the Old Testament. The King James Version translated it 17 times as "giants" or "giant," depending on whether it was plural or singular (*raphe*), but in the other eight occurrences, it was transliterated into English. Here is what we are told in Genesis 6:4:

> The Nephilim were on the earth in those days, and also afterward, when the sons of God came in to the daughters of man and they bore children to them. These were the mighty men who were of old, the men of renown.

Who were these *Nephilim*? There are two primary theories held by evangelical scholars. One of these views, known as the fallen angel theory, states that fallen angels married human women and had children with them. These offspring were giants, known as the *Nephilim*. According to this theory, these *Nephilim* were one of the sources of the wickedness filling the world and leading to the Flood. The sixth and seventh chapters of the non-inspired *Book of Enoch* reflect this view and expand upon the strange passage in Genesis 6:1–4, giving many more details about the sons of God and the *Nephilim*.

Rob Skiba, a prominent promoter of a flat earth, also promotes his own fantastic version of the *Nephilim*, complete with details of *Nephilim* in end-time prophecies. This goes far beyond the fallen angel view held by many scholars, and even the fanciful embellishments in the *Book of Enoch*. Most promoters of this theory believe the *Nephilim* were around 10 feet tall (after all, Hebrew lexicons define the word *Nephilim* as "giants"). However, Skiba and others who so often rely on the *Book of Enoch*, conveniently leave out one detail about the *Nephilim* from it. Enoch 7:2 reports that the *Nephilim* were 3,000 cubits tall (older translations use an archaic term for the cubit, the *ell*).[4] This would be 4,000–5,000 feet, depending upon the length of the intended cubit. I seriously doubt that anyone today believes the *Nephilim* were anywhere near this height. But this one detail greatly undermines any idea that all the *Book of Enoch* is inspired or should be included in the canon. Those who are fans of the *Book of Enoch* conveniently ignore this fact.

---

4. There are textual variants. Some manuscripts have 300 rather than 3,000 here. However, Skiba apparently prefers this reading, because this is how Enoch 7:2 reads in his book, *Genesis and the Synchronized, Biblically Endorsed, Extra-Biblical Texts.*

Once, on social media, a person commented on one of my flat-earth critiques. This person exclaimed that I probably had never even read the *Book of Enoch*. My immediate impulse was, "Of course not — I don't read fiction," though I didn't express it at the time. The truth is, I've read much of the *Book of Enoch*, and I'm not impressed. How we came to accept the 66 books of the Bible is not a simple question, and I certainly will not attempt an answer here. Suffice it to say that the Holy Spirit not only inspired biblical authors so that they wrote without error, but the Holy Spirit also operated to preserve what they wrote and guided the decisions that led to the canon of Scripture. There were many other ancient texts, including the *Book of Enoch*, that various people have thought ought to have been included, but they did not make the cut. I have identified some of the problems in the *Book of Enoch* that demonstrate the wisdom of recognizing that it is not canonical, and, hence, is distinct from the canon of Scripture. It is sad that some Christians want to accept the teachings of the flawed *Book of Enoch*, and then use its teachings to falsely interpret the Bible. Already, some professing Christians who believe that the earth is flat are claiming that the *Book of Enoch* ought to be in the canon. Time will tell whether this opinion will grow.

Chapter 13

Conclusion

The World Is Flat — Thomas Friedman Says So

In 2005, popular author and *New York Times* columnist Thomas Friedman wrote the best-selling book, *The World Is Flat*. Okay, it's not what you think. The book had the subtitle, *A Brief History of the Twenty-First Century*. Friedman used the flat earth as a metaphor for rapid changes that have leveled the playing field in terms of commerce for economies around the world. Get it? A level playing field is flat. Friedman also invoked the Columbus mythology, but I'll let that go. My point is that just a decade ago, almost no one hearing the title of this book would have thought that the author was advocating that the earth is flat. Rather, most people would have assumed that the book's title was a literary device for making a point. I'm sure that the provocative title did its job and roped some readers in, curious about what direction this book would take. However, I'm not so sure that this title would work so well today. With the growing flat-earth movement today, many people hearing the book's title may assume that the book was about, well, the earth being flat.

In his book, Friedman discussed ten factors that helped flatten the world. Number two on his list was August 9, 1995, the day that Netscape went public. One of Netscape's stated goals was to "level the playing field." The revolution in computing that Netscape represented was profound — things went from computer platform to an Internet-based platform. This transformed commerce, going from brick-and-mortar stores to e-commerce, such as amazon.com. The creation of the Internet as we know it also opened the door for all sorts of loony ideas, such as flat earth, to proliferate. Prior to the Internet, it was difficult to disseminate bad ideas. Later in this chapter, I will discuss the reasons for this.

But the Internet has changed all this — almost anyone with a bare minimum of cash can splash all sorts of nonsense on the Internet. Whacky conspiracy theories are a dime a dozen on the Internet. Discussion groups where these ideas can percolate in echo chambers proliferate on social media. Many flat-earthers end up at flat earth after moving from conspiracy theory to conspiracy theory, finally settling on the earth being flat, despite all that you've been told otherwise, as the grandest conspiracy of all. Friedman's book quickly went through two revisions, one in 2006 and the other in 2007. I wonder if Friedman ever writes another update of his book if he'll include discussion of flat-earth theories as a result of the (figurative) flattening of the earth that he has written about.

Zetetic Model vs. the Ancient Flat-Earth Model

In chapter 1, I contrasted the modern flat-earth model (the zetetic model) with the ancient flat-earth models. Some early ancient flat-earth models may have been similar to the modern zetetic model, with a dome over a flat earth. However, those models usually had the sun, moon, and stars set, pass beneath the earth, and then rise again. Eventually, most ancient cultures seemed to abandon the dome in favor of a real celestial sphere surrounding the earth. That celestial sphere, or spheres, held the stars, sun, moon, and planets, and it was the spinning of the sphere, or spheres, that accounted for the rising and setting of astronomical bodies. And that model did a good job explaining many of the aspects of the sky. However, this explanation worked for only one general location on earth. The model could not explain differences in time between points east and west, nor could it account for the changing appearance of the night sky as one traveled north and south. However, the realization that the earth was a sphere solved all these problems. It is no wonder that this model, elucidated by Aristotle and refined by Ptolemy, was the dominant cosmology in the West for two millennia. While this spherical-earth geocentric cosmology could explain time zones, the flat earth could not, for the sun would rise and set at the same time for all locations on a flat earth.

It was the time zone problem that Rowbotham tried to solve with his zetetic model in the 19th century. Even Rowbotham had to concede that there were time zones, but he thought that his proposal of a sort of spotlight sun would solve this problem. And indeed, it can. Sort of. The zetetic model can explain why it cyclically gets light and dark each day. However, it cannot explain why the sun is seen to rise and set each day. That is why flat-earthers today must concoct wild explanations for sunrise and sunset. Nor can the zetetic model explain many aspects of the sky as discussed in chapter 4. It is sad that modern flat-earthers have engaged in a huge retreat from reality.

And there is irony, too. As I discussed in chapter 2, the zetetic model was spawned in the 19th century, when critics were in full assault against the authority and reliability of Scripture. It is as if Rowbotham and other flat-earthers readily accepted the false charges that the skeptics had launched, embraced them, and made them a badge of honor. That is, modern flat-earthers employ many of the devil's arguments. But the irony doesn't stop there. The 19th-century skeptics falsely accused the Roman Catholic Church of teaching that the earth was flat. However, modern flat-earthers argue exactly the opposite — that it was the Roman Catholic Church that taught that the earth was a globe.

A Piece of Satire

On April 1, 2018, I posted the following on my personal Facebook page:

> An Explosive New Revelation
> About the Flat-Earth Conspiracy
> As many of you probably know already, I've been investigating the flat-earth movement for more than two years, and I've written about it several times. However, in recent discussions with several people, I've learned some shocking details that could blow the lid off this entire thing. I can't share all of what I've recently learned, nor am I at liberty to identify publicly who I've spoken to, but I'll reveal what I can at this time.
>
> It seems that many of the leaders in the flat-earth movement are members of a secretive organization that has the initials IPB. It is believed that members of the IPB include Mark Sargent, Jeran Campanella, Rob Skiba, Robbie Davidson, Dean Odle, and Patricia Steere. Undoubtedly, there are others. Some may object that the inclusion of Patricia Steere

in this short list indicates that I don't know what I'm talking about, because it is "well known" that the IPB admits only men. Well, surprise, surprise! It is a little-known fact that the IPB has had women members. This is indisputable. This, too, is kept hush-hush.

Clearly, this is no accident. It is the smoking gun that I've spent more than two years of research looking for that reveals who is behind the flat-earth conspiracy. Yes, I'll call it a conspiracy, because that's what it is. The IPB has been working behind the scenes to get the flat-earth movement going. That movement now has a critical mass that extends far beyond the IPB, but the IPB still is behind the leadership of the movement. You see, not everybody who believes the earth is flat needs to be an IPB member. That's the insidious side of this conspiracy — the fewer IPB members that are identified, the easier it is to hide the IPB's involvement.

I anticipate many objections to what I've learned. For instance, some may complain that they are members of the IPB, but they've never heard the subject of flat-earth brought up at any IPB meetings. Or people may claim they have friends or relatives who are IPB members, but they don't believe the earth is flat. But this overlooks the fact that the flat-earth movement is directed at the top of the IPB. There is no need for the average member to know what truly is going on in the organization. Therefore, ignorance of the IPB's involvement in the flat-earth conspiracy by its typical members proves what the IPB is really up to.

Others may argue that there is so much dissension among flat-earthers, that it could not be such a centralized conspiracy. These differences include personalities, different versions of the flat-earth model, and a wide range in theological positions. People who raise this objection reason that if there is a conspiracy, the leaders have done a poor job by letting so many schisms develop. That is what the leaders want you to think. At the top, things are not so divided. By distracting people by supposed deep differences, it clouds what is truly going on. That is very clever, but with my digging, I've uncovered this deep secret. The objections people will raise prove just how close I've gotten to the truth, and you can be sure that IPB leaders will pull out all the stops to block further investigation of this conspiracy.

I'm sharing here all that I dare for now, but I intend to reveal more shocking details and more information as I uncover it. Probably before September 23. Stay tuned.

Many of my friends caught on right away. For instance, the very first comment came from a friend who, noting the date, simply commented, "April Fool!" A few other friends joined in on the fun, though a few friends weren't so sure, asking, "Is this a joke?" It didn't take long for a flat-earther to find what I had written and began commenting, and soon word of my post spread to other flat-earthers who swarmed onto my FB page. The first flat-earther of any stature to weigh in was Rob Skiba, who wrote:

> [sigh] Once again we find NO "answers in Genesis" from you. Rather we get unsubstantiated nonsense from undisclosed sources? Nice. I believe that's called gossip and bearing false witness. So, consider this a friendly Matthew 18:15–17 confrontation from one brother to another. Since this was a public post, we'll just go ahead and skip to verse 16 as there are plenty of witnesses here. If this is a joke, it's in very poor form and deserves a public apology. If you refuse to do so, we'll skip down to verse 17. At which point, it might be fun to take this to court for slander, libel and defamation. Your choice. We can take this as far as you'd like. This post has been screen captured for the games ahead as Robbie Davidson, Dean Odle, Patricia Steere, Jeran Campanella and others may wish to join in.

Notice that Skiba thought that "it might be fun to take this to court." This is not the proper attitude of a Christian who feels compelled to take a fellow believer to court.

Robbie Davidson quickly joined in:

I agree Rob SMH! I dealt with the legal team at Answers in Genesis for my film Scientism Exposed 2 to get the rights to use the Ken Ham and Bill Nye clip. I'm sure this can be resolved with a public apology unless AIG's legal team would like to take it further as all articles written are under the ministry. Could you please explain your post Danny?

Patricia Steere opined that she thought that my post might have been an April Fools' Day joke that was not very funny. But other than that, the many flat-earthers who commented didn't seem to have a clue that this was satire. Also, notice that they all quickly assumed that what I had written had something to do with my employer, Answers in Genesis. None of them seemed to notice that this was on my *personal* FB page. An uproar of debate went on for a few days, with flat-earthers bringing up many of their usual arguments (and memes), many of them focused on Freemasonry. The irony was lost on them.

After two days of this, I posted this on April 3, 2018:

Quando Omni Flunkus Moritati

Many people have asked about the identity of the IPB. I understand your curiosity, but you must understand my fear of being so explicit in outing this nefarious group. After consulting with some of my contacts (one of which is an Eskimo scout), I have decided that it may be worth the risk to divulge the name. It is the International Possum Brotherhood. Of course, many of you will dismiss this, because "everyone knows" that the International Possum Brotherhood is a harmless bunch of fun-loving guys. That is what they want you to think. Most people don't know of the wicked origins of this organization. Even their flag colors (red and green) denote hate and envy. You need to research this to learn about its history and the evil currently behind this organization. But this won't be easy, for they are vigilant about taking down anything on the Internet that is critical of them. I'm surprised my FB page revealing their role has stayed up as long as it has, but now that I've identified them by name, I wouldn't be surprised if all that I've shared isn't taken down very soon.

At this point, many people began to understand what I was doing. At least the threats of legal action stopped coming. For those of you who don't know, the International Possum Brotherhood was a fictional lodge on the Red Green Show that ran on the Canadian Broadcasting Corporation (CBC) 1991–2006. The faux Latin at the beginning of my final FB post on this is the Possum Lodge motto ("When all else fails, play dead"). Besides the date that my satire went up, I had included a few clues in it, as well as my follow-up (such as the Eskimo scout — that was a reference to one of the comments on my original satire). But still some flat-earthers didn't get it. For instance, one person commented:

> An Eskimo told you Rob Skiba is a member of the International Possum Brotherhood? Seriously, is this a joke or do you not realise Danny Faulkner that someone is trolling you pretty hard? And as a believer I join in others demanding you treat Rob Skiba, and the others you have accused, in the manner the Bible commands you too.

Even when I explained that this was satire,[1] people still didn't get it. So, the following day, April 4, I posted a very clear statement that what I had written was satire. But the comments continued, and I grew weary of them, so I soon made my satire private so that only my FB friends could see and comment on it.

The fact that no flat-earthers seemed to understand that this was satire indicates how spot-on my satire was. To shore up their silly model, flat-earthers insist that there is a secret conspiracy perpetuating the fiction that the earth is a globe. What is the cabal perpetuating this hoax on the world? The most common whipping boy is Freemasonry, though some flat-earthers also implicate the Jesuits, and even a few anti-Semites, such as Eric Dubay, blame Jews.[2] So what better way to satirize this than to claim that the flat-earth movement is itself a wicked conspiracy? And what better choice for a secret cabal than a fictional lodge from a comedy TV series?

And the outrage expressed by flat-earthers was delicious irony. How dare I claim such bad things about leaders of the flat-earth movement

---

1. Many people confuse parody, lampoon, and satire. Though related, they are different. For one thing, satire has a point, while lampoon and parody usually do not.
2. For instance, see p. 39 of Dubay's *200 Proofs*.

without any evidence? Indeed, I've found that baseless salacious accusations against both the living and the dead is a stock in trade of the flat-earth movement. For instance, flat-earthers frequently claim that *all* astronauts are Masons, even though many astronauts are not, or ever have been, Masons. But that accusation is tame. There are all sorts of satanic claims made about NASA and some individuals involved with the development of rocketry. One person is Jack Parsons, who was an early pioneer in development of jets and rockets. Parsons was one of the people who founded the Jet Propulsion Laboratory (JPL), which eventually came to manage many unmanned space probes, though that was long after Parson's 1953 death. Parsons indeed had some occultic beliefs, including being a devotee of Thelema, a cult founded by Aleister Crowley in the first decade of the 20th century. Thelema drew heavily from Oriental mysticism, but it usually isn't viewed as being satanic. In the 1930s, prior to the Second World War, Parsons began correspondence and phone conversations about rocketry with Wernher von Braun in Germany. During the war, von Braun and his associates famously developed the V-2 rocket, the first man-made object to enter space. Upon the war's conclusion, von Braun and most of his team went to the United States, where they became the foundation of the American rocket program, including rockets that launched astronauts into space and eventually to the moon. Flat-earthers frequently have smeared von Braun as an occultist and Satanist, though there is no evidence for these charges. Apparently, in the minds of flat-earthers, the discussions that von Braun and Parsons had are enough to establish von Braun's status as a Satanist. But it gets even worse. Many flat-earthers repeat accusations that Walt Disney was a Satanist and a pedophile.

There are many other examples of the horrible rumors, innuendo, and flat-out lies that flat-earthers endlessly repeat about individuals and institutions. And yet flat-earthers were incensed that I wrote in what should have been obvious satire that flat-earth leaders were members of some super-secret society. An interchange that I had with one person illustrates the hypocrisy of flat-earthers. He wrote:

> Danny Faulkner be very careful sir that you are not bearing false witness against your brothers and sisters in Christ. Of course you Do know that would be a sin, right??

To which I responded:

> What do you think of Charlie Duke, Apollo 16 astronaut?

There was some dodging of the question for a while. This person apparently didn't know who Charlie Duke was and quickly did some "research" on him. I put "research" in quotes, because this person obviously consulted flat-earth websites, which hardly constitutes research. He finally emerged with the stock answer that Charlie Duke is a Freemason (though I don't think that he is). To which I responded:

> Let me get this straight — you caution me about bearing false witness against Christian brothers and sisters, but you feel no compunction in making false accusations against a Christian brother? Get the beam out of your eye, then I'll deem you credible.

To which he eventually responded:

> You posted accusingly about a secret society called IPB and called out individual citizens conspiring. Yet you did it half baked and cannot spell out specifically who and what they are and do [this was before I revealed what the IPB was]. You accuse me of possessing a beam in my eye, yet it's apparent that you have a beam up your you-know-what. You asked me for my opinion about this person Charles Duke. I made a quick research that in modern times is pretty easy to do and behold, the dude's a Freemason. Any Freemason or any other secret society agent can claim to be a "Christian." See POTUS 1, 41, and 43 for prime examples. Beam in my eye indeed. Beam in your ***! [the asterisks were not in the original]

This was from a professing Christian, for he previously had claimed:

> I am nothing but a new citizen in the nation of the true Israel. I've been grafted into the Vine. Why do you find allegiance to Freemasons and NASA? Is it for financial gain or something else?

I don't understand why a Christian would use such crude language. It's ironic that he and all the other flat-earthers that posted on my FB page were oblivious to the fact that I was satirizing the cavalier manner in which flat-earthers repeat false accusations about others.

By the way, I've never asked Charlie Duke if he is a Freemason. I just never thought it necessary, and to tell you the truth, I thought that it would be a little insulting to ask. Plus, it would be a waste of time, because flat-earthers would insist that if Charlie denied being a Freemason, of course he would lie about being a one. Never mind the fact that other astronauts don't seem to think it necessary to lie about being Masons. Notice the weird logic here — if an astronaut admits to being a Freemason, it proves that he's a Freemason; if an astronaut denies being a Freemason, that proves he's a Freemason. I recently proved the pointlessness of asking Charlie Duke if he is a Freemason when his name came up on a FB group dedicated to discussing flat earth and the Bible. I offered to suck it up and ask Charlie Duke, provided that the flat-earthers were willing to accept his answer. No flat-earther took me up on my offer. Not one. They totally ignored my post. I find that flat-earthers tend to do this. When confronted with a devastating argument against their beliefs (or, as in this case, just even the potential of a devastating argument), they completely ignore it.

Finally, others accused me of mockery. Apparently, they don't understand satire at all. That wouldn't be so bad, but flat-earthers frequently repost memes that mock those that they disagree with (for instance, the meme with my photo and photos of two other flat-earth critics superimposed over a Three Stooges still frame that I mentioned in chapter 1). Pointing out that it was inconsistent to accuse me of mockery when they didn't criticize fellow flat-earthers of mockery when they clearly are guilty fell on deaf ears.

Accusations of the Occult, Satanism, and Other Wicked Things

Above, I mentioned the salacious accusations that flat-earthers have hurled against Werner von Braun, Jack Parsons, and even Walt Disney. There is more. Flat-earthers frequently claim that Pythagoras was a sun worshiper, though there is no evidence of this. We know nothing of Pythagoras' theology, but given where and when he lived, if he believed in any god or gods, they probably were the deities of ancient Greek mythology. Helios was the Greek sun god, but that makes Helios merely one god of many, so why would Pythagoras single Helios out for special veneration? Where do flat-earthers get the notion that Pythagoras did? They claim that Pythagoras was the one who proposed the heliocentric theory, apparently to elevate the sun (Helios, the sun god) in importance. However, this once again confuses heliocentrism with the earth being spherical, a common error that flat-earthers commit. Pythagoras may have been the first to propose that the earth is spherical, but there is no evidence that he was a heliocentrist as well. The first person that we know of who suggested that the earth moved was Philolaus in the late fourth century B.C. Philolaus was from the Pythagorean school, and, in many respects, was the successor of Pythagoras. Perhaps it's this association with Pythagoras that has confused flat-earthers. But Philolaus was born a quarter-century after the death of Pythagoras. Furthermore, Philolaus didn't promote the heliocentric model. Rather, Philolaus proposed that the earth orbited a central fire. It was later that Aristarchus (3rd century B.C.) suggested that the earth orbited the sun instead of a central fire.

From this wobbly foundation of alleged sun worship, flat-earthers build a shaky structure of conjecture. They claim that Copernicus was a sun worshiper, too, and thus adopted this supposedly pagan idea. Never mind that there is no evidence that Copernicus was a sun worshiper, unless you consider merely suggesting heliocentrism as constituting evidence. And flat-earthers explicitly make the supposed connection of sun worship between Pythagoras and Copernicus. Similar claims are made about Galileo, Kepler, and Newton. To flat-earthers, the motivation of all these men of science was supposedly to promote pagan worship of the sun. These suggestions were first promoted in the writings of the flat-earth movement of the late 19th century. People in the modern flat-earth movement uncritically accept these accusations as true. Apparently, flat-earthers are inclined to believe almost anything if it conforms to what they already believe.

There are at least three things wrong with this argument. First, there is no evidence for any of it. Merely repeating an accusation many times doesn't make it any truer than the first time it was falsely raised. Second, even if the accusation were true, it commits the genetic fallacy. The genetic fallacy is the fallacy of arguing against an idea based upon something negative about its origin or history. The origin or history of an idea may provide understanding of how an idea came about, but it cannot determine the merits of that idea. Whether Pythagoras, Copernicus, or anyone else who has supported heliocentrism was a pagan or not has no bearing on whether their cosmology is true or false.

Third, flat-earthers are inconsistent in the way they employ this reasoning. They disparage Pythagoras for supposedly being a sun worshipper, but they don't realize that the "eight inches per mile squared" rule for the earth's curvature is an approximation using the Pythagorean theorem. If Pythagoras' ideas are so suspect because of his paganism, why do flat-earthers trust anything that Pythagoras did, such as the Pythagorean theorem? Furthermore, the founder of the modern flat-earth movement is Eric Dubay, a person who has claimed that Jesus Christ never lived and is immersed in Asian mysticism. Why is it that flat-earthers so easily repeat false accusations of paganism in past supporters of the heliocentric model, while giving a free pass to the founder of the modern flat-earth movement who has a demonstrated record of pagan beliefs? The usual response is that flat-earthers don't consider themselves disciples of Dubay. Apparently, it never occurs to them that no heliocentrists today think of themselves as disciples of Pythagoras or even Copernicus either.

There is another example of this inconsistency on the part of flat-earthers. As I pointed out in chapter 5, in many domed, flat-earth cosmologies of the ancient world, the flat earth was the body of a god, while the dome above was the body of another god. So why isn't the modern flat-earth model a return to ancient paganism? In ancient Greek mythology, Gaia was the primordial goddess of the earth. Above Gaia was Uranus, the god of the sky, or heaven. The Roman equivalent to Gaia was Terra, from which we get the words for earth in Romance languages and from which we get the English word "terrestrial." The Roman equivalent of Uranus was Caelus, from which the words for sky or heaven in Romance languages come and we get word "celestial" in English. Therefore, the modern flat-earth model is the resurrection of the ancient pagan cosmology of Gaia (Terra) with the domed Uranus (Caelus) above. Want proof? A commonly cited reference among flat-earthers is David Wardlaw Scott's 1901 book, *Terra Firma: The Earth Not a Globe, Proved from Scripture, Reason, and Fact.* The very first word in this book's title gives homage to Terra, the ancient pagan Greek god of the earth. Obviously, Scott was a Gaia worshipper. He hid his devotion to paganism in plain sight. Of course, I'm not serious about this. However, when flat-earthers employ this wicked logic, they are quite serious. They would declare my claim here ridiculous while simultaneously failing to recognize the same poor reasoning in themselves.

What Is the Appeal of Flat Earth?

Why has the flat-earth movement spread so quickly? As I mentioned at the opening of this chapter, part of the problem is the rise of social media. In the past, it was difficult to disseminate whacky ideas. One could write a book, but finding a publisher willing to go to the expense of editing, printing, and marketing a book on a whacky subject was virtually impossible. One could self-publish a book, but that was a considerable up-front cost. And then there was the problem with marketing and distribution of said book. One could donate copies to libraries, but there is no guarantee that libraries would keep the books, or, if they did, that anyone would read them. But the Internet and social media have changed all that. Many people spend countless hours surfing the web, exposing themselves to many things that, in the past, would not have been so easy to find. That is, traditional dissemination of ideas acted as a filter to sort out the truly bad ideas (and, admittedly, a few good ones).

But social media is just that — media through which information passes. More important are changes in society. The rise of the Internet was preceded by decreasing trust in institutions, but the Internet has intensified this suspicion of authority. Fifty years ago, most people trusted the government to a large extent, but the press coverage of the Vietnam War and Watergate seriously undermined that trust. Even NASA, which in its heyday a half-century ago was one of our most trusted institutions, has not been immune to this societal change. Many people reason that if the government and other institutions are so routinely lying to us, then there must be a reason. This line of thinking can soon give way to elaborate conspiracies. For instance, an amazing number of people now think that the attack on the World Trade Center and the Pentagon on September 11, 2001, was something other than an assault on America and the West by radical Islamists. I suppose that instead they think it was a nefarious plot by our own government to blame Muslims so that we could go to war in the Middle East. At any rate, several speakers at the first International Flat

Earth Conference in November 2017 took it for granted that 9/11 was an inside job, to much approval from the audience. In fact, at least one speaker said that he had only recently latched onto the flat-earth conspiracy after spending a decade "studying" many other conspiracies. I put "studying" in quotes because looking at videos on the Internet doesn't constitute study. In conversations with flat-earthers, I've found that they frequently bring up 9/11. They seem astonished that I don't agree with their conspiratorial beliefs about 9/11. They clearly think that I am very naïve and deceived.

Conspiracies have been around a long time. I first encountered conspiracy theories a half-century ago. One of the first conspiracy theories that I encountered was that Project Blue Book was a whitewash, and that the government was hiding a large amount of information about flying saucers. About the same time, I learned of various conspiracies about the JFK assassination that started showing up as soon as that Warren Commission issued its report. A decade or two earlier, there had been much concern that Communists were at high levels in the U.S. government in a conspiracy to overthrow our system. If such a conspiracy was ever there, it was an utter failure, because no communist revolution overthrew the U.S. Constitution, though the USSR dissolved nearly three decades ago. As I was starting college, this conspiracy morphed into a belief that communism wasn't the real threat, but that there was a much larger conspiracy on the part of the Rockefellers, the Trilateral Commission, and the Council on Foreign Relations to take over the world, with the Soviet Union merely being a pawn in this scheme. A further wrinkle on this story was that this conspiracy had been playing out for generations, going back at least to the Rothschilds two centuries earlier. It wasn't clear what motivation conspirators would have if they knew that they wouldn't live to see the conclusion of their conspiracy. Note that the Rothschilds were, and are, Jewish, which is probably the origin of the anti-Semitic overtones of these conspiracy theories. I also recall Freemasonry as part of this conspiracy. Sound familiar?

In the past, such ideas of grand conspiracies were viewed as being way out there, but now they are almost mainstream. Conspiracies have certainly had an impact on popular culture, such as the 1999 film *The Matrix*, along with its two sequels (2003). In 1978, just four years after the resignation of President Richard Nixon over the Watergate scandal,

Warner Brothers released the movie *Capricorn One*. The movie was a fictional story about faking the first manned landing on Mars. The movie poster showed a spacecraft that resembled the Lunar Excursion Module of the Apollo program on a Hollywood set, along with the question, "Would you be shocked to find out that the greatest moment of our recent history may not have happened at all?" This question was an obvious reference to the Apollo 11 mission in 1969. Again, the movie was about faking the first manned mission to *Mars*, but many people now seem to think that the movie was about faking the Apollo missions to the moon. Claims that the Apollo moon landings were faked began to appear shortly after the conclusion of the Apollo program in 1972. But these early attempts received relatively little notice. The moon landing conspiracy theories began to take off in 2001 when the Fox Network broadcast the documentary *Conspiracy Theory: Did We Land on the Moon?* I watched this documentary in its first run. My impression was that so many of the arguments used were so poor that the producers of this movie made the movie as a gag.

Belief that the Apollo moon landings were faked has steadily grown since. However, with the rise in belief that the earth is flat, the moon landing conspiracy has been subsumed by another, grander conspiracy. Now the most ardent pursuers of the moon landing conspiracy are the flat-earthers. If the earth truly is flat, and if this fact has been hidden for centuries (actually, millennia), then it must be for very nefarious purposes. This would qualify the conspiracy about the earth's shape to be the most diabolical of all conspiracies, subsuming all other conspiracies. Thus, belief in a conspiracy about the earth's shape reminds me of *the ring* of J.R.R Tolkien's *Lord of the Rings* trilogy. When heated sufficiently, the master ring revealed an inscription:

> One ring to rule them all, one ring to find them,
> One ring to bring them all and in the darkness bind them.

But why do so many people find conspiracies compelling? Societal changes explain part of it, but why are conspiracies so easy for some people to entertain in the first place? People have a perverse desire to gain secret knowledge, to be able to say, "I know something you don't know." This is why gossip is so popular.

And this desire for secret knowledge is one of the tenets of the ancient heresy of gnosticism, something that was a grave threat to early Christianity, and, hence, was battled in early church writings, as well as addressed in New Testament epistles. Gnosticism taught that there is hidden knowledge, and that people could attain a higher level of spirituality by learning that secret knowledge. This facet of gnosticism is alive and well in the church today. Many Christians are attracted to all sorts of arcane things, such as numerology, Bible codes, gospel in the stars, and obsession with prophecy or the *Nephilim*, to name just a few. Many of these subjects go far beyond what the Bible says while venturing into speculation. Much of these probably fall under the warning of 1 Timothy 1:3–4 to prevent certain people in the church from teaching any different doctrine and fables and endless genealogies. While some of the warnings that the Apostle Paul gave in his first epistle to Timothy appear a little vague to us today (e.g., 1 Timothy 6:3, which is the introduction of the section that concludes with 1 Timothy 6:20–21), commentaries generally agree that much of what Paul was warning Timothy about was gnosticism. Many flat-earthers claim to have come to much deeper spiritual understanding once they came to believe that the earth is flat. This is very revealing, because it fits the allure of the secret knowledge promised by gnosticism. Therefore, contrary to what flat-earthers claim about 1 Timothy 6:20–21 (something that I discussed in chapter 10), this passage may ironically apply to their knowledge, falsely so called. The attraction of secret knowledge is that it offers a shortcut to spirituality. Discipleship and true spiritual growth are difficult and hard work. By comparison, merely accepting some far-out beliefs as doctrine is relatively easy.

Another interesting facet is the collection of testimonies of people who supposedly came to Christ because of coming to belief in a flat earth. Many of these people claim to have once been atheists. One must wonder if many of these testimonies are genuine or are merely skeptics telling flat-earth Christians what they want to hear in a very successful attempt to make Christians look foolish. For those misguided souls who might be genuine, what will happen if they ever come to realize that they have been misled into believing that the earth is flat? Undoubtedly, it would risk destroying their faith and convincing them that the Bible is nonsense. This is wicked.

As I pointed out in chapter 1, unlike the 19th-century flat-earth movement, the modern flat-earth movement has spawned relatively few books. Rather, the preferred medium for disseminating flat-earth information appears to be YouTube videos. I think that is because many flat-earthers don't read much. Perhaps many flat-earthers don't read much because they find reading boring. And why do some people find reading boring? People who find reading boring generally don't comprehend much of what they are reading. People who lack reading comprehension are just a small step above functional illiteracy. I know this sounds harsh, and perhaps even shocking, but hear me out. People who have no reading comprehension can read a paragraph or two of text aloud, and people listening can grasp everything read. However, if asked questions about the content that they have read, the readers likely cannot answer any of those questions because they have failed to understand what they read. It's not that they don't recognize the letters or words, for they read them aloud. The problem is that they fail to put the words together to understand the meaning of the text. That is, what they've read are just words, and nothing more. No wonder they find reading boring.

I noticed this trend in a "Flat Earth and the Bible" Facebook discussion group that I participate in. In posts to the group, I would describe some of my experiments that refuted flat-earth arguments. I had expected some interaction, but usually few, if any, flat-earthers would respond. When they did respond, the most common comment was a request to put what I had done in a video. This happened repeatedly, and it puzzled me for a while. I finally concluded that the people asking for videos simply couldn't follow what I had written. That's a pity, because I've concluded that people who can't read with comprehension probably aren't very good at reasoning either, because I think that reading comprehension and reasoning ability probably go hand in hand. No wonder these people had fallen for what I recognized as such poor arguments for a flat earth. It's not that these people are stupid; it's just that they've never acquired proper reasoning skills, along with reading comprehension.

Disbelieving

When campaigning for Barry Goldwater in 1964, Ronald Reagan famously said,

Well, the trouble with our liberal friends is not that they're ignorant; it's just that they know so much that isn't so.[3]

This reminds me of flat-earthers. It isn't that they don't know anything. The problem is that so much of what they know simply isn't true. Flat-earthers have their own version of history. They buy into the lie that prior to five centuries ago, most people in the West thought that the earth was flat. They accept the lie that the church taught that the earth was flat. When confronted with the facts of history, it doesn't matter to flat-earthers, because surrender on this one issue would seriously unravel their argument. Flat-earthers consistently conflate the question of the earth's shape with geocentrism, something that the church largely held to throughout the Middle Ages. The continual mixing of these two issues illustrates how much that flat-earthers don't understand.

But this is just the tip of the iceberg. Flat-earthers so easily believe the nonsense about the cooling effect of moonlight (discussed in chapter 5). When I share my experimental results showing that this is not true, I'm met with silence. Flat-earthers readily believe that the many photos that show distant objects that ought to be beyond the earth's curvature prove that the earth is flat. However, when I explain this with temperature inversions and show my photographs taken on a day with no temperature inversion that show a cargo ship disappearing hull-first, I'm met with silence. Flat-earthers believe that the sun's apparent size gets smaller as it sets, but when I show them photos that show the sun's apparent size doesn't change as it sets, I'm met with silence. This goes on and on. Before flat-earthers can realize the error of their ways, they must first realize that much of what they have come to believe isn't true.

Cognitive Dissonance

Many flat-earthers offer psychoanalysis of those that they disagree with. Flat-earthers frequently talk about cognitive dissonance. Broadly speaking, cognitive dissonance is the psychological stress that one experiences when simultaneously holding two or more contradictory beliefs. More specific to the topic at hand, cognitive dissonance is the psychological stress that one experiences when confronted with new information that

---

3. https://reaganquotes.wordpress.com/2008/04/27/our-liberal-friends/.

does not conform to what one already believes. Most flat-earthers readily admit that they experienced cognitive dissonance when they first encountered arguments for the earth being flat, so they think that they recognize it in others. Their testimonies start by stating that they grew up believing the earth was a globe. When they encountered flat-earth arguments, they naturally resisted the arguments, but they couldn't refute them. That is classic cognitive dissonance.

How does one respond to this sort of cognitive dissonance? One approach is simply to ignore the flat-earth arguments, reasoning that the earth cannot be flat, so there must be something wrong with the arguments. While this may be the correct attitude, it isn't a totally rational response. The problem is that the education of very few people included good arguments for the earth being a globe. Instead, most people came to believe that the earth is spherical based upon repetition of that belief, not reasoned arguments for that belief. That is indoctrination, not education. Flat-earthers are right about this at least. However, their solution to this problem isn't the answer. It doesn't help that the flat-earth myth arose in the 19th century, as I discussed in chapter 1. The false history that most people in the West thought the earth was flat until the time of Christopher Columbus makes it even easier to believe that the earth is flat. Consequently, very few people are prepared to refute flat-earth arguments. I wrote this book to provide answers to people who are searching for that refutation. Hopefully, the refutation in this book will provide a second, better response to flat-earth arguments.

Unfortunately, flat-earthers took a third response to flat-earth arguments. They couldn't come up with refutations of flat-earth arguments on their own, leading to cognitive dissonance. They shared what they had encountered with close friends and family. Often, the responses of friends and family weren't very supportive — they didn't have answers to flat-earth arguments either. Many of those other people simply dismissed the arguments for the earth being flat, arguing that "everyone knows that the earth is a globe." Seeing no reasoned response, the flat-earthers-to-be thought that they had identified in others the same cognitive dissonance that they were experiencing themselves. This spurred the potential flat-earthers to study the issue further. Most of this "research" was on the Internet, where there is a huge number of sites promoting the idea that the earth is flat, but precious few refuting that notion. Given the steady diet of flat-earth material and little or no countering information, flat-earthers eventually resolved their cognitive dissonance by accepting the notion that the earth is flat.

A paradigm shift is necessitated by new information that demands the drastic change in thinking. That is, a paradigm shift comes about because of cognitive dissonance. Therefore, changing one's attitude about a matter can be a rational response. However, when one embraces flat earth, it necessitates many additional attitudes that aren't so rational. For instance, one must question how and when widespread belief shifted from flat earth to globe earth. Furthermore, if the earth is flat, modern technology ought to make it obvious to many people that the earth isn't spherical, yet none of them seem to be enlightening the rest of us, apparently content to supposedly continue perpetuating the lie about the earth's shape. These questions introduce further cognitive dissonance that demands resolution. One option would be to abandon belief in the earth being flat, but once one becomes thoroughly convinced that the earth is flat, that option isn't viable. This leads flat-earthers to embrace belief in grand conspiracies involving scientists, pilots, astronauts, and government officials. There is not an obvious reason why this conspiracy exists, so flat-earthers have created reasons. Non-Christian flat-earthers think that governments have promoted the earth being spherical as a form of mind control. This melds with many other conspiracy theories, such as those involving vaccines, 9/11, and so-called chemtrails.

Many Christian believers in flat earth adopt this paranoid thinking with an added wrinkle. Christian flat-earthers generally think that belief in a spherical earth is a satanic conspiracy to hide biblical truth. Supposedly, the big lie didn't begin with Charles Darwin and evolution. Borrowing from modern-day geocentrists, Christian flat-earthers claim the big lie began with cosmology. But unlike the modern geocentrists, flat-earthers conflate flat earth with geocentrism and insist that this is the true big lie that leads to all the others. Christian flat-earthers often go so far as to suggest that belief in the earth being spherical is the great delusion that the Apostle Paul warned about in 2 Thessalonians 2:11. The problem with this interpretation of this verse is that it ignores the context. When considered in the context of the entire second chapter of 2 Thessalonians, it is very clear that the great delusion will be sent to those who reject the truth of the gospel. By interpreting 2 Thessalonians 2:11 this way, flat-earth Christians essentially accuse those who disagree with them of not being born again. This is tantamount to elevating belief in flat earth into an essential doctrine for salvation. It never occurs to Christian flat-earthers that perhaps it is they who have been deluded.

This brings up the *Dunning-Kruger effect*. The Dunning-Kruger effect is a specific type of cognitive bias. A cognitive bias is a bias that people have because of their beliefs. A better term for a set of beliefs is a worldview. People use their worldview to interpret facts. Politics is a good example of cognitive bias. People of different political persuasions will come to different conclusions when confronted by the same facts because they have different worldviews. In many cases, we can interpret information in different ways. However, sometimes new information cannot be interpreted within one's worldview. Cognitive bias makes it difficult for people to assimilate new information properly if that information conflicts with their worldview. We tend to ignore or diminish the importance of conflicting information.

The Dunning-Kruger effect is a term for people who have a feeling of self-confidence and superiority and yet are clueless. I have repeatedly seen flat-earthers confidently state their case when it is very clear that they have no idea what they are talking about. A good example is flat-earthers' response to the simple observation that when the sun is low in the sky, it has the same apparent size as it does when high in the sky. As I discussed in chapter 4, this is what we expect in the conventional understanding of the world, but not at all what one would expect in the flat-earth model. When confronted with this information, some flat-earthers just ignore it, indicating further cognitive dissonance. Others, such as Rob Skiba, attempt to explain it by some mumbo jumbo about atmospheric refraction. The claim is made that water in the atmosphere acts as a lens to make the sun appear larger than it normally would as it moves away from the observer. This attempt is usually demonstrated by refraction of light from water in a container, followed by another demonstration of a Fresnel lens on a tabletop. There are many problems with this supposed explanation. For instance, the amount of water in the air is highly variable, but somehow the amount of refraction supposedly caused by the water is not. Furthermore, how one gets from the container of water to a Fresnel lens is never made clear. To those of us who understand optics, this is total gibberish, yet flat-earthers confidently repeat this nonsense as if it is the people who truly understand optics who are the dummies.

There are many other examples of how flat-earthers think that they are the ones who have figured out the truth, while the rest of us continue to be hoodwinked. This false feeling of superiority is the living embodiment of the Dunning-Kruger effect. The attraction of secret knowledge plays to our pride. Therefore, it is pride that gets people to believe that the earth is flat. And it is pride (the false confidence of the Dunning-Kruger effect) that keeps people entrapped in flat-earth belief. To get out of the trap, a flat-earther must first come to realize that he or she was fooled by some very poor arguments. That is, the flat-earther must come to understand that instead of being among the most enlightened, he or she was among the least enlightened. And the most gullible. That is extremely difficult to do, particularly if one was very vocal about the earth being flat, such as with friends and family or on social media. Consequently, I don't hold much hope for such people. I seriously doubt that what I have written would be of much help to them. Instead, my motivation in criticizing the flat-earth movement is to provide answers to those who are truly investigating this topic.

Blatant Lies

On July 29, 2018, Robbie Davidson made a YouTube video with the provocative title "Flat-Earther Responds to Answers in Genesis & Dr. Danny Faulkner — God DOES NOT Teach ANY Cosmology!" When he posted it to his Facebook page, he included the meme reproduced here. Of course, many people commented on how poor that was for me to say this. Except that I didn't say any such thing. When I confronted Davidson on this, he readily admitted that it was his paraphrase of what I had written. I clarified that this is not what I meant at all, so this was a very poor paraphrase. To condemn what someone has written, it is imperative to accurately quote what that person wrote. To paraphrase what that person wrote using words that person didn't use is a gross mis-

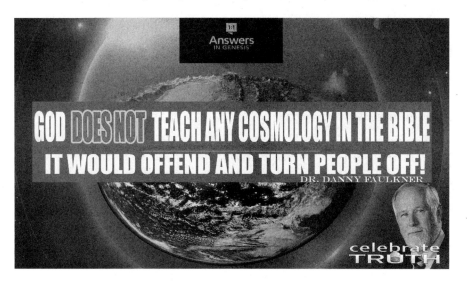

representation of what that person wrote. It is a straw-man argument. I wonder how many flat-earthers out there really think that I wrote "God does not teach any cosmology in the Bible — it would offend and turn people off?" This is so typical of the lies that flat-earthers promote. It wouldn't be so bad if flat-earthers were not condemning NASA and many other institutions and people of lying.

But there are many other examples of false things that flat-earthers frequently assert. I can't begin to count the many times that I've read or heard flat-earthers confidently state that there is no measured stellar parallax. As an astronomer, I know that this is false. Another frequently made, but false, claim that flat-earthers make is that Foucault pendula have been observed to not precess or have precessed in the wrong direction. This hasn't been my experience, and none of these claims are backed up with documentation. At the second Flat Earth International Conference, I heard at least three speakers confidently repeat that moonlight is cooling. As I explained in chapter 5, my three carefully conceived and executed experiments prove otherwise. I don't doubt the sincerity of the flat-earthers who repeat these false claims — I'm sure that they truly believe that the information that they are sharing is correct. However, they couldn't be more wrong about these things. Again, I wish that flat-earthers would examine claims by fellow flat-earthers with just a smidgen of skepticism.

Creation Science and Flat Earth

Many flat-earthers applaud creation ministries, such as Answers in Genesis, for the stand that those ministries take on the authority of Scripture. However, the same flat-earthers think that it is inconsistent for those creation ministries to oppose flat earth. The flat-earthers accuse creation ministries of supporting evolutionary ideas when those ministries agree with other scientists, who happen to be evolutionists, on such questions as the earth's shape. The reasoning seems to be that if evolutionists are so wrong about the origin of the world, then we can't trust anything evolutionists say. This is a variation on the genetic fallacy, an informal logical fallacy. Just because a person is wrong about one thing, it doesn't follow that the person is wrong about other things.

But there are at least two other looming problems with flat-earthers' opinion on this. First, this confuses the distinction between operational science and historical science. Operational, or observational/experimental, science is concerned with how the world works now. One may develop and test hypotheses or theories to test in the here and now. The Baconian scientific method was developed to carry this out. The shape of the earth is a question tailor-made for the scientific method because it is a question of how the world now is. Contrast this with historical, or origin, science. Historical science is concerned with what might have happened in the past. Since the past is past, the past cannot be tested in the manner that science normally operates. If no one witnessed a past event in question, then we really don't know what happened. Ken Ham famously asks, quoting from the Book of Job, "Were you there?" The origin and evolution of life is a past event, so it cannot be tested in the traditional scientific manner, but whether the earth is a sphere is a question that the scientific method can address. Evolutionists are wrong about the origin and history of the world, but we can test in the here and now whether the earth is a globe.

The second problem is that flat-earthers don't grasp that creationists and evolutionists live in the same world. Evolutionists and creationists look at the same data, but they reach very different conclusions because their assumptions are different. This is because the *interpretation* of facts is so different. However, it seems that flat-earthers are truly living in a different world. I have been frustrated in dealing with flat-earthers because so many of them simply choose to ignore data and important information. For instance, as I discussed in chapter 5, flat-earthers argue that the earth's shadow falling on the moon is not the cause of lunar eclipse. Flat-earthers are unfazed by the wealth of data to the contrary. Furthermore, while flat-earthers have dismissed the earth's shadow as the cause of lunar eclipses, flat-earthers don't seem to be the least bit curious as to what causes lunar eclipses if it's not the shadow of the earth falling on the moon. Flat-earthers concoct grand conspiracies to bolster their beliefs. NASA is a wicked organization that has faked everything that it has done. Astronauts are all Freemasons. The world is run by a cabal including the Freemasons, Jesuits, and in some anti-Semitic variations, Jewish interests. This is not the world that most of us live in.

This attitude has a deleterious effect upon the creation-evolution debate. For a long time, some evolutionists have falsely accused creationists of believing that everything in the Bible is literally true. But many flat-earthers proudly proclaim that they believe everything in the Bible is literally true. Of course, as pointed out in chapter 10, there are many nonliteral passages in the Bible. Furthermore, critics of creationists have often accused creationists of being flat-earthers. When there were no true flat-earthers, nearly everyone recognized that this was hyperbole. But now that there genuinely are people who believe that the earth is flat, it is relatively easy for the critics of creationists to lump creationists with flat-earthers, though most creationists strongly reject the notion that the earth is flat. I suspect that the current flat-earth movement was hatched in an attempt, once again, to discredit the Bible, Christianity, and especially creationists. It is truly sad that well-intended Christians have been duped into supporting this unholy agenda. It is my desire that my modest efforts in this book can play a role in combating this great danger.

Index

Io, 132, 134
Iridium (satellites), 247
Irving, Washington, 36, 38
Isidore of Seville, 33
JFK assassination, 366
Johnson, Charles K., 42, 107
John the Good, 34
Jordan River, 193
Josephus, 302–305
Jupiter, 15, 82, 132, 147–148, 174, 191, 336
kaddur, 271–272
Kaku, Michio, 202
Kepler, Johannes, 128, 172, 173, 174, 178, 245, 363
Kepler's first law of planetary motion, 173, 178
Kepler's second law of planetary motion, 173, 178
Kepler's third law of planetary motion, 172–174, 245
Ketu, 88
kinetic theory of heat, 219
Kipfer, Paul, 256
Knibb, M., 341–342
Knodel, Bob, 87–88
Krause-Ogle boxes (see light pipes), 196
Krauss, Lawrence, 202
Lactantius, 30–31, 36
Lalande, Jérôme, 133–134
Large Magellanic Cloud, 118
Larmor, Joseph, 207
latitude, 90, 93, 103, 110, 112, 114–116, 118, 128, 134, 136–137, 139–142, 153, 156, 180, 184–187, 239–240, 245, 249, 251, 253–254, 262
law of cosines, 142
law of sines, 142
Letronne, Jean Antoine, 36, 38
level, 5, 39, 41, 47–49, 54–58, 61, 91, 180, 182–183, 192–193, 195–197, 219, 242, 244, 256, 258–259, 334, 353, 368

light pipes, 196
LIGO, 195–196
limb, 77–78, 97, 147–149, 152–155, 238, 240
line of nodes, 72
Little Dipper, 118
Livingston, Louisiana, 195
longitude, 91, 93, 103, 134, 136–137, 139–142, 153–154, 239–240, 245, 249, 251
Lord of the Rings, 367
Lorentz, Hendrik, 207
Los Angeles, 139, 265
Los Angeles Herald, 265
lunar eclipse, 22–24, 71–73, 75–80, 83, 377
lunar librations, 152–153
lunar occultation, 146–147
Luther, Martin, 34–35, 214, 283
Lynch, D.K., 257
M1 Garand rifle, 186
Mach, Ernst, 186, 204, 209, 214
Mach's principle, 204, 209, 214
Macrobius, 33
Magellan, Ferdinand, 37–38
Marble, D., 192–193
Mare Crisium, 153–154
maria, 150, 152, 154
Mariana Trench, 258
Matthews, K.A., 285
Maxwell, James Clerk, 209
McCracken, Andy, 341
meteors, 322–324, 337
Methodius, 30
Michaelson, Albert, 144, 205–206
Michaelson-Morley experiment, 144, 205–207
Mississippi River, 193–194
Missouri River, 194
MIT, 196
Mobile Bay, 64–65
modern physics, 208–209
momentum, 179, 189–190
moon, 9–10, 18–24, 27–29, 34, 37–38, 40, 44, 71–

85, 87–89, 93, 95–97, 99, 101–102, 109–110, 144, 146–154, 156–158, 160, 170–172, 178, 190–191, 213–214, 217, 221–230, 236–241, 247, 254, 281, 289, 302–303, 314, 317–319, 323–325, 334–336, 347–350, 354, 360, 367, 377
"Moon in My Room," 20
Morrow, Ulysses Grant, 57
Mulgrew, Kate, 202
NASA, 5, 44, 91–93, 217–218, 223–224, 226–232, 235–236, 259, 261, 360, 361, 365, 375, 377
nasha', 217–218
National Science Foundation, 196
natural philosophy, 333–334
Nebuchadnezzar, 277–278
Nephilim, 350–351, 368
New Almagest, 184
Newcomb, Simon, 133
Newton, Isaac, 132, 165–167, 169–172, 174, 177–178, 181, 188, 191, 198, 208, 245, 363
Newton's law of gravity, 178
New York, 30, 41, 187, 267, 285, 353
Nile River, 194
Nixon, Richard, 366
node, 23, 75–76, 83
nomogram, 142
non-inertial frame of reference, 181
North America, 14, 231–232, 234–235, 252
north celestial pole, 100, 114–118, 120–123, 155
ecliptic north pole, 104
northern kingdom, 329
North Star, 10, 114, 117–118, 122
numerology, 41, 368
Nut, 128
Nye, Bill, 358
observational science, 376

Scripture Index